Hitler's Hunting Squad in Southern Europe

Hitler's Hunting Squad in Southern Europe

The Bloody Path of Fritz Schubert through Occupied Crete and Macedonia

Thanasis S. Fotiou
Translated by Stratis A. Porfyratos

Pen & Sword
MILITARY

First published in Great Britain in 2024 by
Pen & Sword Military
An imprint of Pen & Sword Books Limited
Yorkshire – Philadelphia

Copyright © Stratis A Porfyratos 2024

ISBN 978 1 39903 611 5

The right of Stratis A Porfyratos to be identified as
Author of this Work has been asserted by him in accordance
with the Copyright, Designs and Patents Act 1988.

A CIP catalogue record for this book is
available from the British Library

All rights reserved. No part of this book may be reproduced or
transmitted in any form or by any means, electronic or mechanical
including photocopying, recording or by any information storage and
retrieval system, without permission from the Publisher in writing.

Typeset by Mac Style
Printed in the UK by CPI Group (UK) Ltd, Croydon, CR0 4YY.

Pen & Sword Books Limited incorporates the imprints of After
the Battle, Atlas, Archaeology, Aviation, Discovery, Family History,
Fiction, History, Maritime, Military, Military Classics, Politics,
Select, Transport, True Crime, Air World, Frontline Publishing, Leo
Cooper, Remember When, Seaforth Publishing, The Praetorian Press,
Wharncliffe Local History, Wharncliffe Transport, Wharncliffe True
Crime and White Owl.

For a complete list of Pen & Sword titles please contact

PEN & SWORD BOOKS LIMITED
47 Church Street, Barnsley, South Yorkshire, S70 2AS, England
E-mail: enquiries@pen-and-sword.co.uk
Website: www.pen-and-sword.co.uk
or
PEN AND SWORD BOOKS
1950 Lawrence Road, Havertown, PA 19083, USA
E-mail: uspen-and-sword@casematepublishers.com
Website: www.penandswordbooks.com

To the memory of my parents, Spyros and Sofia

Contents

Foreword: Stratos N. Dordanas	viii
Abbreviations	ix
Foreword	x
Author's Foreword	xiv

Part I: Schubert in Crete (August 1941–January 1944)		1
Chapter 1	The Identity of Schubert	3
	The facts	3
	The myth	7
Chapter 2	Schubert; the Spy Activities During the First Period (August 1941–July 1943)	10
	Resistance and German retaliation	10
	Crime in the village of Mount Rethymnon: the beginning of a bloody journey	13
	Schubert in Heraklion: cooperation with the Espionage Office under Hartmann	15
	The incident at the village of Krousonas Heraklion	17
	The first Schuberites from Krousonas	19
	Schubert's crimes and terror in the district of Heraklion	22
Chapter 3	From Schubert to Hartman and the Consequences	30
	German oppressive measures and the weakening of the Cretan resistance	30
	Schubert's integration into the Military Police	31
	Raid on Meskla Kydonia (July 1943)	33
Chapter 4	Schubert as Head of Greek Interception Squad	35
	General Brauer's experiment	35
	The assembly and powers of "Schubert's Hunting Commandos": a state within a state	36
	Social make-up, mission and organization of "Schubert's Hunting Gang"	39

Chapter 5	Schubert's Activities During the Second Period (August 1943–January 1944)	44
	The first brutalities in the provinces of Chania and Rethymnon	44
	The officers of Heraklion under the surveillance of Schubert, capetan Bantouvas and the German reprisals in the province of Viannos	47
	Schubert's role in the annihilation of EOK Heraklion	50
	Schubert's last brutalities in the villages of Rethymnon, Chania and Lasithi Kali Sykia	53
	Kallikratis	56
	Schuberite crimes in the villages of Lasithi, Heraklion and Chania	58
Chapter 6	The Distancing of Schubert from Crete (11 January 1944)	63
	New Years Day 1944: an unfortunate day	63
	German measures of appeasement, the role of Minister I. Passadakis and Schubert's expulsion	65
	Schubert and his gang's toll of monstrosity in Crete	69
Part II: Schubert in Macedonia (February–October 1944)		73
Chapter 1	Schubert and the Armed Anti-communist Forces in Central Macedonia	75
Chapter 2	Giannitsa: Vengeance Begins	79
Chapter 3	Schubert at the Villages of Western Halkidiki (18th April–5th August 1944)	82
	Nea Gonia: Schubert targeted by attacks of ΕΛΑΣ Halkidiki	82
	Enemies and friends of Schubert in Halkidiki	84
	Nea Kallikrateia: Bastion of terror in the area	87
	Peristera	89
	Livadi	90
Chapter 4	Schubert at the Villages of Volvi (5th June–10th August 1944)	92
	Nea Apollonia: Schubert tamed?	92
	Marathousa in flames (19th June)	95
	Raid at Nea Madytos. Retaliation for a Schuberite killing	102
	Asvestochori, day of terror and violence (26th July)	105
	Schuberite deserters: the role of the ΕΠΟΝ women in Nea Apollonia	108

Chapter 5	**Asvestochori, Last Base of Schubert (10th August–28th September 1944)**	113
	Axioupolis Kilkis: Schubert the 'General Coordinator' of Security Battalions	113
	The village of Hortiati during the Occupation	116
	Preface to the holocaust of Hortiati	117
	Why the ambush at Kamara?: the statement of K. Paschaloudis	119
	The critics of the ΕΛΑΣ testimony	122
	Atrocities	128
	Kurt Waldheim and the coverup of the holocaust	131
	Those responsible for the holocaust	133
	The massacre at Giannitsa: Schubert's last act of barbarism (14th September)	135

Part III: Shubert: "Wolf in Sheep's Clothing" — 141

Chapter 1	**From Anixiohori to Vienna**	143
	Krya Vrysi: the mysterious death of the doctor Chr. Mantzana	143
	Austria: Dina Mantzana and Schubert's eroticism	144
Chapter 2	**Return to Greece (5 September 1945)**	146
	At Eleusis Airport: Facing police control	146
	The story of the Austrian ballerina-informant	147
	The identity of "Konstantinides" revealed	148
	The "arrest" of Schubert in Thessaloniki and the mystery-pistol	150

Part IV: Schubert and the Schuberites before the Courts — 153

Chapter 1	**Schuberite Trial in Athens (28 July–5 August 1947)**	155
	Witnesses and delaying tactics	155
	The voice of Crete	158
	The voice of Macedonia	159
	The issue of Schubert's blame	163
	Thessaloniki: Schubert before the firing squad (22nd October 1947)	165
Chapter 2	**Schuberite Trials, Ghost Trials**	168
	Thessaloniki: 'Nine present, forty-nine in absentia'	168
	Crete: Justice and Punishment	174
	The end of the blood circle at Krousonas	181
	Schuberite fugitives overseas	183

Acknowledgements — 187
Notes — 188

Foreword: Stratos N. Dordanas

"Many were murdered and tortured in the cruellest way, homes were plundered and burned. The arrival of this gang (Schubert) caused brutal destruction with tears pain and bloodshed". Thus describes the Special Commissioner in his study of April 1947 the raw terror ravaged through Crete and Macedonia during the Occupation by the Greek educated Levantine, Fritz Schubert, head of the infamous detachment for chasing criminals. Considered one of the worst war criminals, he was convicted and sentenced to death on 27 counts and executed in Salonica. Cosmopolitan, linguist, violent, sadist, cunningly diplomatic – a few characteristics of his deranged character – officer Schubert makes for a unique example in the accounts of the Second World War. Starting early (June 1942) he begins his reign of terror on the Island, the head of a Cretan gang later describing it as the detachment for chasing criminals. Later, by martial command, he is established as the head of a German fronted criminal group of Greeks used to commit atrocities against citizens of Crete and Macedonia in the name of the New German class.

Thanasis Fotiou with his present work, the first on this subject, attempts to demystify the myth with concrete factual material acquired through long research with written and spoken sources. In particular he attempts, in so far is possible, to track his German protagonist through the historical chart of this tragic period, disclosing unknown facts relating to the life and activities of the bloodthirsty soldier and his team.

Lastly Fotiou achieves a unique interpretation thus contributing to the puzzled understanding of this time in history, throwing light on the areas of Schubert's activities as well as Greece more generally.

Thanasis Fotiou is a native son of Marathousa Greece one of the villages in Northern Greece targeted by the Nazi War criminal Fritz Schubert in 1944. A graduate of Aristotle University of Salonica followed by a PhD in Classics from the University of Cincinnati, he became an associate professor of classics at Carleton University in Ottawa Canada, spending his life teaching undergraduate and graduate students in his adopted country. His memories of near death at the hands of the Nazi occupiers at age ten continued to haunt him into his retirement years and led him to piece together the real events of this period from extensive hours of survivor testimonies and long forgotten government documents. The last voices of a brutal period in Greek history cannot be forgotten.

Abbreviations

EAM	National Liberation Front
EAKK	Greek Division for the Persecution of Criminals (Communists)
EAO	National Liberation Organization (Rethymnon)
EEE	National Union (Hellas)
EEΣ	Greek National Army
EΛAΣ	Greek People's Liberation Army
EOK	National Organization of Crete
EOAK	National Organization of Cretan Officers
EΠON	United Panhellenic Youth Organization
FG	Feldgendarmerie
GFP	Geheime Feldpolizei
ISLD	Inter-Services Liaison
MI6	British Secret Intelligence
OYΘ	Plumbing Board of Salonica
ΠAO	Panhellenic Liberation Authority
ΠOET	Panhellenic Organization of Nationalist Battalions
SOE	Special Operations
AΣKI	Archive of modern social history
BA	Bundesarchiv
BDC	Das Berlin Documents
CIS	Italian Consulate of Smyrna
ΓAK	General State Archives
ΓEΣ	General Army Staff
EΘ	Salonica Appeal Archive
IAMM	Historical Archive of Benaki Museum
IAYE	History Archive of the Ministry of Foreign Affairs
IKM	K. Mitsotakis Foundation's Archive
MA	Bundesarchiv
OSW	Osterreichisches Staatsarchiv Wien
SD	Stadtarchive Dortmund
WASt	Citizens Bureau, Berlin

Foreword

In the collective memory of the inhabitants of Northern Greece have been inscribed in indelible ink the names of those who, during the Occupation, worked meticulously to consolidate a German 'feeling of society', simultaneously uprooting any "burgeons of virtue" (a reference to Baudelaire) from the (blossoming) of Greek resistance. Dagoulas, Poulos, Schubert were just few of the 'chieftains' who caused such misery to the lives of the Greeks that even after the nightmare and liberation the ghosts of the past remained to haunt them. To this day, Dagoulaioi, Poulikoi and Schuberites play leading roles not only in scientific research and literary extracts but also family narratives and personal recollections, bloody as was the journey which stained them forever in the contemporary history of the area.

For the most part, the embodiment of these soldiers by newer research betrayed them, identifying them historically and thus distancing them from the accompanying myth. The only one that stood the test of time was that of the German Fritz Schubert, more difficult possibly to erase. And just as the researcher is summoned to collect in his arsenal the only sparse evidence to enlighten his activities before and during the occupation, our aforementioned officer maintains and reinforces his myth with divergences.

So powerful is his presence that he virtually eradicates the facts submitted by others, all contributing to one conclusion; that Schubert was the most ruthless, managing in a short period of time to assemble a private army of barbarism taking hundreds of lives in its wake during his creation of a kingdom of violence in Crete and Macedonia.

So, Schubert persists in the realms of history not as a local perpetrator of crimes in the occupation but, as discussed, due to the varied and fragmentary evidence pertaining to his activities. References to his extreme anti-communist wing in the post war years are many, though others have been lost through time or the destruction of important archives (for example those of the National Greek Office of War Crimes). As a result, all available evidence had to be collected and the bits used to form an overall picture of Schubert and his men. This research demanded methodical determination, patience and persistence to identify primary and secondary sources which describe facts for latent years.

The job was undertaken by Professor Thanasis Fotiou, prompted by personal interest, whose village in Chalkidiki (Marathousa) lay in the area burned by Schubert and the Schuberites.

Before he left to take up permanent residence in Canada, Fotiou grew up with accounts from the Occupation, particularly those about the destruction of his village.

Having completed his long university career, he decided to return – albeit virtually for starters – to his homeland to concentrate on his birthplace revealing facts which were to him inexplicable. He probably did not realise initially that his village would not form the beginning and the end of this but would be included in a long list of inhabited areas of Crete and Macedonia where Schubert's battalion had left their indelible mark.

As much as I try, I am unable to remember the first time Fotiou communicated with me to discuss his willingness to proceed and asking for evidence and information. It is certainly a while ago, possibly more than seven years until the work reached the publisher then the printer. The reader will surely ask why it took so long. The answer is short and simple.

Basically, two reasons:

a) Dark areas which needed enlightenment and added to this a lack of evidence and the fact that the research was undertaken from a distance. Fotiou needed to muster the only means at hand – the internet and the phone – to cut the distance between Canada and Greece and to assemble the first pieces of the complicated, demanding puzzle. After on the spot study on archives in Greece and Germany, for the rest he was obliged to rely on internet and phone often resorting to long phone interviews in an effort to cover the gaps, confirm validity of information and reject mythical suppositions.

b) Because from the outset he wrote whole chapters requiring excessive work in the detailed recounting of facts, often with unnecessary detail. All the material was collected with minute precision and toil demanding long hours, particularly as the author was extremely demanding and strict with himself.

Reading his work, it is easy to see how he achieved such a detailed account for the reasons above. Fotiou indeed covers an important historical hiatus and his work is a positive contribution to the contemporary discussion relating to the assembly of security battalions and the activities of the aggressor. Schubert himself may not have betrayed the country, unlike his men who hastened to join forces for their particular reasons. He drew his armed guard from various sources, places and in different ways often accommodating those with no other options. In any event, these men and their command were responsible for the murder of defenceless hundreds, often in abominable ways. They are considered to be those who introduced the method of assembling unarmed victims in buildings which they then burned. First implemented in Crete, they then perfected their methods in Macedonia at the peak of the crisis at Hortiati.

Fotiou does not limit his account to the events of the Occupation nor those that follow. In an attempt to invalidate one of the established myths regarding Schubert's 'Greek' background, he follows his champion from his first steps, through adulthood and his enlistment in the German army as war breaks out. Fotiou's contribution here is important as the status of the 'Greek' Schubert infiltrates for decades secondary and primary sources with significant assumptions. The question of nationality returns during the accounts around his arrest when he returns to Greece after the war and the story is rekindled.

Schubert's activities during the Occupation and relating to his criminal team in Crete inevitably take up the greatest part of Fotiou's work. Our great island was unfortunate to suffer under the anti-communist guard through their involvement in German attacks. In Crete, Schubert and his men made a name for themselves in armed raids and more widely with the traitors until the German authorities realized that our protagonist was more a creator of abnormalities than a worthy ally of the occupying forces. With numerous plunders attributed to him, murders and varying sadistic methods in extracting information, he was transferred early 1944 with his Schuberites to Macedonia where he had the space to add to the chaotic lack of control. To the extensive and arbitrary violence, he added his own trait introducing sadistic methods in his team's daily routine. He soon gained his deserved place amongst the ruthless Greek fascist names, none of whom nevertheless exhibited so many heinous crimes.

As expected, Schubert's arrest at Eleusis airport was considered a great achievement of the authorities and greatly pleased the victims' relatives who inevitably anticipated his exemplary punishment. His death sentence was accompanied by an unusual conflict between Crete and Macedonia who vied for control of the sentencing procedure. In the end, it was Salonica, where warrants were pending for him and his men which was to be the last stop of his disruptive career. One morning in October 1947, Schubert passed the gates of the Eptapyrgos prison, was transported to the 'usual place of execution' behind the jail and became easy prey for his executioners. His last moments were photographed after considerable publicity throughout the trials relating to his terror thus adding to the abhorrence of the public. Unlike his men; they were transferred to Greece without the exemplary sentence. Fotiou recounts their personal journeys from the court transcripts making them more familiar to the reader who draws his own conclusions.

After so many years hard work and endless conversations with Fotiou – phones and emails – the writer was suffering at the thought of this work never seeing the light of day. Fortunately, his fears were allayed and the final full stop was achieved. Until the very last moment, Fotiou was cutting and pasting, unbeknown to him giving time for the graphic team to enrich his rendering with useful maps upon which a reader can easily track the murderous routes of Schubert and the Schuberites along the drops of blood.

I am convinced the wait was more than worth it. The reader is offered an enticing history unknown even to those specialized in the period which encircles the whole climate of violence in embattled Greece during the Occupation. A history not in the least pleasant from its content but so important for the understanding and reckoning of our recent past.

Stratos N. Dordanas
Salonica, July 2011

Author's Foreword

The present research relates the life and times of Sergeant Friedrich / Fritz Herman Schubert, a unique character, a ruthless terrorist and war criminal who, acting as interpreter, spy and administrator of the famous 'detachment for chasing criminals', committed many murders, tortures, plunders, robberies and kidnappings of innocent people in Crete and Macedonia during the Occupation. Additionally related in detail are the post war years, the emergence, arrest and trial of Schubert by the criminal court martial in Athens and his execution in Salonica. Important references are also made to the Schuberites, the pro-German and nationalist Greeks who were accomplices with Schubert in violence against their compatriots. To this day in certain places[1] the terms 'Schuberites' and 'Schuberitism' commonly convey a stigma of brutality and traitorous activities.

The research strives firstly to report, in so far as resources allow, the practices which Schubert and his associates used in the execution of violence and terrorism. Secondly, to determine from the accounts of Schubert's life and activities, which items can be historically documented and which are myth, suppositions or assumptions. Thirdly, to fill in the gaps of information relating to Schubert's progress in the Middle East prior to 1941 and his extensive role during the Occupation. Fourthly, to bring to light unknown facts to date and expand on what is written with more detail to enable the reader to better judge the extent and severity of Schubert's and his associates' violence which were considered to be some of the worst to plague the Greek population and lastly, to put an end, so far as possible, to reproduction of mythical and fabricated allegations which are evident to this day.[2]

It is for the following reasons that the subject of this research has not been investigated nor considered in the past. First, due to lack of evidence; second due to the particular nature of the "Schubert Association" which Greeks often identified with German ones so attributing the violence to them; and thirdly because the German military authorities (Office Ic) did not consider the Association to be a part of the army of Wehrmacht and mostly avoided accounts in the (Tagebuch) diary, similarly any reports to their command, so now Schubert's absence is evident from Wehrmacht records which are kept in Freiburg.

Mark Mazower, author of 'Inside Hitler's Greece' (1994), in response to my email wrote, "Schubert was a very evil character and whilst I had searched for material I never found anything significant about him. Nothing from Greek records. Vaguely do I remember he was tried towards the end of the war, but I have no idea where you can find court documents. Nor do I think the Wehrmacht records will help".[3]

He was right as none of the German material offers anything relevant. As regards records from Schubert's trial in Greece, the historian Hagen Fleischer, an expert, discovered that "most Greek state documents relating to war crimes were shredded in 1975 with the approval of the minister of Justice".[4]

It is worthy of note that from the records was saved the decision of the criminal court martial sentencing Schubert to death in Athens on 5th August 1947. As regards evidence of collaborators from the court at Heraklion, along with records destroyed at Halyvourgiki in 1989 under A. Papandreou, the Prosecutor, A. Avgouleas[5] discretely declared that these were destroyed though the truth is they were removed to storage. To those enquiring, the janitor responsible insisted that they were burned under Avgouleas' instructions. In 2009, after due process by data protection authorities to Panagiotis Lambrou, a postgraduate student at the university of Crete, the janitor was obliged to admit to the existence of the records and allow access.

These are a wealth of information regarding trials of Schuberites doing military service in Crete and Macedonia.[6] To conclude, the absence of material proved a major problem for whoever decided to undertake substantiated research about Schubert. My interest was born many years ago and increased to summit with Greece's 'new regime' when I decided to discover from relatives and compatriots how my parents' village was destroyed in the summer of 1944. The plunder of Marathousa, a small village by the northern borders of mount Cholomondas in Chalkidiki, was mostly familiar to me whilst as a young child I escaped with my family to the mountains, hours before the homes and few inhabitants became fuel to the fire.

After the war, a dark age of oblivion[7] rendered memories taboo even in family conversations. My mother sometimes undid the silence to express her sorrow being a refugee from a young age saying "cursed are the Collaborators, the Germans and Bulgarians who once again are to blame" referring to the other times 1914 and 1922 when it was the Turks.

Lambrou was examining the collaboration documents as material for research of Heraklion society during the Occupation. The excellent cooperation with him proved constructive. Not only for an exchange of views, but to corroborate based on the findings information about the trials of numerous Schuberites. These documents are today kept in Heraklion.

The memory of the destruction remained in my mind as a recurring nightmare. So nearly three decades after the war, the events were reincarnated in the summer of 1979 at the home of Uncle Nicholas in Marathousa. He had a good memory and his narrative was live and dramatic. When he finished his detailed rendering I asked who was the head of the Germans or collaborators who decided to burn the village and his reply, "Who knows, he was Unknown".[8] That same day I left Marathousa and went down to Nea Apollonia, the base of the Germans and collaborators, thinking that possibly Uncle John could feed my curiosity. His response revealed that "it was here that the German, Schubert, settled with 150 men, all Cretans and they burned Marathousa. I met his second in command, a young German who tried twice to arrest us in our hideout in Besikia".[9] I knew nothing more about this

German and his activities prior to his arrival in Nea Apollonia in June 1944. My first attempt at collecting information relating to the destruction of Marathousa had ceased here. I was then merely curious. Due to my university commitments, I returned to the subject 20 years later.

In 1999, a decade after the collapse of communism, I returned to Nea Apollonia from Canada to record interviews with older and younger generations who I assumed would now feel more comfortable talking about their experiences during the Occupation.

Those who didn't know me seemed reticent and unwilling to talk when I explained that I planned to recount local history of the villages to the north of lake Volvi which suffered by the enemy, not only the Schuberites, but the Germans and Bulgarians. Finally, I withdrew behind the wall of silence before me. I then realized that "traumatic experiences have greater negative effect on the soul than natural disasters"[10] with the result that private events become clouded and censored.

One of the villagers, still a youth in 1944, showed willingness to talk about Schubert beginning his narrative with the following introduction: "Schubert was a Greek German who assembled a group of Cretans released from jail. When he came to Macedonia he added some Pontian Turks from Ombar. I chanced upon one of the best, named Lazaros, at the village coffee shop in the fifties when I went there for wood. He spoke about his time at Nea Apollonia and how proud he was under the Schubert group.

Schubert would recruit by force several kids from villages of West Chalkidiki. Two youngsters from Petralona revealed to my mother that they wished to desert and she sent them to Amalia who provided shelter. It was here that Schubert also brought his wife, Katy, a teacher from Giannitsa who helped us as she could. At the end of the war, she was tried for collaboration and executed. Schubert and his officers, Germanakis and Kapetanakis, were the most bloodthirsty. They tortured and killed many from our village and nearby. In August the unit left and settled in Hortiati which they burned along with women and children. At the end of the war, Schubert left for Germany and in 1946 returned to Greece using the name Georgiades. The EAM discovered him in Piraeus, arrested him and he was tried, then executed".[11]

For the most part, the information, both revealing and interesting, was a reproduction of others' reports and the press as my witness disclosed. Naturally his narrative contained inaccuracies which only later became evident through the process of research. Admittedly, this new evidence from the Nea Apollonian awakened an interest in me to discover more about Schubert. The Occupation, my new chapter was a generally unknown topic. So, I searched for persons who I thought could help.

The mention of several Cretans in Schubert's band fuelled my curiosity to unravel Schubert's relationship to Crete. Manolis Frangiadakis, an old friend with whom we served in the Navy, and with interesting facts about the history of Crete, responded eagerly to my request and was able to access an extract of the court proceedings of Schubert's trial adding "a friend gave me this extract and said it is all he has".[12] It was the first and indeed very important document – although the introduction is missing – as it contains a long list with the names of places and victims of Schubert in Crete and Macedonia between 1941 and 1944. Small villages are named like Eleftherochori, Asvestario, Gorgopi and Karpi in the eastern hills of Paikou, but no mention of Schubert's crimes in the villages by the southern side of lake Volvi (Nea Apollonia, Nea Madytos, Melissourgos, Marathousa).

For the moment, I've left Crete aside and I am concentrating on Macedonia looking for material relating to the region of Volvi. From the Archaeological and Historical division of the Aristotelis University I welcomed the kind input of Professor Giannis Hasiotis, an old student friend and his colleague, Basil Gounari. The latter introduced me to Stratos Dordana who eagerly sent me a copy of his doctoral paper whose title is the retaliation of the Germans in Macedonia, later to be published.[13] The work, impressive particularly in its content, validity and quality, draws material from many foreign and Greek sources. As regards Schubert and his gang, the writer supported his findings exclusively from the Greek records. Dordana[14], more importantly, found from the Salonica appeal court, proceedings and decisions relating to Collaborators and Schubert's volunteers in the years after the Occupation. This document, along with historical records of the Ministry of Foreign Affairs and the Benaki Museum where reports of the International Red Cross are kept, formed one of the most important sources relating to Schubert and his group in Central Macedonia. Apart from a brief mention, the Volvi region surprisingly is absent from the above. The Greek records were a further disappointment so I started wondering how I could connect Schubert's activities in Volvi with those in Central Macedonia. For the moment, the link was impossible as in Dordanas's paper the extent of Schubert's activities is incomplete.

As a result, what is missing can only be found by perseverance and work on the Greek records, particularly the collaborators' files of the Salonica appeal court.

Early 2004, Dordanas continued his research at Salonica to find information relating to trials of those collaborators who formed different Security Groups in occupied Salonica. In the mass of files was one relating to Schubert and his group.

The researcher made available to me particular photocopied documents which I studied in Salonica. The contents consisted of orders, proceedings and decisions of the special court of collaborators of Salonica between 1945 and 1948, police and authorities' reports, sworn prosecution and defence witness statements and examinations of accused who served for the Schubert gang. This court material proved extensive enough to fill the gaps and to complete with more accurate details the activities of Schubert and his team in Macedonia. Indicatively, a more accurate schedule of Schubert's movements in different areas came to light including those in West Chalkidiki. As for Volvi, although sparse, the material was used to corroborate witness statements from the villages of North Chalkidiki. Based on the research Schubert's activities in Macedonia were reviewed and published in article.[15]

In subsequent meetings and discussions, Dordanas encouraged me to undertake the research of Schubert's criminal journey from his arrival in Crete in 1941 till his sentencing in 1947. I considered this request a challenge but also a serious obligation for someone entering a new realm of historical research, particularly of Crete for which without assistance it would be difficult to achieve. Early 2005, Frangiadakis brought me into contact with Kostas Mamalakis, curator of modern history at the Historical Museum of Crete in Heraklion, who had made available extracts of the proceedings of Schubert's trial enticing my interest in the German villain and his activities in Crete. From then, Mamalakis remained one of the closest and most valuable supporters of the research, without whose advice unknown facts relating to the activities of Schubert and his team could have not come to light. In the four years since our first meeting, there was an exchange of endless emails and phone conversations with particular emphasis on discovering tracking and identifying Schuberites and "Gestapites", a role in which Mamalakis was unique. His help proved particularly important as firstly, he made available material from his personal collection including copy proceedings, witness interviews, reports of British and Cretan officers of EAM and EOK, documents from the file of G. Kavvos photocopies of local press during and after the occupation, photos and objects of a military nature; secondly, he responded to my request to interview persons in distant villages of Crete and Heraklion which interviews he kindly made available to me and thirdly, he arranged a program of meetings with people selected for their particular experiences and secured their agreement to discuss with a 'foreign' researcher.

It should be noted that Cretans generally more so than other Greeks – of those who indeed are able to remember – "in fear, do not dare talk to anyone or about anything".[16] Influenced by the brutality of hostilities towards Cretans and of Cretans towards their collaborators, they remain quiet avoiding inflammation of past suffering and opening unhealed wounds.

It was from Mamalakis I first heard details of the origin and activities of Schubert in Turkey (Smyrna). He reassured me he was told of Schubert by Ralph Stockbridge, an officer and director then of the British secret intelligence service, Inter Services Liaison Department who led the inquiry when Schubert first settled in Rethymnon the summer of 1941. The basic facts are these: Schubert was born in Smyrna from a Greek father, Spyros Konstantinides and a Turk mother and christened Petros. The father was "no good" and abused his mother who left him taking Petros with her. She re-turkeyfied and encouraged her son to hate anything Greek. Petros at a young age was enlisted in the Turkish army and fought under Kemal against the Greeks at the river Sakarya. He excelled in the battle and was awarded a medal in the shape of a half-moon which made him very proud. In the 1930s he emigrated to Germany where he applied to change name to one more pronouncable, Frits Schubert. In 1941 he appeared with the occupied troops in Rethymno as a second officer or mere soldier. Here he frequented old neighbourhood near the Venetian fortress to speak Turkish with old people of Asia Minor.

It was to them he divulged his Greek origins, his time in the Turkish army and proudly showed his medal.[17]

The information about Schubert's Greek origins had not been checked for their validity. Around this time, I received a note through Dordana from Hagen Fleischer who had found in a Berlin record the "death certificate of Schubert Frederick of Augustus and Wilmhelmina, aged 50, born in Dortmund Westfalen" and signed by the director of the criminal jails of Eptapyrgos in Salonica.[18] Due to Fleischer's findings, I concentrated on records from Dortmund and Berlin thus discovering all Schubert's past before enlistment as a veteran in 1941, aged 44 in the auxiliary army (Erzatzheer) of Wehrmacht. In short, the public record of Dortmund (Stadtarchiv Dortmund) shows family entries relating to parents, recording a wedding in Smyrna to an Italian, resident in 1926 in Alexandria, the birth of two sons and finally Schubert's return with the family in 1939 from Alexandria to Dortmund until his wife and children's' departure in 1941 to Palermo in Sicily.

In the Berlin Citizens Advice Bureau (Deutsche Dienststelle/WASt) were discovered identity bracelets, TAP (corpse recognition) upon which are engraved the brief army record of Schubert relating to transfers to different units in Crete and Macedonia from 1941 to 1944.

Schubert was sent to Greece as an interpreter and spy but in early 1943 he was enlisted in the military police (Feldgendarmerie). In the Berlin federal records (Bundesarchiv) his partisan id was identified (NSDAP Mitgliederkarteikarte) which bears the date 1st January 1934, the first registration in the Nazi Party and various contact addresses in Germany.

Research in the historical archive of the foreign Ministry (IAY-E) shows a few entries relating to the procedure and start of Schubert's trial without the actual proceedings. The most important and unique to Crete court document (extract) in the archive is a decision (March 1948) of the special court of Collaborators of Chania, which amongst others includes a list of the names of 36 Schuberites with details of the locations of their crimes.[19] In the same file, the researcher can follow through extensive documents the procedure of the recognition, arrest, incarceration in an Italian camp and suicide of the famous Schuberite, G. Kapetanakis.

The archive of modern social history (ASKI) in Athens proved sparse. A report of army intelligence exists, one of the few documents amongst endless reports and witness statements then submitted to the national office of war crimes to support the summons against Schubert.[20]

The Board of military history (DIS) offers extensive material, mostly including action reports which Cretan commanders of resistance and armed groups submitted to the authorities after the Occupation. It comes as a surprise to the researcher to discover that in most reports, as those of Bantouva, Petrakogiorga, and teams of Grigoraki, the 'Satan' and others, Schubert is not mentioned at all or merely named. To point, the Rethymnian commander Chr. Tsifakis in his report mentions German forces as perpetrators of the crimes shown to be Schubert's with his team in particular villages of Crete and merely refers to Schubert's gang as the "executing branch" of "the most beastly crimes".[21]

The reports and other written sources prove a serious problem to the researcher as the information is often invalid, exaggerated and inaccurate to suit the subjective motives of the writers.

Finally at the historical archive of the Benaki museum (IAMM) in Athens are kept the reports of the Swiss, Emile Wenger, representative of the international Red Cross throughout the Occupation, responsible for food distribution and generally assisting innocent populations struggling under the forces and their accomplices. His reports are a valuable source for Schubert's crimes, particularly in Giannitsa and Hortiati as apart from descriptions of destruction they include witness accounts of survivors.[22]

The papers which circulated in the years after the Occupation contain articles about the trials of Schubert and the Schuberites which contribute in different ways to the overall picture. The quality and thoroughness of these articles differ from paper to paper and the researcher needs to be aware as frequently witnesses are misinterpreted or dramatized and names, dates and other information abbreviated missed out or conveyed distorted. As such, the material, so far as possible, needs to be checked and cross referenced with other sources where these exist to establish their validity.

The necessary corroborative source of this primary material proved to be witness accounts which for a decade I have assembled after face to face interviews with people from different backgrounds and political beliefs. Some interviews have been recorded by phone as the only suitable way to easily gap the huge distance between Canada, my permanent residence, and Greece. This method proved rewarding and less time consuming. Of those who accepted to interview over the phone, some were known to me and others were contacted beforehand by a colleague to prepare them for the encounter. Whilst some initially showed hesitation, the fact that they were speaking with a Greek living abroad interested in the history of their country, encouraged them to speak more freely from the comfort of home – rather than a café – and far from local compatriots. Inevitably there were witnesses, particularly from Crete, who expressed concern that my intention was to drag them through the courts accusing them of defaming and dishonouring the dead.[23]

Others kept to generalities on the basis that "we don't need to repeat old stories to be found in books and newspapers".[24]

Challenged by a Cretan witness, I found his article only to discover it indeed was a reproduction of excerpts from the court decision sentencing Schubert in 1947.[25]

As regards more recent bibliography, there is no complete research relating to Schubert. Admittedly there are few reports about him and his gang in works that relate to the Occupation and those writers merely use old evidence and material from publications and newspapers. Regarding Macedonia, the work of Stratos Dordana about the German retaliation is an exception which, as mentioned above, includes a section dealing thoroughly with Schubert's activities there in 1944. Regarding Crete, the most complete and validated accounts about Schubert's activities are included in the works of Cretans I. Manolaki[26] and G. Kavvos.[27] Manolakis supports his brief rendering mostly on witness interviews which he methodically edits whilst the legally trained officer, George Kavvos, in his elaborate work, without reference to source, gives a full picture of Schubert's activities in Crete. From his privileged position as interrogator of German and Italian war criminals in Crete, Kavvos had access to many witness statements and reports submitted to his office in 1945 by political, military police and church authorities of the island relating to criminals like Schubert.

Additionally, Kavvos submits uncensored many documents of occupation forces, Germanophile Greek authorities, British agents and resistance organizations with the result that his renderings offer more validity and esteem. Lastly the rich historical material he consciously submits, he uses as a valuable source for the creation of an epistemological framework within which Schubert and his group are placed. Of the resistance content the booklet of the Krousaniot fighter Har. Giannadaki[28] is worthy of note, which describes the massacre of his village between the pro-German Schuberites and Gestapo on the one side and the Anglophile groups of captain Grigoraki, the "Satan" on the other.

Of 80 in total who interviewed, about one third spoke with me on the phone. Most were with Cretans, whose names and numbers were provided by my colleagues K. Mamalakis in Heraklion and Epim. Platsidakis in Chania. Of the Macedonian witnesses, noteworthy were the accounts of Nea Apollonian Laki Kokkota, a youngster in 1944, relating to Schubert's activities in his town and more generally in the region of Volvi. I maintained frequent telephone contact with witnesses like Kokkota upon realizing that their experience in the village and environs contributed to a deeper understanding of their society's influence in circumstances I was researching.

The establishment of a 'steady base' in villages and around was a policy which mostly I believe brought results as the reader will acknowledge that the analysis of events goes beyond a mere shallow description. Apart from Kosta Mamalakis and Stratos Dordana other witnesses with whom I conversed were the lawyer, Dion. Kasapis from Giannitsa, Stavros Tsiotis from Asvestochori, Theodoros Valahas from Hortiati, George Papadopoulos from Nea Triglia (for Western Chalkidiki) and Basil Voyiatzis from Marathousa. The detailed input of these initial witnesses was cross referenced with those of other interviewees. Frequently the options after cross referencing were difficult. To be noted every effort was made to have at least two witnesses for each village. Then input from these were compared to accounts in the primary source to check inaccuracies, mostly due to gaps in memory and reminiscences of previous political suffering in one of the darkest hours of modern Greek history.

During the long and painful research to reach this result, several people assisted in my efforts whom I would like to thank publicly. Firstly, the aforementioned Stratos Dordana concerning Macedonia and Kostas Mamalakis for Crete and the Occupation, who eagerly replied appropriately to the barrage of emails and phone calls. Additionally, both read my paper chapter by chapter and the whole and made useful comments. In improving the literary content, the advice of Dionysus Tani, an experienced editor, was most valuable. Similarly, the academic Gregory M. Sifakis and the researcher Panagiotis Lambrou, who is analysing the court documents of the collaborators in Heraklion for his doctoral paper. For mistakes in expressing innuendo, it is solely the responsibility of the author.

Additionally, I owe warm thanks to the staff Dieter Knippschild of Stadtarchiv Dortmund, Heinz Fehlauer of Bundesarchiv Berlin and Stephan Kuehmayer of Deutsche Dienstelle (WASt) Berlin, whose professionalism and familiarity with the primary source greatly assisted in the search for revealing documents and information for this research. Special thanks to Ms. Ute von Livonius, contract researcher at the federal military records of Freiburg (Bundesarchiv Militararchiv Freiburg) who researched the respective files looking for activities of Schubert in Greece to no avail. In analysis and factual elaboration, I was assisted by the academics Hagen Fleischer, Mark Mazower and Basil Vourkoutiotis. For the provision of the works of Giannadakis to Mrs.Georgia Katsalaki, researcher of the library and archive of the historical museum of Crete, I owe warm thanks. Further thanks to my friend from Chalkidiki, Vaio Kalogria who from the start helped byresponding to my emails and sending photocopies of respective documents about Karlsruhe in Germany where he studied. Lastly, I can't thank enough my friend Manolis Frangiadakis for his valuable and consistently reliable support throughout my long task.

Aside from the aforementioned, I should like to thank the remaining witnesses who agreed to communicate with me and in their own way contributed to the completion of this work. I owe them particular thanks. From Macedonia I wish to thank Stratos Theoharis, the teacher of Marathousa who from day one showed continued enthusiasm and interest and accompanied me to the villages of Chalkidiki for the interviews. Lastly the work enjoys its publication thanks to the patience of the publisher Petros Papasarantopoulos who showed understanding to the end. The distance parting the writer from the sources of material was the main reason for the delay in completing this work.

Thanasis S. Fotiou
Ottawa, Canada, July 2011

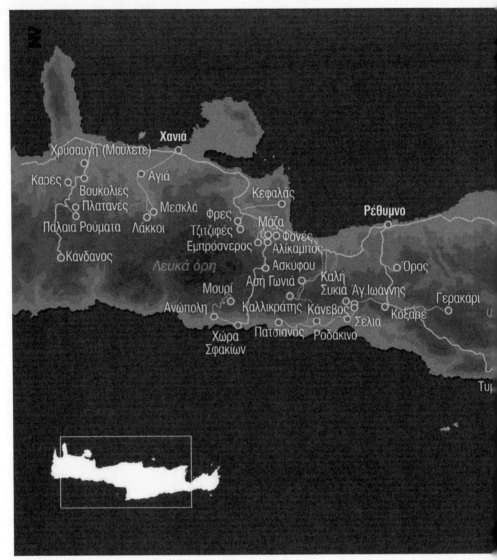

Activities of Schubert in Crete (August 1941–January 1944).

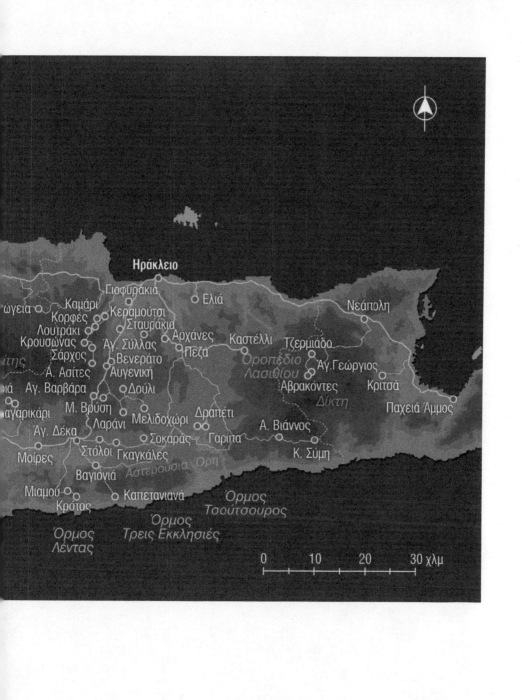

Activities of Schubert in Macedonia (February–October 1944).

Part I

Schubert in Crete
(August 1941–January 1944)

Chapter 1

The Identity of Schubert

The facts

Dortmund is a medieval German city of the 13th century, lying in the province of the North Rhineland in Prussian Westfalen (North Rhine-Westphalia) and in the heart of the area of the river Ruhr in West Germany. During the industrialization of Prussia Dortmund formed the largest centre of production of coal, steel and beer. The extensive coal mines and significant steel mills employed in pre-war years the biggest portion of inhabitants. The city fed the war machine of the 3rd Reich with plenty of steel. For this reason, it was 80% destroyed in the first months of 1945 by the allied bombings.[29] It was liberated by the Americans on 13th April 1945 then reverted to the control of the British.[30] Today it is the largest city of the area and the seventh in population (around 600,000 residents) of Germany. In this city was born on 21st February 1897, Friedrich Hermann Schubert of working-class parents. His father, August, worked in the coal or steel mills of the area and resided then with his wife, Wilhelmine at 16 Hirten Road.

The Schubert family moved in 1900 from this address, possibly again to workers' housing communities near the mines. The move may have been due to the addition of the fourth member of the family, Ida who in 1980 with her married name Reimann lived in Dortmund-Mengede, at 14 Stinne Street. The Schubert family avowed to the Protestant dogma of Evangelicals.[31]

With the outbreak of World War 1 in 1914 the young Schubert was of age to serve with the German forces and was probably enlisted then. His presence after the end of the war in Smyrna indicates that he possibly served his time in Turkey, which in August of 1914 had signed an alliance treaty with Germany and "from 1914 till 1917 was able to appropriate increased concessions from Germany".[32] It programmed a series of German special missions upgrading with military material and leading ottoman units in retaliating enemy attacks, as the invasion of Adad in Gallipoli in 1915. Indeed, those distinguished then Germans and Austrians of the Orientkorps were honoured with the Eisene Halbmond, an iron crescent bearing an enamelled half-moon.[33]

If Schubert indeed then served in the Eastern Unit and he was awarded the distinction of the Sultan for gallantry in Gallipoli or elsewhere, the source that he displays this star with pride in 1941 to refugees of Asia Minor in Rethymno, probably bears a dose of truth. However, by the end of the war the Armistice of Mudros of 30th October 1918 required all German and Austrian citizens, military and civilian, to vacate ottoman territories within a month. Whilst Great Britain made every effort to ensure abidance to the terms of the Armistice, its total compliance proved impossible especially regarding abandonment (article 19).[34] Despite the Agreement, many Germans conducted active roles in the economic affairs of Smyrna before and after 1922.[35]

It's very likely Schubert returned to Dortmund in 1918 to complete his two-year training at technical college prior to going back to Turkey within 1920 as a machine assembler (Maschinen-Monteur) as this 'skill would then have been in demand in Turkey'.[36] Inevitably German constructed military machines which had been dispatched to allied Turkey during the war needed the knowledge of persons like Schubert for maintenance and operation.

All this is reinforced in the evidence of "the allegations of origin" that Schubert still young was sent to study in Germany after which time returning to Smyrna where "for many years he works with the German authorities".[37] However, his repatriation could be down to his emotional tie possibly emanating from his military service in Turkey. The presence of Schubert in Smyrna after World War 1 is supported by archived sources. In 1925 he marries in Smyrna – probably in a Catholic Church – Giovanna (Johanna in German sources) Lucia Mirone, whose father, a musician, originated from Catania in Sicily and her mother, Maria d'Ortera born in Smyrna. The Mirone family resided with other minority Italians forming part of the Greek community. Giovanna was an only child and at her wedding already had a four-year-old daughter Maria. It is not known whether the father of this child out of wedlock was Schubert – in which case his presence in Smyrna dates back to 1920 as Maria was born in September 1921 – or whether Giovanna acquired her daughter from a first marriage dissolved prior to 1925. Another possibility, less likely, that the little girl was illegitimate. All in all, the impression whilst vague that is projected later in the relationship of Maria and Schubert is good implying a father and daughter bond.[38]

Generally, she is described as the "daughter" of Schubert.

It is strange however how Schubert and Giovanna with her family did not abandon Smyrna immediately after the torching of the Christian precincts, the ravaging of properties, the massacres and uprooting of minorities from the city. It may be that binding commitments to his work kept Schubert until apparently, he fulfilled 'his duties with the Turkish authorities'. Giovanna's stay with her daughter may be due to the bond that had in the meantime developed between her and Schubert. What is certain though is that immediately after their wedding in 1925, the Schubert couple settled in cosmopolitan Alexandria in Egypt, where the Italian minority at the beginning of 1930 rose to about 25,000, second in population after the Greeks.[39]

In Alexandria were born the two boys of the family, Anton in July of 1927 and Wilhelm in December of 1931.[40] Inevitably Schubert, as a mechanic, would have no problem becoming employed in some factory, Italian or Greek, producing cotton. Little evidence exists about the 14 year stay of Schubert and his family in Alexandria. On 1st January 1934, Schubert registers as member of the National

Socialist Party (NSDAP) with number 3397778, meaning he had been influenced by the beckoning of nazi ideology and propaganda so albeit late, he decided to enrol to the "main lists" of the members of party (Parteimitglieder) which had almost doubled since 1933, when Hitler took up dictatorial powers. His address as resident of the "foreign section" (Gau Ausland) is written on his party card: rue Federigo Pascha 49, Alexandrien, Agypten.[41]

As Schubert was multilingual – he spoke Greek, Turkish, Italian and Arabic, unfamiliar languages for your average German – he must have been a valued member of the Organization and as such could have undertaken the role of a spy in Egypt. Whilst this is of interest, the relevant evidence is lacking. On 1st September 1939, the date of Hitler's invasion of Poland and the beginning of World War 2, Schubert departed without his family from Alexandria for Dortmund where he lodged in the home of his sister Ida, at Stinnestrasse, 14. The possible reasons obliging him to abandon Alexandria were, firstly, as a member of the National Socialist Party he was responding to the call of Hitler to German nationals abroad to return to serve their country. Secondly, he was in danger of being stuck in Egypt if he extended his stay as Egypt in September 1939 was declared a war area and provided, as per the Treaty of 1936, facilities to Britain who, after the declaration of war against Germany on 3rd September, transformed it into a base of operations for the east Mediterranean and Northern Africa.

On 22nd September 1939, Giovanna also emigrated and was lodging in Dortmund with the two boys, Anton and Wilhelm, at her sister-in-law's Ida's home. The 18 year old Maria is not mentioned in the group and had possibly travelled earlier with Schubert to help find a home.

As it turned out, due to prevailing war conditions, securing a suitable roof was not at all easy. Hence the frequent moves of the family within the city. Only after about a month stay at Ida's home, were the Schubert family able to move in to Friedrich-Naumannstrasse, 17.

Already however the first clouds loomed over the Schubert family life. Securing a home was not the only problem the family had to face: there was the language, schooling, traditions and customs, attitudes, the political climate, employment and possibly more. In February of 1940, Schubert settled in the market town of Dessau in Saxony possibly to find work in the war factory of the Luftwaffe, the military Air Force of the Wehrmacht. His daughter Maria in an effort, it seems, to smooth over her parents' relationship, subsequently visited him in Dessau and, a few days later, the two returned to Dortmund in the hope of reconciliation. But the effort was in vain and the family disintegrated: Giovanna with the children at the end of May moved to Schutzenstrasse, 107 (no.103 also mentioned) whilst Schubert remained with his sister until the end of July 1940 when his presence in Dortmund disappears from sources. The ascertainment that a sound relationship with his wife was impossible to renew led Schubert back to Dessau for employment until the beginning of April 1941 when he was enlisted (his involvement in the forces of the Wehrmacht coincides with the invasion of German troops in Greece on April 6th) as a volunteer, as he was then reaching his 44th year of age, in the Replacement Army (Ersatzheer) based in Berlin. Giovanna with her children, on 25th November 1941, finally abandons the city of Dortmund to settle in Palermo of Sicily[42] where most probably her parents had also emigrated after the destruction of Smyrna.

In April and May 1941 Schubert trained at the School of Interpreting of the Replacement Army with the qualification Stabsabt. B.d.E. -5165- meaning he was a member of the Personnel of the Administration of the Replacement Army with the rank of Sergeant (Unteroffizier), granted to him on 13th June 1941,[43] the lowest of the five rankings of officers. So, until mid-June Schubert remained in Berlin from where he probably departed the same month for Greece. The choice of Greece and particularly Crete by Schubert was not by chance. These positions were closest to the Middle East where Schubert had spent his best years and it seems the nostalgia to return remained strong. As Hitler destined Crete for a broader role within North Africa (Egypt) and the countries of the Middle East with the rich oil wells,[44] Schubert's dream was to transfer as member of German reinforcements of the African Army under Rommel to Alexandria, the city where he lived and worked for near fifteen years. It is worth noting that even after the war in 1945, Schubert planned to use Greece as a stopover to Alexandria.

In the Military Administration of Southern Greece, Schubert appears to take within the local headquarters (Ortskommandantur) the role of "head of interpreters"[45] for a short time. In the summer he was transferred to the local headquarters of Chania under Air Chief Marshal Alexander Andrae, Military Lead of the Cretan Guard.[46]

That same summer – possibly August – Schubert was placed in the District Headquarters (Kreiskommandantur) of Rethymnon as an interpreter.[47]

The National Organization of Officers of Crete (EOAK) in its report gives a realistic picture of Schubert when he started his career in Rethymno: "… he did not belong to the group of German military secret police nor the service of counterespionage… arriving in Crete, he serves in a unit of Rethymno as a sub officer addressed by us the Turk as he speaks apart from Greek also Turkish which he prefers".[48]

In Rethymno, Schubert lodged at the requisitioned home of the teacher Economakis. Here the 15 years old Maria Roumeli met him; several indelible characteristics of his appearance remain in her memory. Anyway, her testimony is not only realistic but chronologically the first that exists: "It was still summer and very hot. A seamstress friend of mine said "let's go to Economakis' house to take an order for a German officer who wants his shirt collars changed. Chrysoula K. asked me who has befriended him and his name is Schubert".

I remember that as I associated it with Schubert's serenade. In the house we found Chrysoula and three other Germans. Schubert sat on a chair silent. He looked around 45 years old, long narrow face, thick myopic glasses, bald when he removed his cap, grey temples, probably short, thin with a large hooked nose, blue eyes and clean as a mirror in his clear white uniform. What impressed me was his appearance and the name they called him. I remember as if he's there. He didn't look very German. He was dark in colour with a crooked nose as many Turks. Anyway, without the uniform you could take him for a Turk".[49]

The Rethymnians discovered something more important, that in fact this "Turk" was really of Greek origin from Smyrna and his true name was Petros Konstantinides. In Rethymno was born a myth which, with the course of time, grew into legend conscripting other interesting characters. So, it is worth examining the different components of this myth as they disclose the psychology of their creators and those indigenous to them.

The myth

In Rethymno, where Fritz Schubert had settled as a mere corporal, he had assumed a strange habit. When he went out, he became accustomed to visiting the old neighbourhoods near the Venetian fort, the Fortetza, where many refugees from Asia Minor resided, several from the areas of Smyrna who spoke Turkish. He befriended a few of the older men there as it gave him particular pleasure to speak in Turkish which he preferred to the other foreign languages he knew. To these groups, he related that he was born in Smyrna from a Turkish mother and Greek father named Spyridon Konstantinides. He himself was christened and named Petros. As still a child, he suffered many psychological traumas as his father was a violent character and often abused his mother who finally left him. The young Petros stuck with his Mum who returned to the Muslim faith and fanaticized her son to hate the Greeks and all things Greek. All this due to the conduct of his father. As a young boy, he was recruited to the Turkish army and fought by the side of Kemal Ataturk. He excelled in battle – possibly at Sangarios – so was awarded a medal for gallantry, a crescent half-moon which he extracted from his vest and showed with pride to the old men and women who spoke Turkish. Later he emigrated to Germany, studied, became nationalized and applied to change his name from Petros Konstantinides to Fritz Schubert.[50]

The British Inter Services Liaison Department, alias MI6, under Captain Ralph Stockbridge, upon receiving information that a German soldier named Schubert was attempting to associate with the town residents, suspected that he possibly wanted to defect and sent out his sleuths to investigate what exactly were his intentions.

The agents involved in the case assembled the above information in a report they submitted to the head of ISLD, who then confirmed that this soldier was merely interested in speaking Turkish and dismissed their concern.[51]

The first who wrote in 1951 about the Greek origin of Schubert was Ioannis Manolikakis, a journalist at that time of a paper in Chania. All the biographical evidence around the "awkward German corporal who acts as interpreter to the Commandant of Rethymno" is related below: "To determine his origin we need to go back many years: to 1900, when Fritz Schubert was born and named Petros Konstantinidesa name of Greek origin. Under the protection of the German consul of Smyrna, the young Konstantinides is sent to Germany and obtains German nationality along with his new name. Later he returns back to Smyrna and for many years works with the Turkish authorities. In fact, he serves in the Turkish army and receives a medal from the Turkish government. Then he returns to Germany to settle after a few years in Alexandria. In 1937 he becomes a member of the National Social party"[52] Manolikakis, who was convinced, as many Cretans, of Schubert's Greek origin does not clarify the nationality of Schubert's mother, Greek or Turkish[53] and to what extent the father Konstantinides was to blame for the alleged hatred of his son towards the Greeks.

One sees Manolikakis refer to a second stay by Schubert in Germany after serving in the Turkish army and before settling in Alexandria in 1926. It is an additional element to the myth. One other journalist, also from Chania and a contemporary of Manolikakis, in an article published in 1998, adds, enhances and gives a different dimension to what Manolikakis has written. In this article, the father Konstantinides is a Pontian named Phaedon (Spyridon sounds too Corfiot easily associated with the Saint of Corfu) a tobacco merchant from Trabzon who settles in Smyrna at a somewhat elderly age and becomes besotted with a young Turkish girl, Gyoulser,[54] marries her giving the Christian name Maria and in 1900 Petros is born, who at the age of 14 loses his father due to old age. The mother returns to the Muslim faith, fanaticizes her son against the Greeks, becomes a lover to the German consul of Smyrna, hence Petros under his protection is sent to Germany where he serves in the German army where he conceals his Greek name to gain citizenship as Fritz Schuber (not Schubert as he wanted to distinguish himself from the composer). After his return to his old homeland he is enlisted in the Turkish army and after the battle of Sangarios (August 1922) where he excelled, the government of Kemal decorates him. The writer of the article, as Manolikakis, does not disclose the sources used for the information relating to Schubert's biography.[55]

It remains an unsolved mystery as to what details of 'Greek' origin Schubert himself moulded to feed his curious audience and what were added or exaggerated and for what reason by subsequent informants. In any event, the history of his origin, as generally outlined from the above sources, must have invoked great feelings and surprise to the refugees from Asia Minor. Schubert must have seemed to them a triple enemy, first as a German invader, second as a denier and defecting Greek and third as a mongrel barbarian (Turk from his mother) and anti-Greek. Further contempt would have been provoked in the Rethymniot refugees by the fact that Schubert took part in the war against the Greeks – possibly also the destruction of Smyrna – and his decoration by the Turkish authorities for his gallantry and anti-Greek stance.[56]

The issue of the nationality and identity of Schubert's supposed parents attracted much interest especially in Crete, less so in Macedonia. People wanted to understand thw reasons why Petros Konstantinides could outperform even the Germans in violence and crimes against the Greeks.

The name Konstantinides was very common in Smyrna. References exist of wealthy Konstantinides as traders, industrialists, bankers, professors and doctors[57] who were obliged in 1922 to abandon Smyrna and find refuge in Greece. One

Konstantinides, in industry from Smyrna, settled with his sons in Heraklion and became involved in the manufacture and export of sultana. "They had a big business and all honourable. It's just the wife of George was a German citizen".[58] So, for some Cretans, Konstantinides / Schubert was identified with one of the sons of the Smyrnan family Konstantinides of Heraklion thus sowing the seed of a new myth, that of the Cretan who was transformed into a janissary. One woman of Heraklion recalls the following: "He was from Heraklion, from a prominent family. The father was a currant merchant. The son he sent abroad to study and he became a German. He changed name and character. He turned out something worse than useless, a Gestapo. His mother was so embittered she denied him. I was still young when I watched her frequenting the graveyard and crying so much and used to ask my mother "why does she cry so much" and she replied "Well, she's crying for her husband but she also cries for her child who changed from a Greek and became German". The mother was very bitter about her child. Whilst a good family, he turned out useless, a Gestapo. And yet he was Cretan and very cruel from what they tell me here (in Avgeniki).[59]

This myth relating to Schubert's Cretan origin did not spread to the extent of Schubert's myth instigated by himself in Rethymno. And yet, some villagers from Oros, a small village south of Rethymno, where Schubert committed his first crime in August 1941, happened to know this version. "He was, they say, a Greek from Heraklion. His real name was Petros Konstantinides and he had family in Heraklion".[60] Yet another version claimed that Schubert was born in Smyrna, he maintained a permanent residence in Vienna and before the War he lived in Greece working in trade. With the invasion of the German forces in Greece in April 1941, Schubert "wore the uniform of a German corporal".[61] There exist even more versions far less known, such as those who have him originating from Thessaloniki or Veroia. To conclude though, the story of his Greek background could not have gained such dimension and intricacy firstly, if Schubert didn't speak Greek even with slang as a Greek[62] and secondly, if his appearance was like an eastern Levantine. These two main characteristics distinguished him from Germans and made him plausible to the average person.

A Heraklian, G. Karras, a 22 year old electrician, describes Schubert from personal experience, "I had seen him many times when I went to his house on Valestra Street whenever there was a power cut. He was pale with thick myopic glasses, nose a bit crooked, a touch hunched. He didn't look much of the Arian race, more eastern, Levantine. There were lots like him in Smyrna".[63] And so, this German soldier who since the summer of 1941 found himself in Rethymno serving as interpreter and spy (interpreters were trained to perform the duties of spies), heard and found out about the resistance the Cretans were conducting against the German invaders and possibly became first hand witness to the retaliation against the villagers in the provinces of Chania and Rethymnon. The account which follows offers a general view of the situation predominant on the island after the "Battle of Crete" during the time Schubert served in Rethymnon.

Chapter 2

Schubert; the Spy Activities During the First Period (August 1941–July 1943)

Resistance and German retaliation

During the ten-day Battle of Crete (20–30th May 1941) the island population, men, women and the young displayed a truly stubborn resistance against the German parachutists, using whatever means available to them, weapons, knives, pickaxes, clubs and even stones. German bulletins speak of "the rage and ferocity" with which the people encountered the invaders. Their fury surpassed the usual limits of the past numerous uprisings against the Turkish occupiers. The invasion's success cost dear. The dead and missing from the elite 7th Division of Paratroopers (VII Fallschirmjager) under air marshal Kurt Von Student,[64] exceeded 3,000 and, with the losses of the other divisions (total 22,000 Germans against 32,000 of the allied armies) of the air force and the 5th Mountain Infantry (V Gebirgsjager) approached 4000 soldiers.[65]

The high number of casualties surprised Hitler in the Wehrmacht leadership and particularly Student, the "Conqueror of Crete" who immediately from his first day undertaking the role of Military Commander "Commandant" of Crete ordered "retaliatory operations".[66] In a public announcement, he declared that "the toughest measures have to be taken and I order the following reprisals executions, fines, the total destruction of villages by burning and the annihilation of the male population in the areas concerned".[67] Next, he authorized the military divisions to implement the measures arbitrarily with absolute freedom of choice justifying his decision by blaming all for the "brutal mutilations"[68] caused by the villagers upon the parachutists.

Student's successor, General Alexander Andrae, continued the same policy of mass reprisal against the civilian population. The executed Cretans during the first three months are estimated to reach 1,135, about one third of the total amount of casualties during the whole four-year German occupation of the island.[69] So many villages around Chania, less around Rethymnon and Heraklion, where parachutists' executions were comparatively small in number,[70] paid a hefty price in bloodshed, the most typical example being the total destruction of Kandanos, a town in the municipality of Selino, on 3rd June 1941.[71]

As a rule, the terrorist tactics and reprisals used during this period, particularly in the villages of the provinces of Kydonia, Selino Chania and Mylopotamos Rethymnon, were suited to the usual method of operation: a German detachment at dawn would proceed with shots in the air and encircling of the particular village to prevent men escaping and terrorize the villagers; then oblige the residents to abandon their homes and assemble at a specific spot, normally the main square where, at the will of the responsible command, a number of men were selected, from 16 and above, as wanted or suspected anti-German offenders. Those chosen were submitted to notional questioning then executed before the assembled crowd or at a spot within or close to the village. Prior to their execution those about to die were obliged themselves – less frequently their tasked villagers – to first dig a mass grave in which they were rifled individually or in groups. Before they left, the soldiers, supposedly in search of arms, would plunder the homes taking whatever valuable and useful item they found. Depending on the decision of each commandant the operation would complete with the partial or total torching of the village.[72]

Variations of the aforementioned methods were often due to the particular circumstances requiring the intervention and the judgment of the responsible German command depending on the type and extent of retaliation in each case.[73]

In the end, the wave of terror and mass executions diminished after the actions of the occupied Government Tsolakoglou and protests of a designated Cretan committee to General Andrae, who by decree of 14th September conceded a general amnesty to the suffering islanders.[74] From then and until the spring of 1942, a relative calm prevailed. It is worth noting that during this period the troops of the Wehrmacht were counting numerous successes on all fronts of the war.

In announcements to his higher officials, Hitler emphasized that "Crete holds a pivotal role in the southeast area" and after the war planned to make it a base not only for the military but also for Germany's commercial fleet.[75] To this end and intent on establishing the Great Island an "impregnable stronghold" he commissioned the construction of large fortification works and the reinforcement of the guard to a proportion of 1:5 Italian/Germans to bolster an anticipated support of the African Army of Marshal Erwin Rommel. Note that General Kurt Student hoped that the 'leap into Crete' (Sprung nach Kreta) would follow the leap into Cyprus and from there the Suez Canal.[76]

The Fuhrer's plans were quite ambitious and were never wholly fulfilled. The number of occupying German forces on the island differed considerably from period to period depending on the demands from the other fronts of the war.

As per existing sources, the Wehrmacht retained at least two divisions of infantry reinforced with units of different expertise, a coastal artillery force of 2,500 men and other services as the 611 division of the Secret Field Police (GFP) known to Greeks as "Gestapo," a force of about 150 men and units of military police (Feldgendarmerie) or 'Butterflies'. In the summer of 1943, the total number of German forces amounted to around 45,000 men of which about 15,000 made up the air force and navy. The Italian division Siena under general Angelo Carta exceeded 30,000 men enlisted mostly at the province of Lasithi.[77] The municipality of Heraklion counted the highest number of land forces, 15,000 Germans and 5,000 Italians, whilst Chania had 10,000 Germans and Rethymnon 6,000.[78]

Evidently the reprisals of Generals Student and Andrae were planned to crush every attempt of Cretan resistance and oblige them to yield to the Nazi yoke. But the results were very different from those the leadership inevitably expected. Instead of bending, the will of many Cretans was fortified and they resorted to lawlessness, fleeing to the mountains in resistance. Their weapons, mostly old but some newer left behind by the allies, were sufficient for now. Anyway, gun possession on the island had such a long tradition that General Andrae did not manage to vanquish, notwithstanding his insistent requirement that all weapons be surrendered prior to conceding the general amnesty.[79] It is for this reason that the national and allied resistance against the occupation in Crete continued without the interruptions typical to mainland Greece.[80]

A number of Cretans, who resisted the German invasion and feared German retaliation if they returned home, remained in the mountains and made up the nucleus of the resistance movement in Crete. Initially the main purpose of these independent groups, from 15 to 20 men, was the rescue, protection and evacuation of those remaining Britons in the Middle East with allied surface craft and submarines which harboured at the southern shores of the island. Later, when the German forces implemented Hitler's decision to establish Crete as "the main hub for the dispatch of human and material resources"[81] to the African Army under Erwin Rommel, the resistor groups directed their efforts on hindrance and specifically preventing the major construction works such as the building of a modern airport, the largest in the Balkans at Tympaki in Mesara.[82] The tasked workforce at these sites was mostly from villages used as supply centres and enlistment by the rebel forces, particularly around Heraklion where the most significant works were carried out. The projects signified oppression and drove many to resistance.

From the spring of 1942 the community teams began multiplying and adopting an obviously rebellious face, a fact which worried the respective German authorities, specifically the 3rd Staff Office and the Department of Espionage and Counterintelligence, who attempted to convince the leaders of the most significant groups, such as Bantouva and Petrakogiorgi of Heraklion, to surrender their arms in return for amnesty and promotion to high political positions.[83]

The German plan of "disarmament" did not have the expected reciprocity and was soon abandoned, allowing the local groups to induct more volunteers. In the spring of 1943, after the collapse of the African front, the resistance groups appeared with considerably increased numbers of members with heightened morale and better weaponry. The force of the Petrakogiorgi and Satana teams in the summer of 1943 amounted to around 50–60 respectively and Bantouva around 160.[84]. General Wilhelm Muller, military commander of Heraklion, at his trial admitted that "from June 1943 the rebel groups had extended their influence against the Germans and the number of (German) soldiers killed had multiplied".[85]

The resistance remained unified virtually throughout the period of occupation. The British representative of the Allied Headquarters of the Middle East in Crete, Lieutenant Colonel Patrick Leigh Fermor, described the Cretan resistance as the "most successful, harmonious and decisive resistance in Europe".[86] The cooperation of the two factions, nationalist and left wing was held unsplintered until June 1943 when, after British instigation the nationalist groups joined the welcoming National Organization of Crete, EOK. EAM formed a separate faction without the break leading to serious dissidence and conflict as, according to the historian H. Fleischer, "in both organizations there existed a solid foundation of Venizelism".[87]

In the municipality of Heraklion, three armed gangs were active, the most significant on all the island under captain Emm. Bantouva from Ano Asites, Ant. Grikorakis better known as "Satana" from Krousona near Malevizi and Georgios Petraki, widely known as Petrakogiorgi from Magarikari of Pyrgiotissa. Their haunts were situated on Psyloreiti from where they were supplied with food, gained information from owners of the shelters (for livestock) and met up with the English agents of the secret services SOE and ISLD. Officers, as Tom Dunbabin, leader of the Allied Mission, Ralph Stockbridge, Xan Fielding and Patrick Leigh Fermor – some of the prominent members – were acting as intermediaries between the Allied Headquarters of the Middle East and the resistance organizations giving guidance, directions and material assistance so the struggle against the occupying forces became more effective and was coordinated as required and according to the military tactics of the Allied Headquarters (Preston Force 133) affiliated to the Office of Cretan Policy.

One of the main concerns of the English was to maintain the morale of the Cretan people at a high level. And they were successful by looking to the protection of the Cretans from German collective retaliation which initially still scared them. The English agents managed, using the Cretan love of the English, to hold the warriors in check and avoid attacks against the occupying armies with any executions of collaborators becoming selective and organized.[88] Note that the main aim and preoccupation of the rebel gangs was the collaborators who supported in various ways the purpose of the German authorities to suppress the resistance movement with arrests, imprisonment, deportation, executions and the terrorizing of civilians.

The damage inflicted by the gangs on the occupiers was minimal, restricted in particular to military material and means of transport.

Crime in the village of Mount Rethymnon: the beginning of a bloody journey

Corporal Fritz Schubert, during this period of relentless reprisals, served, as aforementioned, as an interpreter at the District Headquarters of Rethymnon.

Most likely, due to his posting, he accompanied military detachments tasked with the implementation of reprisals to the villages near Rethymnon, so he himself witnessed the events and personally experienced the method of terrorizing and group executions. His initiation to a bloody career started from Oros, a community of about 30 families, lying in the steep southern slopes of the verdant mountain of Vrysina at an altitude of 820 meters and around 20 kilometres south of Rethymnon. At this village there existed an organisation, which at the time harboured English who after the Battle of Crete did not manage to escape on ships to be diverted through the Middle East. A large number of these British – it is calculated around 4,000 soldiers and officers through Crete[89] – and other Allies, to avoid imprisonment at the camps, hid in mountain villages, such as Oros, and in caves waiting for the signal to be smuggled away to the Middle East by submarine or ships from the southern shores of the island.

The Cretans, throughout the long period of the British being present, showed not only great willingness to care for them but also harboured them, putting their own lives in danger as the German authorities announced that whoever was found hiding or protecting the English would be punished severely.[90] The Germans never forgave the Cretan unbridled love for the English. The first victim of Schubert happened to be an "Anglophile" Cretan from the area of Rethymnon.

On 28th August 1941, four 'Germans', of whom one was a Cretan dressed as a German, appeared in the village of Oros and asked to see Pantelis Papadakis, 67 years old president of the community. As Papadakis was away from home with his large family at a nearby farm, the Germans ordered the young Antony Xydakis, who happened to be the nephew of Papadakis, to go and notify him to return to the village urgently. Papadakis, as president, suspecting the Germans wanted him for official reasons returned to his house, leaving his family at the farm. Later that afternoon, a relative of Papadakis, Antonis Halkiadakis, heard groans coming from the side of the road about 200 metres from the village and a weak voice asking for help Close to the road at the spot "Mezaria" he found Papadakis bleeding, he bound his wounds provisionally, loaded him on a mule and left him, as suggested by the victim, at the home of a neighbour for assistance. Papadakis, who suffered a fatal wound close to the heart, died the morning of the next day, 29th August, with his final words being "Don't go to the house as these people may return".

They buried him the same day out of fear in case the Germans should suddenly appear again and arrest members of the family or others of the groups hiding and protecting the English.

These were members of the Xydakis family, relatives of Papadakis. The sources, six surviving children of the deceased, agree that Papadakis assisted in the concealment and protection of the English, with being paid "with gold sovereigns" as suspected the informer of Papadakis named Prinaris. Schubert and his gang were led to Oros by the young peddler Miltiades from the neighbouring Goudeliana, whom Schubert obliged to become his guide. The Xydakis later searched for 16 years old Miltiades from whom they gained information about the tragic loss of their uncle. Miltiades told them that Schubert and his accomplices drove Papadakis outside the village and started threatening him with abuse and torture to testify where he had hidden the English and the gold sovereigns. In order to escape the victim tried to run into the thick woodland, so "the Germans turned their rifles towards him and fired. They let him be thinking Papadakis was dead".[91]

The account of Papadakis' execution starts and ends with Schubert. In December 1945, Schubert was moved to Crete to defend his crimes.[92] A nephew of Papadakis heard from the imprisoned Schubert that his fellow villager Stelios Prinaris, known with the nickname Vasilomanolakis, was the one who had betrayed Papadakis for harbouring the English and earning sovereigns.

It is interesting that Prinaris' whereabouts were lost the moment he heard that the family of Papadakis sent a relative to Chania to interrogate Schubert.[93] The incident at Oros is recounted in detail as it reflects, though still at the beginning of his career, the modus operandi of Schubert as spy-counterspy. The main elements of the German lieutenant's method can be summarized in the following three stages: first, he planned his surprise attacks on the villages heading a small gang[94] usually consisting of Cretans dressed in civilian gear or more rarely as Germans; next he selected his victims ensuring beforehand a secret coordination with informers, as a general rule co- villagers of the target. "Schubert would go to places directed by snitches" according to a Heraklian witness.[95] It was rare, at even the most distant village, for there not to be at least one hidden informer known as V-Mann, in other words an undercover confidant[96] and third, the targeted victim after his arrest was subjected to cruel torture to testify to hidden weapons, rebel hideouts or British agents and generally his involvement in the resistance. Finally, he was executed, be it alone or before the terrified residents of the village who had been obliged to view the whole macabre drama. It was particularly the methods of terrorizing and torture that distinguished Schubert and his gang from the other Germans and rendered him "the fear and terror of the whole of Crete".[97]

Schubert in Heraklion: cooperation with the Espionage Office under Hartmann

It is stated that in the autumn of 1941, Schubert was transferred from Rethymnon to Heraklion as the area was "rich in glory and plunder".[98] But the more likely reason for his move was military. Aside from his function as an interpreter, Schubert fulfilled the duties of a spy-counterspy on account of the German espionage service, Abwehr III, a role undertaken by interpreters through their basic training.[99] Due to his qualifications and interest in this role he was soon affiliated to the respective Office in Heraklion responsible for the municipalities of Heraklion and Rethymnon. This Office was run under the administration of the Greek speaking Major Hartmann[100] who, as Schubert, was reputed to be Levantine with the real name Roberto Ruggiero.[101]

Apart from his association with Hartmann, Schubert also changed military units. He was transferred from the Reserve Army Command (Befehlshaber des Erzatzheeres) where he served from May 1941 and enlisted in the 4th staff corps of the 433rd infantry Regiment which formed part of the 164th infantry Brigade of 15,000 men strong, which in December 1941 settled in Heraklion under Major

General Josef Foltmann.[102] Its main purpose being the anticipated support of the African Army under Erwin Rommel who, after heavy losses in December 1941, was obliged to retreat and withdraw to Tunisia. As such the 164 Brigade remained in Crete on standby and only by the summer of 1942 were the larger part transported by plane to North Africa where it was reorganized into the 164th Light Africa Division.[103]

Schubert however did not follow the 433rd Regiment to Africa, but in mid July 1942 was transferred to the staff corps of the 746th infantry Regiment which at the time formed part of the Fortress Brigade Kreta. Here the German lieutenant bore the title Sonderfuhrer Z, or "Special Leader", designate of team Z to which belonged the interpreters and espionage agents such as Hartmann.

So according to his records, Schubert served at least from January 1942 till April 1943 in the staff corps of infantry Regiments 433 and 746 in the capacity of interpreter-spy. From June 1941 the Commanding General of Crete, Air Chief Marshal Kurt Student, was ordered to implement the decision of the Fuhrer to construct numerous fortifications to transform Crete into a fortress.[104] One of the scheduled projects was the construction of a modern airport at Tympaki Mesara for the anticipated supply of the African Army, which in January 1942 began to be promoted for the supremacy of North Africa. For the job the community authorities selected around 7,000 Cretans who worked increasingly under dreadful living conditions exploited by the occupying forces.[105] The main road between Heraklion and the Mesara/Tympaki valley offered the best means for the transport of manpower and material to the southern areas of the district so the enemy took protective measures at this time for the road network.

Fortresses and guard posts staffed by German units were established in hamlets and villages lying close to this road artery from Venerato to Tympaki. A number of villages, however, by the eastern slopes of Psiloreiti, due to their rough terrain remained outside the plan of military guarding. As such, the problem of surveillance of these villages, which offered ideal grounds for the development of the resistance movement, was a matter of grave concern to the German authorities in Heraklion.

Hartmann, an officer with notable abilities, was the organizing mind and motivated driver in assembling an anti-espionage network in the province of Heraklion and controlling the area by appointing to respective positions in the community Cretan "scouts" friendly to the Germans, who would be useful as submissive pawns and informers.[106] Important that for the most part these go-betweens were supporters of the People's Faction upon whom the Germans relied when they first came to Crete.

In the first months of 1942, Hartmann concentrated on Krousonas, a substantial village of the municipality (2,600 residents in the census of 1940) lying at a distance of 25 kilometres southwest of Heraklion and on a premium spot in the foothills of Psiloritis.

The incident at the village of Krousonas Heraklion

The people of Krousonas, faithful to the tradition of arms possession and ownership, had a passion for weapons and since the period of the Turkish occupation acquired the reputation of brave warriors for freedom.[107] The case of Krousonas undoubtedly concerned and worried Hartmann and the German contingents as it could create big problems if it remained outside German control. Hartmann knew very well the influence of captain John Pendlebury, member of the British Secret Service MI6, in Crete from 1940 who later armed Krousonas as a future stronghold of resistance in case Crete fell to the German invader.[108] To create a rift between the opposing factions and ideologies, Hartmann relied on a threesome of men who agreed to cooperate to further his plan. Captain Ioannis Polioudakis was the mighty collaborationist General Command of the Constabulary who "cooperated closely with the German authorities most particularly with the head of the German counterintelligence Hartmann".[109] The second member of the triumvirate in Hartmann's close circle of accomplices was the Krousaniotis Georgios Soultatos, a lawyer from Heraklion, member of the People's Faction and professor of kindred spirits in Krousonas through whom he kept close ties particularly with the family of Mic. Tzoulia.

He had acquired freedom of movement within the higher echelons of German and Heraklian society with whom he maintained close ties.[110] In January 1942, he acted as intermediary to introduce the Krousaniotis Nikolaos Tzoulia, the third member of the group, to Hartmann and the Military Commander of Heraklion, Lieutenant Josef Folttmann. At the meeting they discussed various issues particularly relating to the requisition of hidden weapons and the control of the rebellious Krousonas.[111] Hartmann appears to have said to N. Tzoulia, "we know you have fought us but this we forget and we ask to have cooperation".[112]

At around the same time, "Satanas" met with his clan at Krousonas and the nearby villages to prepare them for the pending resistance. With the blessings and support of Hartmann and Commander Folttmann, Nikolaos Tzoulia in January or February 1942 set the foundations of the first secret Germanophile team in Crete, consisting of, aside from his relations, several hundred co-villagers. Noteworthy that until May the group did not proceed to arrest or execute residents but sufficed to commit acts of violence in cooperation with the occupying forces.

So, on 10th February, Captain Polioudakis arrived with a detachment of 40 gendarmes to discover hidden weapons and arrest wanted Krousaniotes. In their search, they requisitioned as much weaponry as they could locate and arrested suspected resistors from whom Polioudakis selected whoever his local accomplices chose, as he himself wrote later: "There we found Georgios Michael Tzoulias and Dimitris Stivaktakis who were later enlisted in Schubert's detachment, indicating to Douralas (Commander of Gendarmerie) who should be released and who not. I realized immediately that these were the persons whose orders we would follow".[113] After this, the Germans discharged the appointed community president under the pretext that he had failed to collect the hidden weapons and nominated Michael Tzoulia as president, the patriarch of the Tzoulia family.[114] By March, using threats and fear, the new president called by named list the Krousaniotes to surrender the English arms distributed to them before the Battle of Crete. Those who refused were locked in the jails of Agia Chania whilst the collected weapons, many old, were moved to the armoury of Polioudakis.

At Krousonas at the time the men of both factions roamed armed with pistols and at public gatherings kept utmost secrecy. On 7th April, Kostis Mic. Tzoulias, a member of the Germanophile clique, in the village square, for reasons of honour fatally shot the resistor Kostis Tzouliadakis or Tzougkris. Before the assembled mass, I. Polioudakis had arrived making a chilling announcement "that's what happens to those who go against our grain".[115] This incident "lit the fire at Krousonas".[116] All at once the Tzoulias propagation created an oppressive atmosphere and insecurity amongst the oppositionists and particularly the resistance, who were obliged to gradually flee to the woods joining the ranks of the rebel clan of Ant. Grigorakis, more widely known as Satana. With the other camp, a group of Krousaniotes influenced by the ever-increasing strength and impact of the Tzoulias, cooperated more closely with them ready to contribute to the new range of activities opening before them.

Soon the supporters of the Tzoulias' numbers increased so much that, by May, they were able to control Krousonas and the area around.[117] Until then, useful as accomplices and snitches of the Germans, the Tzoulias were from now on preparing for an armed mission. Satanas, who had assembled under his leadership about 15 armed men mostly from Krousonas families, appears to have reacted to the murder of the rebel Tsougkris declaring, "Nikolas Tzoulias must be killed. He will burn Crete".[118]

Satanas also undertook the annihilation of significant collaborators in Krousonas following the decision taken with the initiative of the English Tom Dunbabin, the representative of the Allied Mission along with the leaders of four resistance movements, that was Ant. Grigorakis, Em. Bantouvas, G. Petrakogiorgis and the "Independent Group of Anogeia".[119]

On 22nd May, on the road to Heraklion at the spot 'Voutes', rebels of Satanas, in an ambush, killed Michael and Kosti Tzoulia, father and son, but Nik. Tzoulias who was their main target, escaped safely. The executions of the Tzoulia and other officials established a landmark in the history of Krousonas during the occupation.

When Commander Folttmann was informed that Nikolas Tzoulias had survived, he appears to have said, "As long as he lives, all is well".[120] As a result, many sympathizers rushed to enlist with the Tzoulia gang and the germanophile Kon. Makridakis was nominated new president of Krousonas. On 24th May a German legion along with the 'Gestapo' of Krousonas torched 17 homes of wanted rebels of "Satana" and of the terrified mass assembled, selected around 50 people, men and women, some of whom were locked in jails and others sent to work camps at Tympaki.[121] A few days later followed the execution of six Krousaniotes relatives of the resistance amongst whom were also two women of captain Grigorakis' family.[122] The era of blood which started in May 1942 is to continue till May 1945.

The first Schuberites from Krousonas

There are no reliable sources as to whether Lieutenant Fritz Schubert had any connection with the events which developed during the first months of 1942 at Krousonas. According to one statement,[123] Schubert's traces, early 1942, were tracked down to Agia Varvara Monofatsio, the base of a German unit of supplies networking spies and informants from local Germanophiles selected by Hartmann.[124] This was a large village about 30 kilometres southwest of Heraklion and at a strategic junction of highways leading towards Mesara and the southern slopes of Psiloritis. Due to the major military work already started at Tympaki, Schubert had become active in the area of Agia Varvara and with local cooperation, especially the president designates Mic. Houstoulakis, he sent many patriots and resistors to the jails of Heraklion and Alikarnassos. One of the hostages was also the professor Michael Z. Sifakis who prior to his arrest probably late March or early April of 1942, had received threatening messages from Schubert himself, in the presence of his daughter, that 'if he's not careful he'll leave his daughter an orphan'.[125]

After his activity in Agia Varvara and the area around, Schubert by the end of May turned his attention to Krousonas when due to the murder of the two Tzoulias, relatives and supporters sought revenge from their bitter enemies. The Tzoulias welcomed Schubert believing that they were securing a more certain and powerful support from the Germans to annihilate their opponents. Later, Schubert himself, from jail, confessed how he began assembling his gang: "I didn't. It was the Tzoulias who came armed from Krousonas and we searched together for hidden weapons. We discovered them from the Greeks again snitching on each other".[126]

So, no coincidence that Schubert connected with Krousonas at a crucial turn in the conflict between the occupying forces and their enemy. To the executions of their accomplices, as Mic. Tzoulias, the German authorities reacted vigorously with reprisals aimed at terrorizing the people and the utter condemnation of those responsible. It is however unclear how Schubert was officially 'nominated' as leader of Nik. Tzoulias' small gang, the latter remaining 'coleader' with equal, so it seems if not more, powers initially than Schubert, "if Nikolas didn't give the order, Schubert did not kill" emphasizes a Krousaniotis.[127] Krousonas is considered to be one of the villages which took part in liberation efforts during occupations since Turkish rule.[128]

It appears however that it was the sole village in the whole of Crete which supplied Schubert's legion throughout his activities in Crete with a respectable number, around 45, of volunteers and accomplices.[129] On the other hand, to Satanas' clan were enlisted gradually about 50 persons, resistors and patriots, subjected to the violence of the Germans and their collaborators. Krousonas' particularity was due mostly to the following two reasons:

First, the German mindset of the Tzoulia family: Michail Tzoulias with his five sons were the number one family in Krousonas. The family belonged to the wealthy elite of the village and exercised influence over the Krousaniotes with whom it shared family ties, in-laws, marriage connections and similar political beliefs. In politics, the Tzoulias always took the opposite side from other Krousaniotes. Initially from 1905 already, they had taken a stance against the Union of the island with Greece arguing for autonomy. Later with the creation of factions, although the majority of Krousaniotes and the Cretan people were venizelian to the bone,[130] the Tzoulias and few other families like Baltzakides, Gridakides, Makatounides and Makridakides were royalist and active in the Peoples Party. The patriarch Mic. Tzoulias, an enthusiastic admirer of Germany during the First World War, was christened by the people "Allemaniotis" in other words, "German". His children followed the Germanophile inclination and with Hitler's prominence during the 1930 decade, they embraced the ideal of nationalist socialism. In 1936, Nikolas, the eldest son, in a political squabble killed his opponent, Emm. Antonogiannaki or Tsourli.

When a venizelian Krousaniotis provoked them "Come join us, even the king is with us" their reply was abrupt, "We have our Hitler".[131] The occupation of Crete by the German armies opened for them a new realm of action. Other Krousaniotes followed suit.

Second, the dominant Anglophilia of Antonis Grigorakis or Satana and generally in Krousonas: these were for the most part loyal venizelians who had this reason to consider themselves more Anglophile than the others. Their leader Antonis Grigorakis, from 1940, was amongst the first to enlist with the team of English intelligence MI6, organized and run by the English archaeologist, Captain John Pendlebury.

Just before the German invasion in Crete, Pendlebury, with whom Satanas had created strong bonds of friendship and cooperation, agreed to arm the Krousaniotes with about 400 English weapons to fight the Germans under Satanas' leadership.[132]

After the takeover of the island, these weapons were hidden. Soon after, Satanas and his clan were pursued and took to hiding once it became clear that the Tzoulias with the support of the German authorities (Major Hartmann) planned to obstruct their Anglophile enemies and prevail in Krousonas.

In all, the overview of the political situation which characterized Krousonas until the Occupation, as with other villages in Crete on a smaller scale, was usual conflicts and disputes for personal, family and political reasons which resulted in violent encounters such as that between the gendarme Alk. Ieronymides and Ant. Grigorakis in 1935, during the Venizelos movement, ending in their wounding each other. The small portion of royals within the People's Party which felt marginalized and oppressed until 1941, instigated by the German domination sought to take revenge from the majority of the venizelian Anglophile faction for blight of 'honour' and suffering in the past. With the result that Krousonas appears as a unique example of a Cretan village where, at the level of personal, political and ideological conflicts, the minority prevails – with the help of course of the occupying force –

and succeeded in deploying an impressive number of hard accomplices who under Schubert's leadership will later become "the dread and fear of the world".[133]

As regards the makeup and strength of Schubert's initial gang, the picture which evolves from the available sources is confusing. In the condemning decision of 1947 Schubert was accused that until September 1943, he committed crimes "each time with a gang of soldiers" but without the number being determined.[134] In more recent sources and testimonies, the number of armed and "German clad" Schuberites differs according to the source, from 5 to 70 volunteers. Indicatively, the British Captain Ralph Stockbridge in July 1945, wrote that the "Hunting Commandos" Jagdkommando, of Schubert "during 1942–3 consisting of 60–70 plain criminals and Germanophiles" were responsible for many killings.[135]

Concern is also created by the accounts of Har. Giannadakis who names 43 Krousaniotes who "belonged to Schubert's gang and the Gestapo"[136] without clarifying which were German clad "Schuberites" and which "Gestapo", or the Germanophile accomplices and informers who didn't follow Schubert on his missions but resided permanently in Krousonas. In general, though, Giannadakis' extract gives the impression that the Krousaniotes, who from June 1942 were equipped and stuck with Schubert based in Avgeniki, were a small team, possibly four or five, whereas the 'Gestapites' who cooperated and assisted Schubert and his gang were far more. The latter denounced or arrested patriots and resistors of Krousonas and surrendered them to Schubert and his gang more rarely to the Germans, who imprisoned them, placed them in work camps or also executed them.[137]

A more specific impression of Schubert's initial gang can be formed from his witnessed activities during June and July 1942. Putting aside the executions of Krosaniotes, Schubert effected, whether alone or with German divisions, attacks accompanied by Georgios and Stylianos Tzoulia, also Dim. Christodoulakis or Stivaktakis and Ioan. Epanomeritaki or Koutouto. In July, also from Krousonas enlisted as a volunteer the rural constable Chr. Kourakis.[138]

According to the Krousanioti witness Kon. Giannadakis: "During German divisions" attacks, Schubert, with a small team of 4–5 overt Krousaniotes, played a secondary role to do the dirty work. He himself was not present at all the attacks and the casualties were few, about 17 in all. Before August 1943 no one really knew Schubert save his victims.[139] After July 1942 follows a dark period during which accounts relating to Schubert's activities are scarce. After this period, in July 1943 is recorded an undercover attack by Schubert at Meskla Kydonia where twelve German dressed men took part. The dreadful torture to which Schubert's men submitted the Mesklians, many of whom were elderly, forms evidence that the team were German clad Krousaniotes.[140] It is inevitable, particularly after his independence from Hartmann and enlisting to the Military Gendarmerie, that Schubert should decide to increase the number of his small team to convincingly meet the challenges faced with the new opponent, the revamped ΕΛΑΣ, and the ever-increasing forces of the resistance organization EOK.

As a result, to the initial harsh nucleus of companions were added a few more Krousaniotes who formed the permanent team, around twelve to fifteen men as graphically testified by Rev. Manolis Manousakis at Schubert's trial.[141]

Schubert's crimes and terror in the district of Heraklion

It is apparent that the ties Schubert initiated with Major Hartmann were so close so as to make him known to the Cretans as the 'executing arm' of Hartmann.[142] As such, in performing his undercover task he usually acted under Hartmann's command in a secondary role to German military divisions or detachments of the Greek Gendarmes. His method followed during this first period aimed:

1) to reveal and requisition hidden arms,
2) to extract information from patriots and resistors who were cognizant of hideouts and the haunts of resistance teams and English agents with their wirelesses and
3) to terrorize the villages to stop them supporting, in whatever way, the armed rebel clans and the undercover nationalist organizations. Schubert's missions to the various villages were carried out relying on intelligence gathered by Hartmann's Office of espionage from local accomplices within the villages and towns. Note in virtually every Cretan village there existed some collaborator who informed the German authorities responsible about everything going on locally. Their presence in Cretan villages is reported by the clan leaders themselves in their memoirs: throughout Crete, where every village has Germanophile undercover agents, who did not dare wear German khaki as the rebel teams would ravage them as they met them".[143]

The following are those of accounts of criminal activities which Schubert committed in June and July 1942, the most bloody months of the first period. After this time, reports are scarce and Schubert's whereabouts almost vanish. Asi Gonia, of the municipality Apokoronas in the Chania region is a mountainous village lying east of the Lefka Ori mountain range and 35 kilometres southwest of Rethymnon.

Through here passed, were sheltered and enjoyed care and assistance many a British soldier roaming the mountains of Crete prior to their dispatch to the Middle East. The village became a significant hub of the resistance movement under the leadership of the dynamic captain Petros Papadakis or Papadopetraki or Petraka who had intermittently undertaken the protection of the wireless which the British representative of SOE, Xan Fielding or Alekos had entrusted to him.[144] The Germans considered the allied network of intelligence on the Island to be "undoubtedly a miraculous network which spreads even to the smallest areas".[145]

Above the village, Lieutenant Andreas Papadakis had his lair, with his clan who cooperated with the English to protect the English wireless. During this period, spring 1942, the wireless and its guard moved from hideout to hideout around the areas of west and south Psiloritis. When the German authorities of Chania and Rethymnon, through their respective intelligence services, were informed of its existence they decided to explore these areas to reveal and annihilate the guard of about 70 rebels tasked to its protection.

So, May and June of 1942, detachments were sent to find the English wireless and pursue the leaders with their rebel clans. The first of the three detachments on 2nd May terrorized the residents of Asi Gonia with their night attack – mostly women and children as the men had managed to flee to the mountains – and after questioning of the assembled crowd, to find Papadakis or his family and searching homes for hidden weapons, they departed in vain. Similarly, the other detachments in other areas had the same result. In all cases, the men were warned of the Germans' arrival in time and managed to reach the heights of the villages and disrupt the plans of the German leadership.[146]

After the failure at Asi Gonia, Schubert – probably again under Hartmann's order – adopted a different tactic to reveal the hideouts of the English agents and hidden weapons. He resorted to shepherds, the best source of information available to an undercover agent. Hundreds, like Gypari, usually armed to protect their flocks from thieves, were considered by the occupying forces to be friendly towards the resistors but simultaneously most suitable to extract information as regards the haunts of the resistance clans and their English associates. Their familiarity with the mountain spots and connections with the clans to whom they supplied food and information about the enemy's movements, were the greatest asset they possessed.

Markos Gyparis, a farmer from a large nationalist family in Asi Gonia, had recently made friends with Manouso Thymaki from Embrosneros Apokorona. Thymakis, although a life prisoner before the occupation, had been pardoned by the Germans after first agreeing to work with them. Towards the end of May 1942, he fled to Asi Gonia in search of asylum alleging he was a fugitive and wanted by the German authorities. For the residents of Asi Gonia, as Gyparis, Thymakis was known as Venizelian and an Anglophile, a person they could trust. Now however the villager of Embrosneros acted as a pawn of Hartmann and Schubert to dig out the hideouts of the English and their wireless. On 2nd June, Thymakis with Schubert who dressed in English officer's uniform, visited the farm of Markos Gyparis.

Thymakis introduced Schubert to Gyparis as an English officer, just arrived from Cairo who was seeking to meet his colleagues at their hideout. Gyparis believed that indeed he was dealing with an English associate of the Allied Headquarters of the Middle East and happily offered to provide information about the English hideouts, arms, ammunition and whatever else they sought. Promptly Schubert summoned the armed Krousaniotes lying hidden by the farm to achieve his purpose. Upon refusing to lead them to the English hideout, one of the Schuberites emptied his pistol rounds against Gyparis' chest whilst another rushed to arrest Gyparis' partner, Ioannis Psyhountakis who ran off and managed to get away lightly wounded.[147]

Gyparis was the first evidenced victim of Schubert since taking the role of leading the Krousonas gang.

From their new base in Avgeniki, a village lying 15 kilometres south-east from Krousonas and by the road network connecting Heraklion to Tympaki, the Krousaniotes Schuberites, during the first fortnight of June, under the leadership of lieutenant Schubert decided to avenge the death of Michail Tzoulia and his son Kosti by members of the rebel team of capetan Satana. The killing of Tzoulia was one of the scheduled executions decided at a meeting which Lieutenant Tom Dunbabin had called at the end of April in Psiloritis.[148] In attendance were the clan leaders Emm. Bantouvas, G. Petrakogiorgis, Ant. Grigorakis or Satanas and Ioannis Dramountanis or Stefanogiannis with their officials. Dunbabin announced to the assembly the secret plan of the Special Operations Service (Force 113) of Cairo by which they would sabotage the airports of Heraklion, Kastelli and Tympaki and the bunker stores at Peza to disrupt the anticipated reinforcements of Marshal Rommel who was planning in 1942 to attack the defence lines at El Alamein.[149]

In addition, the allied plan included the execution of senior Germanophiles whom the German authorities at Heraklion under Hartmann had placed in positions of strength, particularly mayors, at strategic spots throughout the Heraklion area where "the collaborationists had become after their appointment more suspicious and despised".[150] One such decision of the Allied Headquarters of the Middle East supported by the rebel clans constituted a historic turning point in the relations between the occupying forces and the Cretan people.

Of the officials the resistors selected for execution the community presidents as most dangerous for they coordinated the collection of information and betrayed the activities of the resistance teams. During the first days of May, the clan leaders sought to warn significant members of the nationalist organizations to beware of anticipated German reprisals. Bantouvas concentrated his efforts on Heraklion sending "letters to prominent citizens of the town and particularly Tito Georgiadis" who decided the decision of the leaders to 'hit' the Germans was pointless and dangerous.[151] It is not clear however whom and how many resistors in Heraklion the leaders chose to contact whether in writing or directly. By the end of May they had executed only six of the twelve targeted Germanophile collaborators.[152]

The German authorities reacted decisively, particularly after the attempt by Bantouvas' men on the life of Colonel I. Polioudakis. Under the order of Commander Alexander Andrae, questioning followed and based on compiled lists Anglophiles and resistors were arrested and generally persons suspected of cooperating with organizations and English associates. On 3rd June, twelve hostages, amongst whom several prominent Heraklians and from Agia Varvara were executed outside the town of Heraklion by a mass grave, dug by themselves.[153]

The wave of retaliation was out in the open and provoked such fear that many turned against the rebel clans and particularly Bantouvas "the best team for tracking and annihilating the collaborators".[154] Captain Andrae obliged political and ecclesiastical authorities in Crete to make press announcements and distribute circulars denouncing and condemning the activities of the rebels. "Exterminate these criminals, these murderers". Colonel Polioudakis encouraged the Cretans.[155]

In this climate of terror and reprisals, Schubert initiated his activities with his Krousaniotes accomplices. Krousonas became the hub of criminal pursuit. The main target of the Tzoulias was to avenge the death of their father and brother. In case they couldn't manage to track the actual perpetrators, they considered as much to blame other persons who had any relationship or association with the Satana clan.

On 2nd June, a unit of Germans reinforced also by 'Schuberites' ventured towards the spot "Vromonero", a hideout of the Satana clan at the slopes of Psiloritis, planning to annihilate them. The rebels managed to get away, the Schuberites though arrested five persons some of whom were related, others cooperated with resistors. At his plot, they arrested the elderly I. Xylouris or Xylouroyianni, father of the rebel Menelaos Xylouris whom they tied with a hair rope by the neck to a donkey and "dragged him so both his eyes popped out until they reached Avgeniki".[156] Schubert's men transported the Lydakis, Spyridakis, father and son, Mic. Epanomeritakis and A. Tsorakis, all associates or related to Satana, to Avgeniki, Schubert's new base, where after torture they executed them by a ditch dug by the condemned themselves.[157]

The second round of reprisals followed immediately after the sabotage carried out at the airports Kastelli and Heraklion on 9th and 13/14th June by French and English teams respectively with the help of Greek drivers.[158] The next day, 14th June fifty detained hostages at the jails of Heraklion and Alikarnassos were executed in a mass grave outside Heraklion at the spot "Xeropotamos". In the meantime, the German authorities in Heraklion sent detachments to the suburbs of Monofatsios and Kainourio to pursue and arrest the saboteurs (the French were arrested a few days later), to annihilate the rebel clans, to reveal armouries and obstruct the dispatch from the southern shores to the Middle East of the three clan leaders of Heraklion with their families and team.

This distancing was deemed necessary by the Allied Mission for reasons of security and to avoid reprisals pending the anticipated major German operations at Psiloritis. Aside from the ailing Satana who fled, Bantouvas and Petrakogiorgis in the end remained with considerably reduced forces following the advice of the English agents.[159] Schubert's activities in May and June at the mountain villages of the Heraklion province are viewed within the framework of the executions of German accomplices by resistors and the collaborators by commandos of the allied Army.

At Agioi Deka Kainourio, a village lying at the 46th kilometre of the road artery between Heraklion and Tympaki, they paid for the allied sabotage with three victims recorded amongst the 50 executed on 14th June.[160] On 15th June at this same village Schubert arrived by car along with four Schuberites. He threatened Panagiotakis, the community secretary, to surrender 35 weapons which he had been notified were hidden in the village "otherwise I'll prop against the wall your president, the reverend and the secretary: as I did to Makrymanolis at Stolous, I'll do also to you.[161] Panagiotakis and his villagers surrendered whatever weapons they could assemble thus avoiding the inhuman torture carried out on the previous day, 14th June, to

Emm. Makrakis from Stolous Monofatsi (a mountain village of Asterousia, 15 kilometres east of Agioi Deka) for the same charge that he was hiding weapons.[162]

On 13th June at Drapeti Monofatsi, Schubert arrested Ioannis Manousakis, a 25 year old teacher who worked at Stolous and tortured him to reveal the resistors' hideouts.

"The Schuberites stripped him, threw water with a bucket onto his shoulders whilst Schubert beat him to confess to the whereabouts of the rebels"[163] testified papa-Manolis, the father of Manousakis, at Schubert's trial. In turn he was taken to Agia Varvara where he was obliged to open his grave terrorized repetitively by shots in the air. From Agia Varvara the same day, Manousakis was led to Heraklion and included in the 50 detainees executed the next, 14th June.[164]

Kapetaniana Monofatsi is a small village by the western slopes of the Asterousia mountains, 70 kilometres south of Heraklion and very close to the village Krotos.

These villages lie a small distance from the coves Tsoutsouro and Lenta from where the capetans Bantouvas, Petrakogiorgis and Satanas with their families and entourage were going to be dispatched to the Middle East. In the area between Krotos and Kapetaniana "we had hidden there at the mountain under some cliffs where it was difficult for the Germans to find us" wrote in his chronicle a resistor of the Petrakogiorgis clan.[165] Major Hartmann, around the end of June, sent Schubert with his gang supported by a German unit, under orders, to form a ring around the Lenta cove to thwart the mission of the resistors and explore the area to reveal and pursue them.

Passing through Kapetaniana, the Schuberites arrested Myron Mavroudi who, after a cruel beating to reveal hidden weapons which Petrakogiorgis had entrusted to him, "they rendered useless and maimed. Their method of execution terrorized the whole village and whole surround".[166] They executed him outside the village with Mic. Magrikoli, a travelling Heraklian peddler whom they met on the road to Krotos and considered suspicious. Metohi Vorou in Monofatsi lies in the area of Megali Vrysi and a short distance east of Agia Varvara where a German unit was stationed. The hamlet of Voros was surrounded by ridges with many hiding spots. Here the Bantouvas cultivated cereals along large areas and employed around 50 workers from bordering villages. At the time of threshing at Metohi, Kostas Z. Bantouvas, brother of the clan leader Manolis thought it wise to remain for the cereal harvest and the care of his wife who was bedridden.

So, he ignored the warnings of his brother to abandon Metohi immediately with his workers as the German authorities in Heraklion had planned an attack to reveal hidden weapons and arrest the Bantouvas. Kostas had hidden 100 Italian weapons and ammunition around Metohi, which the Allied Headquarters of the Middle East had supplied in November 1941 for the team of clan leader Bantouvas.[167]

For Schubert's mission at Metohi, the lead role was taken again by the head of espionage, Hartmann. Bantouvas not suspecting that Schubert's gang could take part in the attack, relied for his safety on his forged identification document bearing the name Georgios Nik. Mangousakis.[168] But he didn't reckon on a distant relative of the Bantouvas, a Manolis Hainakis, a secret agent of the Germans who, as becomes clear later, revealed details of the daily life of K. Bantouvas.[169] Metohi was surrounded at dawn of 27th June by a German unit stationed at Agia Varvara and Schubert's gang amongst whom the leading role in torture was played by G. Tzoulias, I. Epanomeritakis and D. Stivaktakis. Schubert and G. Tzoulias held the general command. With terrorizing methods, they assembled the people in the churchyard: "Schubert and the Tzoulias terrifying and swearing upon gods and demons, where are the weapons, where are the English hiding, where the Bantouvas". No one spoke.

They selected the young Zaharias Iatrakis (Yatraki), a worker from Kato Asites and before the assembled crowd and his parents "the Krousaniot beasts, equipped with jagged batons, began sawing them with the speed of a steam engine against Yatraki's body".[170] They crippled him within minutes. He was saved from certain death when G. Tzoulias ordered Stivaktakis and Epanomeritakis to stop the beating.

In the meantime, Yatraki's father who recognized Tzoulia had intervened and approaching him, introduced himself as an official of the People's Movement in the village of Asites. Schubert remained silent at Tzoulias' decision to refrain from Yatraki's execution.

Next was chosen the 22 years old Georgios Spyridakis or Manouros, who with his parents and siblings worked at the farms of Gianni Bantouvas. Whilst the Krousaniotes tortured him in the same way as Yiatraki, suddenly Tzoulias stopped his torment and told him to turn his back and move towards the crowd. A shot was then heard and a groan. Tzoulias had shot him in the back and, before collapsing to the ground, Schubert gave him the fatal blow in the head. His mother bawled in grief without being able to approach her son bleeding to death.[171] The army doctor, Emm. Peristeris who had been summoned to Metohi to tend to the wife of Bantouvas, replied in German to Schubert's insult "What do you want here, succour?",[172] so Schubert spared his life.

Last the ten-year-old godson of K. Bantouvas, Zaharias Kambitakis, after being slapped around by a Schuberite revealed the identity of Kostas Bantouvas from the crowd who, along with the other hostages, was led the same day to Avgeniki.

The next, 28th June, Bantouvas, then 44, was submitted to horrific torture by the Krousaniotes to reveal arms and ammunition.

The abuse by Schuberites happened before his 15 year old son, Zaharias, and women detainees. "In less than half an hour, they had transformed my father into a pile of bloody flesh. They broke all the joints in his body, they ripped out his right eye with a bayonet on but they didn't manage one 'yes' from his mouth; on the contrary, although groaning in pain he appears to have replied "I have them so you're not getting them"[173] meaning the arms and ammunition. To his denial they reacted throwing salt on the wounds and plucking the nails of his hands. Finally, Bantouvas was executed in the square before the residents of Avgeniki. The inscription on the marble memorial standing at the place of execution is terse: "He was tortured and executed by the Nazis of Fritz Schubert on 28th June 1942".

The next day Schubert sent a detachment to search Metohi for the hidden weapons. Upon failing to find them he torched the hamlet. In the meantime, Schubert had requisitioned the farms, the vintage vines, the animals and flocks of the Bantouvas. At Avgeniki around then, meat from the slaughtered animals was plentiful not only for the Schuberites and their families but also those 'sympathizing' with the newly introduced team of residents.[174]

Grigoria Kainourio is a small village on the southern foothills of Psiloritis about 75 kilometres southwest of Heraklion where capetan Petrakogiorgis kept his hideout. The village became a target of retaliation planned by the German authorities in Heraklion after the sabotage of the airports of Kastelli and Heraklion. The mission of Schubert heading Schuberites and a unit of the gendarmerie was scheduled by Hartmann. On July 9th 1942 Schubert arrived very early at the village and ordered the president of the community to point out the home of Emm. Kouklino or Tsouni, a resistor and supplier of Petrakogiorgis. The Schuberites arrested him and in turn beat him to reveal and lead them to the hideout of Petrakogiorgis. As he refused "they tortured him with the most inhuman means and broke his legs and arms so rolling like a lamb in blood from his wounds" recounts a rebel from Petrakogiorgis' clan.[175]

Schubert managed to take by surprise the small clan of Petrakogiorgis at the spot "papa-Perama Temeneli" and of the eight resistors in all he arrested half, amongst whom was also the former deputy of the military police Emm. Perakis. When he refused to respond to the questions as to where and who were the other resistors, Schubert used scissors cut off the tips of two fingers of Peraki's hand. After brutal torture they executed the resistors, G. Mavrakis, E. Kouklinos, M. Stathorakis and V. Pervolarakis. Perakis' execution was temporarily postponed at the request of the commander of the Greek gendarmerie detachment. During the meal held, following orders, by the president of Grigoria, Schubert appears to have been so overjoyed with the wine and German friendly songs of the police force former colleagues of Perakis that he kept his promise to spare his life, a favour going against his avenging instincts.[176]

A few days after the incident at Grigoria, Hartmann planned to avenge the clan of the Patriotic Organization of Petrakogiorgis at the mountain village Vagionia Monofatsi. Due to its position at a critical point between the roads leading to the southern coves of Crete (Lenta) it formed a stop for the transfers and care of British soldiers. The village priest papa- Nikolas Neonakis with the president, the teacher and other villagers had already been targeted by Hartmann early in 1942 when they were arrested but after questioning, released.

For dissolving the clan and annihilating its senior members, Hartmann entrusted the mission to lieutenant Schubert. Before his arrival with his gang, the fugitives after a warning fled to the mountains. Irate Schubert arrested Adam Neonakis, the 75 year old father of papa-Nikola, whom he surrendered to the Military Police of Moirai. But he was saved by Nik. Magiasis, an interpreter and renowned collaborator of the Germans who later at his trial claimed that Neonakis was saved due to his intervention.[177]

Agios Syllas Temeni lies at a crucial spot on the road network between Heraklion and the southern suburbs of Monofatsi and Viannos. It is about 13 kilometres south of Heraklion and just four kilometres north of Archanes where the German headquarters of the municipality of Heraklion had been stationed. It is testified that at this village, after the Battle of Crete, several patriots assembled and decided to organize a resistance hub.[178] Later, mid-March 1942, at Agio Sylla 18 leaders and resistance officials of Heraklion assembled, who under the guidance of Miltiades Porphyrogenis, a powerful member of KKE, signed an agreement for the unification of the resistance struggle under the common name EAM.[179]

On 16th July 1942 Schubert, placed in a German unit, invaded Agio Sylla in search of hidden weapons. Many residents were maltreated and the homes of seven resisting villagers were burned. E. Karageorgakis, resident of the village Metohi, was arrested as a suspicious "foreigner" and after torture, Schubert surrendered him to two Italian soldiers to execute him. When the Italians seemed uneasy, Schubert with threats ordered them to proceed to execute Karageorgakis.[180] It is strange that on this occasion here Schubert stopped the men of his gang to test, so it seems, the 'avenging' attitudes of the Italian soldiers who were possibly camping in the village.

Chapter 3

From Schubert to Hartman and the Consequences

German oppressive measures and the weakening of the Cretan resistance

The documented incidents show how close was the relationship between Schubert and Hartmann, particularly during the period of June and July 1942, one of the most chaotic throughout the German occupation of the island. From August 1942 Schubert and his gang's record as regards killings appears from the sources almost blank, which at first glance seems unbelievable. The lack of evidenced crimes does not necessarily also mean the absence of activities of Schubert and his small band of men. Taking advantage of the general debility of the resistance gangs, it seems Schubert was able to engage principally in the job of counterintelligence to cripple the English spy network, to find hidden weapons, the hideouts of resistance teams and British communications and to terrorize the mountain villages. Using varying trickery and informants, he stubbornly pursued the highlanders. "Schubert did us a lot of damage to the resistance particularly undercover" was the comment of K. Mitsotakis.[181]

Schubert's exclusive turn towards the field of counterespionage, at which he was adept, can be correlated with the military image, as it appears through the sources for this period. Save for sporadic attacks of German divisions in the mountain ranges of the three municipalities to reveal allied wireless and their operators and apart from a few spasmodic moves by the weakened rebel clans on bunker warehouses, military vehicles and local jails in the provinces of Malevizi and Kainourio, no other resistance activities and reprisals are recorded against the occupying forces.[182] In general, the political and military conditions prevailing at the time combined so that the population kept a stance of passive resistance. The main factors behind this situation can be put down to the following:

1) In October – November 1942 there arrived large military reinforcements in men and material as the German command planned to join the African Army of Rommel in its advance to occupy Egypt. The situation, however, soon turned. Rommel was obliged for a second time to withdraw, upsetting the German plans. Due to this, the 22nd Infantry Division of Bremen-Sevastopol under the brutal General Friedrich Wilhelm Muller took up station in the municipalities of Heraklion and Rethymnon. Muller adopted strict political control in the areas where they had placed the experienced

units of infantry.[183] During this period from January to June 1943 Crete was possibly rendered one of the "most densely occupied areas of German occupied Europe".[184]

2) The Commandants Andrae and Broier announced a series of prohibitive measures by which they placed strict controls on communication with the Middle East and restrictions on traffic and people's movement, in general, through the towns and villages.[185]

3) The armed resistance clans of Heraklion, after continued pressure by the British mission, either almost dissolved or fell into "total lethargy without motioning any activity" for a long time. Specifically, Bantouvas, for one, surrounded by a cloud of suspicion after his secret meeting with Hartmann (March 1942) and his dispute with Tom Dunbabin, abandoned Psiloritis in November 1942 and created a hideout at the Lasithi mountains (Dikti) without any worthwhile activity. As for Petrakogiorgis, in February 1943 moved with his clan to Egypt where he remained till early June. During this same period there was a large mission of resistor fugitives from the German intelligence in the Middle East, following the initiative of Cretan officials to the English representatives of the Allied Headquarters of the Middle East.[186]

4) The deceptive plan of the pending invasion of the Allies in Crete obliged the German authorities to intensify the security measures.

Notwithstanding their military moves, the insecurity of the occupying forces had provoked such a psychosis that even in a time of relative calm, they insisted on destroying the resistance, offering amnesties in February and March 1943.[187] The Folttmann-Hartmann plan was adopted which from early 1942 strove to persuade the resistance clans, whilst still small, to lay down their weapons, rewarding the leaders with amnesty and senior political posts.

Schubert's integration into the Military Police

Early April 1943, a very significant change appears in Schubert's military records. The German corporal was transferred from the staff office of the 746th infantry Regiment of the Cretan stronghold (Festungs Brigade Creta) to the Local District Command (Ortskommandantur) based in Chania.[188] This Command was embraced the military police (Feldgendarmerie) headed then by Lieutenant Herbert Gleblin.[189]

As such, from the spring of 1943, Schubert appears in the forefront with increased powers and reinforced authorities albeit still with the rank of corporal.[190] This unit belonged to the military administration of Chania and so Schubert considered himself possibly more secure beyond the control of Hartmann with whom, in the meantime, he had cut ties.

Note Schubert didn't choose to enlist with the Secret Military Police, the GFP, no doubt because this authority appertained directly to the Abwehr, or German

Military Intelligence in which Hartmann exercised great power and influence. His post in the field police now offered him greater powers and authority than those of a mere interpreter- counterspy particularly in matters of tracking the civilian population and pursuing rebel clans, duties of those enlisted to this unit.[191]

Exactly what reasons led Schubert to join the police division in Chania remain unexplored. Some faint light is given by the British "Report" which mentions a reason as the "professional rivalry" between Schubert and Hartmann and adds: "Schubert's relationship with the German espionage was dreadful. Their men often came into conflict with Greek agents of the (German) counterintelligence".[192] Further, the National Organization of Cretan Officers (EOAK) in its "Report" of June 1945 notes that the "office of counterespionage revolted. It arrested him along with other Greek accomplices and surrendered him to the Secret Police for questioning from where he was released triumphant. After his release he moved to Chania from where he emerged all powerful".[193] The EOAK apart from Schubert's brutalities against civilians adds a second reason for his imprisonment "probably envy led the office of counterintelligence to take such action". In the conflict between the two Levantines, Hartmann and Schubert, the Chief of Police played a part, Captain I. Polioudakis in his "Report" affirms that he imprisoned Schubert for mainly personal reasons.

"Always be he (Schubert) Greek or German, whoever covets the lives of our compatriots and their properties we hasten to report to the respective authorities as a criminal (amongst whom I mean the Tzoulias, Tzoutzouriki, Stivaktakis, Schubert) as I wish to prove also with official documents. For this action my life has repeatedly been threatened. If I hadn't exploited the rift between Hartmann and Schubert and put Schubert and the Tzoulias in jail, the harm that would have resulted would have been infinite. Fortunately, the conflict between these two Germans coerced me against Hartmann so not only did he stop threatening me, lying traps for me and blackmailing me etc. but whenever I asked him a favour for my compatriots, he was obliging".[194]

Their rivalry and envy must have peaked in the spring of 1943 to such an extent that Schubert decided to enlist with the police unit 981 of Chania though his activities were restricted to the municipality of Heraklion. On the other hand, the assertion of the "Report" of the Officers of Heraklion that his brutalities "enraged the population"[195] and obliged Hartmann's Office to order his detainment in the jails of Agia probably seems exaggerated. The "brutalities" should be construed not so much as killings but acts of violence, terror and plunder against the Cretan population.[196]

Specifically, at Krousonas, the village indicative of Schubert's activities, whilst before August 1942 those murdered within three months amounted to about 20, the numbers then reduced to five between August 1942 and August 1943.[197] As such it was not the number of killings that provoked the rage of the Cretans and Hartmann's decision to order the imprisonment of Schubert. The rift is justified mostly as a conflict between the two Levantines in the field of counterintelligence where, in time, Schubert and his small gang gained such independence as to distance from Hartmann's band and finally enlist with the Military Police of Chania. The violent arbitrary acts and plunder of Schubert and his team, as the ones against Meskla early July, probably triggered Hartmann to react. It was then he acted through the Secret Police to arrest, imprison and question Schubert.

Acts of violence, also snitching, abuse, blackmail and general terrorizing of the civilian population were charges brought against the Krousoniotes Ioannis and Evangelos Makatounis or Tzoutzouroukos who were sentenced to death in 1945. Typically, during their raids on villages, they would find out which butcher slayed cattle or which local recently sold oil or currants, would arrest him and after terrorizing with threats, would appropriate the meat or the money.[198] According to another testimony, Schubert even wanted to blackmail commandant Gleblin, his senior at Chania, when he attempted to bribe him.[199]

Schubert and the Tzoulias were detained in the jails of Agia Chania around mid-July and it is not exactly clear how long they remained detained.[200] Upon the orders of commandant Bruno Broier they must have been released in the first ten days of August 1943, as on 13/14th August there is evidence of a raid by Schubert against the villages of Kare and Platane Kissamos.[201] It is the opinion of the author that the bone of contention as regards Schubert's imprisonment was the big fiasco he suffered at Meskla in July 1943.

Raid on Meskla Kydonia (July 1943)

Meskla in the suburb of Kydonia, about 20 kilometres south of Chania, was one of the villages tested by the undercover tactics of Schubert. The village lies in a lush valley by the northern foothills of the White Mountains with a population which exceeded 800 inhabitants.[202] During the Occupation many of the Mesklians enlisted to the resistance, some to EAM and others to EOK. For the first time in July 1943, the residents encountered Schubert's violence and terror.[203] Schubert arrived unexpectedly one afternoon at the village square by the central cafe. In the truck were 12 German clad men and one civilian carrying a large bag of weapons for the Schuberites, as it appears later.

Schubert announced to the men assembled, mostly elderly, that he had come on a mission of the Agricultural Division of Chania to investigate the existing irrigation of the plots along the length of the river Keritis and propose the construction of irrigation systems to improve the productivity of their properties. The assembled villagers did not, of course, recognize who was this Greek educated German tending to the good of their village. But some quickly suspected that behind his words hid the real purpose of his visit and began talking. Then at the order of Schubert, his soldiers immediately arrested all the Mesklians present, around 30 men and a few women they found on the streets,[204] and led them to the Primary School where they subjected them to dreadful torture, beating and even razoring their soles and putting salt on the open wounds to make them confess to the hideouts of weapons.[205]

In this way, they were forced to surrender whatever old weapons they found and the wireless of the village. G. Lagoudakis was executed as the weapon, which he admitted after harsh abuse to have in his possession, was not found where he had hidden it. Rather it had been moved in the meantime by a relative believing his initiative would save Lagoudakis.

Schubert invaded Meskla equipped with a list of the names of those possessing weapons. The list had been provided by the German spy Tzimis who had been lodging at Meskla pretending to be an English soldier in search of asylum and care.

Tzimis spread the word to the locals that he was an experienced gun repairer and, in this way, he got to meet, during his four months stay, most of the gun owners and even the serial numbers of their guns.[206] On the day of the attack, however, those Mesklians who had been listed as wanted managed to escape to the neighbouring woods.

When Schubert realized their absence, he was enraged and in vengeance ' and in vengeance meted out brutal beatings, mostly to elderly people who were not those on the list. As such the dreadful excessive violence used against civilians satisfied his sadistic instincts rather than any strategic plan. More particularly though, Schubert's epic failure to arrest even one of the gun owners from those listed by the secret agent Tzimis, gave Hartmann the ideal excuse to give the order to the Secret Police to have him locked up in the Agia jailhouses.

Chapter 4

Schubert as Head of Greek Interception Squad

General Brauer's experiment

In view of the deteriorating situation in the area of undercover issues, the Commander of Fortress Crete, General Brauer decided to intervene in the conflict between Hartmann and Schubert. Pursuant to his order, Schubert was released and rewarded generously with powers rare in the history of the Wehrmacht. Thus, he created an independent competitor of Hartmann and tough leader of an armed gang. The possible reasons leading Brauer to take such a decision can be categorized as follows:

1) The shocking events of July permanently disrupted the comparative quiet prevailing on the island since August 1942. The first tough reprisals were enforced by the German authorities in retaliation to the attack of British commandos against the airport of Kastelli and the bunker stores at the village of Peza on 4th July 1943. Within a few days 190 people were arrested, men and women, whom they deemed left wing or communist thinkers.[207] most from the municipality of Heraklion, to be placed in German concentration camps from where few survived or returned. Additionally, 50 prisoners through Crete were executed.
2) The deceptive plan of the English as regards an impending allied invasion in Crete – a plausible stunt believed by the Germans and even the Cretans – and the allied landing in Sicily on 10th July 1943 created a tense atmosphere within the German leadership who took tough pre-emptive measures against the masses in general and more particularly the resistance groups.[208]
3) During this period, prompted by the British agents during this period, began the gradual split. EAM without though resulting in the intrigues which ensued in Greece. In towns and villages patriotic organizations developed to support the rebel clans, which by the spring grew rapidly in numbers and equipment.[209] Compared to EOK, EAM offered less strength though during its dissolution it didn't take time to develop into a substantial force throughout which the German authorities took their precautions.
4) On the Greek front, the new Germanophile prime minister I. Rallis, prompted and with the agreement of the Germans, decided in June of 1943 to found the legions of evzones to undertake "the protection of our endangered social establishment" from "the sinister purposes of

communism".[210] At around the same time, the Wehrmacht decided to assemble ten independent volunteer battalions of Greeks in Macedonia reporting directly back to the Wehrmacht.

The first anti-EAM formation, the "Greek Volunteer Army" (ΕΕΣ) which Colonel G. Poulos organized and led, began its activities in the spring of 1943. The remaining Anti-communist battalions assembled gradually starting from September 1943 until the first months of 1944.[211] The above circumstances constitute the framework within which is also placed the formation of Fritz Schubert's volunteer gang. Thus, Commandant Brauer encountering "unfavourable conditions" decided to experiment. For starters he tried, without success, to impose through Community Select Committees "the absolute neutrality of the residents against the Occupation Forces as the activities of even one can destroy the whole Community"[212] Within the same decree he demanded of each Committee in case of any allied operations against the island, "to supervise undisciplined active offenders" meaning the rebels and generally resistors. Brauer's second experiment, as he himself admitted at his trial, was the formation of "Schubert's Hunting Battalion" as he respected him as one of Hitler's select soldiers[213] and a leader of Greeks most suitable to terrorize and obstruct the villages from the supply of rebels and the support of the allied landing.

The assembly and powers of "Schubert's Hunting Commandos": a state within a state

The decree with which the Superior Commandant of Fortress Crete, General Bruno Brauer, authorized Schubert to assemble an anti-rebel band, read as follows: "Hereby established in Crete a body under the name 'Hunters of Schubert'. Its administration will have Sergeant Fritz Schubert. As regards weapons, clothing and supplies of the above body, I will handle by another decree. The purpose of this body is the consolidation of order and the crackdown of offenders, communists etc. in the area by whatever means deemed suitable by the leader of the body Sergeant Schubert, having hereafter the total authority and freedom of action.

No bodies nor units have the right to obstruct the execution of the above body's services. To the contrary, they are hereby obliged to offer whatever help is requested by Sergeant Schubert in execution of their aims".[214]

Brauer supplied Schubert with more powers and authorities than possibly he himself requested or hoped of his new patron. He was crowned head of the new gang with the official title Commandant and the rank of sergeant to fit the high position and greater power in the eyes of his subordinates and colleagues. The men of the gang received the fancy title 'hunters', imitating the special units of the German army charged with saboteurs and the pursuit of offenders behind the enemy lines. Then he was given the power, unique and unprecedented in similar circumstances, of absolute freedom to decide and act at will without owing any responsibilities or answering to anyone.

It is worth noting that there is no term within the decree that determines the authority or official to whom Schubert was accountable for his actions. In short, the decree created an all-powerful sergeant to decide between life and death. According to the historian Hagen Fleischer, "indeed the power ceded to him is rare and unique in the military framework".[215] K. Mitsotakis reminds us that "the assembly and activities of Schubert's Battalion was unique in Crete Schubert enjoyed great autonomy and independence. He never reported to the general Commandant of Fortress Crete".[216]

As regards the aims of the new 'Hunting Battalion', they reflected the role generally entrusted by the Wehrmacht to the Military Police, in other words the abidance of order and the manning of death squads and units to pursue the rebels.[217] As such Brauer's decree left open a window with the addition of the abbreviation etc. which gave the right to him discharging an order to add whomsoever he deemed to be his enemy including, obviously, women and children and the elderly. Similarly interesting is the addition of the word "communists", a term encountered for the first time in a decree of Brauer. The Cretan communists which Brauer differentiates in his decree in the summer of 1943 as a resistance organization was not significant to concern the Germans.

Only since September had the Pancretan Committee EAM decided "to assemble forces suitable to act against the occupation".[218] Possibly influenced by the decision of the I. Rallis government to form Anticommunist security gangs.[219] Brauer, for diplomatic reasons, added the word "communists" aside the term "offenders" by which were described the rebel clans and generally the activists of Crete.

It is interesting for the reader to recognize how Schubert himself wished to present his person before others in relation to the 'Hunting Battalion' and his place within it.

Major Johannes Barge in a letter he sent in August 1951 to the respective German authorities, recounts what he heard from Schubert himself when in 1947 they met in the jails of Kallithea: "In the summer of 1947, for some months I remained with Schubert in the jails of Kallithea. There he was detained under the process of questioning for offenses that as head of a Greek anti rebel gang, he had committed many war crimes in Crete and the area of Thessaloniki against civilians. This gang consisted of nationalist Greeks whose mission was to fight communist and anti-German clans during the German occupation. Initially because Schubert spoke faultless Greek due to his knowledge of languages, he had been enlisted to this gang as an interpreter and collaborator with the German intelligence. In time, Schubert increasingly headed himself the activities of the group".[220]

The most significant part of the extract is that Schubert began as an interpreter and collaborator and gradually usurped the lead of this group. The same argument he is to use also during his trial, that in Crete the head of the gang was not him but different Krousoniotes. So according to his assertion, only in Macedonia did he undertake full control and administration of the group, a statement not far from the truth.

The dating of the group's founding creates prickly questions. Most sources date it to the middle of September 1943 immediately after the destruction of the villages in the province of Viannos[221] or even in October.[222] The most reliable source relating to its establishment is drawn from the Report of the National Organization of Cretan Officers (EOAK) The Report presents in full the Order authorizing Schubert with the following comment: "In August 1943 and by the beginning of September, he summoned under daily Police surveillance citizens of the town of Heraklion, about 20 in number. Of those he invited the German speakers and ordered them to read to those present and immediately relay to them the text of an Order".[223]

Major Nik. Pikoulas, as per his testimony at the trial of Generals Brauer and Miller, was one of the German educated officers who translated the Brauer decree to the other officers invited to attend.[224] So, Schubert, by the end of August, was already empowered by Brauer and invited the officers. Another indication confirming the founding of the group in August is the testimony of the Krousoniotis Kon. Fanourakis whom his relative D. Stivaktakis, a Schuberite since 1942, met in Heraklion on 28th August and tried to enlist him saying "Kosti, this (Schubert) is an officer. He has an order to assemble a team as an army to kill renounced individuals and restore order".[225] So his authority must have been granted around mid-August, a time which coincides with Schubert's release and the gang's invasion of Rodakinos on 20th August 1943. One assumes that Schubert had already started recruiting to enlarge his small team by mid-August and by 20th September 1943 he managed to assemble a "unit for special missions" as first indicated in a German report to the commandant of Heraklion, Wilhelm Miller.

"Captain Kreuzer, head of operations of the military gendarmerie of Crete, advised as regards the activation of a special mission unit Schubert which shall primarily be used for missions in search of weapons. The unit consists of Greeks wearing German uniforms without indications of rank".[226]

In the same report is displayed the information dated 26th September 1943 that the Minister I. Passadakis was planning the formation of an anti-rebel band: "the formation of a designated Greek legion for fending off the clans (Banditen) in cooperation with the German army is welcomed by the division".[227] General Brauer's authority had incalculable consequences on the status and activities of Schubert during the last months of 1943. One of these was his headquarters move from the village of Avgeniki to the city of Heraklion. Here Schubert with his close team of officials settled in the mansion at 19 Valestra Street in the neighbourhood of Chanioporta whilst his men camped on the upper floor of a corner house at 12 Petratzaki (on the border of the neighbourhoods Chanioporta and Kamaraki) situated by the next parallel to Valestra. The ground floor at Petratzaki was used as detention areas for torture. The buildings chosen by Schubert as his official base were situated in the most strategic and sensitive spot of the western area of Heraklion from where he could control the main road network through the town to the west and south. At this spot today are situated the avenues of Kalokairinos and 65 Martyrs.

Avgeniki now degraded, remained Schubert's second base until the end of his stay in Crete. Additionally at Chania, Schubert established a detachment of his team at the hotel Brittania (on the floor which today houses the cafe "Muses") in the central square Syntrivani and in a requisitioned house in the precinct Topanas in the old town.[228] This unit was mostly active within the municipality of Chania.

Social make-up, mission and organization of "Schubert's Hunting Gang"

When Schubert received the authorization to found his "Hunting Team" in reality he reorganized and augmented the existing small group of Krousaniotes. The commonly named "Gestapites", Germanophiles and until then close accomplices of Schubert from Krousonas and other villages around Heraklion were of the first to be recruited and armed. To quickly increase numbers, it is said he found willing and suitable workforce from the jails of Crete. Amongst those released were included some serving heavy sentences. With the addition of the prisoners the total force of "Schubert's Gang" is assessed to have reached in the autumn of 1943 around 140–150. The most mentioned number is around 100 men. They are described as 'patriot deniers', 'scum of society', 'anthropomorphic beasts', 'knife pullers', 'monsters' and other such names.[229] (v. List of Schuberites, II A and B) the exact number of criminals released remains disputable, however it is believed to be around 30 – 50% of the total strength of 150 men.[230]

According to an unconfirmed Schuberite testimony, many of those released, when they realized that they were turning against, wanted to abandon Schubert but were executed.[231] It was also alleged that Schubert released German volunteers who had been convicted "for common crimes and killings".[232] In the group were even embodied a few dark clothed Italians. No doubt the few Germans and Italians only served a short while until replaced by new Cretan recruits. It is worth noting that those who committed the most brutal crimes were not released criminals but the Germanophile volunteers who became the favourite officials of Schubert due to their cruelty. To this second group belonged the classy G. Tzoulias, D. Stivaktakis and G. Epanomeritakis from Krousonas, reverend Lefteris Kalergis from Keramoutsi and the most dreaded criminals in Macedonia G. Germanakis from Miamou Kainourio G. Kapetanakis from Moulete Kissamo and I. Kambas or "Turk" from Heraklion. The best description of the group is given by the sergeant of the Military Police R. Haar in his sworn testimony in 1945. "In Schubert's gang which committed so many crimes to the detriment of the Greeks and where resorted all the scum far from Greek were they The reverend Eleftherios Kallergis from Keramoutsi as far as I'm concerned, the personified devil in gowns".[233] From Krousonas 35 Schuberites[234] belonged to twelve clans as Makatounis Tzoutzouroukides, Tzoulias and Makridakis.

No doubt strong family bonds apart from political and personal reasons played a significant part in the recruitment. Approximately 50 Schuberites were gradually enlisted from the town of Heraklion and mountain villages nearby such as Stavrakia, Garipa, Agious Deka, Gagales, Megali Vrysi, Miamou, Komes, Asites, Avgeniki, Keramoutsi and a few from villages of other municipalities. The greater proportion of Schuberites were people of lower economic status – modest farmers, rural officials, unemployed buccaneers, animal and other thieves – and often of low intellect prompted to cooperate with the enemy basically from the desire to get rich through systematic plunder. For a smaller portion of volunteers, other factors combined to justify their joining whether being Germanophiles, personal or family differences,[235] political feuds and in less cases, necessity. That the motive of plunder was most powerful is evident from the conduct of the Schuberites themselves as recounted by the contemporary sources. Anti-communism as a factor in joining the Schubert gang played a small role as in Crete, unlike what happened in mainland Greece, it did not find suitable grounds to develop by then into an accountable concern.

One of the usual charges against the Schuberites, when later tried before the special courts for collaborators, was that "they committed plunder and appropriations of valuable objects of the residents at different villages".[236] The misappropriation of goods was one of the most powerful incentives of all members of the gang.

At whatever village they visited, they would find out who had money or sovereigns and if they couldn't find the person himself, they would arrest his children or the whole family and hold them hostage until the requested amount was paid. The Schuberites G. Tzoulias and D. Stivaktakis arrested G. Gepesakis, a Krousonas pharmacist, plundered his shop, abused him then locked him in jail with his family and he was released by paying them 16 gold sovereigns.[237] Apart from gold they plundered other items such as clothing, food and livestock. Each carried a bundle, some for sale others to eat, for them and their families.[238] D. Stivaktakis trying to recruit to the team his relative K. Fanourakis, promised him: "I'll give you boots and clothes so you're not cold and hungry".[239] Their professionalism at plunder they perfected later in Macedonia where a source from Nea Kallikrateia confirms: "they would travel by car to the various villages, looting and taking cheeses, girls' dowries, goats, sheep, pigs, chickens and whatever else they found and gold".[240] The precious items commandant Schubert shared with his deputies and the other loot they sold to individuals on the black market.

German uniform was established as the official dress for the Schuberites after the founding of the 'Hunting Commandos'. Initially there are indications that the Schuberites in their attacks on villages sometimes appeared in civilian clothing[241] and on other occasions, less frequently, dressed in the uniform of a German soldier.[242] Apparently special reasons determined whether the Schuberites would wear civilian or German uniform during their respective attacks.

In his decree, Brauer considered the issue of dress quite important and left the decision for later. Finally, it was decided that the team dress in German uniform as shown by the picture of the Schuberite detachment in their foray on 5th November 1943 at the school of the village Tsermiado Lasithi.[243] The standing Schuberites wear the German cap with the German logo in concentric circles sewn in to the front fold without the eagle of the Wehrmacht. On the cap of their leader G. Tzoulias (sitting) apart from the logo is also the eagle with the swastika. The buckles of their belts carry the label embossed in a circle GOT MIT UNS (God with us) and the German eagle with swastika in the middle.[244] They are armed with the classic rifle of the German army, the Mauser K98k and the pistol Luger P08. Those wearing the jacket on the left arm bear a white strip and on the collar a badge with the abbreviation of the battalion with the armband -here missing- with the letters E.A.K.K. in Crete declaring the "Greek Detachment in Pursuit of Criminals" though in Macedonia "Greek or National Detachment in Pursuit of Communists". Note Schubert in his Manifesto in the New Year 1944 names himself Commandant of the "Greek Detachment against Criminals" and not "Communists".

The tactics initially were basically one of 'spying-counter spying' whereby Schubert using varying tricks of the trade, such as dressing in British officer's uniform, tried to reveal the hideouts of the English or the rebels, to disarm villagers or terrorize them to give information about hidden weapons.[245] In virtually every village Schubert and Hartmann had their own man from whom they gained information about everything going on. The Germanophile officials played a double game, on the one hand being the most loyal snitches of the enemy and on the other the best protection of the village against German reprisals.

On the other side was the English intelligence who in cooperation with the rebels acted exactly from the opposite camp. So developed a war of espionage and snitching most characteristic of this period.

A Cretan Schuberite summarizes Schubert's method as he recognized it: "He had many agents (who report to him) and he sped to surround the villages, arrest the residents, torture them and execute them at will".[246] Of the known examples of counter-intelligence Schubert relied on the assistance of many accomplice-snitches as Emm. Thymakis from Embrosneros, Kitros or Kitrakis from Kourna Rethymnon, a certain Komnino or Komna from Apokorona Chania,[247] Savva Koutanto, community president of Kamari, S. Stefanakis from Prinia, Dim. Pantedakis from Avgeniki, E. Kapna from Vagionia, Kon. Vardakis and Nik. Magiasis from Moires,[248] Ioan. Hainaki and Mic. Triantafyllakis from Asites, Ioan. Kouvo from Heraklion[249] and of course the Tzoulias and other Krousaniotes.

For achieving his aim, aside from Germanophile Cretans, Schubert used illegal methods and interference with German officials as in the gendarmerie. The incident below, described by Sergeant Richard Haar when in the summer of 1943 he was serving as commandant of the Krousonas jails, is a typical example of Schubert's conduct. At Haar's office in Krousonas Georgios Tzoulias, known as 'the capetan' announced that Schubert requests him "to go to a certain house" to talk to him. Haar however hierarchically superior to Schubert refused to obey. Then Schubert, accompanied by G. Tzoulias and D. Stivaktakis, visited him at his office where he showed him a sheet of paper with four names of Krousaniotes and another two beneath a dividing line. He told him to arrest the first four persons and before executing them "to justify their rifling, put a few cartridges in their pockets to hint that was why they were shot".[250] In case he doesn't find any one of the four he is to replace the number with those chancing under the dividing line. Haar calls the plan satanic and the Krousaniotes deputies protagonists of treason and accomplices in deceit.

Particularly impressive is Schubert's arrogant intervention in a German authority where he has no power as the Krousonas guard belonged to the Gendarmerie of Heraklion whilst Schubert to that of Chania. Further Schubert made a show of strength beyond his rank, causing a problem to Haar who reported him to a superior German authority resulting in an order forbidding Schubert's involvement in the Gendarmerie of Heraklion.[251] The incident at Krousonas no doubt widened the rift in the relationship of Schubert with Hartmann so that, after the fiasco at Meskla, Schubert ends up in the Agia jails.

After August 1943 Schubert adjusts his methods to the new situation: his new tactic more global in nature targeting the terrorizing and abuse of people in distant areas and more villages of Crete. To terrorize as many villages as possible which in any way helped the resistance, his team split into smaller groups, of 10 to 30 men, which camped at strategic spots in the provinces effecting surprise attacks on the mountain villages with or without German forces' support. Each deputy had the freedom to act independently and at will.[252] The main known heads of units were G. Tzoulias, D. Christodoulakis, and M. Kourakis. Schubert was absent from many of the units' attacks as he was exercising from above his newly acquired powers at his base Heraklion, concentrating his interests on the control of EOK and policing of officers in Heraklion and Lasithi.

Because of the many commands, the team generally suffered from bad organization and lack of centralized administration and leadership. Information about the relationship between the Hunting Squad, after its founding in August 1943, and the German military Occupation forces is confused. According to K. Mitsotakis, "Schubert's team had a special position and that is strange. I could not understand how it was integrated within the German system".[253] The judicial authorities of Thessaloniki concluded that Schubert's team "belonged to the armed forces or the political services of the Germans".[254] An interesting fact comes from Schubert himself, who at his trial testified that the 'Hunting Team' included two distinct services, the unit of secret police and the counter-intelligence team and "reported directly to the Feld gendarmerie which was responsible for its activities".[255] So after August Schubert became all powerful, amassing powers which belonged to the Abwehr, in other words the Counter-intelligence Office of Hartmann and the Secret Police, the GFP. The most plausible explanation is that by conceding him wide jurisdiction, Brauer simultaneously positioned him to balance Sergeant Hartmann whose power had gradually increased until Schubert's appointment. So Brauer's decision to assemble the 'Hunters Gang' can be seen to an extent as a reaction to the sharp competition between Schubert and Hartmann.

On the other hand, the position of the team does not seem to have differed from that of the Greek Volunteer Battalion under Colonel Georgios Poulos in

Macedonia and the Staff Office (Ic) of the Army Unit E, which in the spring of 1943 led the creation of the Poulos battalion.[256] Though an independent force with wide initiative it reported to the German administration for issues of operation, weapons and maintenance.[257]

A similar relationship as regards reporting and independence from the German authorities, in general, applied – more so in Macedonia than Crete – to Schubert's case save that Schubert, as a German, officially held a specific position within the German military hierarchy, in other words the Gendarmerie though in practice he was independent and self-authorizing in issues of terror and reprisals against civilians as also Poulos. It is worth noting that Poulos on the one hand was first to assemble a volunteer security legion in Macedonia whilst Schubert on the other founded the Hunting Squad in Crete with a few months' difference.

Chapter 5

Schubert's Activities During the Second Period (August 1943–January 1944)

The first brutalities in the provinces of Chania and Rethymnon

After his release and just before receiving the authorization from General Brauer, Schubert, using spy tactics, on 13th August effected his attacks on two villages of Kissamos, Kare and Platane (Palaia Roumata) to reveal weapons. The information relating to the hidden weapons and their owners at Kare was given by the village's collaborator Ant. Kartsonakis.[258] Schubert with his deputies took the village by surprise and arrested Marco Fantaki and Michail Christodoulaki and locked them in the German jails of the market town Voukolies without announcing the charges. The next day, August 14th, Schubert moved on the neighbouring village of Platane where he executed Nikolao and Elias Bombolakis "because they were listening to a wireless secretly operating".[259]

Upon returning to Voukolies, he summoned Fantaki for questioning in relation to possession of a weapon. Fantakis, who had in the meantime surrendered his weapon to Christodoulaki to conceal it, denied it so "Schubert attacked me and beat me round the waist, caning my legs and the rest of my body; helped also by the Greek Dimitrios Stivaktakis from Heraklion they battered me till unconscious. I was obliged to give in. They led me detained to the Chania hospital. Schubert threatened to rifle me if he didn't receive 15 weapons which happened within three days". In the end, Christodoulaki was executed because he refused to admit where the weapons were hidden.

More than a week after the incident at Kissamo, in the province of Agios Vasileios Rethymnon, Rodakiniotes resistors in conflict with a German detachment provoked the intervention of a German unit from Rethymnon supported by the Schubert gang. The target of the attack was Ano and Kato Rodakino, neighbouring hamlets of about 150 residents, lying on the slopes of mount Kryoneriti, a frequent haunt of the English agents and their wireless and at a short distance from the southern coves suitable for transit with the Middle East. Rodakino is at a distance of 47 kilometres southwest of Rethymnon and was the first village which on 20th August felt the reprisals of Schubert and his gang a few days after his authority by Sergeant Brauer. It is also the village where for the first time Schubert made the use of fire as a method of killing. The justification for the German attack and Schubert's support gave the Rodakiniotis Emm. Giannas.

On 17th August, Giannas killed the German leader of the guard of neighbouring Selia when the latter leading a detachment invaded the shelter of the Gianna or Giannadakis brothers in an attempt to arrest them as reported resistors.[260] Schubert, leading a gang consisting mostly of Greeks in German uniform,[261] surrounded Ano Rodakino applying the usual method of terrorization.

The Schuberites assembled the residents, women and children and the elderly – the males from 15 and above, in fear of reprisals, had fled to the mountains in the previous days – and led them to the square of Kato Rodakino. To the oppressed assembly he pronounced "wherever my foot steps on grass it does not grow".[262] From the crowd they selected the elderly Stavro Fronimo, Christo Loukogiannaki and Nikolao Loukogianni whom they executed for everyone to see. Ioan. Manousakis, old and consumptive, did not have the strength to descend to the square of Kato Rodakino as he was bedridden. A Schuberite discovered him, drew him out of his house and whilst he dragged him along the road to the square, Manousakis fell to the ground and pleaded with the Schuberite to pity him and leave him in his misery. Instead, the Schuberite, irate, drew his revolver and shot him but pointed the bullet to his face and made a wound through one cheek to the other! He did not die.[263] The Schuberites even killed their guide, a Chr. Konstantoudaki from the village Alones.

Then they burned twelve homes – nearly half the village – and threw into the flames alive the elderly Smaragda Kapetanakis and the infirm Despoina Vardaki who managed to escape the flames but yielded to their wounds a little later. The village was plundered and the area, by order of Guard Captain of Crete Brauer, declared a forbidden zone.[264] The residents dispersed to the villages around and only during harvest did they return with special permission from the German authorities. These restrictions resulted in making the docking of allied craft at the cove of Rodakino all the more difficult. Schubert, bolstered with his newly acquired powers, recorded his greatest success at Chania. Three young men were executed in cold blood in central streets of Chania and another four pursued individuals of the town and surrounds were arrested and abused in the Agia jails. The incident at Chania is interesting from a historical and legal standpoint and is worth examining more thoroughly as it is one of the seven crimes where, most surprisingly, the Special Martial Court of Athens decided that there was no evidence of the guilt of the accused (Schubert). On the other hand it is the only example where there exists enough evidence showing Schubert, with Brauer's consent, was responsible for the crimes at Chania. This relates to the execution of the teacher Emmanouil P. Mantakas, 35 years old, a leading member of EAM and related to General Emm. Mantakas, head of EAM in Chania.[265]

Emm. Mantakas was arrested after his betrayal by a collaborator from Chania on 24th August at his sister's house and executed in "the area of the Orphanage on the road leading to Souda".[266] Also, on the same day and around the same time, so early afternoon, the Manousakis brothers were executed in the central street of Chania, the 32 year old Georgios, a butcher, and the 18 year old Manolis, a student.[267] It is testified that later the same day five important officials of EOK were arrested:

Nik. Skoulas, president of the Prefectural Committee of Chania and mayor of the town during the occupation with his son Manoli, Major Emm. Nikoloudis, military attaché of EOK in the prefecture of Chania, Colonel of the Gendarmerie I. Volanis with his son, both members of EOK.[268] Whilst the circumstances surrounding their arrest is unclear, according to reports the aforementioned five had been trapped in a house in the area Pelakapina on the west side of Chania[269] where they had assembled for a meeting. Whilst the Skoulas were left free[270] (others say they escaped) the remaining four after imprisonment were submitted to brutal torture. Indeed, they plucked the nails from the hands of capetan Nikoloudis.[271]

The accounts are clear that the arrests and executions of the Chaniot resistors were effected by men of Schubert's gang without it being clear whether Schubert himself was involved.[272] It is testified however that Schubert's appearance at Chania during the last ten days of August became so noticed so as to worry the leading officials of EOK Chania "to a great extent". As such the Office of intelligence under Captain Markos Spanoudakis undertook intense monitoring of Schubert intending to kill him.[273] Indeed a meeting was called of the joint committee of EAM – EOK during which it was discussed whether the building where the gang camped should be blown up.[274] Schubert, however, it seems had been warned in time of EOK's plan and 'he proceeded immediately to the headquarters of the Command and received certain instructions.[275] These no doubt related to the decision of Brauer to authorize Schubert to annihilate the newly established resistance organizations and destroy those plotting against his (Schubert's) life and generally the Germans.

Schubert executed Brauer's instructions with lightning speed, thus showing his senior his counter-intelligence talents. Thus, Schubert's arrival at Chania was directly related to the recent activation of the secret resistance organizations EOK and EAM inside and out of the city. The Macedonian warrior capetan Nikoloudis, based in Lakkous Kydonia with the support of the Volanides, had organized and armed officers and contributed to the creation and strengthening of small armed clans in different areas of the municipality of Chania.[276] The teacher Mantakas had the initiative to induct the young of Chania, as the Manousakis to the ideology of the recently independent EAM.[277] It is worth noting that Schubert achieved a timely blow to the leadership of the local EAM whilst the leading members of EOK paid a smaller price and particularly Nik. Skoulas, as mayor and former officer of the Gendarmerie maintained excellent relations with commandant Brauer. So, what led the justices to doubt that Schubert was responsible for the arrest and executions of Emm. Mantakas and the Manousakis brothers? Schubert no doubt argued that he himself was situated at his base in Heraklion and under Brauer's orders who was solely responsible for the safety of the Chaniots, the German military police achieved the blows against the patriotic organizations of the city. None of the witnesses appeared to support the sworn testimony of Vasiliki, the widow of Emm. Mantakas who was absent from the trial. As such, on 24th August Schubert proved to his new patron General Brauer how effectively he had managed the new powers which he had recently granted him.

The officers of Heraklion under the surveillance of Schubert, capetan Bantouvas and the German reprisals in the province of Viannos

In general, the full time and reserve officers of the municipality of Heraklion in the first years of the Occupation abstained from the efforts and battles undertaken by resistance clans against the enemy, particularly during the critical periods, as that of the allied obstruction in June 1942.[278] In the lists of those executed and outlawed there is no mention of even one officer's name in the mass of testimonies. M. Bantouvas himself admits that he tried in November 1942 "to convene a meeting of the to date inactive Officers to achieve their contribution in the struggle but yet again failed".[279] The activation of the officers in Heraklion was triggered by the significant decision of the time of the Allied Middle East Command and particularly the subsidiary Force 133 to create on the Island a nationalist resistance organization distinguishable from the EAM organization to which from the spring of 1942 virtually all resistance organizations would report.[280]

To this end early 1943 in Heraklion, four important military officials ranking as majors and above and three Heraklian citizens decided to depart from EAM and found, or rather reconstitute, the National Organization of Crete (EOK) to reinforce the resistance conducting acts of sabotage and assembling new populous resistance clans to systematically trace information from the Intelligence Team reporting to the Allied Middle East Headquarters.[281] The Cretan officers who never applauded the efforts of the communist M. Porphyrogenis and the unification of the resistance clans and organizations under the common umbrella of EAM, now satisfied with their dissociation, saw plenty of opportunities before them for action and leadership.

In the next months this patriotic Organization achieved great success in the induction of a considerable number of military and political members, particularly from the higher echelons of society within and outside the city of Heraklion. The municipality was organized on stable grounds with a collection of provincial committees taking orders from military prefects.

These administrators – the official title was council leaders – were appointed by the exiled Greek Government of Cairo: Colonel Ant. Beteinakis from Archanes for the Municipality of Heraklion, for the municipality of Lasithi Colonel Nik. Plevris a Lasithiotis (from Agio Georgios). The Heraklians Men. Lignos, Emm. Petrakis and Kon. Petrakis were appointed as members of the Judicial Prefecture.[282] The most serious problem the ever-expanding EOK faced was the surveillance of its members' activities by the respective German authorities such as the Secret Police or Gestapo (GFP), the Office of counter-intelligence under Hartmann and the intelligence service of Lieutenant Fritz Schubert.

These three bodies made great efforts to mark out high officials and annihilate the Organization prior to its expansion. Schubert's contribution to the task of policing and crushing the EOK of Heraklion whilst partly known was not insignificant. Initially Schubert did not strictly follow the method of surveillance of officers initiated by General Bruno Brauer early 1943 and applied by the respective German services. Brauer's decree in part read as follows: "All former Greek officers (permanent, reserve and police) must, until further notice, appear in person every Saturday between 9–11 beginning from 20.2.43 at the respective Kreiskommando".[283] As a result of the decree, the German officials compiled lists of names and respective folders with useful details particularly regarding the involvement of each officer in resistance organizations. Undoubtedly when they decided to effect individual arrests of officers it was facilitated by the Saturday 'roll call'. Brauer's method however seemed ineffective to Schubert as it left several days where the military remained unobserved and without controls. For this reason, he took the initiative independently of the other respective authorities to innovate and "during August and by early September enforced a daily presence under Police surveillance on citizens of Heraklion, about 20 in number".[284]

These citizens were officers to whom Schubert for the first time showed off his powers as beneficiary of Brauer's decree of authority. The German educated Mechanical Command Nik. Pikoulas translated the decree to the officers of Heraklion whom he (Schubert) had invited to roll call.[285] Conveying the contents of the decree to the officers had one purpose: it was a chilling warning to them that Schubert was now self-authorized to persecute on his own with arrests, imprisonments, torture and executions for whatever acts of resistance whenever circumstances demanded.

Soon the right conditions appeared. During the first fortnight of September there arose a very critical situation within the German authorities provoked by the surrender of Italy on 8th September 1943. The events of the ensuing days, 9–12 September, provided the spark for the brutal German reprisals against the villages of the Viannos province.[286] First the possibility of Italian deserters and their induction to the Cretan resistance scared the German officials. The Italian General Angelo Carta who had earlier initiated a line of communication with the British mission and officials of EOK, until the last minute, left the possibility of the Italians joining the allies open. On 9th September, Patrick Leigh Fermor had talks in Neapolis Lasithi with Carta himself and three days later accompanied by Colonel Nik. Plevris with Carta's representative Captain Franco Tavana, head of the 2nd Division of the Italian headquarters. But he was unable to promise allied assistance to Carta neither to Tavana.

The decision of the allies not to proceed to a landing was now final but for military reasons was kept secret.[287] Finally, Carta, disappointed, advised his forces to concede to the German orders to surrender as an Italian revolt against the German forces, as had been discussed, without the immediate landing of allied detachments and air support would have proved not only pointless but also disastrous for the Italians. He himself with his deputies was exiled in the Middle East whilst the Italian units, even those which had fled to the mountains to join the resistance clans, like that of Bantouvas, around mid-September, surrendered to the Germans.[288].

The misleading tactic of the English allies fired the ambitions of capetan Manolis Bantouvas who, more than all the resistors, from early on firmly believed the English any minute would affect the landing, to take advantage of the Italians' willingness, mostly anti-fascist, to revolt against the Germans. The surrender of the Italians exposed some of the enemy's weaknesses and encouraged enthusiastic clan leaders like Bantouvas to exploit the newly created situation. Things rolled out of control. Bantouvas urged by his recent supply of arms and ammunition (allied delivery of 20th August) put into action his own plan to prepare the way for the legendary landing and bridgehead.

In early September he notified via messengers the clans of the Community warriors to assemble at specific spots for action with each Community Committee of EOK sending two units to Dikti to rendezvous.[289] As a result of this 'enlistment', more than 200 armed rebels had assembled at the camp "Hameti Vrysi", mostly members of EOK from Heraklion. Bantouvas also summoned select officials of EOK to Geraki Pediados to make decisions regarding "the full revolt of the armed clans and their consolidation at Dikti".[290] Colonel A. Beteinakis accompanied by another five responded to Bantouvas' behest.

Subsequently Bantouvas, encouraged by the numbers, upon requesting support proceeded to the second part of his plan that was the insurrection against the German forces who were camped at the easternmost posts of the province of Viannos. In his opinion, this province benefited by the creation of a bridgehead along the southern mountain range Heraklion-Lasithi with the extensive beaches suitable for the anticipated allied landing. On 12th September at a meeting in Neapolis Lasithi the agreement of 30th July was confirmed between Major Patrick Leigh Fermor and the Italian Captain Tavana for the activation of the Italian units and the creation of a defensive line across the naturally strong posts at the mountain borders of the municipality of Heraklion Lasithi.[291] In the meantime, Bantouvas, to encourage the Italians and English to proceed, took the initiative to act. So, on 10th September, Bantouvas' rebels destroyed the guard posts at Kato Symi killing two of the three German soldiers. Two days later, on 12th September, Bantouvas' men having ground advantage sneaked up on a force of about 200 Germans on reconnaissance around Archanes.

At the environs of Kato Symi, the Germans got trapped in a gorge and in the skirmish that ensued aside from about 30 (less than 20 in German sources)[292] German dead, another 13 soldiers were taken prisoner, whom Bantouvas intended to use to persuade the German officials to refrain from chance reprisals against the villages of Viannos.[293] Proud of his success, that same day, he sent a badly written note to Tom Dunbabin wherein asking: "When will the English make a landing to help us fight the Germans".[294] Bantouvas, who had not notified the British mission about his planned actions, pointlessly and recklessly, according to Tom Dunbabin, created a very dangerous situation for the residents of the province of Viannos. As such and in their interests, he was obliged to distance his men as quickly as possible. In the end, after leaving the larger portion of his unit to disperse, by 20th September with a few armed men he abandoned the mountains of Lasithi and chased by the German detachments, he fled to the mountains of Tsilivdika on the southwestern side of Psiloritis around Kali Sykia Rethymnon awaiting his transfer to the Middle East from the closest southern shores.

In the meantime, on 17th September, the Germanophile General Commander of Crete, I. Passadakis in his proclamation to the Cretan People gave the following advice and simultaneously warning: "If the Cretan People united does not take the decision and pledge to help in the disappearance of the clan (Bantouvas), they will disappear themselves".[295] German retaliation was effected with lightning speed. During the period between 13 to 15th September, the forces of Commandant Walter Miller executed around 400 persons,[296] mostly men, they plundered many villages and destroyed seven in the province of Viannos and subsequently similar numbers in the province of Ierapetra. In his declaration, Commandant Bruno Brauer used language reminding the Cretans of the German reprisals of 1941: "Very serious measures have been taken on this portion of the Island and a number of its Communities have ceased to exist".[297]

Schubert's role in the annihilation of EOK Heraklion

Within the time frame, certain of Schubert's activities are placed in this period.

Immediately after the destruction and mass executions in the provinces of Viannos and Ierapatra, the German security services extended their efforts to reveal and arrest members of EOK, who in whatever way had some involvement in the activities of the despised Bantouvas 'clan'.

The searching had particularly intensified due to the execution, on September 20th, of 13 German prisoners who, after pressure from Cretan officials, M. Bantouvas had set free but his brother Christos, to avenge the murder of Kosta Bantouvas by Schubert, executed them on their return trip.[298]

The Germans' efforts were quickly effective. Prior to abandoning his camp in the mountains of Lasithi, Bantouvas sent briefing messages to several officers, officials of EOK, through liaisons with people who were arrested by the Germans and obliged to name the persons for whom the messages were destined. One of the first arrested on 27th September at Mohos Pediados was Major Emm. Giakoumakis who was betrayed by reserve deputy Lieutenant Ioan. Zografakis and arrested by a German patrol relaying Bantouvas' message to Giakoumakis.[299] In all 22 persons, mostly officer members of EOK Heraklion, were locked up in the jails of the Gestapo (GFP) and submitted to strict questioning.

Initially Giakoumakis started as one of the founding officials of EOK Heraklion and later as active member of the Prefectural Committee, he played a significant role in the consolidation of resistance clans against the enemy. Although he himself did not take part in Bantouvas' operations at Viannos, as did Beteinakis, he was not indifferent to Bantouvas' personal plea to send armed forces to the mountain.[300]

Along with officers Beteinakis and Plevris, he was considered one of the biggest fish the German nets had caught and, for this reason, Hartmann and the officials of the Secret Police used every form of psychological pressures in their questioning to force him to disclose the members of the EOK organization and to admit 'that we aimed to prepare an armed revolt to hit at the occupying forces'.[301] For three continuous days of questioning, Giakoumakis abided by to the oath of EOK to not betray associates and plans even if submitted to harshest violence. On 30th September, he was moved from the 'Gestapo' prisons to Schubert's Headquarters at Valestra Street near Chanioporta. The following is the full narrative of Major Giakoumakis. It is apparent from this how the huge effect of the appearance, words and general conduct of Schubert – and G. Tzoulias – on his disposition resulted in him yielding and admitting what he had kept secret at the Gestapo jails.

"This German (Schubert) wore thick myopic glasses, short, hunched he gave me ghastly looks as if he wanted to crack me with his hostile stare and said to me in faultless Greek: 'Welcome Mr. Giakoumakis. Do you know who I am?' I answered no. 'I am Schubert' and simultaneously he takes me by the hand and leads me to the end of the yard to the room he used as a lounge. 'Sit', he says. Then I fell into the seat like an empty sack, the thought that they surrendered me into this beast's mouth paralyzed me. Such was my panic and uncontrollable fear, as I was not emotionally prepared for this turn, that I had no reality of my situation. So, he, standing always gesticulating and frothing from evil says to me: 'You Mister Major Giakoumakis, don't think you can follow the tactics you kept in the Police. Here you're going to churn everything up otherwise you'll leave chopped up for the dogs.

In turn he calls: 'George, come so I can surrender you scum'. Within a minute appears at the entrance to the lounge a tall hulk, 1.80 and more, with a scarf on his head, black shirt with boots who comes next to me and asks me to follow. I got up but couldn't control my legs, I was a wreck, I walked with him to the yard, hypnotized and was led to an outdoor staircase leading to a loft. At the first step I tripped falling forwards so the Krousaniotis removed his revolver from its case and hit me on the head with the butt leaving me a lump. Once I realized that my fate was decided to be killed like a dog, I promised the Krousaniotis I would speak. Georgis returned me to Schubert without us climbing to the room and I disclosed all".[302]

According to the testimony of Nik. Plevri, Giakoumakis named 14 persons of whom 12 were arrested early October and locked up in the jails of the Secret Police where in the meantime Giakoumakis had been transported. One of the detained was the reserve Deputy Nikodimos Kritsotakis, an EAM lawyer from the village Krasi Pediados who, upon being questioned, realized he was imprisoned due to Giakoumakis, in a rage, shouted: "You traitor, what have you churned out to the Germans? What's all this about a clan and stuff?".[303] Then Giakoumakis relayed his experience with Schubert shouting from his cell for all to hear: "Guys, understand I suffered much torture by Schubert and his accomplices, my soul was broken, I was a wreck and I revealed all betraying you to save myself from certain death so take your precautions. I ask forgiveness and I regret it but need to purge myself by telling you. Take your precautions".[304]

On 25th October, the 22 detainees were committed to trial before the German court martial at the Agia jails of Chania and five officers were sentenced to death, amongst whom Emm. Giakoumakis along with the liaison conveying the notes I. Zografakis.[305] The remaining prisoners released were placed under surveillance and ordered to appear before the Headquarters and Schubert, who was then wound up in espionage.[306] Major Hartmann, after their return to Heraklion, addressed them the next day emphasizing that they miraculously escaped and that he had enough on each of them which if used would send him back to Germany. He finished with the warning: "Now go home and know that you are being followed continuously and we are able with our contacts to track your every move".[307] After a few days, early November, Hartmann assembled, in the hall of the municipality of Heraklion, around 100 officers from the whole municipality and coached them regarding the basic principles of the nazi propaganda as it had modified after the collapse of the eastern front and intensified actions by a stronger ΕΑΜ/ΕΛΑΣ. He concluded highlighting the threat of communism on an international scale: "The allied forces are trying to submit the world to Bolshevikism. That is our common enemy against which you must fight".[308]

He believed he could sway the more conservative officers whose anti-communist inclinations were stronger, as in the case of the recent obvious defection of Major Mic. Diakaki and less evident of Nik. Plevris.[309] It is worth noting that the acquittal of N. Plevris by the German court raised many questions amongst the officials of EOK, who suspected that prompted by a strong anti-communist inclination "he aligned to the Germans",[310] specifically to organize security battalions in the municipality of Heraklion to annihilate the ever increasing forces of EAM. Indeed, after Schubert's departure from Crete, early January 1944, Plevris recommended a Security Unit in Heraklion under his command. His suggestion however met the disapproval of all the patriotic organizations and the Allied Headquarters. Later, in September 1944, General Miller rewarded Plevris for his anti-communism with the supply of arms and clothing to fight against the communists.[311]

Once Hartmann finished his speech, a German officer announced to the assembly that he had been sent by Schubert to lead them to his Headquarters. Soon the officers heard Schubert raging against communism: "The communists want to eradicate your free wellbeing and submit you to the most brutal dictatorship ever encountered".[312]

He demanded of the officers "for the good of the homeland" that they denounce Miltiades Porphyrogenis, a significant ideologist of the KKE, a spiritual inspiration of the resistance in Crete and the professor Ioanni Mathioudaki, also an active official of EAM from Koxare in the suburb of Agios Vasileios Rethymnon. For the first time it is witnessed that Hartmann and Schubert attacked communism so severely, evidently aiming to sharpen the enmity of the conservative portion of EOK against EAM so that these two parties would embroil in civil war, as happened in mainland Greece with the Security Battalions and other anti-communist groups. Obviously then an attempt by the Germans to apply the known tactic of divide and rule, which failed miserably in Crete.

To conclude, Schubert's contribution to the dissolution of EOK Heraklion can be considered one of the greatest successes of German intelligence in respect of stamping out the secret resistance organizations in Crete. The Secret Police, particularly the counter-intelligence Office of Hartmann, were obliged to appeal to Schubert in the case of Major Emm. Giakoumakis who proved a significant source of information and weapon against EOK. After the execution of A. Beteinakis and the distancing of N. Plevris, the Organization was left without leader for a substantial time without being able to retrieve its old power and glory. The new EOK under its new political leadership worked like "a foundation in the hands of peasants".[313] The big winner in this whole state of affairs was naturally the new star, Lieutenant Fritz Schubert, who proudly showed his newly acquired strength and independence from Hartmann, taking the initiative in the war against the communists and nationalist resistance.

Schubert seemed to kid himself with the idea that as head of a force with policing and intelligence powers, he could worthily compete with Hartmann. As such, he concentrated his interest on policing and intelligence matters, duties where he had particular talent and preferences. It follows that until his distancing early in January 1944, Schubert's criminal record compared to that of the Schuberites seems scarce. He himself in his 'apology' at his trial in 1947, refers to the ceding of full independence to the leaders of his gang to act at will whilst he himself "was a mere interpreter".[314] On the one hand, Schubert's irregular and arrogant air and on the other, the "beastly tactics" of his untamed gang, provoked the hatred of the Cretans and the disapproval of many German officers against him.[315]

Schubert's last brutalities in the villages of Rethymnon, Chania and Lasithi Kali Sykia

The mass reprisals at the mountain village of Kali Sykia, about 40 kilometres south of Rethymnon in the suburbs of Agios Vasileios, are deemed the most 'beastly' crimes which Schubert committed in Crete. He himself ordered his men to throw women, of different ages, onto burning homes. Just before the incident the neighbouring area of mount Tsilivdikas had become a field of skirmishes and conflicts between German detachments and resistance clans who had assembled at this spot to support the flight of Manoli Bantouvas' team and other resistors from the southern shore (cape Plakia) to the Middle East.[316]

The English representatives of the allied mission had decided that Bantouvas who, due to "recklessness and lack of sound judgment" provoked the brutal reprisals at the villages of Viannos, had to be distanced as soon as possible as, according to Captain R. Stockbridge "because of him, the Germans chased us from one end to the other".[317] German detachments followed his trail to annihilate the despised mobster and his small clan. At Tsilvidika, north of the village Kali Sykia Rethymnon, Bantouvas' team, reinforced by small armed divisions from the provinces of Armario,

Agios Vasileios and Sfakia, fought with German patrols causing enemy casualties and killing about ten Germans.[318] Of the approximately 150 residents of Kali Sykia the men, save for a few elderly, had fled to the mountains the previous day, fearing reprisals when they learned that Schubert was in the area. On the morning of 6th October, a German force arrived at Kali Sykia intending to search mount Tsilivdika and pursue the resistance clans who had murdered and imprisoned German soldiers in the previous days. Schubert took part in this cleanup operation with a detachment of approximately 30 volunteers.[319] After a brief search of the village, the German unit continued its route towards Tsilivdika whilst Schubert and his men remained in Kali Sykia.[320]

The Schuberites surrounded the village and in a rage assembled the women and children in the area of Livadi situated at the edge of the village. Then asking to find out where the men were, the hidden weapons and the rebels, they started their threats and insults, "you whores, snitches, where are your men". All kept strict silence whereupon a chilling shout was heard, "We'll have you all".[321] To scare them into speaking, the Schuberites set fire to four homes and ordered their owners to go and extinguish them to save their houses.[322] The owner Evangelia E. Gryntaki was eight months pregnant and was holding a two-year-old baby in her arms. Prior to throwing her alive into her burning home, a Schuberite grabbed the baby and threw it to the ground. In panic, she managed to climb out of the window but both times the guards threw her into the fire again and waited until she was cindered. The other four women (Eleni iNikitaki was holding her young daughter Maria) the Schuberites finally led not to their own houses, but rather they threw them separately into neighbouring burning homes, two alive and the other two shot first with a revolver. Of the assembled crowd, they selected in two groups another ten women, four from Rodakino and some elderly.

Despite the efforts of the detachment to ensure that the selected women become fuel to the fire, still three escaped wounded from the guards as they had crawled into a part of the house of Leonidas Moniaki where the flames had not reached.

Another villager was saved due to the intervention of Schubert. Evanthia Zoumberaki at an advanced stage of pregnancy, whilst being led to a burning home, recognized two of the three Schuberites accompanying – they were also labourers when she met them at the harvest in the plain of Mesara – and taking up courage she said to one: "Don't you fear God, playing me the German?" and the Schuberite replied: "I'll burn you whore alive with that you're carrying." Then Schubert intervened saying: "Let her go to hell as she's loaded" (pregnant),[323] so she escaped burning. Aristea Kostaki also recognized another Schuberite known also to her brother Michael from the harvest in the fields of Mesara, who asked her: "You wench, where's Michael?" Kostaki, guessing his intentions replied: "You should be ashamed seeking my brother – what for?".[324] She was lucky that the Schuberite decided not to punish her. They threw into the flames the formerly wounded Eustratios Damoulakis, an eighty year old who later died from his burns. To the casualties were also added two men from the neighbouring village Agios Ioannis

Schubert's Activities During the Second Period (August 1943–January 1944)

whom the detachment found working in the fields (another version of the story claims that they were discovered up a tree where in their fear they had climbed to hide) outside Kali Sykia and executed them in cold blood. In all, they burned 12 women, one man, Vardi Nikitakis, they torched 10 houses and plundered the rest, about 20 homes. It seems that the president of the village at the time, Manolis Gryntakis, brought proceedings in the German martial court of Chania against Schubert and five of the Schuberites whom three of his villagers had recognized.

At the trial, held from 16th to 19th March 1944, with the aforementioned women as witnesses, two Schuberites were sentenced to death and executed at the jails of Izzeddin (near today's Kalami) Chania in the presence of Gryntakis. His testimony remains uncorroborated and doubtful.[325]

HERAKLION (city centre). The positions of the main German military offices and that of Schubert.

During his trial in 1947, Schubert placed all the blame for the killings at Kali Sykia on the Greeks "who we had in the detachments, whom some women, reacting to the torching of their homes, insulted, shouting: 'Traitors, not only do you surrender us to the Germans but you burn our livelihoods.' They rushed to save their homes from the fire when the Greek guards opened fire on them, killing a few women. Not only was I not involved in the crime but I and my officers conducted questioning".[326] In truth, these 'Greeks' were the men of Schubert's Hunting Squad, who served under his orders and the responsibility for their crimes was borne wholly by Schubert, although at the trial he insisted that he was a mere interpreter without administrative powers.

The German forces had planned to block Bantouvas and his clan at Tsilivdika from three sides. One battalion, as aforementioned, advanced via Kali Sykia to Tsilivdika; another blocked his advances from the area of Kallikrati Sfakia, whilst a naval force obstructed his escape from the southern beaches in the area of Rodakino. The three German units created a tight hold around those assembled at Tsilivdika who, divided into small groups, managed to get away. Bantouvas, pursued by the Germans, crossed the area of Sfakia – some villages were too afraid to respond to his request for supplies – and ended up at Kalos Lakkos, a hamlet of farmers near the Sfakia gorge. But even at this hideout the trained dogs of the Germans hunted him out, forcing him to withdraw in the direction, upon the advice of the English liaison, to the southern shores of the municipality of Heraklion.[327] Finally with his team on 31st October, he fled to the Middle East from the cove of Lenta Kainourio. The distancing of Bantouvas for the Germans meant an opportunity to celebrate: "The arch mobster Bantouvas abandoned the island with his bodyguards the cad who caused such damage to a peaceful population", proclaimed Commandant Brauer.

Whilst for the English representatives and the Cretans it provided a temporary respite from the fear caused by the harsh reprisals at Viannos. According to the British Report, Bantouvas "twice before wanted to entangle Crete in rebel war without support and without the hope of supplies".[328]

Kallikratis

After Kali Sykia, Schubert with his detachment followed the German unit[329] pursuing Bantouvas and the British support into the province of Sfakia. Two other units consisting of men from the air force (Luftwaffe) and alpinists (Gebirgsjager) from Askyfou coordinated their movements so as to meet up with the German team from Kali Sykia in the early hours of 7th October outside the small village of Kallikratis. The village with a population of about 350 residents is situated on the eastern heights of Lefka Oroi and at a height of 750 metres. The Germans discovered that Bantouvas with his clan had escaped the blockade and during their march west had been supplied by Sfakia villages, like Kallikratis. The residents were accused "that rebels had escaped their village and this was not reported to the

German Authorities".[330] In the meantime, the morning of 7th October, the men of the village, who had been informed of the German approach, fled to the surrounding hills just as the German forces advanced. The barrage of gunfire didn't succeed in scaring them to return. The Germans, sedately entering the village, announced that their target was the pursuit of rebels and the collection of weapons. Without disclosing their intentions to harm the village, they gave orders to the villagers to notify the men who had fled to the hills to return unpunished, otherwise they would be deemed rebels and executed on the spot. Few believed the German promise and returned the same day.

The morning of the next day, 8th October, Kallikratis was surrounded after heavy shooting. From this moment on, Schubert with his detachment had the general command.[331]

All the residents were ordered to assemble in the churchyard, men separately from the women and children. From the crowd some women swore at them thinking they were Germans then they asked why they swearing, revealing their Cretan dialect. Notwithstanding the threats to reveal Bantouvas' hideout and hidden weapons, the residents kept total silence. Schubert, enraged, ordered his men to select villagers, mostly elderly whom they sent for execution at the 'lodge', a deserted house.[332]

There they finally executed around 10 men and another 6–7 were found dead, strewn along the streets, evidently trying to escape. Specifically, Manolis Hairetis tried to escape, grabbing his guard's gun, but the second Schuberite managed to shoot him. The young M. Vouyioukalos went and brought a rifle and surrendered it where they were being collected. Upon turning his back, they fired a shot and killed him.[333] Another two men from nearby villages, arrested at Kallikratis, were shot as liaisons and suppliers of the rebels. They also executed an Askyfou shepherd, I. Lykakis, who was forced to serve them as a guide.[334]

The Schuberite priest Lefteris Kallergis was seen shooting a Kallikratis and before departing grabbed the mule of the local priest whom he knew from seminary school.[335] About twenty women were taken as hostages to the Agia jails where they were detained for over a month.

With the village nearly deserted, the Schuberites departed, taking the few hostages. Later the same day they returned to complete their task. After first plundering, they then burned around 80 homes.[336] During the plunder, whoever they found in the houses, elderly women, old bedridden and disabled men, they executed before burning. In all twenty men and eight women were executed, mostly elderly and infirm. The area of Kallikratis was declared a forbidden zone and the residents were strewn around the different neighbouring villages. In the report of 8th October, the respective staff office of the 22nd Division noted the following facts, obviously distorted.

"At Kallikratis, after the search of Kdo (Kommando) Schubert, 8 guns and 3 pistols were found. 50 men were arrested there, all from distant villages and those suspicious were executed. The village is destroyed. The dispatched navy and staff units arrive tomorrow noon back behind Askyfou. The Agia unit returns to Kanepo

(Kanevo). End of the anti-rebel operation'.[337] Schubert under German protection followed in the direction Bantouvas' team had advanced. On 12th October, Schubert's Unit arrived at the hamlet of Kaloi Lakkoi, Bantouvas' last stop, which he found deserted and plundered it." (today the hamlet is abandoned)

The next day at the villages of Chora Sfakia and Anopoli, he executed a few men and continuing his journey north he surprised the village of Mouri, which he avenged for Bantouvas' escape the previous day. He arrested five men whom he submitted to appalling torture – indeed he blinded one – then executed them.[338]

The crimes of Schubert and his gang in the province of Sfakia provoked, it seems, much concern to the German Captain, Garrison Commandant Askyfou, to whom the province reported, so he requested General Brauer to distance Schubert, as the Cretans were showing enmity to the German military forces. It seems Brauer promised That he would ensure Schubert left as quickly as possible.[339] Indeed, the mass executions and the destruction of Kallikratis was Schubert's last big criminal operation as until his departure there is a significant decline in his activities though in contrast an increase in the activities of his gang under the leadership of the Krousaniotis deputies.

Throughout the remainder of his stay in Crete, according to the decision of the Special Court Martial, Schubert was adjudged responsible for the death of only three persons. In October at the location of Gefyraki outside Krousonas, he executed Georgios Grigorakis, the brother of capetan Ant. Grigorakis or Satana.[340] He was also accused that as lead of a detachment for the first time, he invaded the municipality of Lasithi and specifically against Kritsa of Mirabello. On 6th November after assembling the Kritsas in the square, he selected a few men and one by one summoned them to a room where his officials tortured them to reveal where they had hidden weapons. During the assembly, the Schuberites, pretending they were searching the houses for weapons, stole whatever valuables they found.[341] This was the last witnessed raid of Schubert in Crete.

Schuberite crimes in the villages of Lasithi, Heraklion and Chania

In early November 1943 Schubert's gang appeared at the villages lying to the east side of the Lasithi Mountain range. The municipality of Lasithi until mid-September 1943 was run under the administration of the Italians (Siena Division). Generally, the relationship between the Italians and the Lasithiotes was peaceful for the whole of the period. The Administrator of the Division, General Angelo Carta, was instrumental in creating this atmosphere. He had exhibited anti-fascist feelings when he voluntarily surrendered to the English, along with his deputies, and exiled to the Middle East. Similarly, several Italian officers and soldiers requested protection and asylum in the mountainous villages with the rebel clans, such as that of Bantouvas, to avoid their surrender to the German authorities. So, a lot of the Italian weapons ended up in the hands of the villagers and resistance teams, despite the threats of reprisals by Commandant Brauer against whoever bought or obtained weapons, firearms, military items of apparel or equipment from the Italians.[342] Information relating to equipment of the villagers and resistance clans – the most well-known being that of capetan Adam Krasanaki or Krasanadami from the village Agios Georgios – no doubt was the reason for the raid which about 20 Schuberites effected in early November under the leadership of G. Tzoulia. Note that the Italian General, Carta, and his team, protected by the English, had passed through these mountainous areas in September. The terrorizing mission of the mountain folk began on 3rd November from the villages Avrakontes and Koudoumalia and ended the same day at Agio Georgio. Once the Schuberites had assembled the people of Avrakontes in the square, they then led them to the nearby hamlet Koudoumalia. On the way, they picked out from the mass Georgios Tzirakis and a group tortured him in front of the crowd. On the road from Koudoumalia to Agios Georgios, a Schuberite suddenly shouted to the civilians "say farewell to your men", so the women started grieving and mourning. Fortunately, the threats were the usual tactics of Schuberite sadism. In the square of Agios Georgios, where they assembled all the residents of the three villages, the head of the detachment climbed on a nearby well and threatened to destroy the village if its residents didn't reveal the hidden weapons and the hideouts of the rebels. Then a villager addressed his compatriots saying: "Guys, whatever you have, German or Italian, bring it to save ourselves". The people started carrying even scrap iron, such as accessories from capstans, but nothing was enough to change the plans of the executing squad.

At Agios Georgios, the Schuberites separated from the crowd Emm. Kalykakis, postmaster of Avrakontes, the locals Dimitri and Adami Krasanakis, members of the respective EOK and 6–7 villagers whom they led to the village cafe for questioning.

> "… and there they pushed them in one by one where they were met by four Schuberites, two to the right and two left. As they passed, they beat them with sharp sticks until they fell to the ground then kicked them with their boots, piling them like sacks under the shop benches. They then received Emm. Kalykaki and, as they led him outside the village to execute him, his five daughters followed him mourning and pleading to the Gestapites, but they gave them no attention as if they didn't exist".[343]

The worst torture was suffered by Adamis Krasanakis whose loud groans could be heard throughout the village. They say that one of the perpetrators was a known Schuberite with whom Krasanakis had past differences.[344] They also executed Adam Karofylakis, a young man recently married, after first beating him so badly that his eye hung only from one nerve.

On 5th November (in other testimonies 3rd November),[345] the same detachment of Schuberites terrorized the village of Tzermiado where they assembled the residents in the square and asked for hidden weapons and resistors. To reveal the arms, the Schuberites selected five men and after torturing them, covered in blood they executed them in a mass grave near the cemetery. They killed G. Papadakis, a notary and member of the local EAM, outside the village. Amongst those executed were also the young brothers Georgios and Konstantinos Pytharoulis. The latter recently married at Avrakontes, wore his mother-in-law's clothes so escaped the village blockade. For better safety he fled to the village of Tzermiado where by quirk of fate, he was later arrested and executed with his brother Georgios and Nik. Spanakis and I. Tsamandoura.[346]

Schubert was accused of being involved in the killings of Tzermiado, but the Special Court Martial in its decision deemed him innocent because according to the verdict there was not enough evidence of guilt against the accused.

The case of the village of Miamou Kainourio assembles the most evidence of tactics adopted by the Schuberite squad in its raids during the last months of 1943. Miamou is situated on the northern heights of the Asterousia Mountains, at a height of 500 metres on the road leading to the harbour of Lenta, where occupied craft and submarines often berthed. The village which in 1940 numbered around 500 residents, due to its difficult terrain – communication with the nearer villages was possible only by mules – remained outside the area of activities of the occupying forces.[347] Another reason was that Miamou was one of the few villages in Crete where weapons were not held and as such did not attract the attention of the enemy. Notwithstanding that, a detachment of about 30 Schuberites, led by G. Tzoulias, after first blockading the Monastery of Apezanon where they beat the monks and shot the housekeeper,[348] in turn surrounded Miamou on 17th November 1943.

In the morning, the Schuberites assembled all the residents in the square and demanded that they surrender hidden weapons. From the crowd they selected four men and led them to the nearby Primary School where the Germanophile president of the village Antonios Har. Germanakis had gone with his 30 year old nephew Georgios Ioan. Germanakis.

At the school, the four chosen "they brutally beat them as we heard them groaning through the square" describes a witness on the spot.[349] With the drama over at the school, G. Tzoulias approached the assembled crowd, grabbed two men by the collar and as he dragged them, he shouted to the crowd "Look at them, you won't be seeing them again". But the moment he was preparing to shoot them with his revolver, a local suddenly intervened and pulled aside one of the victims without provoking a reaction from Tzoulias. Evidently it was the collaborator of the village till then unknown to his compatriots but known to Tzoulias, possibly as a labourer in the farms of the Malevizi province. The second victim he selected, Emm. Krousaniotaki, a father of four children, Tzoulias executed before the crowd and indeed gave him the fatal shot in the head as he fell to the ground. Upon departing, the detachment took with them some hunting guns, old weapons and three residents whom they executed outside Miamou along with another three persons from neighbouring villages. Two were shepherds arrested in the grazing grounds of Apezanes monastery.

The best outcome however of the whole raid was the enlistment of Georgios Germanakis to the 'Schubert Hunting Squad' supported by his uncle, the community

Schubert's Activities During the Second Period (August 1943–January 1944)   61

leader Ant. Germanakis. G. Germanakis, one of six children of Ioannis Germanakis, was penniless and unemployed, unable to support his wife and two young children in difficult times. As such, Uncle Antonis, on the one hand, offered a solution to the economic woes of his nephew. By the same token, he was trying to purge the dishonour he caused the family before the war, when he left pregnant his married niece, the sister of Georgios, in return for a favour he did as community president, when she had asked him to appoint her husband to the rural police force.

Generally, the villagers had a very low opinion of the Germanakis family and their morals.

The enshrining remark of a witness was: "I'd like to know what kind of christening these people had".[350] The next day a villager of Miamou, Stylianos Manidakis saw G. Germanakis in German clothing in a street of Heraklion and as he approached him Germanakis disclosed to him the apparent initial plan of G. Tzoulias: "You there, you know that the Germans would have killed you all?" Evidently a rhetorical farce of a man emboldened by the force of a weapon and uniform. From that moment, all traces of Germanakis disappeared amongst the villagers of Miamou. After the Occupation it is said that Germanakis committed many brutalities in Macedonia, "he tortured women cutting the nipples from their breasts and burning people in ovens".[351] His wife, Despoina, immediately after the liberation, left with her children to Athens never to return to the village. In the meantime, Germanakis' mother often frequented Athens, raising suspicions amongst the villagers. In Macedonia, Germanakis, along with Georgios Kapetanakis, evolved into gang leaders with officer ranking supplanting G. Tzoulias and the older Schuberites. Here he embarked on a career of a violent and bloodthirsty mobster who often exceeded in brutalities, even Schubert himself.

The activities of Schubert's gang, as noted by the sources, continued through December 1943 at the same pace. Detachments of the group effected raids in mountain villages for which Schubert was accused but acquitted by the Court Martial. In their terrorizing attacks, the detachments it seems concentrated their efforts more on plunder and blackmail rather than mass executions. In total only 14 killings are recorded compared to 23 at the same number of villages the previous month. Typical examples of villages where methodical plunder occurred were at Maza, Fones and Douli.

On 3rd December, a detachment of Schuberites headed by G. Tzoulias assembled the residents in the square of Maza in the suburbs of Apokorona Chania, threatened them and tortured them to surrender hidden arms. Iosif Kasapakis maintained that he did not possess a military weapon and then, by order of G. Tzoulias he was taken away by two Schuberites to be executed. On the way he tried to escape but his executioners shot him down. On the way back to the square, as the perpetrators had not proclaimed the murder of Kasapakis to the crowd, Tzoulias, enraged, confronted them: "You guys, scared to tell them out loud?" So, he made a public announcement of their actions. Throughout the time the assembled residents were being threatened to surrender arms, other Schuberites searched the homes for weapons and to simultaneously plunder: "They came to my house which they searched and stole from me six pairs of pillows, two blankets, plates, forks, saucepans and various other items" testified the widow of Kasapakis in 1945.[352]

That same day, Tzoulias' detachment invaded the neighbouring village, Fones, where they assembled the residents in the square and threatened them with death unless they surrendered hidden weapons. Those who had old weapons brought them forth and surrendered them to save themselves. Those who declared they did not possess weapons were harshly beaten. Markos Grylakis, after torture, was dragged out of the village and executed.[353]

The small mountain village Douli Monofatsi, situated on the inclines of Psiloritis at a height of 440 metres and a small distance north west of Agia Varvara, twice became the target of plundering raids of the Schuberites during December. The first time, the detachment assembled the residents in the square, selected three men, beat them, dragged Dim. Chaniotaki outside the village and executed him. Before they left, they plundered homes. A week later the Schuberites went back to the village. This time their motive was to steal animals. The residents in fear locked themselves in their homes and using the opportunity, Schubert's men grabbed from the stables and sheds cattle and sheep for their own consumption and for sale.[354] Similar incidents were repeated and in other mountain villages of the Heraklion municipality such as Gagales, Garipa, Kato Symi, Krousonas, Korfes, Loutraki, Melidochori, Episkopi and of the Chania municipality as Alikampo which were terrorized by Schuberite detachments during the last months of 1943. No mass killings were noted, the raids of the detachments increased under the leadership of members of the squad and the plunder and threats peaked.

Chapter 6

The Distancing of Schubert from Crete (11 January 1944)

New Years Day 1944: an unfortunate day

On 1st January two significant events, one political and the other military, sealed the end of Schubert's activities and presence in Crete. Firstly, the Germanophile newspaper of Heraklion, The Cretan Herald (Κρητικός Κήρυξ) published on its front page a long announcement of Schubert entitled "Proclamation and wishes of the Leader of the Greek detachment hunting criminals" which with the arrogance of a senior officer addressed "the Cretan people".[355] The point of the Proclamation, which seems to have annoyed General Brauer most, was Schubert's unwillingness to act within the framework of attempts to calm and pacify the residents which the German authorities employed after the dreadful events at Viannos. Schubert tried in the 'Proclamation' not only to absolve himself of the responsibility for the criminal acts of his squad particularly during the last two months of 1943[356] but also requested of law-abiding citizens to become snitches "of any criminal", in other words resistor, so as to avoid "the strictest punishment", and to surrender arms and military material within a defined time frame.

The final straw in his autocratic conceit was the statement "don't be mistaken, all these and those who possess such items are known to me and none of them are destined to escape". The proclamation was signed with the grand title Leader of E.K.A.K. Schubert.[357] The second event which heralded Schubert's end in Crete was the fiasco at Meskla.

After a time lapse of six months, the Schubert squad revisited Meskla. On New Years Day of 1944, ten (eight according to other witnesses) Schuberites, in civilian clothes and emanating from the detachment camping at Chania, suddenly appeared outside Meskla. This team is not reported to be led by the known deputies of Schubert, who indisputably did not take part in this raid and probably had no knowledge of it, judging from the method of planning and execution of the raid. Neither was the point of the mission clarified.[358] According to the depositions of Mesklians the drama began and developed as follows.

On the morning of New Years Day, at Meskla square – next to the Primary School and the bridge of river Keriti – there appeared two unknown visitors pretending to be resistors. Dressed in civilian clothing each held a bag as if a Santa. They asked to meet Mesklian patriots 'following the introductions of the resistor Anton. Frangonikolaki from Fournes'.[359] Those residents who heard the names of persons to which the visitors referred became concerned as those sought were resistors, members of the organizations EOK and EAM. Indeed, this particular day many of these, hiding in fear in the mountains around, had returned to celebrate with their families. Three resistors, Nikolaos Tsamantis or Tsamantakis, Alekos Papilaris and Manolis Batakis, on receiving information about the arrival of the two suspicious foreigners, armed themselves with revolvers and went to meet them; they soon discovered that they themselves were on the wanted list. Then under the threat of the weapons, the foreigners surrendered and in turn admitted that they belonged to Schubert's squad and along with them were another eight, armed and hiding in the plains[360] waiting to be given the signal to enter the village. The bags they held were a trap as they did not contain new year's presents for the "rebel" villagers but military items such as grenades, pistols and German documents. The Schuberite detainees themselves revealed the reasons for their raid; the arrest and execution of resistors whom they believed – possibly following information from a snitch – that they would find in the village attending the New Year celebration. And they were right. Very soon a team of armed Mesklians assembled and were dispatched in search of the eight Schuberites.

A second team of armed villagers along with a team of ΕΛΑΣ under Captain Kriton Kyanides[361] took up strategic positions around the square and at the Main Street, in wait for the remaining Schuberites, who upon arrival immediately started heavy gunfire whilst simultaneously shouting and threatening, "Where is your damned president? If you don't release the two detainees, we'll burn your village",[362] along with other abuse. Then the armed Mesklians and Kyanides' ΕΛΑΣ attacked the Schuberites who, unaware of the strength of their opponent, scattered trying to find shelter in nearby homes where they also risked the beating of women who went for them with farm tools and household ware.[363] Upon both sides ceasing fire, five Schuberites were captured and three others fell dead during the fight.[364] The detainees along with their two bag carrying companions were executed by the rebels at Lefka Oros and their bodies thrown by the bank 'Voulisma'. Immediately after the incident, most villagers, for fear of German reprisals, abandoned the village and fled to the woods by the village of Zourva. Early that afternoon, a German force arrived who carried out an on-the-spot inquiry into the incident and buried the dead Schuberites. After establishing a temporary guard, they departed without burning or plundering the village. This lenient handling it seems was due to a presentation by an assembled committee under the Bishop of Kydonia and Apokorona Agathangelos Xyrouhakis to General Brauer after the incident.

It is reported that the committee to justify the Mesclian actions gave the following argument:

> "The activities of Schubert and his Squad, consisting mostly of Greeks, often becomes the reason for residents becoming enraged and revolting against the occupying armies. An example to the point, the events at Meskla noting that if they were genuine German soldiers the villagers would have obeyed

them but because they were Greeks, they reacted, resulting in most of the residents climbing to the hills".[365]

The incident at Meskla was the last straw signifying the basic weaknesses of the squad; the bad leadership, organization and obedience which plagued Schubert's gang as General Brauer himself notes at his trial: 'The team was badly organized, that's why he dissolved it and outplaced him'.[366] We can conclude that this time Brauer acted decisively. First, he stunned Schubert when he tried to disclaim responsibility for the events at Meskla and throw it onto the deputies of his squad.[367] He could no longer provide any counter argument to what he was being accused of or justify the crimes which the squad committed during the last months of 1943. In addition, Schubert was accountable for a serious breach of his military authority relating to the 'Proclamation' which he published at New Year in the Heraklion daily press. Whatever he said to Brauer would be difficult to defend his position as a lieutenant before a general. Indeed, Brauer seems to have been convinced that he was dealing with an individual suffering from a psychological disorder. So, he ordered that "they catch him and lead him to the secret German police where they also injected him to stupefy him" according to Schubert's own admission at his trial.[368] During the medical examination to which he was submitted he was diagnosed as suffering from third degree syphilis, an additional reason for his prosecution.[369] After his brief treatment at Chania and his detention, Schubert was admitted to an Athens sanatorium, most likely the Daphne Mental Hospital – for a psychological symptoms treatment, for a few days. For reasons of pride, he no doubt claimed his detainment was merely punishment by his superiors. Another reason which contributed to his isolation, according to the British Report, was that "the Germans hated Schubert's squad for their extreme methods" which created obstructions to the pacification of the island.[370]

German measures of appeasement, the role of Minister I. Passadakis and Schubert's expulsion

The arch Germanophile I. Passadakis, appointed Minister General Administrator of Crete, seems to have played a part in the issue of Meskla and by the same token in Schubert's expulsion. Passadakis, in his article of 7th January 1944 to the Germanophile press of Heraklion, announced that the "murder" committed at Meskla by Cretan (Schuberite) servicemen in a German unit should be punished "exemplarily".

But diverging from the methods he had previously followed in similar circumstances, Passadakis, pleaded to the Commandant of Fortress Crete Bruno Brauer to not proceed to the group punishment of the Mesklians but punish only those responsible. According to Passadakis' assertions, Commandant Brauer responded to his plea then Passadakis summoned the Mesklians to return to their homes and jobs. The point of the intervention in favour of the Mesklians, added Passadakis, was to avoid detracting from the efforts of appeasement and reconciliation between the occupying forces and the Cretan population which the German authorities had already developed.[371]

It is a fact that the bloody events at Viannos really scared Cretan society and at the same time provoked anger and hatred against the Germans. First Commandant Brauer in his plea, after the departure of capetan Bantouvas for Egypt, repeated his wish to calm the waters and reconciliate: "To the peace-loving population I again extend my hand for the restoration of a principle, the respective acquisition of a protected zone. The plight of the comparatively poor population will benefit through generous measures of social welfare".[372]

The German philanthropy published in the daily press at the time from mid-October 1943 extended to a series of alleviating measures which the German authorities of the island undertook to appease and reconcile the population. So, on 15th October, Commandant Brauer announced that 400 million drachmas would be available for the improvement of the economic situation of those working at German projects and charity foundations. A bit later, 135 million was distributed to charitable foundations of Heraklion and mass distribution of food began for destitute and poor residents of the city. In addition, Brauer made a plea to the wealthier population of Crete to contribute "to this task of active fellowship", offering money and necessities.[373] In December of 1943, the occupying authorities, for the first time, paid a Christmas subsidy to Greek workers of the German army and increased days off to three for Christmas and New Year. Also, at this time there was a regulation and moderation of compulsory work and a pardon for those in breach of labour laws. Lastly, and for the first time, Brauer gave permission for the bells to ring at the churches.[374]

Within the bounds of the Nazi attempts for a "friendly symbiosis of German occupying forces and the Cretans"[375] particular activities of Lieutenant Fritz Schubert are included.

On 8th November, it was published in the daily press that "Mr. Schubert, Director of Jacte Commanbo (sic) deposited in the Hospital account for the infirm of the foundation the amount of 475 thousand drachmas for their needs. The Hospital gives warm thanks".[376] This amount then matched the monthly wage of a high-ranking employee in a German office and the deposit must have been at the same time as the grant of 135 million drachmas of Commandant Brauer to the charitable foundations of Heraklion, amongst which was also the Hospital. One asks why this gift was made by Schubert, who was not known for his gestures of philanthropy and anyway played no part in the events of Viannos? Schubert's intention becomes more comprehensible if his philanthropic announcement is related to the 'Proclamations' he later published in the same Germanophile paper of Heraklion.

On 28th December 1943, an invitation was published in the Heraklion paper, Κρητικός Κήρυξ, in which Schubert hides behind the pompous title of Administrator of the Greek detachment of criminal hunters.[377] Undoubtedly to the Cretans he was best known by name rather than his administrative title. Further, the 'invitation' is styled in such a way so as to be used as a trap for the Cretans who would possibly come forth to denounce directly to Schubert men of his detachment who committed crimes or blackmail against them. The Cretans were invited to denounce "always similarly a criminal who came to their attention," in other words to report active resistor compatriots to avoid collective reprisals against their villages.[378]

The invitation on the one hand encouraged wronged Cretans to voice their complaints to Schubert; on the other it discouraged them as it obliged them to become snitches and consequently incur the enmity of their compatriots. In Schubert's mind, his invitation would render unjustified the accusations of Germans and Greeks to higher ranks, that the abuse of the 'Greek detachment' had extended the hatred of the Cretan people against the occupying forces.

Three days later, on New Year of 1944, Schubert republished the extract of the 'invitation' in another form, as "Proclamation and wishes to the Cretan people",[379] in which the characteristic feature was the domineering character of Schubert. His autocratic arrogance overtook every boundary. To the 'proclamation' he added one more threatening paragraph relating to the punishment of those who fail to surrender arms and forbidden military material within a defined time otherwise "no one will chance to escape".[380]

But how could these announcements reconcile with the spirit of appeasement and conciliation which Brauer and the German authorities then advocated? Their result must have been exactly opposite. The activities of the various detachments of the Schubert squad during the months of November and December clearly showed that the policy of the German Sergeant had in no way adjusted to the policy of peace and appeasement which the military authorities of the 'Fortress' were trying to apply.

Undoubtedly there were many residents who, though maltreated or abused by deputies of Schubert, would voice their complaints not to Schubert himself but to the local authorities. As such there was pressure on the German Sergeant to restrict the abuse of his squad and impose some control. Schubert however, in order to show that there was no Cretan complaining about the acts of his team, published the 'Invitation' and 'Proclamation'. Consequently, the German Sergeant had no intention of changing his policy of terrorizing and violence which his diverse squad exercised at the time.

There is no doubt that the strict reprisals with which Schubert threatened all those who failed to denounce anti German efforts represented the outright undermining of Brauer's and his officials' efforts to create a climate of reconciliation and cooperation with the Cretan people. In direct contradiction to the harsh language of Schubert, in his aforementioned announcements, is the diplomatic and appeasing language of General Brauer who, in his "Plea" of November 1943, after first extending a hand of friendship, exhorts the population of the island to support the German army in its race against Bolshevism, concluding: "whoever offers help to the army in this effort is welcome"[381] evidently an effort by the General to turn, as the example of the German authorities in mainland Greece, the resistance organizations of the nationalist EOK and communist EAM to civil conflict.

It is worth noting that Schubert, though recognizing the policy of appeasement of Brauer, still decided to diverge from it, a tactic he followed throughout his military career. The British, in their Report, make a significant observation that the German officers nurtured hatred towards Schubert because "his beastly methods obstructed the attempts at reconciliation".[382]

As aforementioned, his autocratic "proclamation" exceeded established boundaries for the position and rank of a sergeant. It could only provoke the intense reaction of the German officers and Commandant Brauer, especially after the fiasco at Meskla. The arrogant announcement of Schubert's donation to the Heraklion Hospital must also have provoked a lack of sympathy by the German military hierarchy as the hospital was perhaps obliged to mention him by name and title, an exception made it seems only for him. So, the announcements relating to philanthropy and Schubert's New Year wishes, superficially edged within the framework of the German system, but in fact bore boldly the mark of his character – a strong desire to project himself – and the autonomy of the Sergeant, one he acquired from Captain Brauer himself.

It is not known what opinion I. Passadakis generally had about Schubert and particularly the New Year "Proclamation". It is very likely he considered him essential for the terrorizing of the mountain residents as, just ten days after his expulsion, Passadakis announced the formation of Security Squads at Chania and Heraklion.[383] It could be, though, that he contributed to the distancing of Schubert when he spoke to General Brauer. Further, some degree of truth may exist in Passadakis' exaggerated declarations that when Schubert was informed about the murder of men of his team at Meskla, "he became enraged and decided to take revenge destroying the village entirely and slaughtering the residents of the area".[384]

Once Passadakis heard of Schubert's intentions he intervened to Captain Brauer and "managed to obstruct the human beast". It should be noted that Passadakis, imprisoned in 1947 as a collaborator, tried to project himself as "saviour" to justify his position. The British were trying to find a Schuberite, then after 'Schubert'; they were always looking for a Schuberite who could be persuaded to murder Schubert and then enrolled without punishment to the resistance movement. Lieutenant Colonel Tom Dunbabin, when he discovered that such a candidate could be papa-Lefteris Kallergis, very close to Schubert in December 1943 wrote to Ioanni Dramountani or Stefanogianni, head of the resistance team of Anogeia: "Hasten to contact Papalefteri that his services are welcome with great pleasure and once the job is done, if he can, let him kill Schubert himself Can we trust this dirty priest?".[385] In truth, the English Service of Special Operations (SOE) laid down many plans for Schubert's murder but he took adequate security measures, "Schubert appeared to live as a medieval despot at Heraklion residing in a building guarded as a fortress".[386] Brauer gave Schubert ten days'[387] grace to prepare before departing by ship for Athens. As far as the "Hunting Squad" is concerned, it is said that the General ordered its dissolution.

In reality, he gave the option to the Schuberites to choose whether they preferred to follow their leader to his next post or reorganize and remain to continue their activities in Crete. The 'Greek Squad' divided nearly in the middle with 35–40 volunteers following Schubert to Macedonia whilst the remaining Schuberites continued their criminal activities, mainly in the municipality of Heraklion, until the German forces pulled out of the area in early October 1944.[388] Immediately after Schubert's distancing, the Germanophile political authorities of Crete, pioneered by the Minister I. Passadakis and with the support of the German Occupation authorities following the example of the Greek Security Battalions of the I. Rallis government, decided to create similar battalions also in Crete to annihilate, according to the common proclamations EOK-EAM of Crete "the disaster of Schuberitism" against the Cretan people.[389] Finally in February 1944, in the municipality of Heraklion the "Security Unit" assembled about 90 German clothed anti-communist, convicts and criminals,[390] under the leadership of a lieutenant Dede and one Ioan. Xylouris, whilst in the municipality of Chania the "Hunting Mobster Squad" under the gendarme's leader Dim. Papagiannakis resumed for a while the despised 'Schubertism".[391]

In the final analysis, the attempts to assemble security battalions in Crete failed miserably as the resistance organizations EOK and EAM formed a common front and, with the support of the Cretan population, achieved the self-destruction of anti-communist formations.

On 11th January, Schubert abandoned Crete for Athens where he remained about one month for medical care and recruitment. There are no details regarding his activities during his stay in the capital. Men mentioned as being enlisted to the gang include Kon. Economakis or Economou, G. Kokkinis or Athinaios and possibly I. Kambas or Tourkos.[392] Around mid-February, Schubert, leading about 40 Cretans, departed by ship for Salonica where he was placed under the orders of the Befehlshaber Saloniki-Agais. Strangely, in Schubert's military records his transfer to Macedonia in January 1944 is not mentioned but is construed by the record of 29th May when the unit was renamed Korpsgruppe Saloniki that Schubert had enlisted from the start to the mechanical unit of 985 division of the Military Police.[393] During his short stay in Thessaloniki it seems he embarked on some recruiting; "the force was augmented with various ranks and different criminals he collected from Thessaloniki" testifies the Krousonas I. Gridakis.[394] Nik. Konstantinou and his two sons were then enlisted to the gang. From Thessaloniki Schubert was transferred in the last ten days of February to Giannitsa Pella.

Schubert and his gang's toll of monstrosity in Crete

In answer to the question of how many became victims of Schubert and his squad from the beginning of his activities until his departure, the numbers differ according to the source. In the indictment against Schubert in October 1946, the

Royal Commissioner of the National Office of War Crimes calculated the number of victims at above 3.000:

"Intentionally and deliberately, he effected the killings of many residents of Crete and others murdered killing more than three thousand Greeks in different ways".[395] To the 3,000 murders which appear to have been committed exclusively in Crete, the Commissioner G. Demakopoulos at Schubert's trial in 1947 added the murders in Macedonia: "3,000 are the murders weighing him and it would be a crime to delay his punishment".[396] The second piece of evidence is the "Report" of the National Organization of Officers of Heraklion. In the list of German war criminals Schubert comes 54th with the following description: "He holds first place in the slaughters in Crete, he executed more than 250 without any procedures; his victims are strewn from one end of Crete to the other".[397]

Last The Military Information Service in June 1947 sent a report to the National Office of War Criminals in which Crete ascribes 35 victims to Schubert and 10 to G. Tzoulias![398] In the third document, Schubert's conviction decree, 75 murders are listed for which Schubert was adjudged guilty of committing them from August 1941 to December 1943 in 16 villages in Crete, mostly in the municipality of Heraklion.[399] According to the fourth court document, according to the Special Court of Chania during the period 1942–1943 those executed exclusively by the various Schuberite detachments number around 65.[400] In addition, the Schuberites terrorized a number of villages known from other sources which are absent from the aforementioned judicial decisions. The number of victims in villages as Metohi Vorou Douli, Loutraki, Korfes, Grigoria, Avrakontes, Agio Georgios, Chora Sfakia, Anopoli Maza, Fone, Kefala Apokorona and Kare Kissamo approach 35 persons and could have been even higher. To the final number of victims must be added 10–12 Krousaniotes executed by Schuberites, usually compatriots who are not mentioned in the court papers.[401] So, the total reached by adding the above numbers exceeds 200 persons, to be exact 210, executed by Schubert and the Schuberites in a period of eighteen months, that is from June 1942 till the end of December 1943. The victims can be divided between Schubert – when present he gave the order – and the Schuberites when Schubert was absent.

It is worth noting that Generals Brauer and Miller were deemed responsible and condemned to triple death sentences "for the execution of at least 200 persons by the Schubert squad".[402]

How then can the atmosphere of 'dread and fear' which Schubert and his gang created amongst the population of Crete be reconciled with the low numbers of casualties in a difficult period of the war? Evidently in Schubert's case the criteria for the assessment of his activities are determined: 1) not by the extent but by the depth of his criminal activity and 2) by the decision of a considerable number of

Cretans to enlist under the German deputy cooperating in criminal activities against the civilian population. Below are offered some possible explanations.

First, Schubert, a violent character with sadistic instincts, chose torture as the most effective way of terrorizing Cretan villages. In the exercise of bodily harm against their victims, Schubert's men were pitiless and unsparing. The violent beatings took the form of public shows and their reach exceeded the boundaries of the village where the torture took place. For this reason, the German lieutenant in his raids concentrated his interest more on cruel abuse than mass executions. According to the decision of the Special Martial Court of Athens, out of the total of sixteen villages, Schubert executed one person at each of nine of them and between two and four people at the remaining seven. Exceptions are the villages Kali Sykia and Kallikratis, punished with mass executions most probably due to the intense hatred of the Germans against capetan Bantouvas, whose presence in the area spurred Schubert, with German approval, to collective reprisals.

During Schubert's trial the most graphic descriptions of brutalities are contained in the testimonies of Cretans, as that of Arist. Kastrinogiannis, who relates that to the plea of one about to die to allow him to write down two words to his wife prior to his execution, Schubert answered with cynical stance: "you're now preparing for the next world and you're in the mood for writing letters?"[403] To an arrested Cretan he announced his immediate fate with the phrase "wear your shroud to die".[404] After the war, such phrases prompted many characterizations of the German Lieutenant in the daily press, as "bloody slaughterer of Crete having the soul of a hyena" "beastly sadist",[405] "despised executioner with the chilling glance of a snake"[406] and "anthropomorphic beast".[407]

Next Commandant Brauer gave Schubert the rights over life and death. The name Schubert was the fear of the Cretans. His name was disliked as much by the German Court Martial as by the German Police as he interfered in their task.[408] Schubert, head of a shadowy team, used the rare, even unique in military circles, strength to execute dirty business which the usual German army normally avoided, in other words terrorizing the people in the villages and cities.

Kanavakis, then 16, resident of the precinct Kamaraki Heraklion, where Schubert had established his base, in his memory associated Schubert with fear. "He was our dread, when we met him in the street. He'd grab whoever he wanted and jail him or beat him or even clean him out. The name Schubert was the fear of the Cretans".[409] "He'd kill you for a joke without accounting to anyone"[410], according to K. Mitsotakis. His strange appearance also provoked fear, "we were scared to look upon him", remembers old Portalakis, also resident of the same area.[411] So, Schubert's tyranny, mostly a corollary of the autonomy he had been ceded but also his particular idiosyncrasies, formed the source of continuous dread and fear for the Cretans.

Third, Schubert possessed particular 'attributes', which distinguished him from other Germans: "He spoke Greek perfectly, he knew the backstreets well, he walked high, he'd approach people, take his precautions and would become very shrewd in matters of intelligence".[412] He was a hard "devil" and the Greeks who followed him tried to imitate him, even exceed him in devilishness and cruelty.[413] His greatest 'artistry' he often manifested in forced assemblies of residents and questioning of suspects. In these situations, he provoked such psychological shock combining abuse, anger, foul mouthing, excessive threats, sneering and gestures to raise the dread and paralyze inner strength.

A characteristic example of one who 'Poured out the names of officer members of EOK to Schubert and Tzoulias was Major Emm.Giakoumakis.[414]

Fourth, Schubert and his squad in truth committed more crimes in more villages than is known from the sources, but people generally attributed them to the Germans as even in the first period, but mainly in the second, the Schuberites dressed in German uniform could not easily be distinguished from the genuine Germans. Their speech of course could betray that they were Greeks but generally they avoided speaking their language when circumstances demanded as at Schubert's raid at Meskla in July 1943. According to a source, a small team of German clad Schuberite 'spies' appeared at the village cafe of Gerakari Amarion and "at the table where they sat, they were chatting (speaking an incomprehensible language) Then they left. Outside the village a shepherd heard them speaking Greek and contacted the Gerakari that they were not real Germans but Schuberites".[415] Even today some older witnesses who lived the events, in their narratives interchange the name of Schubert with the Germans, justifying their emotions that as far as they were concerned, 'they were all German enemies'.[416]

Last, the Central committee ascertaining brutalities in Crete, in its Report of 1945 provides witnesses from 76 cities and villages. Schubert is listed amongst the biggest war criminals "for countless executions" and is named the sadist which "all of Crete shivered"[417] without detailing his crimes.

Also, at the collaborators' trials of 1945–1946 there are repeated mentions of Schubert as "the dread and fear" of Crete and of those who followed him as evil "wandering" Greeks.[418] Further, at Schubert's trial in 1947 the biggest impressions made in court and to the journalists were the dramatic narratives of witnesses present and absent from Crete who blamed nearly all Schubert's crimes with short mentions of his accomplices. Schubert in such a way became the scapegoat for the Cretans. The Cretan society could not reckon with the idea that it was possible for their own people to play collaborator roles in such an early period (1942) when in mainland Greece the collaborators appeared much later, towards the end of 1943 and particularly 1944 at a time when the Germans began surrendering from the different fronts. Evidently the tendency of the Cretans to attribute many criminal activities to Schubert served as an ulterior motive, the creation of a shield behind which those who played some German friendly role during that troubled time wished to protect themselves.

Part II

Schubert in Macedonia
(February–October 1944)

Chapter 1

Schubert and the Armed Anti-communist Forces in Central Macedonia

Schubert and his team, now augmented, arrived in Giannitsa during the last ten days of February 1944. Apart from the permanent German guard there of around 100 men under Capt. Max Pescho, a small armed team of Greek volunteers had been recruited, under the command of Kyros Grammatikopoulos, a fanatic nazi from Drama.[419] The latter willingly joined the ranks of the German guard to join in proudly terrorizing the people of Giannitsa and around. Apart from Grammatikopoulos, Schubert found a plethora of armed anti-communist groups with whom he periodically joined forces to achieve his goals. Unlike Macedonia, in Crete early on, Schubert commanded a unique armed force against the resistance with Cretan volunteers, who were enlisted, armed and nurtured by the occupying authorities of the island. Crete did not cultivate such allegiances, unlike Northern Greece, for two reasons: the Cretans were mostly absorbed in the ideology of Venizelos which suppressed the growth of other doctrines particularly communism.

The Royals, those with Metaxa, supporters of the popular and Communist groups wherever they lived, were a low-profile group who generally remained neutral during the Occupation and additionally in Crete, compared to Northern Greece there was a small Pontian population, both Greek and Turkish speaking, whose particular doctrine and tradition played a pioneering role against fascist communist cooperation with the German invader. Whereas in Northern Greece, 70% of the armed nationalist anti-communist guard were Pontian, whose substantial portion were enlisted in the nationalist groups and Captain Schubert's 'detachment'[420].

The oldest group assembled in the spring of 1943 under the auspices of the martial command of Salonica-Aegean,[421] was that of the dismissed Colonel George Poulos, a fanatic beholder of German nationalist ideals, head of the nazi organization EEE (National Union of Greece) and a relentless hunter of communism and the most predatory nationalist leadership. In his guard were recruited about 300 German clad men, mostly buccaneers for quick gain, various criminals and persons chased or pursued by ΕΛΑΣ (Greek Liberation Army) as rebels from Salonica and areas of Macedonia, mostly refugee villages of Ptolemaida[422]. The Wehrmacht considered this detachment as part of the German army since "any violence against Poulos' detachment will be considered as violence against the German army".[423] Poulos worked methodically with words and actions for the success of the German forces, often joining them in raids against areas of central and west Macedonia where the Poulos forces pioneered in crimes against the unarmed.

In the province of Kozani, in July 1943, Poulos forces plundered and burned around ten villages, executing groups of their inhabitants.[424]. Salonica, Poulos' base till the spring of 1944 (from summer 1943 Poulos used temporary bases in smaller towns of central and western Macedonia) became the stage for their crimes where they practiced freely and arbitrarily not only against proclaimed enemies but also those whom they suspected may be resistors, though often nationalist.[425]

Many from Salonica suffered terrible torture in the prisons on 32 P. Mela Street, others lost their lives from the bullets of Poulos' men. In May 1944, Poulos settled in Krya Vrysi in Pella, which he transformed into an impregnable anti-communist garrison to control the area of Giannitsa in cooperation with other nationalist groups such as those of Kyros Grammatikopoulos, Stergios Skaperdas and Fritz Schubert.

The Pontian Grammatikopoulos, a motorist from Drama, from the start was so taken with the ideology of nazism that he became "more German than the Germans", fighting with a position in the Wehrmacht in Finland, Crete, Africa and the Russian front.[426] As Poulos, Grammatikopoulos became one of the most fervent predators of the 'Jewish Bolshevik cohesion', effortlessly striving for the imposition of German imperialism. "Let us wish for all European nations, particularly we Greeks, the absolute Victory of the armed Alliance" he wrote in March 1943 in the Germanophile paper, New Europe[427]. In Salonica, where he settled with his family at the beginning of 1943, as agent of the Gestapo (Secret Martial Police) he made many arrests and executions for which the German authorities rewarded him with the lease of a Jewish shop[428]. It was then he assembled an armed team, mostly Pontians, from the areas of Drama and Kilkis, which he made available to the Germans, taking part in their activities. It was at Paiko in early January 1944 that Grammatikopoulos armed Turkish speaking residents of Aravissos (Ombar) disposing of 'rebel collaborators' to the jails of Pavlos Mela, thus instigating strong retaliation from ΕΛΑΣ in Aravissos in early February[429]. At the fields of Giannitsa, Grammatikopoulos from the spring of 1944, appeared with the title of coordinator of the local nationalist groups. During this time, he settled in Giannitsa, where for the first time he met the recently arrived Fritz Schubert, with whom he became close friends and cooperated until the end of the Occupation.

Vlahos Stergios Skaperdas, a large farm owner from Drosero in Pella, didn't ally to the occupation, moved by the German ideology of nationalism, nor the dream of the powerful 3rd Reich, unlike the aforementioned leaders. In contrast, Scaperdas from the beginning of the German occupation actively showed his tendency towards the resistance helping in the formation of the first groups of ΕΛΑΣ in Paiko. When in 1943 he was informed that ΕΛΑΣ was reliant on KKE (Greek Communist Party) he then defected to the nationalist organization ΠΑΟ, which in turn dissolved late 1943 under the continued pressure of the more powerful ΕΛΑΣ. Reacting to the persistent threats of ΕΛΑΣ against his person and his family and the confiscation of his assets by ΕΛΑΣ, Skaperdas was obliged to take refuge with the Germans of

Salonica for protection. Here he built strong ties with the powerful leader G. Poulos, who encouraged him to assemble his own armed team and collaborate with him in the war against detested communism.[430] Skaperdas enlisted mostly Sarakatsani from the villages of Drosero and dressing them in "scaperdan attire" in May moved them to Krya Vrysi, Poulos' base, to begin, in an ideal cooperation with his patron, his anti-communist activity to its bitter end. Later the two of them would join Schubert in the fields of Giannitsa to create an establishment of violence and terror with arrests, beatings and executions of suspects.

From the summer of 1944, in the Giannitsa area, arrests were made, in this climate of violence and terror, by the armed team of Pontian Apostolos Tsarouchides and capt. Iordanis Haseri (or Hasiari) from Kallifyto in Drama.[431] Haseris, a violent individual, was pursued by the Bulgarians after his involvement in the attack in Drama in September 1941 then settled first in the Giannitsa area, where he cooperated in the activities of the resistance group ΠΑΟ, and after its dissolution at the end of 1943 he defected to the group ΕΕΣ of Michalaga.[432] Prompted by Michalaga, he assembled an armed team from the Turkish speaking villages of Kozani and from January 1944, with divisions of ΕΕΣ and the guard of Col. G. Poulos, he took part in the attacks of 'rebel villages' of Kozani where the Haserans violently abused and executed the unarmed and resorted to the plunder of property and burning of homes.[433] In July or August, Haseris abandoned Aravissos[434] and settled in Giannitsa where, as leader of about 100 random men, invaded nearby villages "in search of communists, not always without victims and executions".[435]

A close friend of Haseris in Giannitsa was his compatriot Ap. Tsarouchides, the leader of a small armed anti-communist team.[436] In the summer of 1944[437] the sum of treacherous armed lords, leading at least 10,000 men, is reckoned to be over 300 in Macedonia and Thrace. Most (60%) of them were active in Eastern Macedonia and Thrace due to the large amount of Pontian refugees in the provinces of Drama, Serres and Kilkis under strict Bulgarian occupation. Similarly in areas of Kozani, Edessa and to a lesser extent around Giannitsa and Pieria[438]. Around Kozani, Pontian anti-communists, mostly Turkish speaking, formed the Greek Volunteer Unit, assembling early January 1944 under the auspices of the Wehrmacht. Late,r these leaders of ΕΕΛ and other local nationalist groups of Macedonia responded to the efforts of the German authorities to structure "a framework of coordination and functionality"[439] for the better performance of their targets and enlisted to an unofficial organization under the bogus name 'National Greek Army'.[440] This ΕΕΣ leadership was handed to the three Papadopouloi, Kisa Batzak (Kyriakos Papadopoulos, 60 year old farmer from Kouko Katerini), Michalaga (Michael Papadopoulos, 42 year old cattle trader from Serbia Kozani) and Constantine Papadopoulos, a 30 year old student from Rodona Kilkis.

The management of ΕΕΣ, probably symbolic, was given to the older Kisa Batzak who, in August 1944, to be closer to the root of administration, moved the base from Kouko to Salonica[441]. At the time the numbers of ΕΕΣ armed men amounted to 5,550.

The team of ΕΕΣ were mostly active in the outdoors and were led, according to the leader of the SS Heinrich Himmler, "to an ideal cooperation with our German divisions in the fight against the Bolshevik plotters till the very end".[442]. In the first six months of 1944, units of ΕΕΣ took part in large raids of the Wehrmacht at Krousia (February), Pieria (March), Vermio (March and April), Paiko (March) and North Pindos (July) in which they took the lead in executions of the unarmed, abuse, imprisonments in camps and jails, plunder and burning of homes and villages as at Ermakia, Pyrgous, Mesovouno, Eleftherohori and other mountain villages known to the authorities as "rebel villages".[443] The extreme cruelty of the Germans and their accomplices brought about tragic living conditions to thousands of fire victims and the homeless as described in the Report of the Agricultural Bank of Greece. "In general, the conditions of the fire victims of the provinces of Serbia, Grevena, Voios, Kastoria, Kozani is such to provoke genuine dread to their unaffected neighbours, who live with the daily threat of suffering the same fate. Homeless in rags, unshod, hungry, abandoned by all and helpless and worst of all, unable to find any State Authority or Service to report, they live days of agony, fear and without hope for the next day".[444]

Chapter 2

Giannitsa: Vengeance Begins

The population of Giannitsa, between 13,000 and 15,000, was a mosaic of populations from different origins, as local Greeks, Eastern Thracians, Pontians, people from Asiaminor, Karamanlis supporters and others who lived in their individual separate hamlets. It is worth noting that, at least according to a local from Giannitsa, this mosaic did not show faults such that would lead to ideological, political and social conflicts and disputes.[445] Generally, the Giannitsiotes stood by the national Resistance, many serving in the 30th corps of ΕΛΑΣ[446] whose area of activity was the plain of Giannitsa and Paionia and its base at Paiko mountain.

The control of this area with its many villages and road and rail networks became the bone of contention between the forces of the Wehrmacht and the 30th corps, whose numbers in the spring of 1944 amounted to 500–600 men.[447] It's also noteworthy that amongst the royal and patriotic Giannitsiotes, none became members of the treacherous militia.[448]

Possibly this stance of the Giannitsiotes, which for the Germans and their allies formed a kind of impregnable wall to their efforts to attract informers and recruits, explains in part the harsh methods the enemy used against this town.

In many of the villages here the predominant vein of the population was Pontian refugees, particularly Turkish speaking residents of Bafra of western Pontus, most of whom, due to language and cultural differences, felt marginalized and could be discriminated for their fanatic anti-communism and allegiance to the occupied force[449] Just before Schubert's arrival, the armed Turkish speaking Pontians from the mixed population of Aravissos had taken refuge in Giannitsa (Obar) after an attack by ΕΛΑΣ on 3rd February, in which there were many casualties. Amongst the Giannitsiotes they were known as 'Obar Gestapo' and for their characteristic phrase "hands have pockets out"[450] used when checking citizens. About 15 men were recruited into Schubert's guard, mostly Pontian and Karamanlides from Aravissos and the villages of Pella, Kilkis and Drama who from fear and hate towards ΕΛΑΣ and the Bulgarians had settled in Giannitsa for better safety.[451]

The Aravissian Lazaros Kommatopoulos and his wife Eudoxia were the most notable recruits to Schubert's squad.[452] The strong nationalism, particularly of the Bafrans, will cause hereafter serious backlash to the Giannitsiotes as regards their treatment from the volunteer gangs of Schubert, Grammatikopoulos, Skaperdas and others. "The Pontians of Aravissos from February caused a tense atmosphere in the city. Terrorizing with the Germans and their armed accomplices they are intent on dissolving the resistance organizations".[453]

Before Schubert, there were few retaliatory executions or torture against suspected supporters of the Resistance. The only incident was the arrest of about 100 to 200 men by German divisions on 13th November 1943 and their imprisonment in the 'Pavlos Melas' jails for a short time. Amongst those selected for imprisonment were senior employees of the provincial offices, the courtroom and the Agricultural Bank.[454] Apparently many of the hostages victimized as in September 1943, they had signed a note of protest against Bulgarians' expansion in central Macedonia.[455] Immediately after his move to the home of Bulgarian speaking G. Kaiafa, Schubert created such terror that the Giannitsiotes had never before encountered. "From the first day he stepped his foot in Giannitsa, he sowed fear into the whole area! He immediately assembled 180 residents and beat them" states St. Triantafyllides at the trial of Schubert, a civil servant and witness to the events.[456] From the mass of those assembled, Schubert, with his committee, chose the most 'suspect' and locked them into the basement of the Turkish bath, known as Medrese, part of the guarded camp of the German guard. The questioning was a riddling trap: "Are you a communist? Do you know other communists?"[457] Whether answering yes or no the questioned 'suspect' would accuse himself, thus surrendering to inhumane torture. The imprisoned Giannitsiotes were beaten hard 'over several days' with pistol butts, clubs, lashes and other means. The Schuberites, with the help of the armed force of Grammatikopoulos, filled the prisons from those taken at road blocks in various parts of the town and surrounding villages throughout the two-month period they were stationed in Giannitsa.

After the torture, followed the selection: "Some were dismissed, others were sent to the Pavlos Melas camp and others to work in Germany".[458] Even more abominable were the crimes committed by the Schuberites against the unarmed in various surrounding villages, such as Pylorigi, Sandali and Asvestario,[459] of particular the case of the village Sandali, a small refugee hamlet on the road between Giannitsa and Edessa. During an attack here Schubert chose 13 men, executing two on the spot, the remainder he moved to the Giannitsa jails where he put them through "medieval torture for those days",[460] threatening them with death. It was here that, 'during the uprising of the villagers of Sandali, the teacher Katina Aggelidou consenting to become Schubert's lover sacrificed her honour to save the lives of those arrested, whom she saved".[461]. Local Giannitsiotes endorse her decision to become Schubert's lover and disapprove of ΕΛΑΣ, who later executed her.[462] The local authorities of Giannitsa soon realized that Schubert was a brutal, sadistic terrorist unlike any of the known hitherto nationalist leaders of armed Greeks. Even though a mere German sergeant, he appeared to act autonomously, unrestricted by the local German authorities on whom often citizens relied for a form of order and protection from the bigotry of fanatic individuals in society.

Under the initiative of the mayor, Thomas Maggriotis, a flawless person lacking in ideologies and discriminations, the local authorities of Giannitsa acted through the German command of the town Max Peschko so that "recalled, apparently, by German Authorities in Salonica"[463], Schubert and his unit were distanced on 18th

April. The mayor's success he considered as one of the worst blows he received as a leader and "for this reason, Schubert detested him to death"[464]. Two days before leaving for his new base, Nea Gonia Halkidiki, he barged into the mayor's office, Locked the mayor, his secretary and a clerk in one room and threatened them saying: "Homos, you're ridding me. You're all to blame. When I return, you won't get away"[465]. Continuously reminding them of his return with vengeance. From Halkidiki, he sent a threatening letter to Maggriotis commanding him to harvest and thresh the farmland of two Schuberites from Aravissos and deliver the crop, 400 kilos of wheat per acre, to their families in Salonica. "Unless the Mayor abides to this letter, this act is considered a sabotage and according to German law punishable by death".[466] The letter was submitted to the German Commander of Edessa who undertook to respond himself.

Mid-June on his way from Giannitsa, Schubert entered the mayor's office, assembled in one room the threesome, Maggriotis, Haritides and Triantafyllides and, in a threatening tone, warned that things were not well in their town. According to his own sources, the deterioration was due to his absence: "I should have killed you, Mayor and them, meaning us and the priest, to confess to who are the communists here and to put a stop but you won't get away, I would have done it here and now but those German rats, whom you dosed with ouzo, didn't let me".[467] Indeed, true to his word, Schubert on 14th September committed the atrocities which he would have during his first visit to Giannitsa.

Chapter 3

Schubert at the Villages of Western Halkidiki (18th April–5th August 1944)

Nea Gonia: Schubert targeted by attacks of ΕΛΑΣ Halkidiki[468]

Nea Gonia, a hillside village (157metres) of refugees from Eastern Thrace (527 inhabitants in 1940) in an area which didn't stand out for its strategic position nor its prominence for the Germans, compared to Giannitsa. In these villages lying across the mountain range from Nea Kallikrateia to the southern tips of Hortiati, as Nea Gonia, Rodokypos, Petralona, Krini, Vassilika and Peristera it is evident that the chance visits of ΕΛΑΣ forces were restricted mostly to the supply of food. Then because most living there were conservative, any resistance organizations were symbolic. These villages were located a short distance from the area where there were important, established German (Nea Kallikrateia, Vassilika) and Bulgarian (Nea Kallikrateia, Nea Triglia, Nea Moudania, Nea Silata) forces, charged with continued supervision of the coastal area against sabotage and the awaited invasion of the Allies.

Most likely though, the main reason Schubert settled in Nea Gonia was to control the road network Salonica – Halkidiki (two basic road arteries crossed this area) and protect the southeast safety zone around Salonica from possible resistance raids. This area was possibly considered quiet and humiliating for Schubert. At his new base, Schubert and a band of about 65 men[469] worked with a German unit known as Topographic Service, from whom "was supplied with ammunition, money and food"[470] In reality, the cartographers made up a small minority whose functions relied for security on the battling Germans, making up the majority of this unit. Their men often joined Schubert's forces in raids against local villages. One such team, arriving from Giannitsa, settled in Nea Kallikrateia around the same time Schubert armed in Nea Gonia.

The Schuberites inhabited the Primary School of the village, while Schubert with his gang – in the requisitioned home of Klada. The night of 24/25th April, 2nd after Easter, they were attacked by a unit of ΕΛΑΣ.[471] The police Headquarters of Halkidiki, once informed of Schubert settling in their precinct, decided to hit, hoping to expel him. Placed in charge of the unit (reinforced by men from the 2nd guard of G. Raftoudis from the Nigrita – Sohos area) were Capt. Vouros and Capt. Filotas (pseudonym of Vavdinos K. Papargyri/Papargyriou). The surprise attack against the Schuberites was planned for midnight. Food and guides were provided by the active Kriniotis Yannis Kopanos.[472] But the surprise faltered and the operation was a total failure. The persistent barking of the dogs betrayed the presence of the resistors to the Schuberites, who took up arms in the building and caused them to begin the raid earlier than planned, only exchanging shots without succeeding in approaching the school and making use of grenades and dynamite. Finally, the waning group were obliged to retreat when powerful German spotlights from Nea Kallikrateia flooded the whole area. Thus, the battle of Gonia ended ingloriously, lasting less than an hour.[473] Though without any casualties, Schubert immediately closed off the town, assembling all its residents, men, women and children in the square and threatened to execute in revenge 50 people unless they surrendered hidden arms and revealed the persons responsible for the attack.

In fact, he separated the first four for execution keeping the President of the community Athan. Kazakis and the priest to 'treat' them last. "Then Schubert told us whoever has a weapon to go bring it and surrender it to take his family and leave".[474] Whoever possessed whatever weapon, old or new, surrendered it to avoid the punishment. Whilst this process was still going on, capt. Polte, the head of the German unit in N. Kallikrateia arrived to move locals to individual labour in the fortification work of N. Kallikrateia and Epanomi. When he encountered the mass of people waiting in fear, who and how many were finally to be executed, he approached Schubert and explained to him that the residents of Nea Gonia had no relation to the resistance and rebel forces, rather they seemed very cooperative, particularly the president, with enforced labour. Schubert, always contrary to every German official's intervention, was obliged reluctantly to allow the people to return home. Kazakis himself in his statement, refers to the incident concluding "after much toil and negotiations, the executions were avoided.[475] Some Goniates reacted to Schubert's invitation to those in the square 'Whoever wants to enlist to the guard to save his family and take them, can enlist now'".[476]

To avoid possible execution, three youngsters enlisted to Schubert's gang. A fourth was a 21 year old Stavros Giannoglou, who had deserted from ΕΛΑΣ the day of the attack and, fearing retaliation, enlisted voluntarily to Schubert's force with which he served to the end.[477]

The victims of that day were two outsiders whom the Schuberites arrested that morning outside the village whilst Nea Gonia was enclosed. One named Aristeidis Bavelis, a shepherd from Sarakatsani, was passing with his flock, the other Asterios Valanas, resident of neighbouring Krini, arrived with his donkey to buy flour. The first accused as a supplier and the second accomplice of ΕΛΑΣ on a mission to verify Schubert's casualties during the raid, were executed outside Nea Gonia that same day.[478]

Putting failure aside, ΕΛΑΣ of Halkidiki had a second attempt one week later at ridding the area of Schubert. It appears[479] the mission was undertaken by the bold Capt. Kitsos (George Tsitourides an enlisted officer of the armed force in Kilkis) leader of the 2nd division of the 31st League of Halkidiki, who on the night of 1–2 May blockaded the village and pounded the stone-built school where the

Schuberites sheltered. From an official source a hard battle in the village ensued over three hours without casualties.[480]

Disheartened Kitsos is obliged before dawn to retreat to his hideout in Hortiati. Wishing to avoid the reproach again of capt. Polte, Schubert the next day did not harm anyone. "Next we pursued to rid this gang which settled in N. Kallikrateia"[481] states the then president of Nea Gonia A. Kazakis.

Enemies and friends of Schubert in Halkidiki

During this time that Schubert settled in the villages of Western Halkidiki, the inland peninsula was under the control of the 31st division of ΕΛΑΣ whose command was capt. Vouros (Thomas Tzelepis or Tselepis, enlisted officer of supplies from Pieria) and the captain was Kitsos. In the spring of 1944, the number of serving armed forces in the ΕΛΑΣ guard is estimated at around 250.[482]. Central Halkidiki, with its predominant mountain areas of Holomonda and Hortiati and its many peninsulas, with its many peninsulas, was then virtually impenetrable to transport for lack of road networks so ideal for the expansion of resistance groups. The problem though that the propagandists of the National Liberation Front, EAM movement, initially encountered was that the population of the mountain villages for the most part were local, conservative and suspicious.[483]

As a stalwart bastion of anti-Venizelos factions, the population opposed the attempts at novelty and enlistment. "Quite the opposite in the villages where refugees from Asia Minor resided, there we had a better response", notes an EAMist supporter. Of the 6,000 or so such refugees in Halkidiki[484], few settled in the mountain villages, the majority by the sea. Many refugee communists, who contributed to the growth and establishment of EAM organizations, escaped to villages of southeast Halkidiki from East Macedonia after the failed uprising in Drama against the Bulgarians in September 1941. Though many of the instigators of the EAM movement assembled in many villages, it was not until the summer of 1943 that they clamoured to grow into active resistance groups.[485] Until then anyway, the mountain villages were not under German pressure. Apart from the control of Polygyros, Mount Athos and the other two peninsulas of Halkidiki, they concentrated their attention on the safety and protection of the complicated southern shore from allied ships invasions and the anticipated British landing. Two incidents triggered the growth and spread of the armed divisions of ΕΛΑΣ in Halkidiki. First, the decision of the nationalist organization of the command of ΠΑΟ (Panhellenic Liberation Organization) to assemble in the summer of 1943 an armed resistance force of 100 men, to whom was entrusted, inter alia, the interruption of EAM[486] influence and assumed control of the Peninsula.

Note that ΠΑΟ as YBE (Defenders of Northern Greece) then, since 1941 had assessed the demographical and geographical advantages of Halkidiki and laid down an ambitious plan to use her "as a centre of recruitment with the aim of finally expelling the Occupation".[487] The mission was entrusted to Capt. Athan. Skorda from Nea Madyto, who heading about 30 armed men, mostly ex police, "made purgatory attacks against EAM" in the villages of Northern Halkidiki[488].

More specifically, his terrorizing raid at the village of Marathousa in September[489] was the reason that the Macedonian Headquarters of ΕΛΑΣ ordered the 30 year old capt. Strato Giannis Haritides from Rodopoli Serres to transfer from Krousia Kilkis to reinforce the armed teams under capt. Zacharia Zagoriti from Arnaia,[490] before the ΠΑΟ men reached Halkidiki and determined their aim. The group of about 60 infantries under capt. Strato joined Zagoritis forces and formed an army of over two hundred men. On 3rd November, in a battle outside the village Vrasta or Vrastama in the southeast heights of Holomonda, the larger and, in weaponry, forces of ΕΛΑΣ managed a heavy blow against the divisions of ΠΑΟ who escaped pursued to the Middle East.[491]

The battle at Vrastama wrecked the plans and dreams of ΠΑΟ to establish Halkidiki as a stronghold and gateway against the enemy and communism. Immediately after, the Headquarters of ΠΑΟ, in an attempt to regain control, ordered its armed forces in Eastern Macedonia to join ranks in Halkidiki 'for exceptional reasons'. With this in mind, around the end of November, the divisions of ΠΑΟ camped at the heights of Hortiati but received attacks by the ΕΛΑΣ division of Capt. Kolokotroni (pseudonym for 26 year old Kostas Kolintzas from Vlaherna Arkadia) and skirmished.[492] Officially ΠΑΟ declared the final dissolution of armed activities on 25th January 1944. From November 1943, almost all of Halkidiki was under the control of ΕΑΜ/ΕΛΑΣ save the peninsula of Kassandra. From February 1944 under the auspices of the occupying authorities, all (15) villages of Kassandra were provided with arms and the peninsula, with Valta as a base, became the stronghold of armed anti-communist militia.[493] Amongst this regime were selected the Kassandran officers, G. Varelas, Pant. Mourmouris and Asterios Michalakis, the latter a member of the nationalist division of the notorious G. Poulos.

The 31st Regiment of Halkidiki, (named so early August 1944) which never grew into an active force, included three divisions operating in strategic areas of Halkidiki. The first under Vouros controlled the north and east side of Holomonda with its hideout in the area around Megali Panagia, the third active at the southern slopes of Holomonda protected by the woody area north of Polygyros while the second under capt. Kitso operated in western Halkidiki at the heights of Hortiati with its hideout at Kerasies, between the villages of Livadi and Petrokerasa. The force in total in the summer of 1944 approached 350 men.[494] Thus, they needed support in numbers, equipment and arms from the 2nd division (part of 13th Regiment of Krousia) in the area of Nigritas-Sohou under G. Raftoudi and G. Pavlidi (capt. Mavro).[495] Often Raftoudi's men would cross the passes by lake Volvi to reinforce the divisions of ΕΛΑΣ Halkidiki.

The second incident (triggering ΕΛΑΣ growth) was the authority given by the German authorities in 1943, due to the imminent surrender of fascist Italy, to the occupying Bulgarian army to extend into Central Macedonia, including Halkidiki.

The presence of the Bulgarian army in Halkidiki obstructed the growth of EAM organizations and the like yet encouraged ant-icommunist brigades. From October 1943, Bulgarian forces, in total 5,500- 6,000 men, began to camp by the shores from Stavro to Epanomi charged with the "defence of Halkidiki shoreline against allied invasions".[496]

Two infantry regiments were bolstered with coastal Bulgarian artillery, whilst the Bulgarians acted under the control of the German martial authorities, who remained accountable for the inherent political defences of the peninsula.[497]

All along the eastern shoreline from the straits of Rentina to Ierisso, at opportue spots, grew the divisions of the 13th Regiment of Bulgarian infantry based at Stratoni, whose iron pyrite mines were of vital importance to the warring industry of the 3rd Reich.[498] The Germans entrusted to the Bulgarian army the construction of fortifications (ditches, tunnels, guard posts and cannons) at the narrow band of Rentina between the eastern shores of lake Volvi and the edges of Holomonda and Kerdylia, the aim of which was to deter the communications of resistance divisions through Eastern Macedonia to Halkidiki and vice versa.[499] At the western shores of lake Volvi, at Ghiolbas or Ghiol Baxe, where there existed the large agricultural installations of the Bulgaromacedonian Boris Tsolantsevits, camped a squadron of cavalry about 200–250 men.[500]

To this squadron was entrusted, from spring 1944, the control of the passes between lakes Volvi and Langada (Koroneia) which the resistance forces of Central Macedonia used to reinforce the divisions of ΕΛΑΣ Halkidiki.[501] At the southern coastal belt from Epanomi to Nikiti were stationed four divisions of the 41st infantry regiment based at Nea Triglia.[502] At strategical spots were positioned larger or smaller units of Bulgarian soldiers depending on the area's demands, as at Nea Kallikrateia, Nea Moudania, Vavdo (a unit of about 50 men)[503], Gerakini and Nikiti.[504] Temporary camps of Bulgarian divisions are registered at Plana, Nea Silata and Nea Flogita[505]. So, the larger part of the 41st Regiment were installed along the eastern shores of the Thermaic Gulf for the control and safety of the beaches and Salonica from allied invasion. From January 1944, Bulgarian divisions, often reinforced by larger units based at Langada and Kilkis, began to conduct clearing operation,s particularly at the villages lying at the northern and northeastern slopes of Holomonda. The aim being the pursuit of resistance teams, the dismantling of EAM organizations, the tracking of hidden weapons, the arrest and punishment of wanted rebels and generally the bullying of the villagers to deter supplies to ΕΛΑΣ divisions.

The policy and tactics the Bulgarian forces used during their operations and raids – often in cooperation with German divisions – failed miserably through Halkidiki for two main reasons: for one, the rebel teams tended to harass,thus avoiding up front conflicts with the Bulgarian squads. The method is described by a leader of ΕΛΑΣ "we continuously harassed (the Bulgarians) hindering their movements and supplies".[506] Then secondly, the Bulgarian authorities did not plan to Bulgaria-ise' Halkidiki, as the population was not Bulgarian speaking or thinking.

As such the Bulgarian forces did not show the cruelty and violence characteristic to their methods in Eastern Macedonia and Thrace.[507] Their soft policy allowed the villagers to continue undeterred their provision of accommodation, food and support to the resistance force throughout this period. It is noteworthy that even the Germans had little esteem for the Bulgarians who lacked not only organization and discipline but also motives.[508] According to the words of one from Polygyros: "To be truthful, the Bulgarians were not so cruel as amongst them were many opposing their own royal establishment".[509]

It is not known whether Schubert kept any ties with the Bulgarian military units in the places he settled. It is proven without doubt though that in June 1944, he used the Bulgarian cavalry stationed at Ghiolba, lake Volvi in the destruction of Marathousa. Most likely the rising of Bulgarian squads against Arnaia on June 2nd[510] was planned to coincide with the establishment of the German Topographic Service and Schubert's league at Nea Apollonia early June. According to reports, "from nightfall the people Left the village in fear saying, "is coming tomorrow to do much harm". We left towards Melissourgo, but fell upon Bulgarians the next day".[511] The Bulgarians cajoled the people to return to their village.

Nea Kallikrateia: Bastion of terror in the area

At his new base, at Nea Kallikrateia, the population (1,550 residents by the census of 1940) mostly consisted of refugees from Eastern Thrace and some from Asia Minor. There is no evidence that Schubert committed any crimes during his month-long stay though the anti-resistance organizations of EAM and ΕΠΟΝ had shown some activity in the village.

The explanation behind Schubert's stance no doubt is due to the fact that this village was under the control of a permanent force (one unit formed the German guard reinforced by a smaller Bulgarian unit)[512] and commander Polte who, as aforementioned, detested Schubert and his practices, and maintained a good relationship with the local authorities. As such, Schubert concentrated his activities exclusively against other surrounding villages. According to reports, fragments from the Schuberites would conduct surprise attacks on various villages "with the German topographic service and arrest people abusing them generally threatening and torturing".[513]

Petralona. On 21st May Schubert with his gang invaded Petralona, a refugee village of mostly Pontians, situated on a hillside at 270 m, "because he found that rebels were passing there".[514] Enforcing terrorist tactics, he assembled the residents in the square and selected 22 persons who he accused of having associations with the rebels. Abuse began with the townsman there, Aristeidis Katirtzides, who was beaten so badly "that he literally groaned in pain". Using the excuse that they were connected to the resistance, eight young men in all were tortured by Germanakis and Kapetanakis amidst the crowd. Next Schubert ordered that Ar. Katirtzides and a fellow villager be taken outside the village for execution. Though late to the assembly arrived Christos Gardikas, a metallurgist professor at the University of Salonica, who had a summer house at Petralona, spoke German and often mediated between the occupying forces and the villagers on various issues. So Gardikas pointed out to Schubert that the Petralonites "are nationalist and anti-communist and not related to the rebels. They are peacemaking people and friends of the Germans".[515] To Gardikas' declaration, the local policeman, Leonidas Sarigiannides, added his own, telling Schubert, "We are all with you" and showed him a note from the German authority, which confirmed him a Germanophile. Then Schubert replied, "If you are all with me, come and enlist to the squad". Sarigiannides accepted his proposal. Schubert first sent a young man to run and prevent the execution of Katirtzides and his companion. Then, from the team he had selected for execution, he held only five unmarried youngsters aged around 18–20 and allowed the remainder to return to their homes. These new recruits were transferred to Nea Kallikrateia and that same afternoon wore Italian uniforms, having first been obliged to wash in the sea. That evening, to a skull head drawn on a helmet, which Schubert kept in his notorious suitcase, they gave the oath of the brigade, which ended in the phrase 'freedom or death'. "Out of fear and to save our village, five youngsters were enlisted and they brought us to Nea Kallikrateia where they dressed and armed us" narrates one new recruit.[516]

Krini. A week later, 28th May, Schubert, with a portion of his squad, invaded Krini, a village of locals (about 500 residents in 1940) at a distance of just six kilometres north of Petralona and an altitude of 280m. In the morning, he enclosed the village and with terrorizing tactics assembled the residents in the village square where "brandishing a large pistol" he insulted and threatened them with beatings and execution unless they identify the resistors. Noteworthy that EAM had established in Krini a small corps of support, who helped the resistance when they had recently hit at Schubert in Nea Gonia[517]. The smaller force however had already escaped to the mountain before Schubert had cordoned off the village. Konstantinos Kazakis was the only leader who was arrested in the village, taken to the assembly where promptly Schubert called him by name and ordered his execution after torture.

The Cretan Grigoris Karyotakis, priest of Krini, having refused to enlist, Kapetanakis pulled by his beard from the crowd; the Schuberites beat him and finally kicked him down whilst he continued to pray. Then Schubert "appointed him guard of the faction to prevent his execution".[518]

Schubert considered the presence of priests to be a necessity, as he wanted to portray himself not only as the enemy of communism but a burgeon of religion. To compel the villagers to enlist to his gang, Schubert followed the method used at Nea Gonia and Petralona; that is, submitting his victims to torture with threats of death Even though this did not always occur. "Get up you who mock us",[519] Schubert angrily screamed, addressing Heracles Kazakis and Moscho Moustaka. The Schuberites took them aside, announcing the cold warning to the crowd, "Look at them, you won't see them again".[520] They were driven to an old house and abused.

Soon Schubert chose more, whom his accomplices beat in front of the crowd. Moustakas, who hadn't understood why all the violence, dared to ask "Why are you beating us" to which came the reply, "So you join us". "Yes, we'll join"[521] he assured them and immediately the torture ceased. Schubert then dissolved the crowd, satisfied by the result of his raid, as he returned to Nea Kallikrateia accompanied by five new recruits, whom he dressed, armed and swore to the Schuberites. One of these I. Kehagia, he left free when his father paid a ransom of one gold sovereign.[522] A few days later Moustakas and Soubasis defected, uniformed, and hid in their villages.

A squad was then sent by Schubert, burnt their homes and threatened the Krinians with the destruction of the village unless the deserters report to the unit immediately. Before they departed, the Schuberites plundered the village for food and livestock.[523]

During their raid on Krini, on the road between Nea Silata and Krini, the Schuberites arrested G. Minoglou, a 60 year old travelling trader from Salonica, whom they first beat at the prisons of Nea Kallikrateia (in the basement of N. Fanarioti) then 'took him walkies' to an existing open ditch outside the village, where they executed him with the accusation that he was an accomplice and supplier of the rebels, the official reprimand for pedlars, gypsies and vagabonds falling into the hands of the Schuberites[524]

Peristera

One foggy day in May, a division of the Schubert league headed by Germanaki and Kapetanakis surrounded Peristera, a village lying on the southeast side of mount Hortiati at an altitude of 570m with a population of about 450 native residents. Whilst most of the residents were conservative favouring the royals, a small number of Peristerians were loyal to EAM.

Implementing the usual method of terrorizing the unarmed, the Schubert command announced that all residents, men women and children, abandon their homes open and assemble at Alonia, a spot near the Primary School. During their identification controls the young Heracles Tasos, Nikolaidis and Christos Adamis had not sought to issue id's; thus labelled 'foreign' as accomplices and believers in EAM.

Whilst the Schuberites dragged them from the pile, they proclaimed "See them? You won't see them again" and immediately began beating them before the crowd with such passion that they tumbled to the ground. Though groaning from the beating of the clubs, "the leader Germanakis, placing a plank on two chairs for a platform, stood up and declared: It is I who have the power to cut off noses, to extract eyes, to cut off ears, to pull nails".[525] Upon hearing the chilling message, the local leader Athanasios Kottis and reverend Nikolas tried to explain that these youngsters were innocent Peristerians and were being unjustly punished. To this came the prompt reply "There you are, it was you we were after" then beat them as well, "groaning in pain".[526] Kapetanakis threatened reverend Nikolas, pulling him by his beard: "Priest, I'm going to have your nails".

After the thrashing, the leader announced that whoever had a weapon should surrender it for his family. Whatever old weapon they had, they surrendered, believing this way they would save their lives and protect their family. Mid-afternoon before leaving they had collected 15 old weapons, several muskets and two hunting guns. And they didn't forget the usual looting, indeed stealing some valuable items.[527]

Livadi

During their time at Nea Kallikrateia, Schubert also invaded Livadi via Galatista[528]

"They came from the side of Agia Anastasia and Galatista to find hidden weapons" testifies one from Livadi.[529] The gang of 20–25 men headed by aides of Schubert achieved a bold mission as there is no evidence of German backing in an area near the hideout of capt. Kitsos, leader of an EAM division.[530] Possibly the reason the mission was brief. The village was surrounded by heavy firing and the residents forced to assemble in the square, leaving their homes open. Most were women and children and the majority seniors, as the young and men had escaped to the nearby woodland. After the terrorizing, the leader announced to those assembled that whoever had a weapon should surrender it to save their family. "The people to escape brought whatever old weapon they found even rusty knives".[531] The invaders then returned with their plunder to base.

In general, it seems Schubert's force, whilst in Crete, often resorted to the plunder of villages they terrorized. Coincidentally, testimonies from Macedonia relating to this are more specific and detailed. As when Schubert left Giannitsa for Nea Gonia he carried with him "a mass of looted items, beds, mattresses, sewing machines clothing etc."[532]

Nik. Fanariotis from Nea Kallikrateia relates on looting from his requisitioned home where G Germanakis and G Kapetanakis resided. According to Fanariotis, "from the various plundered villages, they carried cheeses, girls' dowries, chickens, goats, sheep, pigs and gold items".[533] Indeed, these leaders kept back at his home two large trunks each full of loot, their proportionate share from Schubert's hand-outs. They plundered all the neighbouring villages. From Peristera, Germanakis brought gold tied in a scarf which he entrusted to the wife of Fanariotis. Two days later he asked for it back and surrendered it, probably fearing Schubert, for the usual hand-out.[534] The sale of plunder was a lucrative source of funding for the Schuberites.

During his 40 day stay in Western Halkidiki (deducting five days for his involvement in the clearing operation at Paiko) Schubert, apart from mainly cruelty in his terrorizing methods at the villages, kept executions to a minimum: his victims were only six, of whom two were passing 'outsiders'. Evident though is a substantial increase in the number of recruits, about 20 youngsters, from whom 15 were recruited from Crete, Nea Gonia and Petralona, the others from neighbouring villages. The number exceeds those from Giannitsa. Almost all were obliged to enlist under the threat of their execution or that of their compatriots. Apart from the volunteer St. Giannoglou, all defected, some from Nea Kallikrateia and the others from Nea Apollonia, each at different times.

Two Krinians, G. Soubasis and M. Moustakas, under pressure from their compatriots and to avoid the threatened destruction of their village, returned to the force at Nea Apollonia but Schubert remained pitiless to their pleas "Don't you feel for us at the bloom of our youth to kill us"[535] as they were driven to Calvary. Evidently Schubert's efforts to forge the alliance with Halkidikiotes Pontians failed miserably as the recruits neither possessed the loyalty of the Cretans nor even the fanatic anti-communism of the Turkish speaking Pontians from the areas of Giannitsa and Kilkis.

Chapter 4

Schubert at the Villages of Volvi (5th June–10th August 1944)

Nea Apollonia: Schubert tamed?

Nea Apollonia, or the Turkish Egri Boutzak, 57km east of Salonica, is the main village of the area (1,390 residents in the census of 1940) where people from Asia Minor settled during the exchange of 1922- 1923, mostly from the villages of Aksaz and Deirmentzik of Propontis with some from Bigali and eastern Thrace. At a close distance southwest of the village in densely wooded heights are the hamlets of Mesopotamo (Altsali) Xirorevma (Darmimis) and Asprohoma (Aktoprak) where in addition to those from Asia Minor, locals from Zervochoria, a few refugees from the area of Sampsounda and a few families from Sarakatsani also settled., a few refugees from the area of Sampsounda and a few families from Sarakatsani. These hamlets, whose total number of residents did not exceed sixty families made up a part of the municipality of Nea Apollonia. For the most part, the residents of Nea Apollonia during the occupation were Venizelikoi, with friendly attitudes towards the resistance. According to reports, the organizations of EAM and EΠON gathered a considerable number of members with recruits to EΛAΣ less than ten in number.

Due to its geographical position, Nea Apollonia did not offer itself as a base, camp or supply station of EΛAΣ whilst the hamlets were from time to time used by the resistors for supplies and hospitalization.[536] The small portion of nationalists in the village had most likely been absorbed into the nationalist organization ΠAO without notable activity.[537]

From the perspective of its position, Nea Apollonia was an important spot as regards the control of the area. It lies next (at a distance of about three kilometres) to the road network linking Thessaloniki to Kavala and the train line known as the Trenaki from the harbour of Kato Stavro to the station of Arakli, about 18 kilometres northeast of Thessaloniki. This transport network was of vital military importance for the movement of German and Bulgarian forces and military equipment during the Occupation. The village also lies in a suitable spot to control the passes each side of lake Volvi, which were often used by the EΛAΣ squads to cross from the northern areas of Macedonia (Kilkis, Nigrita-Sohos and Kerdylia) to Halkidiki and vice versa. Further, the lake itself was used for the transfer of resistors and injured as well as a source of fish for the rebel gangs.[538] A third important factor for the choice of Nea Apollonia by Schubert was that it provided a valuable spot for terrorizing the villagers in the northern heights of Holomonda, who assisted the rebel teams in general and their passage in particular.

A few days before Schubert's arrival at Nea Apollonia, about one unit of Germans of the topographic service arrived from Nea Kallikrateia and fortified, who fortified the area around the primary school where they camped. Apart from the military vehicles they brought with them a small number of horses who were looked after by the Schuberite S. Diktabanides from Kallifyto Drama. Attached to the force was also the young Giannitsian Kriton Grammatikos who was obliged to serve as interpreter.[539]

Accounts told that the unit was followed by a gang of Greek collaborators, headed by the notorious Schubert, who spread fear, death and destruction wherever he went.

First the established gangs of resistors abandoned the village to find hideouts in the surrounding mountains and swampy parts of lake Volvi. But also, most residents, in panic prior to Schubert's arrival, loaded their animals and carts with food and clothing and with their families hid outside the village, which had virtually emptied. In the meantime, on 5th June, the date of Schubert's gang's arrival, the local authorities under the instructions of Pashalis Paschalides, a peace abiding citizen and diplomatic local official, organized a reception and held a meal for Schubert and his men. During this the German leader seems to have assured Paschalides that 'he had not come to do harm to the village and no one need fear. All those who left, to return immediately and know they will not be punished'.[540] What mostly convinced the villagers to return was the news that Schubert was no passer-by, rather he planned to stay and make the village his permanent base.

The Schuberites, around 80 of them, camped on the ground floor of the primary school while Schubert, with Katina Aggelidou and the couple Lazaros and Eudoxia Kommatopoulos, stayed in the requisitioned home of Voutsa opposite the school and very close to the house of president Paschalides, who was also the owner of the local bakery so very familiar and popular with his compatriots. Schubert awaited the return of those who had abandoned the village and on the morning of 7th June with church bells and loudspeakers the villagers were alerted to assemble in the school yard under threat of execution for those found hiding. Approaching the assembly "one could see and experience himself what he had heard about Schuberite terrorism".[541] The Schuberites formed in a circle, had their weapons pointed against the crowd and Schubert, gun in hand, and surrounded by a team of his officials, with a harsh tone gave instructions to which of the three groups, men, women and children and youngsters each arrival was placed. Behind the Greek guard several Germans observed the whole play. To the panicked crowd, Schubert made a great effort to appear cooperative, concluding in his speech, "Go to your homes and keep quiet as I don't want to harm your village but if anyone counters me, they should know they won't get off".[542] Next, following a family register, he invited each family head to appear before him with all his family and if there were no records, he sent them off. He wanted to find of those present who were considered resistors, who were absent and why.

Next to him Paschalides, accompanied by the despotic secretary, John Matselas, ex-Police force, responded to his questions and, where he could, justified the absence of his compatriots. In most cases though, particularly with the 18 declared EAMites, to whom Schubert referred as "those with the stained shirts",[543] he would reply, "I don't know why they're off. They abandoned their homes and left".[544]

The case of Paschalides is interesting as Schubert strangely did not react angrily, threatening him with torture or execution, acts committed on officers of other villages for 'not denouncing communists'. All accounts accredit the comparatively low crime rate committed by Schubert with his gang against the residents to the skilful tactics of Paschalides and the discreet relationship his (Paschalides) family cultivated with Schubert's lover. Paschalides' son describes his father's contribution so: "The reason my father had such influence on Schubert was his (Schubert) wife Katina, who was on good terms with our family. This Katina had a hold on Schubert She was a very good woman. Schubert took her reluctantly. As an oppressor he had her confined as he feared her leaving".[545] Anna Devreli, an ΕΠΟΝitissa who experienced a shocking incident at her village noted that "Katina was very friendly with the wife of president Paschalides. She influenced Schubert. When he arrested my sister and myself and accused us of conspiracy, Katina intervened to save us from certain death. I was saddened to hear that they stoned her to death at Giannitsa. Wrongly as she saved many people in the village".[546]

Apart from Paschalides' effective methods, what helped a lot were the hideouts of Volvi where, despite his attempts, Schubert did not manage to arrest about 30 wanted EAMites with their families hiding in the wooded slopes of mount Besikia. They lived in caves and abandoned fishermen's huts and kept on the move in fear to the heights of the mountain and along the shore in the reeds. At least twice, Schubert sent gangs headed by deputies Germanakis and Kapetanakis, reinforced with a small German force, to arrest them. At the first ambush in June, the pursued succeeded in escaping in time from the block after a tip- off. At the second foray in early July, about 50 Schuberites embarked on three barges and, under cover from the Bulgarian cavalry stationed at Ghiolbas on the west side of Volvi, they penetrated through the village of Mikri Volvi to gather intelligence and a guide. The first resident they arrested they executed as he refused cooperation; they raped his daughter, then killed her.[547] In the meantime, the rebels with their families had been tipped off, so they had time for some to scatter to the nearby hills, others to dive in the lake, breathing from a reed held to their mouth, and finally others pretending to be fishermen. The garrison commander of EAM of Nea Apollonia, John Tsolakis, with his wife and two young children, fled to an abandoned fisherman hut on the east shores of the lake where he thought he would be sheltered from the raid of Germanakis. Once he heard shots, he ran to the nearby boat pretending to be a fisherman.

The Schuberites jumped from the barges, surrounded the area, placed guards and one of the commands with list in hand asked Tsolakis his name. As he was searching the fake name he had given, a guard in panic started shouting, "Rebels are descending and will slaughter us"; in the woodland he had glimpsed some gangs and feared them to be rebels. At the same time, a loud whistle of a shepherd who happened to be nearby came as a gift from God. The Schuberites, terrified, "nearly killed themselves, fearing who would first escape in the barges and forgot about me on the edge of the lake".[548] Tsolakis owed his life to the pathological fear holding the Schuberites the moment they heard the phrase 'rebels coming'. Those hidden in the wood – men, women and children – were lucky as the Cretan deputies of Schubert had a bad reputation for brutalities against the unarmed.

Marathousa in flames (19th June)[549]

His method of terrorizing with raids at nearby villages Schubert applied immediately after settling at his new base, Nea Apollonia. Virtually every day there were rumours in the villages within about a ten kilometre radius of Nea Apollonia that Schubert's gang were to spring a surprise raid to dig out hidden weapons and arrest "communists". Initially the target of these raids became the three small hamlets to the north of Nea Apollonia, where he often returned with "suspects" whom he put to torture at the makeshift prison barn of Varveri the Kaklamani. Twice the Marathiotes, terrified by the news of an imminent raid by Schubert, abandoned their homes and hid at the nearby riverbeds. Soon Marathousa would become the first village of the area to experience the raw violence of Schubert.

Marathousa (the former Turkish village of Ravna) one of the Zervochoria of northern Halkidiki, just 8.5 kilometres south of Nea Apollonia, lies on a plateau (altitude 180m) at the northern foothills of Holomonda. In the census of 1940, the village consisted of about 430 inhabitants,[550] of whom two thirds were refugees from Asia Minor and Thrace and the rest native Greek settlers from the nearby villages with a very few Sarakatsani (six households) As with other areas of Greece, the Sarakatsani of Marathousa were conservative people, royalist and neutral or contrary to the resistance. In contrast, the Marathiotes, refugees and natives for the most part, supported rebel resistors.

Most likely the first in Marathousa, in the spring of 1943, to organize the resistance was 'capetan' Michalis (known as Nikos Soustas from Neochori, one of the exiles at Ai Strati during the Metaxa dictatorship).[551] There followed the military K. Konstantaras and Z. Zagoritis from Arnaia, who during their forays at the villages of northern Halkidiki in the summer months of 1943, overhauled and boosted the morale of the members of EAM organizations.[552] In this same area at the time the armed team of captain Ath. Skorda, member of the nationalist ΠΑΟ, opponent organization of ΕΑΜ/ΕΛΑΣ, was also active.

To encounter ΠΑΟ for the control of Halkidiki in the last ten days of October 1943, Capetan Stratos (Giannis Harittides) was dispatched from Krousia via Marathousa, heading about 60 well equipped men from the 13th Regiment of Kilkis.[553] During his stay capetan Stratos added flesh and blood to the Marathiotes organizations and in addition became the founder of the district network of supply, which developed into one of the most remarkable aid centres of the newly established Headquarters of Halkidiki, with its facilities at the Kamela near Megali Panagia at the northern heights of Holomonda.[554] Head of ETA (Resistor Commissariat) capetan Stratos appointed George Varveris, who soon became the driving force of Marathousa and was elected the main official of the village, especially as capetan Vouros (Thomas Tselepis or Tselepis) undertook the administration of the 31st Legion of Halkidiki,[555] which grew into a Regiment from August 1944. At first, few Marathiotes were embodied in the small team capetan Vouros first offered in November 1943. Gradually eighteen Marathiotes were recruited to ΕΛΑΣ and other residents served periodically with the resistance organizations of EAM and ΕΠΟΝ.[556] Indeed, whilst Marathousa is not per se a mountain village, it played its part as an excellent hub of supply and communications of the resistance teams: "It was our number one haunt. Whatever we willed we found there" confirms characteristically a woman of ΕΠΟΝ.[557]

From time to time, the local organization was notified to befriend the passing divisions of ΕΛΑΣ (rebels from the area Sohos-Nigritas under capetan G. Raftoudi) who were summoned to reinforce the comparatively small forces of Halkidiki. Schubert, who had information that Marathousa was being used as a support base and supply of the passing resistance teams of ΕΛΑΣ, decided to punish the village. The terrorization of the village was undertaken, possibly with Schubert's approval, by G. Germanakis, his most trusted chief, who, for better results, it seems contrived the following strange trick: On 16th June, about ten days after the Schuberites' arrival at Nea Apollonia, two cavalry men dressed as ΕΛΑΣ reached Marathousa and asked to see the local president and priest to convey the message that their company would pass by the village on Sunday and, before continuing their route up the mountain to meet other resistance bodies, would stop to dine. As such they were summoning the authorities to prepare food to join their comrades for a meal in the village.[558] The president passed the message to the local team, who in turn relayed it to the head of ΕΛΑΣ, capetan Vouros. Apparently Vouros suspected that the 'hospitality' was probably a plan of Schubert or one of his staff, possibly to trap them if the authorities responsible and the village caterers hadn't questioned the request for food.

But because their facade looked fishy, prompted by Varveris, Vouros agreed to send to Nea Apollonia the nationalist Katerina Papadaki, sister of Varveris, to find out whether the horsemen had really been dispatched by the Schuberites.[559] Papadaki returned without being able to unravel the mystery. Nevertheless, in case Schubert wished to go ahead with his plan, capetan Vouros decided to set an ambush on the Sunday at Platana, a strategic spot on the main road Nea Apollonia-Marathousa, about three kilometres outside the village, whilst he himself, with a small force of rebels, lingered at the spot named Milos. Germanakis, heading a gang of about 50 Schuberites, planned his exit from Nea Apollonia to arrive at Marathousa around noon, about the time of the meal which supposedly the residents would have prepared. During their march towards Marathousa, the Schuberites met a stray fisherman named Karabouzouki from Melissourgos or Lotziki, from where a Bulgarian infantry unit after six months stay had recently withdrawn (April). The unlucky fisherman was put to torture to testify the names of communists and the homes where the resistors of Melissourgos convened. With the information extracted from the fisherman, Germanakis decided to make a small deviation[560] and follow an eastern route to surprise Melissourgos.

"It was Sunday afternoon, lunchtime when the Schuberites with shots in the air surrounded our village".[561] They ordered the villagers to abandon their homes immediately and assemble in the square. There they selected seven or eight people of those denounced by the fisherman. Placed in line, they set up the shooting squad performing the cursory sentence.

They drew the EAMite, Cornelios Eliadis, from his hideout and beat him with the priest in front of the crowd. The leader then announced that "whoever have weapons to bring them in return for their families".[562] Many, to save themselves, brought whatever old guns they had hidden. Around 3–4 in the afternoon, they headed off eastbound, following the path to Marathousa. Thus, the division bypassed the trap at Platana and approached the village from a point where the overgrown riverbed provided better protection.

In the meantime, the disgruntled Marathiotes began wondering whether the "collaborators" had postponed their visit for another day. In any event, many housewives, prompted by a local counsellor, left out any attractive items they had in the hope that the invaders would restrict their looting to these items and not search the entire household. Late in the afternoon the village was awoken to intense frequent shootings and exploding grenades and flares up above. Shortly the church bells alerted the residents to assemble in the village main square, otherwise those found hiding would be executed on the spot.

Many in terror, not knowing the reason behind the bell ringing, hid wherever and however they were able. Those who reached the square, mostly women, children and the old (the men had time to escape to the nearby riverbank), about 200 of them, quickly realized the danger upon seeing the guards and the machine guns surrounding them.[563] No one knows whether the Schuberites, as they had threatened, executed those discovered hiding whilst searching their homes. They had little time.

The resistance force headed by capetan Vouros, guarding the spot at Milos, upon hearing the gunfire rallied for an attack.

Their attack didn't proceed as planned. A Schuberite positioned at the edge of the village upon seeing the rebels at the clearing opposite the river, started shooting and before being wounded by a rebel shotgun, he had alerted his companions of the imminent danger.[564] Once the Schuberites realized their comrade's wounding was due to a rebel attack, they ran off in panic, abandoning their casualty bleeding and the crowd in commotion. Many Schuberites had luck on their side as the standing crops still offered protection and safety for their flight. One Cretan Schuberite was arrested as he ran to escape, after first executing in cold blood the plumbing official,

Vassili Tsoukalas, who, in trying to distance himself from the village, was arrested and deemed a suspicious 'outsider' because of his occupation.[565] Some collaborators in fear found makeshift hideouts in the village where they remained till the next day. Through a fig tree the events were observed by the arch-executioner 'Turk' John Kambas. The terrorizing of the village lasted about one hour.

Germanakis' plan for Marathousa remains unknown. A holocaust as at Kleisoura Distomo and later Hortiati must be ruled out since there had been no preceding rebel attack resulting in German or Schuberite casualties. The discovery and confiscation of hidden weapons was Germanakis' main mission. Usually, he would brutalize a few people and select a few men as hostages.

As time was short, Germanakis had to hurry to achieve his purpose. The only written narrative of the incident at Marathousa comes from the volunteer St. Giannoglou from Nea Gonia, who writes the following in his statement: "From N. Apollonia part of the division headed by Germanakis moved to Marathousa and there assembled the residents after weapons. Rebels attacked them and killed 4 of their youngsters and the next day, apart from this division descended the Bulgarian Cavalry to substitute two men held back, the Turk Kamba and another then because the resistors killed a Bulgarian Officer and some residents had escaped, they ordered the village to be burned. The next day I heard said that the Bulgarians caught a team of 6–7 rebels with arms and executed them".[566]

After the existing commotion, the Marathiotes wondered whether they should stay or abandon the village. Finally, they followed the advice of Capetan Vouros to leave and go as far into the mountains as they could. Vouros, knowing how Schubert reacted in similar circumstances, gave a short but harsh warning saying, "Marathiotes, see you leave tonight as your village tomorrow is being put to flames. Tonight take your animals and whatever it is you take, take it before it burns".[567] Dusk was soon arriving and the people's only thought was how to reach the farms at the slopes of Holomonda before pitch darkness fell. Most, exhausted, left only with the clothes they were wearing.

At dawn next day, risking their lives, many returned to their homes, loaded their donkeys with some clothing and food and rushed back to the mountain. Those who delayed and were arrested in the village by the enemy met a tragic end.

The Marathiotes from the heights of Holomonda noticed the smoke and flames raising from the village and obstructing the horizon before them. Fearing that the enemy would search for them, they took to the hill towards Arnaia, about twenty kilometres from the farms. Arriving late afternoon, they were met by frightened residents who closed their doors and showed the fire victims towards a nearby wood to spend the night.

In the meantime, Schubert heading his gang – reinforced it seems with a few Germans- in the early hours of the Monday met in Marathousa with a force of Bulgarian cavalry stationed at the estate of Slavomacedonian Boris Tsolantzevits at Ghiolbas or Ghiol Bakse, on the western shore of lake Volvi.[568]

The author with the former Prime Minister, Konstantinos Mitsotakis after his interview at his office in Athens.

View of Krousonas.

Memorial of Kon. Bantouvas at Avgeniki.

General Bruno Brauer.

Schubert's headquarters at Valestra 19, Heraklion.

Memorial of casualties at Kali Sykia, Rethymnon, October 1943.

Memorial of casualties at Platana, Marathousa.

Memorial of casualties at Asvestochori.

Hortiati elementary school.

The aqueduct, Kamara, of the Rikoudi ambush.

The vehicle of the French Water Board.

Hortiati, after the holocaust, ruins and mourning.

The Holocaust Memorial.

Giannitsa.

ΔΗΜΙΟΣ ΤΩΝ ΕΣ-ΕΣ

Schubert after his arrest in Eleusis.

Schubert's Mauser C 96 revolver.

Schubert's trial.

Schubert listening to his death sentence.

Schubert's tomb.

Schubert in the dock.

A morbid depiction of Schubert.

A small portion of cavalry proceeded with Schubert's gang in the direction of Nea Apollonia, whilst the rest of the total force of 300 riders[569] proceeded west through Zagliveri. The Bulgarian horsemen, whilst tightly surrounding the village, found three women who were hiding and planning to return to the village to collect food and clothing from their homes. They urged them to disappear "before the Greeks capture and kill you".[570]

Protected by the Bulgarian cavalry, Schubert had at his disposal the freedom and time to act as he pleased.

Outside Marathousa, two divisions of ΕΛΑΣ took up positions to strike the enemy as it arrived, without of course knowing what forces Schubert brought with him that day One unit stationed about three kilometres north of the village at Grekia. (at the hillside of the hamlet Asprohoma) According to a Marathioti resistor, "when we saw the Bulgarians coming with their wagons towards Marathousa, we stopped. We could no longer proceed from here at all".[571] From warriors they were transformed to passive observers, watching the village in flames to its end. The Marathiotis with binoculars saw his house on fire: "Yes, I told them. That is my home. You see it now being burned last".[572] Once they realized the village had been turned to cinders and ruins, desperate they took the road through the dale of Krimni to their hideout at Holomonda. A second unit bolstered by the force of the 13th Regiment of Krousia (Kilkis) under capetan Gianni Ephraimides were stalking not far from the village.[573] A squad from the unit, ignoring the real strength of the enemy, attempted a reconnaissance operation of the Bulgarian guard at Paliabela. It was exposed though to the superior force of the cavalry, which served to manically pursue the rebels to a long distance from the village. Two resistors trying to protect their companions and ease their escape, countered the enemy near the village but fell dead. Another three or four ΕΛΑΣites were killed near the farms, the border of the bloody pursuit. In the skirmishes a Bulgarian officer was also murdered.

Monday 19th June, marching on Marathousa, at Platana, Schubert collected many Sarakatsani he found in the surrounding huts[574] and brought them with him to the village, where they witnessed the events. Olga, the wife of Kotsos Haideftos, who had just given birth and had a forty day old baby, remembered Schubert's reaction when he heard Schuberites reporting the death of some of their men during Germanakis raid the previous day: "Outside the village were thrown three youngsters hidden in the hay so they say 'chief, the boys snatched, the pillows in blood". To which their leader declared, "torch the village and to the infants in their cots death. Leave no one".[575] Soon the homes, more than one hundred, were plundered and burned down. Whoever remained in the village, mostly elderly, were either executed on the spot or thrown into the flaming houses. K. Tsakaleros, old and bedridden, was first ripped open through the stomach then burned on his mattress with sacks of rye. The old El. Terzoglou was found by her relatives slaughtered and hung by a fig tree. The old Sarakatsani, Dimitris and Paraskevi Mitrousi, were brought to the square where Schubert asked who wanted to deal with them.

"I", said one and took them by the hand to Fountouki's house. At the door, a shot was fired and he pushed them inside, so he killed them all, and put fire to the house.[576] Old man Stylos and his wife refused to abandon his hut believing they would listen to him: "But they're Greek, aren't they? I'll have a word and they won't harm us".[577] They burned them alive too in their home. Of the total eleven dead Marathiotes six were burned. The holocaust of Marathousa was completed late in the afternoon of Monday 19th June.

The abundant plunder was loaded into carts[578]. To two of these, instead of donkeys they yoked the prisoners Pavlos (pseudonym of the notable rationalist Dim. Christoforou from Epanomi) with the Salonican teacher and guide I. Orfanides to one and to the other the Krimniot EAMitis Gr. Kontos with the Thasitis teacher St. Pita. K. Vosnakis, a former Marathiotis and recent recruit to Schubert's league from Epanomi, with others tortured the cart bearers until they collapsed to their knees (the debonair Pavlos fainted early on and was replaced) from the brutality two and a half kilometres outside the village.[579]

At a point where a steep downhill began, Schubert with a whistle instructed that the men carts be emptied. Then many Schuberites "carried on their shoulder some sacks, others packs and saddle bags with plunder".[580] The loot, especially Vlach rugs and girls' dowries, the men on their return tried to sell off to the villagers of Nea Apollonia, who often refused the offer out of fear of retaliation from ΕΛΑΣ or for lack of cash. With one Schuberite who insisted on selling a rug to a housewife, received the response, "I with no bread to feed my children, this (rug) will I buy"[581] The Schuberite reacted angrily "So, that's how you want it, I'll see to you" and disappeared. The next day two collaborators arrested Devreli and locked her up. After her interrogation Schubert let her return to her family.

On the way back to Nea Apollonia late that Monday, in addition to the loot, Schubert also brought hostages with him. The Bulgarian horsemen on their way through the villages of Platanochori (Dere Mahalas) arrested for treason the guides D. Christoforou, I. Orfanides and S. Pita and from Krimni the notable Grigoris and Asterios Kontos. In addition, the raiders discovered hidden the Marathioti Vas. Theocharis and Vas. Karakasi from Riza and arrested two chance traders, whom they deemed to be affiliates and suppliers of the resistors. The next day, 20th June, Schubert decided to execute these nine hostages at Platano of Ladeni, the Calvary of Nea Apollonia, but it is said that the president Paschalides insisted "you should take them from where you brought them and not kill them in my village".[582]

So, nine people[583] (some sources give the number increased from 14 to 17) were transported outside Marathousa, to Platana where, after torture, they were slaughtered or executed at various spots in the area. The ΕΠΟΝitissa Sonia (pseudonym of Niki Routsi from Polygyros) later passed by the place of execution and, at the sight of the decomposing bodies, felt the horror and chilling fear. "All the corpses showed signs of wounding and slaughter. Pavlos with the teacher (S. Pita) had been brutally tortured. Their bodies naked wearing only the shorts, and on their soles, they had imprints from horseshoes."[584]

Immediately after the destruction at Marathousa Schubert decided to celebrate his great victory. Olga Haideftou's baby, still un-baptized, gave him the opportunity he wanted. He left his detainee, Kitso Haideftos, to go and slay some lambs and bring them to Nea Apollonia. Schubert, with his lover Katina Aggelidou, made it known to Olga that her baby would be christened Eleutheria. When they learnt she already had a daughter Eleftheria, they suggested Irene. Haideftos slew and roasted several lambs; the church full of Schuberites and three priests attended the baptism of Irene with Aggelidou the godmother. There followed a big celebration with roast lamb, drinks and dance. To the ravaging and upheaval caused to the poor Marathiotes, Schubert decided to add irony and ridicule, giving the baby the name Eirini (peace in Greek). After the baptism, the Sarakatsani were free to return to their huts at Platana.

The more immediate problem the Marathiotes faced during their fifteen day stay in chilly Arnaia was hunger. Schubert however, knowing it was harvesting season, decided to extend their pain and hunger as much as he was capable. As such he impounded the residents, declaring the area out of bounds. The representative of the International Red Cross, Emil Venger, upon discovering the miserable living conditions of the scattered villagers, asked to meet Schubert.

"This league we first met in Marathousa of Halkidiki, where it had maltreated all the residents indeed denying us and, with an excessively arrogant attitude towards the International Red Cross, the provision of even meagre assistance to these unfortunate people".[585]

The Marathiotes, in order to survive, had to return as quickly as possible to their fields for the harvest before it was ruined. So, they decided to refer to the responsible German authorities in Salonica to lift the restrictive measures of Schubert. The job of travelling to Thessaloniki to request of the superior German authorities the special permission allowing the villagers to return was shouldered by 23 year old George Voyiatzis who enjoyed close relations with the family Kalou or Kaloudi of Thessaloniki.

In the past, Voyiatzis had worked with members of this family in the smuggling of Britons from their estate through Halkidiki to Asia Minor and as a minor trader he supplied oil in a period of great scarcity of foodstuffs.[586] Giannis Kaloudis and G. Voyiatzis visited the then Director of Military Affairs and Supply, Dr. Markull, replacement of Max Merten, whom Kaloudis knew well and accounted to him the incident of the destruction of Marathousa and the ban imposed by Captain Schubert on the people. It is not known who signed the order to Schubert to lift the restrictive measures against the Marathiotes, possibly Markull himself or the then Military Administrator of Thessaloniki-Aegean under whose orders Schubert served. As no young man dared convey the envelope with the order to Schubert, it was undertaken by old Dimitris Voyiatzis, the father of George. Schubert's reaction to the directive was as expected: "I shall give permission for you to return but hold you accountable to send me 3000 kilos of wheat".[587] Voyiatzis had no choice but to agree.

After 40 days of hardship in the mountains, the Marathiotes could now return to their village. Subsequently the Nea Apollonian, Stergios Baharides, arranged through the International Red Cross to distribute to the fire victims some food and bedding.[588]

The Kalos farm, an area of about five acres lying between old Foros and Pylaia, had been requisitioned by the Germans for herding horses and particularly for its grocery products. The father Kalos and his children Pantelis and Giannis (the latter had studied agriculture in Germany) kept close ties with the respective directors of the economy and supply division of the Military Administration of Thessaloniki-Aegean.

To the question of why Marathousa was destroyed, according to ΕΠΟΝitissa Sonia (Niki Routsi) Marathousa was one of the best 'rebel villages' of the area so Schubert had targeted it for destruction.[589] In other words, the disaster of Marathousa due to its position had been predetermined by Schubert. But Schubert, as in general with each German command of a military force, was authorized by the superior authorities of the Wehrmacht to effect retaliation against the unarmed population using as an excuse the slightest hostile act against the forces of the Occupation.

According to the directive of 1943 of Deputy Walter von Stettner: "in circumstances of casualties in operations against the gangs it is incumbent upon the respective leader of each unit to determine the executions. And here applies the proportion 1:50. In addition the villages must be destroyed".[590] In the case of Marathousa the raid of capetan Vouros against Schubert's league on 18th June resulted in the loss of four Schuberites, including two missing who had hidden in the village.[591] The murder of German clad Greeks of a special force under German command was equivalent to the loss of German soldiers and as a result provided serious cause for retaliatory measures. For this purpose, Schubert sought the help of his superiors, who arranged to dispatch urgently the Bulgarian horsemen.

It was Schubert himself though who decided the form and extent of retaliation once he entered the village and assessed the situation. The assertion that Marathousa would become a precursor to Hortiati if Schubert found more people is conjecture as circumstances had in the meantime much changed between June and September 1944. The accounts of some villagers that three Marathiotes Sarakatsani to the destruction of the village contributed is reliant more on suspicion as most believed the Sarakatsani to be 'very right wing, royalist and passive' and during the post occupation period organized aggravators of the left.[592] In any event, solid sources are lacking to prove that the Sarakatsani had converted their ideology to collaborate with the enemy in the burning of the village.

Raid at Nea Madytos. Retaliation for a Schuberite killing

"One day the league went to Nea Madytos 'Strologgo' and there killed eight people. I was sick and didn't go"[593], declared one Schuberite. On the eve of the name's day of Agia Marina, the early hours of 16th July, Schubert, heading around 50 men, surrounded Nea Madytos, a refugee village 15 kilometres east of Nea Apollonia and, applying the usual terrorizing measures, assembled the people in the village square. Those threshing outside the village – the threshing season – were obliged to go to the square. Six people who tried to get away and hide were executed on the spot. There Schubert beckoned from his list Kyriakos Touvlatzis to step forward from the crowd of men to "sort him out".

Kapetanakis, raising a long baton shouted "You come here. You are the command here" and struck him on the back, his shirt red with blood. Then others grabbed him and beat him with their gun butts, then trampled on him with their boots.[594] Next came the turn of Nikolaos Hatzizisis, also an EAMite official, who was subjected to the same torture by Kapetanakis and his comrades. "Then those two were taken outside the village and with a spade they split their heads".[595] On his list Schubert had more villagers' names for execution – to some he referred with their nicknames – but all had hidden outside the village. Late in the afternoon before departing, he loaded on the lorries whatever military material he collected, mostly blankets from the Albanian front which he forced the villagers to surrender at the square and five or six women whose husbands he selected for execution but had escaped into the mountains. The next day after interrogation he let them return to their village.

According to reports of the residents, Schubert's raid against their village was payment for the behaviour of their compatriots. Two Cretan peddlers, residents of Nea Madytos, travelled frequently to Nea Apollonia to sell their wares and there met Cretans of the league who confided in them that they wanted to desert to ΕΛΑΣ. I. Fanourakis, one of the peddlers, contacted EAM at Nea Madytos and a team from ΕΛΑΣ waited outside the Asprohoma precinct to pick up the would-be deserters.

The Schuberites didn't turn up at the rendezvous 'and the two Cretans were caught slaughtered and dumped under some trees outside the village'. (Nea Apollonia)[596]. According to accounts the desertion plan had been uncovered and Schubert took his revenge.[597] The drama ended with the arrest and brutal treatment by the Schuberites of one resident of Nea Madytos who came to Nea Apollonia to find his donkey which he had been obliged to give up to one of the Cretan peddlers under the orders of the local EAM. "They grabbed him, the brutes, and he was beaten so bad that he was churning up the names of our guys. That's how the misery all started. When they came here they knew who to catch". Of the eight victims, the EAMite officials they found and killed were only three.[598]

A few days after Schubert's raid against Nea Madytos, at a neighbouring hamlet, Xyrorevma, there was an incident which caused such commotion in the area that four lives were lost, the first victims of Nea Apollonia and many others maltreated.

Sarofianos Koumboyiannis, a newly recruited 18 year old Schuberite from Xyrorevma, and a companion from Galatista were out on patrol (others say looting) when the resistors surprised, arrested and executed them. Some villagers, fearing they might be surrendered as responsible, had to escape to the nearby mountains, although their flight, in the eyes of their enemies, incriminated them even more.

Ant. Arnaoutelis was accused as responsible for the arrest of Koumboyiannis so had to flee to the mountain. The Schuberites first looted his home then burnt it with all the year's harvest.[599]

After blocking off the hamlets, Xyrorevma, Mesopotamo and Asprohoma, Schubert assembled everyone, ordered his men to effect an exhaustive search to find hidden weapons and chose 60 men whom he transported to the jails of Nea Apollonia. There "they were beaten and tortured by every way"[600] for several days to testify to the perpetrators of the betrayal of the two Schuberites. In fact, so as to smother their cries and loud roars the Schuberites "played music all day putting the loudspeakers on full blast", a tactic used virtually every day.[601] The arrests increased. On Sunday 23rd July, the Schuberites by surprise (they say a tip- off) arrested the resistor Kon. Kokkota, who earlier chose to abandon the village for the mountain but hunger made him descend to his field for food. During his interrogation at Schubert's office, also present was the communal secretary I. Matselas, Schubert's most trusted accomplice and a blatant traitor of the village.

In the afternoon Kokkotas repeated to his wife who visited him at the jailhouse the words he faced at interrogation: "Argyro, Matsalas came and said that I had been active in EAM, had arms and cooperated with ΕΛΑΣ. I don't know what you'll do. But tonight, I die".[602] Later the same day, Kokkotas, who bore wounds on the neck from the knife of the 'Turk' Kambas, along with three others from the group of 60 prisoners, was executed in a mass grave under the huge plane of Ladeni, the village's Calgary. Of the three victims, all residents of Asprohoma, only Andreas Zahos was a resistor, whilst the other two were shepherds. The next day, Schubert released the other prisoners amongst whom were several Sarakatsani of the Tsonga family. It is said Schubert would have executed more but the Tsongas notified one of their cousins, Taso or Thanasis Tsonga, a leader of anti-communist armed forces in the area of Pangaion, who mediated with Schubert so as to free the others along with the Sarakatsani.[603]

Schubert in the raid of capetan Kitsos (25th July)

A few days before the 26th July, Schubert must have received word from the Military Team E Thessaloniki to take part with German and Bulgarian forces in a clean-up operation against gangs in the area of Asvestochori-Hortiati.[604]

Asvestohori was stamped as the first target of a surprise attack in the early hours of 26th July. A tip-off was revealed to ΕΛΑΣ Halkidiki that Schubert, with his group, was to leave Thessaloniki the previous day, 25th July, so capetan Kitsos, leader of the 2nd division of the 31st Regiment of Halkidiki with about 60 resistors decided to stage an ambush at Mavros Vrahos, a small distance from today's village of Peristerona and a place known locally as Dekatessara, where the Northeast slopes of Hortiati lie by the public highway Thessaloniki-Kavala. The men of the auxiliary ΕΛΑΣ Nea Apollonia set up four posts at opportune spots from where they would light smoke signals at each post as a sign that Schubert had departed.

Similarly, at the posts were informants tasked to relay messages from resistance at Nea Apollonia destined for capetan Kitsos, giving details of Schubert's preparations. From the last post, to transmit the message to the headquarters of ΕΛΑΣ, was the 15 year old Theofilos Kokkotas, the brave son of the recently executed K. Kokkotas, who along with his brother had high hopes for the ambush, believing this time 'Schubert would be caught like a rat in a trap'.[605]

Prior to the afternoon of 25th July, the smoke had begun to relay the sign that Schubert was departing, but soon after an informant villager Dim. Hiotis or Zoulis disclosed to capetan Kitsos that the ambush was betrayed and a division from the German 'Topography Service' had already blocked them from the southern hilltops.[606]

This German force had arrived with military vehicles from Nea Apollonia in the early hours at the Thessaloniki-Kavala highway, passed Peristerona towards Thessaloniki without alerting Kitsos whom they blocked from his rear. In the end Kitsos, after a long conflict with the Germans and Schuberites, was able to break their grip and escape with few casualties. Later Schubert himself admitted that the rebels 'pressed him so badly that, if not for the German team to help, they would have killed him'.[607]. Kitsos' ambush, as far as we know, was the third failed attempt of ΕΛΑΣ Halkidiki to harm Schubert and his men. Once he had burned the few homes of Ano Peristerona, Schubert was free to continue his journey to Thessaloniki.

Asvestochori, day of terror and violence (26th July)

Asvestochori, nine kilometres east of Salonica, due to its geographical position was of military importance for the protection of Thessaloniki as regards the northeast band of the military safety zone. As such, apart from a small police force there had been installed a vehicular German guard whose administration (Komandoura) was housed in the mansion of St. Leta.

The population of the village, consisting of locals and few refugees, (in 1940 numbered around 2,750 residents who, in the summer months, nearly doubled with holiday makers) were mostly Venizelikoi, who had generally sided with the Resistance. Of the committed EAM many were active in liaison and supplies. A small number belonged to the nationalist portion with some, such as the then president and secretary, it seems cooperated with the enemy. Noteworthy that to the local population should be added a respectable number of patients, around 600[608] and employees of the Sanatorium, situated on the east side, at Exohi, at a distance of three kilometres from the village. Until July 1944 no incidents are recorded to have affected the lives of the villagers. For the first time, on the night of 12th July, a rebel gang descended on Asvestochori from their hideout on mount Hortiati, captured nearly all (18 or more correctly 8) the police, killed two and wounded another two soldiers of the German guard who protected the wireless office outside Asvestochori. As immediate retaliation, the Germans on 20th July at the woodland Kouri, arrested and executed three Asvestochorites affiliates of ΕΛΑΣ. The involvement of ΕΛΑΣ so alerted the Military Unit E that they planned a clean up operation as the 'radical and quick restoration of this area was considered imperative for the continued conduct of the war.'[609]

In this operation took part, aside from one German unit and two Bulgarian divisions from Langada aside, the 'league' of Schubert camping then at Nea Apollonia. Evidently Schubert's involvement was considered necessary as he was known to the German authorities for his brutal methods in extracting information for the tracing of communist activists.

The next retaliation was planned to happen on 26th July. Early that day, the village was surrounded and the villagers awoken by the commotion of shots and church bells and megaphones alerting the people to assemble in the local park. In turn, Schubert's men passed through the village, violently dragging the people from their homes, directing them to the square. As they emptied the houses, the Schuberites searched them for hidden weapons and military ware.

Also early on, Schubert's officials Germanakis and Kapetanakis joined with Kateriniotis Dion. Batalas, who cooperated in the operation with "khaki uniform and revolver",[610] selected 11 persons indicated by Batala as communists and they were taken to the local park. In the meantime, at the park, those assembled including locals and holiday makers were divided into three groups, of women and children (women and children up to ten years old), children under 17 and a group of men placed at the highest spot of the hilly park. It is estimated the men amounted to about 300, a small portion of the population as included in this number were holiday makers. A large group, mostly active in EAM, had abandoned the village the night before when it was relayed that "a ghastly terrorist arrived", whilst other villagers spent the night in their farms.

Provoking fear and terror in the assembled mass was their head executioner G. Germanakis who "tromped around with two revolvers in hand and appeared to be enjoying it when he suddenly faked an execution and pointed the pistols against the men who in panic tried to protect each other standing one in front of the other".[611] Three or four machine guns had been positioned in the space between the men and women where "German soldiers" (Schuberites) were stationed.

At intervals, Schubert, who had the general command, (the German offices present were on lookout duty) called to the gunners to lie face down and target the men but the guns "they placed above their heads".[612] These faked executions were repeated three or four times. After the sound of triggers, loud screams could be heard from the group of women. The last time though Schubert, irate because, it seems, after extensive interrogation wasn't able to find more guilty parties for the incident of 12th July, approached from the opposite building of torture and literally bawling: "gives the order that the gunners are to fall face down and load their machine guns with their magazines". They fill them with the cartridges and take up real positions, now with loaded machine guns to start shooting against the assembled men. Crawling and pushing, the men fall on each other, whilst the women start shrieking and, to avoid the massacre, retreat and fall in the ditch with the berries. There was chaos which lasted about ten minutes. After the bullying,

Schubert at the Villages of Volvi (5th June–10th August 1944) 107

again 5–6 men were plucked from the crowd, taken to the house opposite and given a good beating. Their groans reaching the park.[613]

The men that Schubert sent for questioning at the nearby basement, where Komandura was housed, were selected from the crowd by a list of names which it seems the accomplice D. Batalas provided. Amongst the select group, apart from 'stamped communists', were included people at whose homes weapons and military ware had been discovered. All these detained waited their turn to be submitted to interrogation to confess their personal guilt or to other supposed parties. Those beaten in the basement of Leta that afternoon and found 'culpable' were held in a pile to be executed. One of these S. Demakas, though sickly, was taken to the park then to the basement where he was abused so badly as to yield to his wounds. It is unknown how many from the crowd Schubert still planned to send to the basement for torture. To this macabre scene which so pleased him and his accomplices, an end was given by an unexpected event. Around midday, traveling from Thessaloniki, the journalist Eleni Lionta arrived and upon seeing the events in the park and the threat to the lives of friendly Asvestochorites, approached the German Captain and addressed him in flawless German: "Captain Sir, the German people are famed for their humanity and culture rooted in Ancient Greek education. This violence exercised today against these villagers does not conform to German humanity".[614] The captain it seems appreciated the sound judgment of the young lady, intervened with Schubert, stopped the further questioning and announced that all women who had military items at their homes must bring them in exchange for their loved ones.

Soon, the women surrendered shotguns, several pistols, hunting guns, dynamite and various German and Italian military items.[615] As a result, many of the mass of detainees escaped torture and inevitably executions due to the intervention of the German captain, who "received dazing insults"[616] from Schubert.

Of the total 21 persons held for execution at the building of Komandura, eleven employees and patients of the Sanatorium were taken aside with five Asvestochorites. The remaining five villagers, with a few from the Sanatorium, were taken as hostages to the camp of Pavlos Melas.[617] Fifteen of these were taken to the place of execution one and a half kilometres from the park (it seems one patient fainted on the way outside the village). The victims were lined before a ditch, dug by locals in the presence of many Asvestochorites who were obliged to watch the deathly scene. The execution took the form of a ritual. The head executioner Germanakis roll called, one by one, to descend into the ditch and there they were executed, shooting them in the back of the neck. At one point, Schubert ordered one of those present "to go to the ditch and supposedly count the corpses, but with a nod from Schubert, a bullet from Germanakis sent him as well to eternity".[618]

The 16th victim (you will remember Schubert always insisted on 16 in number) was the stout 22 year old student, Kon. Malamas, on holiday, in whom Schubert saw the revulsion for the brutal exhibition of barbarity. This painful blow to the villagers lasted from the early hours through till late afternoon.

At the spot of execution, Schubert made a speech to the men gathered, declaring that only he provided protection from the communists to "whoever wishes to follow. I followed Schubert out of fear, as I didn't want to join the rebels"[619] declared the head of rural police in Asvestochori, who dressed Schuberite immediately after the incident and thereafter took part in all their raids.

Schuberite deserters: the role of the ΕΠΟΝ women in Nea Apollonia

Upon his return to Nea Apollonia, probably late in the afternoon of 26th July, Schubert did not need to question who had betrayed his mission. He knew even before he left that the rat was nesting within his own force, but he kept it secret, possibly lacking the required time to deal with the matter then or more likely, he believed a short wait would produce better results and simultaneously his own greater satisfaction to catch the perpetrators red handed. Captain Lefteris Petromanolakis, "the fear and terror of all" was Schubert's agent in tracking the moves of the Schuberite Gianni Manousaki who had squealed on the plan to desert by a team of Cretans and Pontians from Halkidiki.

The team, it seems, amounted to about 12 people who were to be harboured at ΕΛΑΣ with the help of three women with whom Manousakis had close ties to succeed in his plan. "This Cretan used to pass by our home, would sit there, drinking coffee for a while. Now he probably knew we had connections. My aunt with my sister believed him. My mother would cry and say 'take care, you could end up in trouble'". These words are part of the dramatic testimony of the then 15 year old Anna Devreli, who with Zacharoula, her older sister by two years, and her aunt Maria Hioti, undertook the job of finding suitable escape routes for the men of Schubert with the rebels.[620]

The accomplice within ΕΛΑΣ and the ΕΠΟΝ women was to be Dim. Kalaitzis, a 22 year old from Nea Apollonia, who had helped, towards the end of June, harbour, through the young Domna Tsakali, a dynamic member of the local ΕΠΟΝ, the first lot of Schuberites consisting of four or five young men from villages of western Halkidiki. These desertions inevitably encouraged the resistance forces to approach any of the Schuberites who wished to renounce. "They told us, if we could, to dissolve this band in this way, in other words, gang by gang make them flee to ΕΛΑΣ".[621]

It is said the largest role played in the desertions was of Amalia Flamourtzoglou "a woman who got on well with the Schuberites as she had a boyfriend, they say the (Schuberite) Koxenoglou".[622]

From other reports, it is known that those who expressed a desire to leave were Schuberites from the villages of western Halkidiki and especially Petralona. As such, the Halkidikiotes formed the largest number (8) of the team Manousakis prepared for defection. It seems 28th July was agreed as the date and the spot to pick up the deserters was scheduled by D. Kalaitzis at a point outside the village.

The day before however, 27th July, five young Schuberites from Petralona decided to defect during their night watch near Schubert's home. Kon. Mavrides, upon suspecting or realizing that something had gone wrong with the deserters' plan, without further ado suddenly warns his companions saying "tonight we leave".[623]

He decided that the meeting point would be at the well of Amalia on the road to Holomonda. At around 10 at night, they deserted arms and fled towards the mountain.

Only the lethargic Chr. Poiratzides lost time reaching the meeting point and was obliged to return to his watch. To captain Nik. Manousakis, who effected a raid, Poiratzides pretended ignorance as regards the four colleagues who were missing. The next day Schubert called him for questioning and it was only the intervention of L. Kommatopoulos that saved him from Germanakis' bullet. In the end, it was discovered that the same night, apart from the four Petralonites, in all seven men had abandoned the league. The other three were from Krini, as their defection, according to Schuberite P. Katirtzides, coincides with that of the Petralonites: "Myself and another 4 compatriots along with three from Krini abandoned our arms and fled as deserters to save ourselves".[624] Schubert had never encountered such a wave of desertions in the past. He was furious with the pioneers of this conspiracy, I. Manousakis and one Dardano whom he sentenced to death "as traitors of the league's mission to women".[625]

Around noon of 28th July, Zaharoula Devreli met their colleague Dim. Kalaitzi at Apoulianes, who had ventured two code names. In the meantime, Manousakis had arranged to meet the girls and pass by their house in the afternoon to pick up the note.

Upon her return Zaharoula had just entered her home when suddenly Schuberites brandishing pistols jumped round the house. Upon seeing them approaching Anna called out a warning: "Ah, Zaharoula, they've betrayed us". At that moment Petromanolakis pounced in, pistol in hand, grabbed Zaharoula and searched her, finding the note in her bosom. Other Schuberites arrested Anna and her aunt Maria. In all six women were locked up as conspirators in Schubert's basement. There they also carried I. Manousakis "shaking like a fish".[626] The next day very early Manousakis, whilst being dragged out of the basement by Germanakis, was heard saying "Cousin, have pity, don't kill me, I have two kids".[627] Nothing could calm the fury of Germanakis as he made for the usual place of execution. Soon came the turn of the women to testify.

Schubert summoned Anna to his office last, the youngest but bravest and most eloquent of all. Schubert translated her words to the Germans of the military Police whom he had invited to stand as witnesses of his grand success. Her apology, as she called to memory, reads as such: "So you, what have you to say? Why have you done all this?" "Captain sir, I have nothing to say you don't know. I can't deny what we did. The note is in your hands. What can I say? You, you are German and what you do, you do for Germany. You even give your life for her. Don't you want to capture the whole world? You are a big force. What can we do? We are weak. What do you want us to do? So, I tell you that I am a Greek woman and I did what I did as a duty to my nation. I know the history of Greece as you do. So, what is our big wrongdoing as (the boys) wished to leave and we facilitated that? What further to say, you don't know. When captain Germanakis heard the words 'I am a Greek woman' it seems he was offended, he turned nasty and with a hard slap threw me to the ground. Schubert ordered that he be taken outside immediately. I persisted, saying 'what I did, I did as a Greek woman' and as I could hear the German officers present repeating the phrase 'jawohl, jawohl', I realized they liked my words.

They were polite and attentive. Their presence maybe gave me courage so as to ignore the logo hanging threateningly from Schubert's neck who after my every word or phrase would throw me abuse. I can't tell you, his obscenities. Vile. He'd kill you first by words. Never have I heard or met in my life such a foul man. His Greek was very good, not natural of course. He knew a lot even Greek proverbs."[628] Anna would intermittently interrupt her narrative trying to wipe the tears and hold back the sobs drowning her. As she explained, this was the reason until that day she had not agreed to speak to anyone about her dreadful ordeal and she felt shaken as she brought to memory the face and words of Schubert. "Schubert, as I knew him during the two months of invasion, was in reality a man eater, a beast, an anthropomorphic beast, a creature of the jungle. He reckoned people as nothing, not even a worm. It was nothing for him to take out his revolver and kill you for no reason. He didn't say 'I'll kill you' but 'I'll clean you out'. He was a mad psychopath, a criminal with a callous soul and satanic mind. Anywhere in the world, I don't think there exists such an evil person. Something must be to blame during his life to make him a beast. Maybe from the Asian Minors his hatred is rooted.

How we were not killed he was surprised himself, 'I don't know how you've escaped my hands' he repeatedly told us".[629]

The next day a committee consisting of the priest, the president and the village teacher came to plead Schubert not to execute the sisters. They highlighted their characters, their families and pointed out that as orphans they were led astray due to their age and lack of paternal guidance. After Schubert blurted his usual obscenities against the young girls, he then addressed the committee: "I will give you my word that I won't kill them but neither let them free. I will hold them hostages. Don't ask anything. Get up and leave".[630] Back in the jailhouse the sisters couldn't believe that Schubert would stick to the promise he gave the committee. Indeed, their doubts quickly came true. One item in the questionnaire they were ordered to complete was 'how do you want me to execute you, knife, rope or revolver'. And in reply they wrote 'execute us with a revolver but in the village square in front of the crowd'. It was blatantly clear this man had no qualms.[631] After these women, Schubert also arrested a number of men and women, around 15 who had supposedly been involved in the previous day's events, particularly the betrayal of his gang's moves. Kondylenia Tsakalaki, a cook in their league who had been locked up with other women in the jails, also became a target of suspicion. For three days Germanakis, Kambas, Kommatopoulos and Kapetanakis, the toughest kernel of the group, submitted all the detainees to questioning and terrible torture to confess to informants, suppliers, affiliates and rebels' hideouts.

The shepherd I. Karagianni, as others, had already been beaten as they were bringing him in, accused of supplying resistors. In jail they trampled and kicked him like an empty sack with such frenzy that "blood ran from his ears and mouth". The Devreli sisters intervened and saved him but he was so badly injured he was unable to recover and died a little later. Another prisoner was Theodoros Glavas, 22 years old, who got the beating of a lifetime from the same team of torturers with the result that "I was sick for twenty days to recover. Once the Germans left, it was then I stood up".[632]

The case of Glavas was typical of a lot of people who became victims of Schubert because they happened to be in the wrong place at the wrong time. On the day of the Devreli sisters' arrest, Schubert, surrounded by his officials, Germanakis, Kapetanakis and Kommatopoulos, noticed two youngsters chatting in their yard. He then ordered Germanakis: "Him with the curly hair take him". But when Germanakis approached them he was confused and asked: "Which one? They both have curly hair". "Then take both", came the answer.[633] Initially Schubert meant Leonidas Kiourtsis, whose hair was much curlier than Glavas. Both were unknown to Schubert. Glavas had no connection with organizations whilst Kiourtsis though belonging to a family of resistors was not active himself. During questioning at his office, Schubert asked Glavas whether he knew a compatriot of his "who collected bread for the rebels". As his answer was negative Schubert's bullies reacted with a tough beating. Two names of known resistors which he blurted out did not help to stop the torture. Finally, Schubert asked if he knew one Dimitris Drakos.

"I know one Drakos Antonios. Dimitris Drakos, we don't have in this village" answered Glavas without of course knowing that Dimitris Drakos was a supplier and guard of EAM, known however to his compatriots with the nickname Tsamtzis. Schubert was so sure of the name that he went wild with Glavas' response, saying "This one pretends he's not from here! Give him another beating to realize with whom he's dealing". From the severe thrashing Glavas fell to the floor of the office almost unconscious. As a German there lifted him, Schubert ordered his team. "Take him and chuck him in jail and tomorrow morning take him to the plane tree for the rifle". When he was not summoned the following day, Glavas realized he had become a victim of bullying, the usual method of Schubert. The second night there was the sound of a shot in the village. Schubert quickly entered the jail and addressing his gang shouted angrily: "If they've killed any of our men, do (with the prisoners) what you like. If you want, chop them up, if you want target them with machine guns, if you want, throw grenades at them. Do whatever you want". Fortunately, nothing had happened. The third day, Schubert called Glavas to his office and asked him ironically "You've had a beating? Do you know Kalaitzis? If you see him, will you come and tell me or disappear? I just want a few words with him". He let him leave as his mother had cooked chicken, which she brought to president Paschalides who offered it to Katina, the "wife" of Schubert with her regards. Just before he left, around 10th August, for Asvestochori, Schubert burned around ten houses of villagers active in EAM/ΕΛΑΣ, who had fled to the mountain. He took with him the collaborator I. Matselas and the sisters Anna and Zaharoula with their aunt Maria whom he locked in a dark room and placed the 'Turk' Kambas to guard them.

Within his league, Schubert gave strict instructions: "If you upset these girls even words, know that I myself will clean you out".[634] To their mother who came in tears to plead to set her daughters free, Schubert gave in and freed her sister, the pregnant Maria. On 27th September, the eve of the league's departure from Asvestochori, Schubert invited them to his office to announce his 'generosity': "Gather your things immediately and disappear from before me otherwise I'll clean you out." " At first, we thought he was joking as we knew he was a mad man, a psycho a wild beast. Before he let us go, he summed up with these words: 'In your lives a bigger evil you have not encountered nor do I think you will ever. In my life I have not done good but for you as they say, do a good deed and forget it: I will do good in not killing you'".[635] Germanakis however made his own reckonings and before they were set free relayed his threat "If he leaves you free, I will find you and kill you". After Schubert's order to disappear, they immediately ran to the main road of the village and luckily found a small lorry which transported them to Thessaloniki. Germanakis left to search for them at the bus station of Nea Apollonia but they, in the meantime, had decided to bunk that evening at a relative's house, so without knowing upset his plans. After a few days they were back with their family with whom they all celebrated "not only our freeing but also our resurrection".[636]

Chapter 5

Asvestochori, Last Base of Schubert (10th August–28th September 1944)

Axioupolis Kilkis: Schubert the 'General Coordinator' of Security Battalions

From around mid-August to the end of September, Asvestochori became the permanent base of the battalion. Schubert himself, with Katina Aggelidou and the couple Lazaros and Eudoxia Kommatopoulos, settled in a mansion in the village. Duties of a squire were performed then by the 17 year old tailor from Krousona, I. Gridakis. During this time, important for the German military due to its imminent departure, Schubert used Asvestochori just as a rallying base for raids into Central Macedonia. On August 19th, heading the League of Pursuit of Communists, Schubert cooperated with nationalist divisions of Aristeidis Papadopoulos and German forces of the army, navy and air force in an anti-resistance operation in the area between the estuaries of Axios and Aliakmona. The operation was held under the leadership of Lieutenant Knetsch, Battle Command, at the Garrison Headquarters of Thessaloniki.[637] In the operation, the refugee village of Nea Malgara paid dearly by the particular terror tactics of Schubert.

The Schuberites assembled the men outside the village and mauled them to surrender hidden arms. The community president Alex. Katsarelia they beat to death. During a security check of identification documents, five persons were deemed suspicious as originating from other villages: they had come as paid labour in the fields – and they were executed in a ditch which they themselves had to dig. The execution gave pleasure to Schubert whilst 'he was eating watermelon laughing'.[638] Under Schubert's instructions, whoever from the crowd brought weapons from their homes won, apart from their own freedom that of one more compatriot. In the end, all were left free after first being obliged to hand over whatever valuables they carried upon them. In their report the German authorities in charge concealed the tragic incident of Nea Malgara as if it never happened, a policy they followed whenever Schubert and his gang were involved in missions: "The area between the estuaries of Axion and Aliakmon to the railway line joining Sindos with Plati and Gida is clear of mobsters. In almost every village in this area there are small divisions of Greek nationalist voluntary battalions. The inhabitants are law abiding".[639]

In the last ten days of August, Schubert turned his attention to a key road network of Axioupolis, crucial for the planned departure of the forces of the Wehrmacht. To protect the road network there and limit the attacks of ΕΛΑΣ, Schubert worked closely with other militia groups to create a tougher reign of terror against the unarmed population.

And so, possibly upon orders of the military authorities of Thessaloniki, he invited all the recognized nationalist groups of the area of Giannitsa to assemble at the end of August at Axioupolis of Paionia: "there Schubert spoke to us and defined the positions as necessary to be taken up by the security battalions".[640] Schubert took the place of General Coordinator of the activities of the various nationalist forces and handed the duties of organizer of the local teams to his close accomplice Kyros Grammatikopoulos.[641] Axioupolis was of military importance in the control of the road and rail network which was already being used by the German forces for their departure. At a short distance from Axioupolis, the 30th Regiment of ΕΛΑΣ, from their hideouts on the eastern slopes of Paiko, were extending their attacks to "bleed the enemy even more in that area".[642] So on 21st August, resistance forces blew up a train carriage between Axioupolis and Geugelija and the next day within Axioupolis they fought with armed guards of the village. On 28/29th August, the resistors hit the German guard at the mine near the village of Pigi, causing significant losses and damage to the enemy. On 30th August, a division of the 30th Regiment at the heights of Karpi were preparing for new raids.[643]

In cooperation with small German divisions, Schubert on 29th August raided the mountain village of Karpi in pursuit of rebel gangs. Applying his usual method of terror, he assembled in the square as many women and children as remained and in retaliation for the flight of the men to the heights, he burned the village (150 homes) after first plundering it. Before they left, the Schuberites snatched many goats and sheep and pack animals. Outside Karpi, the league met two travellers whom they executed.[644] On the way to the nearby village, Stathis, Schubert was attacked by a team of resistors without casualties. In retaliation, passing through Stathis the German captain arrested four people and executed them on the spot. Finally, late that day Schubert arrived at the mountain village of Gorgopi where he decided to spend the night with his gang, a decision contrary to the captain's intense concern with safety. Apparently, Schubert had earlier received assurances from the leader/priest of the German guard based in Goumenissa that the Gorgopianoi were "peaceful and nationalist".[645] The morning of the next day, 30th August, the people without submission to violence or terror were notified to assemble in the centre of the village to listen to Schubert, who from the balcony of Blatsi, seemingly restrained, spoke about the final prevalence of the Wehrmacht and the complete defeat of communism.

Suddenly he changed stance and "became a beast. All hell broke loose. Things turned bad. Now people felt the Schuberite terror".[646] With insults and threats he demanded of the community president to divulge who were the communists as he discovered that 'he slept in the nest of communists'. Remember Schubert spent the night in the home of the president who in a panic answered that all present were communists. Then Schubert ordered that all roads be closed and all the residents had to come to the square. He picked out the over 16 year old men from the women and children and demanded that all who had weapons hidden to surrender them immediately. One Gorgopianos with a nephew in the Battalions dared shout out "we have surrendered our weapons" when the Schuberites pounced ready to massacre him. At the crucial moment (around 10 in the morning) Georgios Kamesis arrived, a Gorgopianos, head of a small team of active anti-communists with their base in Axioupolis, who wished to avenge the recent death of his brother in law by rebels of Paiko. After liaising first with Schubert – according to other reports he prepared a list of the names of Gorgopianoi communists – he assumed the job of selecting the communists and those who had weapons. During the process he left out the nationalists, influenced by the constant begging and cries of the women presen,t and held those with relations in ΕΛΑΣ whom he deemed guilty for the murder of his brother-in-law. Of the 12 that were finally executed most were elderly but included were also four youngsters between 17 and 20 years old. One woman managed to save her husband when she cried to Schubert that they had brothers serving in the league of Poulos.[647]

Those chosen to die were led by the arch executioner Germanakis outside the village to a river where Dina Madzana was also present, who describes in her testimony the chilling scene unfolding before her eyes. "One of the sentenced, to escape was thrown in the river but nevertheless Germanakis with his machine gun executed him in the river. The execution was truly horrific".[648] She also tells us that she pleaded with Schubert to exclude from execution two youngsters 16 & 18 years old whom he enlisted to the league. Schubert seemed content by the small number of 'communists' Kamesis chose to satisfy his personal vengeful spirit and ordered his officials to pick out from the assembled crowd 24 youngsters as a second bunch for rifling. One Pontian Gorgopianos, upon the Schuberite ordering his 17 year old son to join the line with the others, boldly complained to Schubert "Why are you unfairly executing us, we requested arms but the German services didn't give us any".[649] Schubert only calmed when Kamesis corroborated the information provided by his compatriot. Thence Schubert disclosed his true intentions saying "We won't execute you, but whoever wishes, they should come with us".[650] So the treacherous plan of the German captain was to oblige Gorgopi youngsters under the ploy of execution to enlist to the league, although the clearing of Greece had already begun and the German military were retreating at all fronts of Europe.

Finally, about six youngsters were obliged to follow Schubert, then deserted in October when the league had temporarily camped at Axiohori awaiting orders for departure towards Germany. Before Schubert left Gorgopi he announced to the assembled crowd that when he returns "even a cat won't remain alive in the village".[651] The residents, fearing that he might stop and burn the village on his way from Axioupolis to Thessaloniki, abandoned it.

In Axioupolis, impatiently waiting to collect his daughter was the doctor Christo Madzana who at the assembly of Axioupolis had been obliged, beseeched by Schubert, to part with her upon condition that Schubert surrender her at the end of the cleanup operations.

Schubert though didn't want to keep his word and insisted on keeping her with his gang with the excuse that she was needed for her medical knowledge. (Madzana appears to have been a first-year medical student) Finally, albeit reluctantly, he let her return with her father to the league of Skaperdas where he served from Krya Vrisi. Clearly Madzana had serious reservations about the German's real intentions. Schubert returned to Asvestochori on 30th or 31st August and was soon to be summoned to partake in the retaliation at the neighbouring village of Hortiati.[652]

The village of Hortiati during the Occupation

Hortiati lies in the densely wooded south west side of the mountain of the same name (ancient Kissos) at an altitude of 560 metres and a distance about 20 kilometres north east of Salonica, six kilometres from Panorama/Arsakli and eight kilometres from Asvestochori.

In 1940 there were around 2,300 residents.[653] In June 1941 the Hortiati together expressed their strong objections to the decision of the government during the occupation to confiscate agricultural produce for the occupying military. In a clash with many residents of the village with a gang of the gendarmerie there were five dead and many wounded.[654] In the autumn of 1942 a German military aircraft destined for the airport of Sedes crashed into the trees at mount Hortiati and from the flames were saved about 20 soldiers who bore serious burns. The Hortiati transported the wounded to the closest homes of the village and tendered to their treatment as best they could with the supplies available. The Germans who came to collect the dead and wounded thanked the president Batatsio who coordinated the care and the whole village for the help offered to their comrades. Ever since, "the village the Germans considered the best in the area for its good relations with them".[655] As such, many residents believed the village had won the goodwill and protection of the occupiers. In August 1943 Captain Max Merten, the military administration counsellor of the Force E Thessaloniki-Aegean visited Hortiati and was photographed in front of the primary school with the students, teachers and community board.[656]

Though the point of the visit is not known, it was most likely tied in with the commencement ceremony of the new school year immediately after the abandonment of the building by the German force based there in the summer of 1943. Due to its geographical position and neighbouring Asvestochori, the German authorities decided to withdraw that division. In November 1943, resistance forces of ΠΑΟ headed by K. Mitsos and A. Tsamaloukas on their mission to reoccupy Halkidiki from ΕΛΑΣ control, camped at the heights of Hortiati. After anti EAM proclamations at the primary school and the supply of the forces, it is reported that a few villagers enlisted to ΠΑΟ.[657] During their short stay at Hortiati, Tsamaloukas and Mitsou accepted a proposal from the German authorities of Thessaloniki to cooperate exchanging the reinforcement of ΠΑΟ with arms and ammunition.[658] These

Asvestochori, Last Base of Schubert (10th August–28th September 1944)

negotiations, in which the then president of Hortiati played a role, did not lead to a deal. Soon the 13th Regiment of Mitsou – the Regiment of Tsamalouka had dissolved due to lack of ammunition – was attacked by the team of capetan Kolokotroni and was obliged to retreat, destined for Heimarros Serres.[659]

For the first time, the Hortiati heard songs of the resistance by men of capetan Kolokotronis during their brief stop at the school. "The happy feast" and new announcements raised the morale of the people and reinforced the developing local resistance organizations.[660] It was during this period that the core of the reserve ΕΛΑΣ was created and "since then the village was split into ΠΑΟ and ΕΛΑΣ", testifies one from Hortiati.[661] In the spring of 1944, the German authorities of Thessaloniki housed at the primary school of Hortiati a military division which they later withdrew, possibly in June.

After the departure of the Germans, Hortiati became a supply centre supporting the resistance teams of Halkidiki. The second battalion 'Hortiatis' of the 31st Regiment of Halkidiki under capetan Kitsos was formed at the woodland Kerasies, a few kilometres east of Hortiati between the villages of Petrokerasa and Livadi. Thence resistance forces began arriving for supplies and raids against the enemy, as that of 12th July against the Sanatorium of Asvestochori. On 27th July followed a German cleanup operation around Livadi during which "the weaker groups of gang forces" fled to Holomonda.[662] Strangely, until the end of August there are no reports of resistance activity around Hortiati and Asvestochori whilst the latter from mid-August became a base for the Schubert league.

Preface to the holocaust of Hortiati

The advance of the Russian forces in the Balkans around end August 1944 obliged Romania – soon and Bulgaria – to swap camps. Hitler ordered the retreat of forces from the Balkans and their concentration in defence of the realm. Due to the rapidly developing situation, the German lead issued the first orders for the gradual evacuation of the Greek territories and declared Greece a military operations zone. In the last days of August, the special military divisions and the German citizens started moving north. Divisions of the 30th ΕΛΑΣ Regiment of Paiko repeatedly tried to attack passenger trains carrying departing Germans to Yugoslavia.[663]

For the protection of retreating occupying divisions, the last ten days of August proved crucial as regards military organization.

First, in the broader area of Giannitsa Schubert, as previously mentioned, became general coordinator of the activities of independent and local anti-communist groups, a force of around 800 men.[664]

Second, under German initiative, all the equipped bodies of Central and Western Macedonia were placed under the orders of ΕΕΣ (National Greek Army) the largest nationalist coalition with around 5,500 men, whose higher lead was appointed, the notorious Kisa Badzak (Kyriakos Papadopoulos) with a new base Thessaloniki.

Third, within Thessaloniki the paramilitary "teams of death", such as those of the brutal A. Dagoula and the looter A. Vihos, gained absolute freedom to impose whatever measures they deemed suitable to restore order. In short, the whole reorganization of the different nationalist-anti-communist bodies of Central-west Macedonia had two targets:

1) to keep ΕΛΑΣ away from the towns and road networks in view of the planned departure of the Germans and
2) to intensify retaliation against the unarmed population of the towns and villages, thus by culturing a reign of terror restricting the rebels' attacks and disruption.

In reacting to the German measures, ΕΛΑΣ already from the summer of 1944, had intensified its attacks on German positions, motorcades, trains, communication networks and towns protected by strong German guards, security battalions and the Gendarmerie. Indicatively in August, Veroia twice became target of resistance raids, resulting in many prisoners being freed and arms and ammunition appropriated from warehouses.[665]

Intense clashes occurred near and within the town of Giannitsa with the German guard and the teams of Poulos, Skaperdas, Tsarouchides and Haseri who sought protection from the ΕΛΑΣ attacks in fortified properties in town.[666] The ΕΛΑΣ attack was down to its new policy brought in force by the leadership in view of the final confrontation with the enemy, that was: to gradually rally the resistance divisions around the towns and create an increasingly suffocating grip with the ultimate aim of possibly deterring the enemy forces from raids against the rural population. Stratos Dordanas summarizes the situation as follows: "On the other hand, the frequent attacks of ΕΛΑΣ compelled the anarchists into the extreme treatment of the unarmed, often manifested in the form of callously thieving intrusions under the pretence of pursuing the resistors. Particular brutality was shown by the gangs of Poulos and Schubert who settled in areas of military priority, attempting to distance ΕΛΑΣ from the towns and road networks".[667] In light of the German departure, the 31st Regiment of ΕΛΑΣ Halkidiki, reorganized, reinforced with heightened morale and under new command, in mid-August 1944 left Megali Panagia, till then its base in eastern Holomonda, to move further west to the village of Paleochora "to be closer towards Thessaloniki as it is anticipated soon the Germans will abandon the city".[668]

With this in mind, ΕΛΑΣ Halkidiki, somewhat prematurely, put into force the decision of its Headquarters: "to guard by any means the roads around Thessaloniki and seal off all whether Germans of Security battalions or Bulgarian or Gendarmerie. It was the 'tightening' we mentioned, in other words the maximum confinement of the forces of the enemy. We had instructions to hit the Germans wherever they be lest they dare push outside the city (Thessaloniki)".[669]

Asvestochori, Last Base of Schubert (10th August–28th September 1944)

In the circumstances, during the last ten days of August, two units of the 2nd Battalion of Halkidiki were placed outside Thessaloniki, specifically at the eastern mountainous area, which was under the indirect control of the Germans and their allies. The 2nd unit of about 60 men under capetan Floria (Antoni Kazakos, 26 year old ex teacher of the Detention Foundation of Thessaloniki) camped outside the village of Hortiati at Scout Camp, also known as Kastanies.[670] The responsibility for the daily supplies of the unit was shouldered by EAM organizations of the village.

The supply of foodstuffs was a heavy burden, borne mostly by the wealthier villagers. In a few days the 1st unit was positioned, headed by the recently appointed lead capetan Hortiati (Georgios Kirkimtzis, 23 year old deputy from a family of Hortiati) who camped northeast of Hortiati at Dragana, about equidistant to the village and the public highway of Thessaloniki-Kavala.[671]

These units took up a comparatively restricted area but of significant strategic importance as it neighboured with the eastern security zone under the control of German forces camping at Asvestochori, also the battalion of the notorious Schubert at Arsakli and Thermi. Consequently, the presence of ΕΛΑΣ divisions in such a sensitive area constituted itself own a provocation to the occupying forces. The mission of the resistors was to "make the area around Hortiati safe and guarded and whatever enemy vehicle was moving in the zone to be hit".[672] Part of Floria's unit consisted of the 'Exemplary Team of Youth of ΕΠΟΝ' entrusted to and guided by Kostas Paschaloudis, 22 years old then, politically active from Pylaia and member of the board of capetan Floria. Due to his position, Paschaloudis was privy to and aware of the decisions taken at their headquarters even as regards military matters as that at Hortiati. He spoke to the author, promising to relate the incident of Hortiati "as I experienced it from within and I know direct from the administration of the battalion I heard the verbal report which Rikoudis made to Floria and Floria's to the Battalion".[673] I asked him not for his opinion but what he personally recognized regarding the plan ΕΛΑΣ mapped out and effected on 2nd September in the area of Hortiati.

Why the ambush at Kamara?: the statement of K. Paschaloudis[674]

"The two units of the 2nd Battalion had been advanced earlier. One was situated at Kastanies, above Hortiati, and the other towards the side of Ardameri, near the public road.[675] That was ΕΛΑΣ plan. It had two purposes: first to block the retreat of the occupiers and second to prove that, for real, the resistors hit the Germans. The mission of capetan Floria was to guard Hortiati from enemy raids as the village lent itself to such protection due to its geographical situation and very close were positioned divisions of Germans and Security Battalions. The defensive measures the unit lead took from the start were geared to guard duties at strategic spots and watchtowers to recognize any enemy movements. Towards the end of August, the military watch at Hortiati went up to Kastanies and warned capetan

Floria that according to his sources the Germans were soon to come to Hortiati to requisition animals. He didn't know the exact day. We all knew though that Battalions, Bulgarians and Germans as they were leaving around then invaded nearby villages and grabbed animals for transport and meat. Particularly well known was the looting gang of Schubert who any day could intrude upon Hortiati for plunder and violence. We also knew that the thefts and appropriations had in the last months peaked.

When the Germans were intent on requisitions, they usually took with them two or three Greek collaborators to liaise with the village authorities. For this reason, the EAM group of Hortiati was perturbed by the news it received and sought the protection of the head of the 2nd unit. Capetan Floria sent his partner with a brief to his principal, capetan Kitsos at Kerasies. Kitsos descended to Kastanies and spoke to Floria. He then asked to see Rikoudi, the person responsible for the ambush on the main road of Hortiati. I was also present at the meeting. Kitsos' order was addressed to Floria and indirectly to lieutenant Rikoudi "to guard the passes so as to prevent the requisition of the animals at Hortiati".

As there existed three passes through which the enemy could enter Hortiati, capetan Floria the night of 1st to 2nd September placed a team of 10 to 15 men at each pass and kept for protection the remaining band of around 20 resistors on guard if the need arose. At the location Kamara, near the main road to Hortiati, he placed the 24 year old Vaios Rikoudi, at Strofi, on the road towards Agios Vasileios another team and a third occupied the position Myloi, whence passed a footpath from the public road outside Panorama towards Hortiati. These were the 'impact teams'. A smaller 'security team' was placed near the road to Asvestochori above the Sanatorium under orders, should the enemy forces be large, they were to take them by surprise and delay them giving time to the other resistance teams/ambushes to detach and retreat in time. It was a warning intervention. That was the plan and I know it well as I was there and party to the conversation. I had the details. Both the plan I knew but also the general tactics we were to follow; that is the team leaders had explicit orders to hit whatever German or enemy car was moving along the road. For the purposes of requisitioning and appropriating animals we did not expect a whole phalanx but a small force with one or two cars. An ambush by 15 resistors could even attack five cars to create a distraction and oblige them to retreat frustrating their mission.

In the early hours on the main road from Asvestochori to Hortiati there seemed to appear a passenger vehicle something between a small bus and taxi. It was a staff vehicle fitting five, six up to 7 people. It had colours you could not easily distinguish from a German military vehicle. The fact the car was for passengers and not a military truck transporting a large number of soldiers made Rikoudi think it could be a vehicle of the Water Supply coming for chlorination. As it approached Kamara, Rikoudi descended to the base of the aqueduct and signalled it to stop whilst the resistors from above shouted "Alt". Instead of the driver stopping for the check, he floored the gas and distanced. Then Rikoudi and his men, thinking it was enemy, shot,

Asvestochori, Last Base of Schubert (10th August–28th September 1944)

upon which they heard shouting 'we are Greeks'. For some reason, the passengers didn't abide to Rikoudi's signal nor to the 'Alt' of the resistors. If they had stopped and said they were going to chlorinate the well, as was discovered later, naturally they would not have hit them. The fact that Germans with Greeks from the water supply came together sometimes – once every fortnight – and unexpectedly was known to us all – to Floria, to Rikoudi and his men. We did not know the day or time it would come. Rikoudi had this in mind, that's why he tried to stop the vehicle but it accelerated and left. Immediately after the first hit, appeared a second, clearly a German military vehicle of those used to transport soldiers. As the two arrived one after the other, there was no time to verify what Greeks were in the first car and their purpose. The second was deemed to be a support vehicle for protection of the one ahead so the resistors hit without indicating to stop.

They were complying to the general order of ΕΛΑΣ to stop anything German moving along the road. The travelling Germans were armed Gestapo. One German got away and two others wounded – the one badly injured, died later – were hastened to the League.

Also transferred were wounded Greeks from the first car. The whole incident lasted less than half an hour.

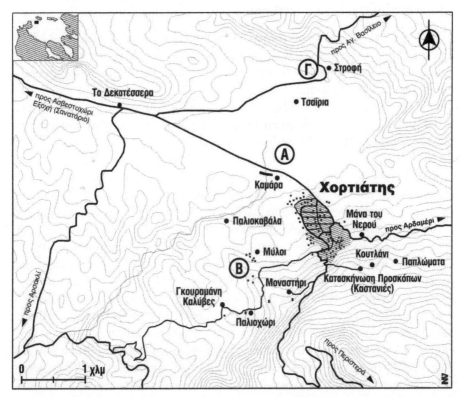

Hortiati: the three points of the ΕΛΑΣ ambush, 2nd September 1944. (Th. Valahas-D. Theocharis, Thessaloniki, 2008)

Afterwards Rikoudi sent an intermediary to ask Floria what to do. Floria ordered that the teams mingle and withdraw to their camp at Kastanies. Upon his return early afternoon, Rikoudi gave a verbal report to Floria which I heard as I happened to be present. I was also present during the report a little later Floria gave to capetan Kitsos at Kerasies. Information regarding the events I also received from other youngsters from the ambush as the Hortiati Zachariades and others who belonged to my ΕΠΟΝ Youth team.

Between 1–2 in the afternoon, 14 military trucks arrived at Asvestochori and stopped just outside the village. The Germans skirmished whilst surrounding the village. In the meantime, the resistors of the backup team descended towards the village and started shooting to halt the Germans thus giving time to the others to detach and the people to distance to the mountain. Most of the Hortiati abandoned the village save a small minority with right wing inclinations who obeyed their representatives, remained and paid dearly the cost of the raid. No one imagined that the retaliation would be so harsh. It was not the Germans who brought the evil. They brought Schubert however and his gang who were thieving thugs, violent and vile. They were the reason for the holocaust of Hortiati".

The critics of the ΕΛΑΣ testimony

After the war, the appropriation of animals was considered the excuse of ΕΛΑΣ in its attempt to cover up the real reason for the ambush at Kamara, thus justifying the protagonists, Floria and Rikoudi, from the accusation that they gave the grounds for the destruction of Hortiati.[676]

Critics say the first real reason for the ambush was the strike at the cars, the Greek and German ones which arrived for the chlorination of the well. Further, those responsible at ΕΛΑΣ knew that on Saturday, 2nd September, those cars would ascend to Hortiati.

Additionally, the resistors, and in particular capetan Floria, discouraged the residents from abandoning the village with the result they remained and about 150 residents lost their lives listening to their advice. The issue of the quest and pursuit of the guilty parties for the holocaust of the village became the charge of the right wing Hortiati, particularly those with many victims. This village which during the Occupation was conforming, later split into right and left, which bequeathed the conflict to the younger generations.[677]. The leaders of ΕΛΑΣ in 1945 were taken to trial for "premeditated manslaughter and provision of assistance to the enemy". According to the order of the Misdemeanour Court of Thessaloniki, the culprits of ΕΛΑΣ, acting in the knowledge that the enemy would proceed to group executions of the residents, "with arms from distancing themselves thus enabling their arrest and execution".[678] In interviews the Hortiati repeat the accusation of the order declaring that "the resistors knew what would follow. They collaborated in the murder of innocent people and didn't allow women and children to leave".[679] Rikoudi was the only one convicted in 1945 by the Criminal Court of Polygyros to 18 years in jail for the murder of the worker G. Sideridi, passenger of the first vehicle.[680]

As regards the issue of requisitioning or appropriation of animals by Germans, Bulgarians and Corroborators, the archive of capetan Hortiati provides a concise and clear picture.[681] Villages in the area of Agios Vasileios just eight kilometres northwest of Hortiati, in the last days of August had pleaded in protest to capetan Hortiati that Germans and Bulgarians had requisitioned or snatched their animals, primarily horses and mules along with carts so necessary for their rural needs.[682] It appears ΕΛΑΣ made efforts, so far as possible, to protect the villages in the area from thefts of animals, as characteristically noted in the report of a lieutenant of ΕΛΑΣ: "A German patrol was coming this way from Ag. Vasileios. Once they arrived at the huts and collected some mules and donkeys they quickly retreated back to fire. They were about 40–45".[683] So, the command of capetan Kitsos must have been aware that appropriations and requisitions of animals, particularly for transporting loads, had climaxed in the area. The village of Hortiati had become a target of ensuing German pillaging because of its position and possibly because of the considerable number of mules necessary for the villagers' hard tasks and transport of forestry, particularly to the town whence their existence".

According to a Hortiati, "There was Information that the Germans would come to requisition animals, mules and horses but also cattle for food. We heard it then before the incident. Once they settled in our village they didn't requisition"[684]

The news regarding the requisitioning of animals at Hortiati, though undefined, did not leave capetan Kitso indifferent.[685] As aforementioned, the latter descended to Kastanies for a personal evaluation of the situation. Further, the German authorities, it seems, were preparing a cleanup operation in the area: on 1st September capetan Floria informed his colleague capetan Hortiati that "a T.A. (collaborators) force was to advance with Germans towards Hortiati destined for Athrameri".[686] It was information which could reasonably be linked to the recent return of Schubert to his base, Asvestochori, and his possible involvement in the mission. For this reason, the plan of Floria to place ambushes at the three positions of Hortiati was aimed not only to satisfy the request of the EAM organizations of Hortiati to avert the appropriation of animals, but also to implement the general policy of ΕΛΑΣ to hit the Germans and their allies when they were advancing within areas under ΕΛΑΣ control outside the town. It is noteworthy that these ambushes were designed on the basis of a possible invasion of German forces on Hortiati. And if the invasion hadn't happened on 2nd September, the ambushes could have been planted another day, whilst new circumstances would demand an adjustment or change of plan.

The second assertion that the portion of right wing Hortiati put forward was that ΕΛΑΣ (capetan Floria) was in the know that the cars, Greek and German would cross to Hortiati to disinfect the well on Saturday, 2nd September, and that's why he placed the ambush at Kamara. Relevant is the account that "the resistors had framed the ambush Friday near the village where they would chlorinate, but because they didn't arrive (the cars) on Friday, on the Saturday they moved the ambush to

Kamara. They knew what was to follow as the Germans declared it unequivocally. They would burn the village and many would pursue the ΕΛΑΣ to the mountain. That was their aim".[687]

Evidently the assertion is based clearly on the result of ΕΛΑΣ actions and ignores the intentions and procedures leading to the result. Below are listed available sources in the hope they offer a base upon which the reader can form his own opinion and decide either way which version lies closer to historical fact. The first source is the testimony which Hortiatis Georgios Trontsios gave in 1976, employee of Ο.Υ.Θ. and a passenger on the German vehicle hit.[688] G. Trontsios, whose job involved the care and daily supervision of the water tank (every morning and evening he'd fill the distilling-tubes with diluted chlorine), discovered that the disinfectant had finished on Friday 1st September. And as he was unsure whether they would bring him chlorine the next day, he decided to walk 20 kilometres to Thessaloniki, setting off as early as he could, in the hope that he would secure the shipment of the necessary chlorine, if at all possible, the same day. There was, however, no guarantee that his wish could be satisfied as it was probably too late – at the Board's offices late morning – to find an available vehicle and coordinate the transport of Greek employees and the German chemist the same day. Luck however was on his side. Before even completing his journey to the offices of the Water Board, at Neapolis, a northeastern district of the town, he met 'the German ride', was recognized and climbed in.

"I told them we don't have chlorine and there are resistors in the village. They reassured me saying they had already sent a lorry with eight barrels of chlorine. So, we returned. Myself, the chemist, the two from the Gestapo and one more employee from the water, Alekos Sotirchopoulos. Outside the village, at the bridge, at Kamara they hit us. We jumped from the car and descended to the river. They caught us and took us to Livadi, above here, where the county court was open".[689]

The second additional source is the evidence of Ioannis Tamiolakis, a more senior employee, who was able to talk to the colleagues of A. Sotirchopoulos, responsible for the chlorination of the Hortiati well, and I. Stanino, supervisor of the network and in charge of shipments to Hortiati.[690] In a recent interview, he gave the following revealing data about the doomed mission of 2nd September:

During the Occupation, they went once a week, whenever suited them and they had a car. That way a specific day wasn't scheduled. Sometimes it was two consecutive Fridays, one Saturday, one Monday or another day depending on other commitments or the car could have a breakdown. Then, they didn't schedule a shipment as no doubt they didn't want the Resistance to know that today, Friday, they would visit. Nor did Trontsios know exactly which day they were visiting for chlorination. Indeed, that day (2nd September), Stanino was telling me, last minute they postponed saying they wouldn't go. He was to go as well. Later they changed and decided to go. They said let's go and Stanino didn't join them.

As I remember, the car of Ο.Υ.Θ. was large 'wheels', a passenger vehicle of the time – there remains the photo – and the German military car accompanied it. See to Hortiati went sometimes one and sometimes two cars as necessary. In war time things couldn't be scheduled. There was a shortage of gas and when the O.Υ.Θ. car had a breakdown, only the German car went with Greeks. As O.Υ.Θ. had no chemist, an Austrian chemist came to Hortiati to measure the mixture of chlorine and water. Before and after the Occupation, this job was done by the expert Sotirchopoulos.

Of course, many times, when we went, there was no chlorine to flush in the well. No the Austrian chemist didn't need to be present at the well but, I assume, he went for the ride and the odd ouzo which we also drank whenever we went. The information I've given you comes from a valid source, from people responsible for the chlorination. I worked with them and was able to unravel a few things".[691]

Based on Tamiolakis' evidence, one can explain the confusion which one discovers in existing sources regarding the time of the dispatch of one car or more for the chlorination of the well at Hortiati.[692] It wasn't scheduled for a particular day i.e. every Friday or Saturday, but could be set for any day of the week.

Generally, the Board arranged to dispatch a car once a week, though not a rule as other emergencies of the Organization did not allow such luxuries. There are circumstances where the dispatch could only be achieved once a fortnight or even twice a week depending on demands and particular conditions. The supply of chlorine (sodium chloride) was made mostly once a week and usually, not always on Friday or Saturday.

We conclude:

1) The dispatch to Hortiati on 2nd September was coincidental and unscheduled as the decision was taken that morning and
2) G. Trontsios who couldn't have known exactly which day O.Υ.Θ. was able to dispatch the chlorine shipment, happened by chance to meet the German vehicle on his walk to Thessaloniki.

The O.Υ.Θ. car most likely was similar to the one in the photo, in other words a small bus like a taxi with metallic roof and open sides which allowed space for at least five passengers and cargo. In some sources it is named a lorry or truck.[693]

In this were loaded eight barrels of powder sodium chloride with three, maybe even four, passengers, employees of O.Υ.Θ.[694] The foreman G. Sideridis with his technicians were to tend to the repairs of the reservoir and water measurements.

The second car is named as the German military 'wheels'[695] in which the Austrian chemist (known in sources as doctor), two men of the Military Police (horseshoes or gestapo) and two Greeks, A. Sotirchopoulos and G. Trontsios, employees of O.Υ.Θ. travelled.[696] It is unknown why Sotirchopoulos travelled in the German vehicle and not in the Greek. Noteworthy that the German chemist in the past travelled with the Greeks but this time – probably since July – he travelled separately with increased security measures. The change was due to the order of Military Unit E who, subsequent to the incident at the Sanatorium of 12th July, imposed emergency protection measures for vehicles and transported soldiers being moved to nearby districts outside Thessaloniki.[697] Anyway, due to the ruling the vehicle of Ο.Υ.Θ. did not offer the required space to carry all the Greeks and Germans. After the respective authorities coordinating by phone, the two vehicles would set off early from their individual service areas and meet at some point of Thessaloniki to travel in convoy to Hortiati.

The German vehicle would follow the Greek from a small distance to offer protection if necessary. At the suburb of Neapolis the German vehicle stopped to pick up G. Trontsios and a little later stopped again at the Kommandura of Asvestochori where Trontsios was asked if "there are partisans in Hortiati" to which he replied "in the village no, but there are up in the mountain".[698] Due to the delay, the car of Ο.Υ.Θ. had in the meantime moved on a few kilometres so it was out of sight to Trontsios and the rest of the passengers in the German car. But the distance between them was a few minutes. The generally accepted view that the German vehicle arrived half an hour after the Greek one is probably a guess.[699]

The concern of the Germans to be informed about the situation at Hortiati was understandable as it related to their safety. Contrary to Trontsios'[700] testimony who knew nothing about the new ΕΛΑΣ policy and consequently the order which Floria was following, the Germans decided to continue their advance evidently unsuspecting that Hortiati and the area had recently become guarded and controlled by a unit of ΕΛΑΣ. Greek or Germans however the mission that Saturday was standard routine like those preceding. Anyone Hortiatian seeing the cars one after the other towards Hortiati would understand their purpose.

To the point though, what did Rikoudi and his band of 12 know about the cars and their mission to Hortiati? Had Floria, if indeed he knew, given him details of the particular characteristics of each car enabling him, from a distance running in a dust cloud, to immediately recognize the vehicle of the Water Board? Remember the Ο.Υ.Θ. vehicle, without any distinguishing logos, could have been seen to be a vehicle carrying Greek accomplices of the Germans in their mission of requisitions.[701]

Then it is unknown what instructions Rikoudi had and how to react if and when he realized the cars were coming for the disinfecting of the well. Would he leave the Greek and definitely hit the German, sticking to the letter of the general mandate of ΕΛΑΣ. Wasn't he able to make allowances for the German vehicle as if it were involved in a peaceful mission?

According to the testimony of an EAM Hortiati "it seems he (Floria) did not give specific information and instructions to Rikoudi what to do. Rikoudi had little experience and without proper instructions did his own thing".[702] Anyway, capetan Floria had no reason to request details of the Ο.Υ.Θ. business as the urgent and flagrant concern was the deterrence of the requisitions. The arrival or not of a car or several for the water did not seem to constitute a high priority in the agenda of Floria nor Rikoudi. In short, neither Floria and especially not Rikoudi were prepared to handle a difficult situation with minimum priority once the plan for the ambush had started.

Asvestochori, Last Base of Schubert (10th August–28th September 1944)   127

It is difficult to form a clear picture as to what exactly happened at Kamara the early hours on 2nd September as the protagonists left meagre, contradicting and confused information. The lead of the ambush, Lieutenant Vaios Rikoudis, was naturally responsible for events at Kamara; his testimony is the only one which goes to revive the events at Kamara. The most important fact in his brief narrative is the point that the first German car, although called down to stop check, "increased speed and headed towards the village. We called them to stop and when we hit them, they started shouting "we are Greeks".[703] It is not clear what made Rikoudi suspect that the car which, on the outside, he described as German, could carry Greeks on their way to the reservoir.[704]

After the hit he didn't have time to ascertain what Greeks were inside and their purpose as soon the second German car would arrive. In which case Rikoudi did not order the car to stop without giving a reason. The lieutenant convinced, after the attack, that the vehicle with Greeks had nothing to do with the reservoir disinfection, reasonably concluded that the car with the armed Germans was involved in a common mission with a hostile motive.

According to K. Paschaloudis, "the whole operation was not considered a mistake but the result of a mandate, in other words that whatever German vehicle was moving had to be hit. If only those cars hadn't arrived that day. It was simply an unfortunate coincidence".[705] The result of the shootings against the truck was the heavy wounding of the foreman Georgios Sideris, who later died, and less badly wounded was the driver, Kleanthis Terzopoulos.[706] The vehicle stopped at 400 meters from Kamara and was then led in front of the cafe of the president Chr. Badadtsios – today the Heroon – where emergency treatment was given to the wounded, who were then taken to the headquarters for care. Terzopoulos was moved to the ΕΛΑΣ hospital of Megali Panagia where he recovered. In the attack against the German car, one German was fatally wounded, most probably the Austrian chemist, whilst a military policeman was also wounded, surrendered or was detained. One German soldier, (others say two) probably also wounded, managed to flee towards Asvestochori (Exochi) where he briefed the German authorities about the event outside Hortiati.[707]

It is strange that only the Germans and none of the Greeks were wounded. The car was torched and the tyres removed to make shoes. Amidst the commotion A. Sotirchopoulos and G. Trontsios got away, only to be arrested later but set free after questioning.

It is not clarified how the residents of the village – many were away at work outside the village – were alerted to abandon their homes and hide in the mountain. From available sources, one can conclude that the majority of Hortiates, especially the active and friendly inclined towards the resistance, fled, urged by the sense of impending danger and their own survival. According to K. Paschaloudis, "there was no thought about how to protect the village after the hit". Usual practice was to vacate the village, especially by the men, a job done by the activists of the village.[708] There is the version that the officials of the local EAM warned the people to leave "shouting through loudspeakers".[709] It is also reported that the president, Chr. Badatsios, refused to ring the bells to vacate the village saying: "You activists leave, I will stay, maybe I'll be able to save the village".[710] He and the village priest, it seems, not only held back members of their family, but encouraged other villagers to stay.

The Hortiati claim that capetan Floria and resistors entered the village that day[711] and urged the villagers to stay: "Those ruffians, they wanted to strike the Germans so they should also protect the village. They didn't even let the women and children leave. And another thing. On the list of victims two or three from leftist families are dead" claims Anastasios Zekkas, who lost his mother that day.[712] Evidently the activists and their families abandoned the village contrary to the minority, the 7% of the whole population, who remained for differing reasons, mostly because they believed the Germans would not harm them.

Atrocities

Most accounts refer to a total of twenty trucks[713] arriving which transported around 350 men including about 80 Schuberites from Asvestochori to Thessaloniki. As regards the time of arrival of the vehicles at Hortiati, most agree that the German phalanx reached Hortiati early afternoon, so around one to two o'clock: "It was several hours, possibly one or two but late noon when we saw the German phalanx" relates a woman from Hortiati.[714]

Lieutenant Rikoudi also confirms that "around noon we saw coming a phalanx of 14 vehicles".[715] After a short skirmish between the Germans and the retreating resistance, the village was surrounded and the usual terror tactics applied. All the residents were ordered to assemble in the central square of the village at the local cafe of Badatsios.[716] The Schuberites picked from their homes several villagers, many elderly and infirm, and led them with foul and threatening language to the square. Any Hortiatis they found sick or bedridden they killed on the spot or burned along with the house. They say that they cut off the fingers of 38year old Maria Tsiagali and removed her rings then killed her in front of her home. Her three young boys were led to the burning whence only the youngest, eight years old, survived to relate his dreadful experience. Any residents who tried to flee to the mountain fell on the shots of the guards who had sealed all exits.

The Schuberites killed eleven people who had fled outside the village and another five as they were trying to escape.[717] They also used the less accustomed method of the slaughter of women and men and the dismemberment of babies.[718] Christos Badatsios, president of the village, did not abandon Hortiati as he believed 'he would convince the Germans that the residents were not to blame and he'd save the village'.[719] His trust was founded on the services he had offered to the Germans in the past and particularly on his good relations with the leader of the unit, when they were camping in the village. Within the cafe they questioned Badatsios, who was heard to have said to the officials of Schubert: "I swear to you, guys, we know nothing. It was outside the village the evil befell; how do we know who did it".[720]

Whilst trying to explain that the village had offered help in the past to the Germans and Greek gangs, enraged Schuberites swore at him and one even stabbed him in the hand. The maltreatment of Badatsios continued. The good-natured community principal there couldn't imagine that Sergeant Fritz Schubert had the general command that day and he would act "at will". According to the testimony of Nik. Tomaras "the village fell into line under Schubert".[721] Germans, officers and soldiers, especially those based in the village, soon realized they were incapable of offering the least assistance to the unfortunate inhabitants whilst Schubert and his gang were present.[722]

One German soldier, Errikos, found some women hiding by the stream and recognized them as he had stayed at the home of one of them. He assured them that they were in no danger and encouraged them to return to their homes as 'the search was only for activists and communists',[723] the usual retaliatory measure the Germans there believed would be applied that day. Soon the Schuberites appeared and despite Errikos' pleas and entreaties, led the women to the square "with the violins playing, others singing and others laughing and saying 'aah what a spectacle it will be today'".[724] At the square, the terror peaked. Those assembled were threatened with staged executions; some on their knees, some standing. One Hortiati woman relates what she remembers from the speech Schubert gave to the panic-stricken crowd: "and his voice got angrier and angrier, but we could not understand a word of what he was saying throwing punches in the air the rabid piercing look and frothing at the mouth".[725]

More than 80 women and children were led from the cafe of Badatsios to the bakery of St. Gouramanis to be burned alive. At the head of the line walked Badatsios "live carnage".[726] Death by fire it seems was, from the start, the decision which Schubert made after endorsement by the German forces' leader.

Once the crowd reached the bakery, Schubert – others say his aide G. Kapetanakis bawled: "Fire, fire. Shut them in and don't let anyone flee. We'll burn them all".[727] Outside were guards ordered to kill anyone who dare show their nose outside the bakery. With the building packed with people and those inside cramped up behind the doors and windows, the Schuberites, to relieve the crowd, placed a machine gun by the small window of the front door and started shooting, killing and wounding many women and children. Next, they spread dry branches by the bodies of the dead and wounded and with a flare gun lit the fire. Maria Aggelinoudi, then 38, recounts to a journalist how she managed to escape the furnace: "I saw around me the first falling to the ground and we all started screaming and pleading not to be killed. One bullet caught my elbow and I also fell. When I recovered somewhat, I saw them covering us with moss and adding gunpowder. Then I heard a shot and the branches caught fire. I lifted myself up with some other women, also wounded, and we tried to get out and save ourselves. But those who attempted first to untangle were stabbed by them who threw them inside again to be burned. The flames were beginning to wipe my clothes. I am in terrible pain and can't see anything. I feel a rolling around my head and without thinking open the door and exit. I fall to the ground. Something soft touches my hands and trying to clearly open my eyes, I realize it is two slaughtered women. One holds in her arms her small child also killed. The other is my sister-in-law. I remain laying on top of them and wish to appear dead. I grab the nine-year-old little child of my slaughtered sister-in-law and we go for the mountain".[728]

The 70 year old Panayiotis Sarvanis was the second adult who managed to save himself: "Schubert's men threw branches upon us which they lit with fire and all were burned, save myself who was saved miraculously, falling on a mass of corpses and faking dead.[729] Six children aged between seven and ten managed to escape from a small window at the back of the bakery. Once the guards realized, they pitched a machine gun.[730] Eleni Nanakoudi, ten years old, lost her mother and sister in the bakery to the firearms of the collaborators whilst she herself was wounded at her knee and hand. Once the atmosphere was beginning to become suffocating from the smoke, Nanakoudi followed a compatriot woman with baby in hand as she pushed the door to exit: Hardly had she opened the door and she was knifed. Then I fell next to a mass of corpses, pretending also to be dead. I didn't move only after hours when already it was beginning to dawn. I had blood everywhere, my own and others. Etched in my memory has remained a tent. A dead mother fallen to the ground holding in her arms her baby still breastfeeding and next to her the Germans laughing. Then I set off for the fields to meet my father. On the way I met two guards. One with gun in hand sees me and prepares to shoot. The other deters him 'let it live. Aren't you full of killing?' To which he replied 'No'. He holds him and calls to me 'run, run I tell you, to save yourself'. At some point later I reached the field where was my father".[731]

Nanakoudi was lucky but not so many other children who found their tragic end. And what an irony! The bakery used to supply the bread of the villagers now used to burn, amongst others, the six-member family of the owner, Stephanos Gouramanis. He was saved escaping to the mountain but his five children, aged 6 to 18 with their mother Iphigenia, 39 years old, were put to fire. Also burned at the bakery was St. Kouparanis, 70 years old, with his little grandchild, a two-year-old, whose parents having to leave for their plot outside the village, left with her grandmother, without thinking that it might become a target of the avenging madness of the enemies.[732]

Around 40 women and children were led from the main square by Schubert's men to the mansion of Damboudi to be burned alive. In front walked, dressed in his robes, the 62 year old priest Dimitris Tomaras with his two young daughters, Aggeliki and Irene and the crowd followed, as if in a funeral procession. In total 34 people were burned at this house. One of those on death row, Eleni Koukaroudi, relates in her testimony how she planned to save herself and some others: "When the roof began to burn, we started shrieking. Then we had to move outside whilst one of the men went to find the Command (Schubert) to find out whether we were to be killed or burned. They led us to the square and forced us to kneel. Then I had an idea and with four or five other women we fell in the arms of the Greeks, saying we had brothers and parents in the Battalions and they must save us. That's how we managed to get away".[733] Another 34 people were burned, shot, slaughtered, dismembered in or outside the village. One corroborator snatched the four-year-old baby of Eleonora Giannoudi from her arms and shattered it against a rock. Then he slaughtered the mother frantically screaming in pain.[734]

At his trial in 1947, Schubert, amongst the other crimes, was accused of raping five women. In the end, the court admitted evidence regarding only one rape "he forced into promiscuity Maria Avafoudi (correctly Giannakoudi) using bodily force against her" then killed her.[735] According to a Schuberite testimony, Schubert himself had executed at Asvestochori[736] the arch executioner I. Kambas because he raped a girl at Hortiati then killed her. One resident of Hortiati, returning late that same day to his village, recounts that "there (by the stream) was also a young lady with her mother. The position of the girl shows that they had raped her before killing her. There are two similar incidents."[737]

As such, Hortiati was punished for the ambush of ΕΛΑΣ with 146 victims, of whom 128 were women and children and the remaining 18 men. Of the women, 23 were mothers of children from two months to 16 years old. Also, about 20 infants up to five years old encountered a horrific death in the flames or against the rocks. Around 35 elderly men and women, all over 60 years old, were burned or executed. From Switzerland, Emil Wenger describes the crimes in his Report 'Dreadful offenses causing horror in the middle of the 20th century'.[738]

The head of the German detachment, a policeman Wili Polman, in his telephone report to his superiors, shows that he was very happy with the result: "We chased the residents of Hortiati to their death".[739]

The spoils from the plunder of around 300 homes before they burned was rich; "they stole horses, cattle, pigs, wheat, clothing and different valuables".[740] Also in the loot was D. Kamisis from Asvestochori. Germans and Schuberites continued the plunder and destruction of the village till 7th September. The Sunday a German unit obliged those Hortiatians who had returned to bury a few of the corpses lying around On Monday 4th September, Schuberites returned and plundered whatever they had left intact the last time round. "At Asvestochori I saw Triantafyllou also holding a load of clothes", testifies a looting collaborator.[741]

Kurt Waldheim and the coverup of the holocaust

In a recent article titled "Memoirs of a hidden mass slaughter at the Greek village Hortiati", the German journalist Von Eberhard Rondholz expresses amazement that one of the beastliest crimes of war was not recorded in any military diary, report or other document of the Wehrmacht. All the research conducted to date in the German Federal Archives of the cities of Freiburg and Ludwigsburg has not located a shred of evidence regarding the holocaust of Hortiati.

For what reason, asks Rondholz, has the destruction at Hortiati, worse than those of Distomo and Kommeno, been silenced from German archives?[742] Besides, near

Arsakli, two kilometres south, one could find the establishment of the American College Anatolia, within which the Headquarters of Army Group E and the 3rd Command Office of Intelligence of the German army had settled. The buildings were just nine kilometres from Hortiati. This office was the responsible division, which should normally have received the relevant report from the respective Office 1c of the military unit, accountable for the slaughter at Hortiati "which news spread to the Macedonian capital like lightning".[743] The 26 year old Oberleutnant Kurt Waldheim served at that time in the 3rd Command, in a key position as 'intelligence analyst of the resistance movement', consequently one of the best-informed officers of Army Group E. Within the administrative hierarchy of the Office, Waldheim held third place. He and his colleagues submitted reports to Office 1a (operations planning) based upon which decisions were taken and respective plans mapped out. Through his hands passed reports relating to brutalities as at Kalavryta, Kleisoura, Distomo and Hortiati. These villages, as many others, were characterized as "villages of looting collaborators" (Banditendorfer).

Waldheim, former Secretary-General of the United Nations (1971–1986) in 1986 won the presidential elections in Austria. He was then considered a controversial character and accusations were raised against him for his latent nazi past, particularly his role in the expulsion of Jews from Thessaloniki to Auschwitz. So, a National Committee of Historians was established, which reviewed the relevant archives of the Wehrmacht and took interviews from Waldheim and others who served together during his time in Hitler's army. The experienced German researcher, Ute Von Livonius, to whom the Committee entrusted the review of the military archives of Freiburg as regards Waldheim's possible involvement in the holocaust at Hortiati, writes after thorough and extensive investigation:

"In history, this man Schubert appears as an evil nightmare. Whilst a criminal who was convicted for many incidents, there is no trace of his doings in the files of the Wehrmacht. For the holocaust (of Hortiati) there is absolutely no record in the military reports or diaries, save for the note "Bandenkamfe in der Nahe Saloniki", in other words, "activities of collaborators around Thessaloniki. Nothing else".[744] More specifically as regards Hortiati, professor Hagen Fleischer, member of the Committee and very well versed in matters of the Resistance, posed the following question to Waldheim: "I have a question regarding the village of Hortiati, which lies just six kilometres from Arsakli. This village was totally destroyed on 3/4th September 1944 with unexplained brutality. The so named 'League', under sergeant Schubert, was the executionary detachment. The incident caused unsurpassed commotion in Thessaloniki and Arsakli, that's at Arsakli the uproar was unmatched".

Waldheim's response was brief: "The incident is unknown to me".[745] He further added that on that day he was absent from Arsakli as he had gone to Vienna for his dissertation.

Typically, Waldheim in his interviews would deny facts which were known if not to all but to those with positions in the Wehrmacht. In his declaration that he knew nothing of the expulsion of thousands of Jews from Thessaloniki to the crematoria of the Reich, one official replied: "How come he knew nothing? This fact was known to all".[746]

In any event, the presence of Waldheim at Arsakli is proven by testimonies of the officers who served then at Army Group E in Thessaloniki. The director at the time of the 3rd Command Office and Waldheim's supervisor, major Wilhelm Hammer, in his testimony in 1947 at the Courts of Nuremberg, referring to the "heinous crimes" of the resistors against German soldiers, raises as an example the ambush incident:

"I remember another occasion when a German working team, charged with the repair of the water installations of Thessaloniki, fell upon an ambush and were annihilated just outside the village Hortiati".[747] Then Theo Lauber, an officer-liaison between the Secret Military Police and the 3rd Command of Army Group E, testifies to the Committee that he had clear memories of the slaughter at Hortiati. In his statement he recalls details, like names of those involved, and he correctly pronounced the name of the village. Lauber, whose office was next to that of Waldheim, admits that the bloodshed provoked "huge commotion (and) general anger at the Army Group". Indeed, there was a decision to ensure the return of the fire victims and render them some 'German protection'.[748]. Why though did the exasperation and indignation of the German military authorities not lead anywhere, in other words to the staging of examinations and punishment of those responsible for the crimes? Then, why did the respective authorities request the involvement of Schubert, known for his barbaric and heartless treatment of unarmed masses?

Those responsible for the holocaust

From the German side, those responsible for the events at Hortiati fall into two categories: to the first group belong he or those who decided to order the immediate dispatch of German units to Hortiati. The decision was taken by an officer (possibly the Command himself, major B. von Studnitz) in the Military Administration of Thessaloniki- Aegean and relayed to the Garrison Command of Thessaloniki (Standortskommandant Saloniki), the sector exercising executive control over the city and environs. The Swiss representative of the International Red Cross, Emil Wenger, on 4th September made a request direct to the Command to grant him permission to visit Hortiati. Two days later the permit was given by major Wilhelm Knetsch, battle command (Kampfkommandant), who possibly joined the mission to Hortiati as head of the military division.[749] Generally, the decisions by the higher sectors included general directives and gave considerable discretion to respective military units to take spontaneous decisions for specific purposes they deemed suitable.

The commands of the units involved in the operation belonged to the second group. Apart from the deputy lieutenant Willi Pohlmann, command of the military police detachment[750] and sergeant Fritz Schubert, command of the Greek pursuit detachment,[751] other names are not mentioned.

To the question of who decided that Saturday that Hortiati had to be punished for the death of one German – and the wounding or captivity, according to another source of another – with the burning of women and children, all indications are directed at the sergeant of the Gendarmerie, Fritz Schubert, to whom, it is believed, the overall command to punish the Hortiati at will was given. The Schuberite Stavros Giannoglou from Nea Gonia, Halkidiki, present at Hortiati, in his sworn testimony throws all the blame for the destruction on Schubert; similarly, in his extract referring to "the blazing and absolute destruction by the Schubert gang of the village of Hortiati of Macedonia".[752]

Where Schubert was involved in German operations retaliating against unarmed victims, the unit commands, though highly ranked, would yield him full authority to determine the method and extent of retaliation. There are scarce examples where a German military command would intervene, not to disrupt but to limit the plans of Schubert, as with Asvestochori. According to the journalist Rondholz, "the Wehrmacht leadership in its race against the Resistance, gave Schubert and his gang absolute freedom to pick, within the boundaries of Hitler's notorious mandate, what barbaric measures he would use even against women and children".[753] The powers he obtained in Crete, he tried to exercise in Macedonia without the same success. The burning of Marathousa in June 1944 with few remaining residents was his only significant barbarism before the holocaust at Hortiati.

Until August 1944, his activities generally remained on a calm scale whilst situate in comparatively quiet areas. In mid-August though Schubert settled in Asvestochori, a sensitive position in the defence zone of Thessaloniki to its northeast side, and at a crucial time whilst German forces were preparing to withdraw. Additionally, in the last ten days of August, Schubert retrieved many powers he enjoyed in Crete. With his immunity, if not express mandate of the German authorities, he coordinated the various nationalist units in the area which, as the end of the war approached, tended more towards anti-communism than allegiance to the Germans. Then Hitler expressly declared Greece a zone of military operations, signifying all-out war against the Greek population.[754] Hortiati was the first village where the Führer's recent directives were applied.

To conclude, the unsurpassed savagery of Schubert against women and children at Hortiati was due to the following main reasons:

1) The unprovoked attack of the resistance team against service vehicles on special dispatch to disinfect the water relied upon by German forces but also many residents of the town,
2) The proximity of Hortiati to Asvestochori, Schubert's base, to Arsakli, base of the Command office of Army Group E, and to Thessaloniki where, "since the summer of 1944 the organization and safety of the innocent population had been disrupted and with German tolerance the Security Battalions took control"[755],
3) Schubert's hatred of capetan Kitsos and ΕΛΑΣ Halkidiki,

4) Hitler's recent directives for the protection of the road network, military stores and services during a time of withdrawal of the occupying forces from Greece, and
5) The tactics of Schubert to harshly punish the unarmed population of the villages (see the burning of women at Kali Sykia, Rethymno) where the men had earlier fled to the mountain.

The massacre at Giannitsa: Schubert's last act of barbarism (14th September)

Schubert never forgot Giannitsa, the core of anti-communist activity in the area. His hatred against the mayor Th. Maggriotis, the reason for him leaving in April, lurked unquenched. In the meantime, the frictions between the Giannitsiotes and the Bafralis Pontians continued with greater intensity. From August, ΕΛΑΣ established permanent headquarters in the town and the standing German guard bore the weight of frequent guerilla attacks.[756] Already since July, anti-communist leaders, such as Skaperdas, Haseris, Tsarouchides (Arkadiou) and others moved their headquarters and forces to requisitioned buildings in the centre of Giannitsa and close to the fortified German camp.[757]

These buildings, housing about 200 collaborators, on the night of 17/18th August suffered attacks by the teams of the 30th Regiment without success. In the town the EAM organizations intensified their efforts to harbour Germans, some of whom due to the imminent fall of the 3rd Reich, inclined towards Em. Tsirelis, an active partner of EAM, to assist in their escape.[758] On 26th August, Tsirelis managed to assist only one of the two police (the other en route sobered up and returned to his unit), and the Austrian corporal Otmar Doern after first accompanying them to the liquor store of K. Boskos, then to that of Papadopoulos Brothers. The news that Tsirelis deliberately intoxicated the men before housing them, though disputable, raised to the German authorities "the suspicion that the liquor stores are dosing the soldiers in order to spirit them away".[759] The authorities were late to react to Doern's defection, possibly because Schubert, towards the end of August, was cooperating with German units in cleanup operations against the villages around Axiopolis and in early September busy with events at Hortiati. Indisputably the frequent attacks of ΕΛΑΣ, the desertion of corporal Doern and the frustrated attempt of Herbert, the second police guard, became triggers for the massacre which followed on 14th September.

A few days earlier, 9th September, at the office of captain Max Peschko, military lead of the Giannitsa Guard, all the Security Battalion leaders of the area assembled in a meeting: F. Schubert as General Coordinator[760] with his deputies, Kapetanakis and Germanakis, K. Grammatikopoulos as general organizer[761], G. Poulos with his secretary P. Triantafyllou, S. Skaperdas, I. Haseris, Tsarouchides (Arkadiou) and others. The issue for discussion, it seems, related to the measures that had to be taken to terrorize the people to such an extent that they cease any form of support to the Resistance and yield fully to the occupying forces.[762]

The 14th September, Thursday, important Name Day of the Holy Cross, was chosen as it was a holiday and most men were to remain in town. Many activists though and members of EAM, also those possibly deemed suspicious, were daily abandoning Giannitsa even up to the 13th September.

The plan of action was decided by Peschko himself in his office. With firing and loud hailers, he forbade all traffic from noon 13th September to 6 in the morning of 14th September. There followed the first arrests of those who assisted in the defection. The Germans led Tsirelis to the Mentrese prison then burned his home, whilst the owners of the liquor stores, Georgios Boskos with his 16 year old son Dimitris and the brothers Maximos and Dimitris Papadopoulos, they arrested in a hold up and transported them to the Kommandura for cross examination prior to imprisoning them.[763]. As dawn of 14th September arrived, the divisions of Schubert from Asvestochori and Poulos from Krya Vrysi, who surrounded the town, announced through hailers that the men and children above fifteen years of age were to assemble in the yard of the 1st Primary School, where the German guard camped, and the women with the young at the Clock square (Parko). Any men who dithered "were beaten pitilessly from their entering the yard to the point of assembly. Many were beaten so. I remember one of them, Apostolos Iliopoulos, though already seated next to me, continued to be beaten till unconscious; on the other hand, he escaped rifling and ended up in the Hospital from where he exited in November or December of the same year".[764]

At the gory spectacle soon to appear before the eyes of the assembled crowd the other leaders with their gangs were also present, in total exceeding 500 men. Schubert, the overall orchestrator, adapted his tactics for dealing with his sacrificial victims. This time the torture with cudgels and iron rods, which brought on a slow and painful death, was employed as a harsh lesson of terror against innocent people.

The men assembled including the youngsters, apparently around 1,000 to 1,500, were divided in two groups, the young and the men. First to speak to the crowd was papa-Grigoris Karyotakis, priest of the league from Krini (always named Papagrygoriou) who encouraged the Giannitsiotes to disclose the communists and refrain from concealing the resistors. Next Schubert spouted such vilifications to expose how his vengeful blaze burned inside him: '", squealers, you who pimp your women, buggers, you managed to snarl me six months ago last at Giannitsa and you screwed me. This time though you will pay. I'll annihilate you all".[765] Finally, he urged them: "We don't want foreigners in Greece, be nationalists and kill the communists"[766]. Then Skaperdas added: " it's to the benefit of law-abiding citizens to disclose the identity of the communists".[767]

Under Schubert's orders the selection of 200 (300 in another testimony) "communists" began. Germanakis and the other accomplices of Schubert and Skaperdas terrorized them with staged executions: "they fired against the communists, whom the nationalists indicated from the assembly, whilst P. Triantafyllou shared out cigarettes hinting 'Caesar to those who are about to die'.[768]

For starters, Schubert made sure he summoned before him the despised team of community officials, Th. Maggriotis, P. Haritides and S. Triantafyllides whom he kept aside for special treatment as privileged enemies. The massacre began from the top of the community pyramid, the higher-ranking local employees of Agriculture, the Bank and the supply centre of the International Red Cross. Urged on by a "get on with it", Kapetanakis and Germanakis picked out G. Papaioannou, a local tax clerk, and, beating him with metal rods and walking sticks before the crowd, they left him dead within a few minutes. Waving his arms threateningly amidst the mass, Schubert gave a chilling warning "In five minutes that's how you'll all end up".[769] Based on a prepared list which every time Schubert handed to his accomplices, in the meantime supplemented by Hanialakis, Economakis, Tzoulias, Christodoulakis and others, he began the selection of "communists" and those with dubious allegiances.

They picked Dim. Papaioannou, a secretary with the agronomy, and whilst similarly beating him, Skaperdas intervened, exhibiting him to the crowd as a lesson to the communists and saying: "I know you're a communist, confess to more as we've killed others who were innocent".[770] Another six people, mostly working for various services, "they began beating with bats and gun butts, all together, and you heard a thud as against an inflated sack. Transformed by the blows into a shadowy mass they would shoot them to finish them off", testifies 18 year old Anna Konstantinidou, an interpreter at the headquarters, who watched the grisly scene from the neighbouring house of Pourgiazi, by the Kommandantur.[771]

Next came the turn of the Mayor, Thomas Maggriotis. During his rounds of the crowd to point to the communists, Maggriotis repeated insistently: "The communists are not here but up in the mountain".[772] Upon being presented to Schubert he heard his irrevocable sentence: "Mayor, first I'll kill you then those rats the priests"[773] and directed towards one of his accomplices he shrieked like a wounded beast "Take the mayor and another 7 to look after them". "Indeed, I'll do so" came the response of the arch executioner Germanakis.[774] Maggriotis and the other eight Germanakis were led to and executed at the deserted tobacco warehouse of Tantzi in the centre of Giannitsa. Before killing them, the perpetrators robbed whatever valuables they held, shoes, socks, clothes even the mayor's trousers.[775]

In the meantime, for the burial of the corpses heaped up before the assembled crowd, a mass grave needed to be dug, big enough to also accommodate the victimized "communists". One team of youngsters was ordered to dig in the nearby property a very large and deep ditch in which "one after the other, they endured the process of beating then each finished off with a bullet. They would tug them by the legs and throw them one on top of the other into the mass grave".[776] In this way they had killed several from the list prepared. Maximos Papadopoulos, owner of the liquor store which Peschko frequented, whilst being led bloodied to execution at the ditch – others say he climbed out of the ditch wounded – started shouting, giving the impression that he wanted to point to communists. Once drawn back to the assembly "in panic he addressed captain Peschko telling him to save him".[777] His cries were hopelessly piercing: "I don't want to die. I've done nothing wrong. I'm still young".[778] Then a farmer, Christo Konstantinides, 50 year old father of Anna, rose from the crowd and addressing Peschko said '" can vouch for this child. He is a good boy". Hardly had he finished talking when a Schuberite grabbed him by the collar and dragged him towards the ditch shouting: "Who will vouch for you? I've been looking for you all morning".[779] Anna, who had been watching and listening to the goings on, in panic ran to beg Peschko to save her father.

Peschko coldly replied: "I'm not in charge. It's Schubert".[780] Following his total disregard, Papadopoulos and Konstantinides were executed at the ditch before the crowd. By early afternoon the first bout of executions was complete with eight victims in the ditch and nine in Tantzi's warehouse. Soon the second round would begin.

Of the total listed, there remained around 40 to 50 men for execution. Running down the list, the Schuberite K. Economakis brought S. Triantafyllides along with the clerks S. Hatzopoulos and D. Stoides and presented them to Schubert, who sarcastically asked in what category they fell. To Economakis' response that they were in the same with the mayor, Schubert shouted, "You homo, didn't I say I'll have you, your Mayor I killed, now it's your turn".[781] Triantafyllides' execution and that of his comrades was postponed due to the unexpected appearance of Poulos, who spoke to those assembled, singing praises to Hitler and Germany and expressing his faith in the victory of the nazi forces, concluding: "I assure you that all who today lived this drama will not suffer from now onwards. The young in a few hours will go back to their homes. You men contact your close ones to bring food and water. Tomorrow you will all go home".[782] During Poulos' speech, a soldier from the guard Headquarters, named Roody, removed Triantafyllides from the lot of listed detainees. Triantafyllides refers to the Incident at Schubert's trial: "He killed the mayor and would have killed me as well at Giannitsa if it weren't for the timing of Poulos arriving who intervened and removed me from death row".[783] Roody led him to Commander Peschko. Forgetting the reason why he had been saved, Triantafyllides asked Peschko: "Commander sir, you are to kill me as a communist", and received the reply "Stay calm".[784] Roody, acting under his Command's orders, led Triantafyllides for security reasons to the offices of the Kommandantur where soon Peschko arrived. Knowing the employees Stoides and Hadzopoulos were listed, he challenged Peschko 'to save them as they are innocent'. But he refused saying "Be quiet. The edict against the township is serious. The Mayor has been executed. I cannot intervene".[785] Soon Peschko himself would admit to Triantafyllides that he doubted whether the executed Mayor was a communist. Poulos departed around 3.00 in the afternoon. Because individual torture took up too much time, Schubert decided that the remaining Giannitsiotes be executed in a group at the dug ditch.

From 'death row' formed by the victims in two parallel lines, the armed accomplices of Poulos and Schubert as the prisoners passed "first beat them with iron rods bent at one end resulting in their brains being thrown out, their limbs broken as their kidneys and ribs",[786] then the executioners waiting by the ditch finished them with the fatal blow. The bystanding German officers as an audience of the torture and executions seemed to enjoy the spectacle as, smiling, they photographed the grimy scenes. Of the women assembled the sisters Sophia and Eleni Papaioannou were executed "after first they abused them".[787] Later that afternoon the women and children were left free to return to their homes. Those who chanced to be outside on the streets or by their fields were executed on the spot. The total number of dead that day exceeded 70 and some calculate nearing or exceeding 100.[788]

At some point, Schubert must have been told about Triantafyllides and Haritides being saved by the German commander. He then demanded of the German deputy performing liaison functions to bring them back for execution. Peschko didn't give in to Schubert's insistence and reassured the prisoners that "under all circumstances and whatever happens, from this moment you are under my protection".[789] Noteworthy that Haritides, prior to Maggriotis being selected for execution, was sent probably by Peschko himself to retrieve "around 400 bread offertories for Poulos and Schubert's men"[790] and he didn't return to the fated group whilst under the wing of the German cook; he was hidden in the building of the kommandatur and later led to a basement where Triantafyllides was hidden. The next morning Peschko summoned Triantafyllides and Haritides and entrusted them with the handling of the Commune and the task of assuring the men still left in the school yard that whatever happened, to go back to their homes and keep quiet, but in case the resistance retaliated the whole of Giannitsa would be burned"[791], a harsh warning holding these officials partially to blame.

Even before dusk, the Giannitsiotes terrorized began drifting towards the mountain and hilltop suburbs of the town. As many were confused what to do, a gathered committee asked Triantafyllides and Haritides to travel together to the village of Pylorygi and report to the EAM official Pavlos (pseudonym of G. Kostopoulos) about the possible consequences of an ΕΛΑΣ attack on the town.

The EAM official remained unconcerned saying "a battle is a battle, what of 70 or 100 casualties, they will anyway hit the Germans".[792] Indeed, an attack by a section of the resistance was suffered by the gangs of Skaperdas and Poulos outside Giannitsa on their return to Krya Vrysi late on 14th September. Two from Poulos were killed and Dina Madzana received congratulations from Poulos for her truculence.[793] Schubert departed the next morning, after loading a car with "swine and other loot",[794] particularly foodstuffs from the Red Cross warehouse destined for the wounded and victims of war. On 16th September, Wenger of the International Red Cross was in town and was shocked at the plunder and mortality: "Giannitsa (is) now a dead city".

Disillusioned, he added the following to his Report: "Unfortunately all our efforts to end these dishonourable acts have borne no result. The excuse of weeding out communism does not suffice to borrow the right to attack so against citizens who are unable to react and particularly women and children".[795]

The 30th Regiment of ΕΛΑΣ laid down a plan to hit the German Guard and its accomplices in the early hours of 18th September. To cut off chance reinforcements of the enemy they mined the roads around the town and positioned ambushes at appropriate spots on the road network.[796]

The divisions of Skaperdas and Poulos hastened from Krya Vrysi to support the pressurized Germans and their allies but ended up surrounded by the resistors and sought the help of the Germans from the neighbouring village Melissi to no avail.

By a quirk of fate, a German detachment on its way from Thessaloniki responded to the flares of Skaperdas and intervened to break the resistance front. Divisions of Schubert and Poulos, which earlier managed to enter the town, succeeded in repelling the resistors. In turn they killed any elderly Giannitsiotes who hadn't managed to escape and torched the town. Schubert "as another Nero observed the dreaded spectacle of the burning city".[797]

The fire destroyed most of the town or about two thirds of the residents and created a tragic crisis for the population. In the meantime, the resistance forces regrouped and led a long nightly invasion against the enemy camping in town, resulting in the loss of four Germans and the injuries of another two.[798] The ΕΛΑΣ attacks continued until 21st September when the gangs of Schubert, Skaperdas and Poulos received orders to return to base, carrying with them the rich plunder. Schubert returned to Asvestochori with a very valuable 'loot', Dina Madzana, who then suffered from appendicitis, and her father entrusted her to him to arrange for her operation in Thessaloniki. But because many wards of the hospital Hirs had already closed due to the continuing withdrawal of the Germans, Madzana remained at the house of Schubert in Asvestochori where she recuperated with the special care of Katina Aggelidou, "an attractive 28 year old teacher".[799]

Part III

Shubert: "Wolf in Sheep's Clothing"

Chapter 1

From Anixiohori to Vienna

Krya Vrysi: the mysterious death of the doctor Chr. Mantzana

Since early September, non-military associates of the Germans and select families of nationalist clans rode the trains for their journey to Germany. After the treaty of Caserta on 26th September by which the Security Battalions were termed enemies and invited to surrender, several warlords, such as Poulos, Grammatikopoulos, Kylindreas and others with their armed gangs preferred to follow the German army, seeking protection from Germany at a time when the 3rd Reich was on its 'last legs'. Indeed, to reposition closer to the road and rail network used by the Germans, Poulos moved towards the end of September from his stronghold at Krya Vrysi to Nea Chalkidona awaiting to be summoned by the German authorities.[800] For the same reason, at the end of September, Schubert moved his battalion to Axiochori, Kilkis, his last station before departing for Germany.[801]

In Axiochori, Schubert awaited the signal to depart for over twenty days and avoided acts of violence used up to now. Following the gang was Dina Mantzana, who elicited Schubert's promise that he would surrender her to her father who resided with his family at Krya Vrysi, with the battalion of Skaperdas.[802] Christos Mantzanas, a specialist paediatrician and pathologist, in 1935 moved with his five member family from Agrinion to Macedonia where he worked in the various districts of Serres, Kilkis and Pella, prior to settling in Salonica and "blackmailed by Schubert" was enlisted in June 1944 in the battalion of the nationalist warlord A. Vihos. After the latter's expulsion by the lead of the terrorist organization ΠΟΕΤ[803], Mantzanas defected to the gang of St. Skaperdas, where his daughter Dina was already enlisted as a military nurse, carrying the battalion uniform and an Italian weapon. Hence father and daughter took part in the raids of Skaperdas and Poulos in the area of Giannitsa. It appears Schubert formed a relationship with Mantzana, a curvy attractive 23 year old medical student, in the brief period she was under his wing, with the result that he abandoned Katina Aggelidou at Asvestochori "with a case of clothing". His plan to keep her conflicted with the insistence of Mantzana herself, but more so her father, that she return to her family. "And the next day Schubert collected me for surrender to my father".[804] In the event, on 30th September, passing by Nea Chalkidona towards Krya Vrysi, she was informed by Poulos' men that her father had been murdered two days before and the family captured by rebels during the takeover of Krya Vrysi.[805]

Mantzana, as she testified later, accepted the news of her father's death by rebels as the truth and surprisingly returned to Axiochori with no further action. But according to the testimony of a Poulos from Drama serving in Chalkidona the news of Mantzana's death was conveyed by P. Triantafyllou, an officer of Poulos: "We had our doubts and asked him how he was killed, as the men of ΕΛΑΣ did not enter Krya Vrysi. It was then he told us they found him killed without knowing how".[806] And as doubts and discussion amongst the gang continued, Poulos "through daily order forbade all conversations about the murder of Mantzana. In my opinion Mantzana was executed by Skaperdas' men by order of Schubert who held his daughter by force".[807]. Mantzana, when returning in 1945, was asked by the Greek authorities if, in her view, her father had been executed under Schubert's order, replied: "From these people one should expect everything".[808] Contrary to the decision of the Criminal Court – Schubert was acquitted from the charge that he planned the death of Mantzana – the doctor's sudden death just before Schubert's departure from Asvestochori for Axiochori suggests a conscious decision of the German officer to rid himself of the father to enable him to keep the daughter as his lover during his impending journey North.

Austria: Dina Mantzana and Schubert's eroticism

Whilst the battalion was still based in Axiochori, G. Germanakis "escaped with 15–20 men for a destination unknown to us".[809] The remaining Schuberites, around 70 men, followed Schubert, it was about October 20th. For their transportation to the Yugoslav border around 80 cattle carts were used which Schubert requisitioned from Axiochori and the neighbouring village Aspros. In a passenger car (saloon) driven by G. Economakis rode, apart from Schubert, Mantzana and the couple Lazaros and Eudoxia Kommatopoulos. At Evzones, the saloon developed a fault and broke down. From Gevgelija they travelled by train to a certain spot in Serbia and from there the Schuberites began a long trek, whilst Schubert with his elite gang rode by car. Around 30 Schuberites with their weaponry defected from the battalion and for nine months served in the woods of Serbia under the nationalist Michaelovits, prior to their capture by rebels of Tito in Slovenia. Dressed in appropriate uniform they pretended to be workers, fugitives from a German work camp returning to Greece. The trick worked and via the Red Cross, Schuberites, as Gridakis, Kamisis and Xanthopoulos in the summer of 1945, were transported to Greece.[810]

Outside the mountain village of Loret (today Sierpo), partisan forces attacked the Schuberites resulting in six being killed and three or four escaping. The remainder, around 30, continued on foot whilst Schubert with Mantzana, Lazaros Kommatopoulos and his wife Eudoxia, K. Domna, the groom and K. Economakis his private chauffeur, travelled through Sarajevo and Zagreb to Vienna where they arrived in February 1945. Schubert with his company moved into a private home whilst the 30 or so Schuberites were left in a German camp for displaced workers.

Mantzana, according to her testimony, en route from Axiochori to Vienna was obliged to withstand the abuse and threats of Schubert to compel her to yield to his sexual desires: "Whore, slut, flirt. Your father, the scoundrel, two-timed, I shit on the living and the dead, if you don't take me, I'll kill you with my own hands".[811]

In Vienna they remained for over a month and Mantzana, thinking that Schubert would stop pressuring her, declared her love for the 35 year old Economakis and her wish to marry him. Schubert in a rage turned his revolver to kill them both but as she herself claims, she attacked, disarming him. Nevertheless, Economakis, as Domna, Schubert set apart immediately, threatening to surrender the former to the SS as a communist.[812] Just before the arrival of the Russian forces in Vienna on 13th April 1945, Schubert, with Mantzana and the Kommatopoulos couple, fled to Schwaz, a mountain hamlet in Western Austria. Here they resided again in a private house for about a month until the surrender of the town to the 103rd American Infantry Division on May 4th.

Schubert and his company, pretending to be displaced persons from Greece, appeared before the Americans as plain clothed civilians; indeed Schubert wore "civilian clothes which he carried with him from Africa".[813] He declared his name to be Konstantinos Konstantinides[814] and that Mantzana was his fiancee, a relationship she detested but was obliged to accept. At Schwaz, Schubert forced her "under threat of his revolver" for the first time, as she testified, to satisfy his sexual urges. Schubert and Mantzana, characterized as "displaced persons", were sent with other Greeks to a camp and transported to Innsbruck where for reasons unknown they were detained till August. During this four month stay Schubert often beat Mantzana to yield to his sexual desires[815] Nothing else is known of the lives of Schubert and Mantzana in the camp of Innsbruck save the information that they met Mastichoula, the wife of G. Poulos, who had surrendered to the American military forces in April of 1945 and had been detained in an allied concentration camp in Kornwestheim in Germany.[816]

Towards the end of August, Schubert and Mantzana were moved to Munich preceding their flight to Greece.

Chapter 2

Return to Greece (5 September 1945)

At Eleusis Airport: Facing police control

After a few days' stay in Munich, on 5th September 1945, Schubert and Mantzana, aboard a British plane, were repatriated to Greece along with other Greek hostages whom the Germans had plucked from the concentration and work camps. Mantzana recommended Schubert not to return to Greece, but he kept saying he was madly in love with her and could not part. In case she abandoned or surrendered him his revenge would be harsh: "If you're intending to betray me, I'll kill you with my own hands".[817] He insisted Alexandria was his final destination.

The plane landed at Eleusis airport. After announcement of the names of those hostages returning by Anastasiades, the deputy Police officer of the Alien Centre of Piraeus and responsible for control that day, the passengers were transported from the airport to a school in Eleusis to submit to police control.

"First before the officer appeared Schubert Fritz under the pseudonym Konstantinides Konos.

Question. What's your name?
Answer. Konstantinides Konstantinos.
Question. What are you?
Answer. Greek
Question. Possibly of Jewish origin?
Answer. No.
Question. Place of origin?
Answer. From Smyrna.
Question. When did you arrive in Greece?
Answer. 1924 or 1923.
Question. What is your occupation?
Answer. Engineer.
Question. Where do you stay?
Answer. Thessaloniki
Question. In what direction?
Answer. Vardaris
Question. Which part of Vardaris?
Answer. Vardaris

Question. Does anyone know you?
Answer. The young lady my fiancée.

After this I was summoned and was asked first my place of origin, where I reside and if I know Konstantinides and what is my relationship. I replied that I know him from Thessaloniki and met him through my father and denied he was my fiancé. Then the officer suggested I go home and to Konstantinides to remain".[818]

So, according to Mantzana, Schubert brought problems upon himself as he was unable to provide a specific home address in Thessaloniki and insisted Vardaris was his permanent residence. (Vardaris is a large central precinct in the west side of the city).

If Schubert hadn't panicked and had given the officer any address in Thessaloniki, most likely he'd have slipped through as was admitted later by the examiner at the Alien Centre of Thessaloniki when speaking to Mantzana: "By concealing this, he could have avoided judicial procedures".[819] Mantzana defended herself, saying she was acting "under the force of intense emotions due to the cascade of threats perpetually thrown at me".[820] It remains inexplicable however why the police officer Anastasiades did not question Mantzana to extract the information she submitted later in her testimony. How was it possible that this officer did not have serious suspicions when he heard Mantzana's denial; that she was not Schubert's fiancée and that she met him through her father in Thessaloniki? And again, the police of the Piraeus Alien Center made the mistake of letting Mantzana slip through their hands at a crucial stage of the questioning process, when on 15th September she visited Schubert at the cells of the Centre and gave him 5,000 drachmas for maintenance.[821] Later the officials at the Centre created a myth.

The story of the Austrian ballerina-informant

In 1976 Sarantos Antonakos, a former policeman, published an interesting article in which he recounts exhaustively the history of the unveiling of Schubert as he heard it from G. Doukakis, a deputy at the Piraeus Alien Centre in 1945.

Doukakis contributed decisively in the examination process leading to the verification of the identity of the German officer. So, according to his account, with Schubert and the other returning Greek hostages was Anna Pinter, "twenty year old beauty, ballerina of the state ballet of Vienna.[822], who, for fear of the Russians married some Greek and came to reside in Greece. This ballerina was the only one of the mass of passengers who came forward to disclose to the examiner Anastasiades that 'Konstantinides was in fact German'[823] thus reinforcing his doubts about Konstantinides' supposed Greek origin". The questioning continued until, two weeks later, the identity of the real Konstantinides was unveiled.

The story of the Austrian ballerina offering valuable evidence to the officer is merely another one of the many myths created to justify certain circumstances relating to the varied and complex life of Schubert. Evidently the 24 year old Dina Mantzana "sexy with dark ruddy face, dark eyes and neat hair"[824] was transformed in the myth into a beautiful ballerina of Vienna. Then, on events known from Mantzana's adventures with Schubert in Austria, were adapted to the life of the Austrian artist. Both Pinter and Mantzana, out of fear, were forced to abandon Vienna just before the arrival of the Russians. Both had developed emotional ties with 'Greeks' and came to Greece for permanent residence.

To conclude, Mantzana, whose presence at Eleusis airport control is not mentioned anywhere in Antonakos' account, is recreated as the Viennese Pinter an unidentified person as a ballerina of Vienna.[825]

The Alien Division of Thessaloniki to whom Mantzana, on 28th September 1945, testified revealing facts about Schubert's identity and activities, for some reason repeated the mistake of the Piraeus Centre and let Mantzana free after her questioning. From here, her traces were lost. Though an essential witness, she did not appear at any of the trials of Schubert and the Schuberites neither as witness nor accused. For the first time, in April 1947, she is mentioned in an indictment of the Special Court of Thessaloniki with the note "Dina or Nita's Mantzara, (sic) resident of Thessaloniki and already unknown residence"[826]. Her disappearance is explained by the fact that early on she left Thessaloniki and settled in Agrinio where she married Chr. Gerochristou working in security.[827] For these reasons, Mantzana remained totally unknown to the media and generally to the Greeks. Inevitably to cover up the violators of their duties at Eleusis airport, it appears the Alien Centres of Piraeus and Thessaloniki colluded so the examination report of Mantzana was kept secret, giving way to the myth of the Viennese ballerina circulating then.

The identity of "Konstantinides" revealed

When Mantzana visited Schubert on 15th September at the Piraeus Alien Centre, the process of revealing his real identity had not yet finished. Details as to how this came about have been saved according to the testimony of Deputy George Doukakis, examiner of Schubert at the Piraeus centre.[828] Anastasiades surrendered 'Konstantinides' to the Police officer Abraham Valsamakis, considered a specialist in the examination of 'difficult clients' like Schubert. But as Konstantinides continued maintaining absolute silence regarding his identity and kept complaining about his unfair treatment, Valsamakis ordered that he be detained temporarily in the cell of the Aliens Centre. On the fourth day, the Deputy G. Doukakis took over the questioning to whom Konstantinides, after pressure, admitted that he was a German citizen returning to Greece to marry a Greek girl with whom he had fallen in love in Thessaloniki whilst serving there. Notwithstanding the prisoner's supposed concessions, Doukakis still maintained his doubts as to the credibility of Konstantinides, when someone knocked on the door and upon entering the office was dumbfounded facing 'Konstantinides'. Doukakis noticed the surprise on the visitor's face and taking him out of the office asked him how he knew the detainee. "It's the German sergeant Schubert. I met him in Chania. It must be Schubert. How did this beast end up in your hands? He's burned villages, shot civilians"[829] replied Joseph Kourkoutis, a marine agent who by chance dropped by the office of Doukakis at the Centre as he had been summoned to testify in a collaborator's case.

When the examiner, A. Valsamakis, who had in the meantime taken over the questioning from Doukakis, conveyed to 'Konstantinides' the damning evidence of the Chaniot Kourkouti thinking that 'Konstantinides' would crack this time, the exact opposite happened. He appeared angry and defiant, emphasizing: "I am not Schubert How is it possible to come to Greece if, as you claim, I am accused of a load of crimes?"[830] At this point of the questioning, a second witness entered the office, colonel Economou, who upon recognizing the head of the "Death Commandos" proclaimed: "Congratulations, officer. You have in your hands the notorious Schubert".[831] He then mentioned various of his crimes in Crete. His testimony triggered the officials of the Aliens Centre to dispatch two police officers, one to Crete and the other to Macedonia, to collect evidence. After a few days, they returned with numerous documents and witness statements, the 'indictment' of "Konstantinides" which Valsamakis used as the new weapon to remove the mask from the face of "Konstantinides". To the respective crimes which the examiner listed, "Konstantinides" initially reasoned that the injection given to him in the Berlin hospital caused him amnesia. Later he argued that those responsible for the crimes were the generals Broier and Miller. Eventually, exhausted by the many days' examination, pseudo- Konstantinides yielded under the weight of evidence and with the voice of innocence said: "I have one soul. Take it as quickly as possible and be done".[832] It was a long and painful process which lasted over two weeks.

Schubert's arrest was first announced on 18th September to various friends in Crete by Tom Dunbabin: "Schubert was arrested a couple of days ago in Athens where he had returned lately under cover of an immigrant labourer".[833] Dina Mantzana was summoned last to testify at Thessaloniki's Aliens Centre on 28th September, when the mask hiding the German sergeant had already fallen. Schubert was moved from Piraeus to the Averof jails to be tried later as a war criminal.

When the daily press announced that Sergeant Schubert was in the hands of Greek justice, Macedonia, and more so Crete, demanded from the Ministry of Justice that Schubert be tried at the places where he committed his crimes. Immediately after the revelation of "Konstantinides" the request of the Cretans was published: "We express the unanimous desire of the Cretan people that he be tried and executed here amongst us and in the presence of those he so tyrannized".[834] The same Heraklian paper announced the next day, September 22nd, that capetan D. Domalakis on behalf of the group Satana sent a telegram to the prime minister and the ministers of justice and economic affairs asking that "they allow a team of Cretan resistors and police to undertake to travel to Piraeus to collect him".[835] The insistent actions of the Cretan agents succeeded. It is said that the persons who finally handled his transfer were Chr. Tsifakis and Emm. Bantouvas, both significant resistors of the island.⁸³⁶ Early in December, it was announced Schubert would be transported by military aircraft, as "fears of lynching had been expressed". Finally, on 17th December, he was transported by plane to stand before the Military Court Martial of Chania "to whom by special law was granted the right to function as a court of crimes of war"⁸³⁷ During his transfer Schubert continuously emphasized to those escorting him that "no Greek had he killed", adopting the role of an innocent dove, to which stance he remained adamant until his death.

Schubert, who remained detained in the Remedial Jails of Chania at least until February 1946, was visited by Cretans, following permission from the military authorities, who sought information mostly about collaborators.⁸³⁸ The decision of the Sofouli Government that Schubert be tried not in Crete but in Athens by the Special Military Court Martial for War Crimes was taken according to the Constitutional Act 90 of 31st December 1945, constituting this Court as exclusively responsible for foreign criminals.⁸³⁹

The "arrest" of Schubert in Thessaloniki and the mystery-pistol

In Schubert's case, there exists a plethora of invented versions of his life, his movements, activities and his death. As regards his origin, he himself, as aforementioned, contributed to the creation of one such mythical surrounding. Issues such as his sudden disappearance, his actions in Macedonia, his escape to Austria and above all his return, recognition and arrest all became a subject of wild fantasy.

For many Cretans, Schubert never left Crete but with his gang continued his activities until the German surrender at Chania in May 1945.

Then, it is said, with other criminals, Germans and Italians he was a prisoner of the British waiting to be transported to mainland Greece for questioning and in turn to be sent to an allied camp in Europe.⁸⁴⁰ Schubert however, disguised as a common civilian, tricked the British guard, returned to Germany where he was decommissioned and consequently settled in Vienna. Thence he communicated with the Greek girl (generally associated in the sources with Thessaloniki) with whom he fell in love during his time in Greece and agreed to meet in Thessaloniki.⁸⁴¹ With the pseudonym Konstantinides he returned by rail to Thessaloniki. At this point, two versions are offered. According to the first, Schubert, upon arriving at the city train station, was recognized by a Cretan policeman, who in civilian clothing followed the moves of suspicious passengers. Schubert initially denied the identification and insisted he was a repatriating Greek labourer from a German work camp. The final identification was supported by evidence produced over the next few days.⁸⁴²

By the second version, Schubert, unperturbed upon arrival, secured a room in a hotel where he was unknown to the guests as Thessaloniki had never been host to his activities. However, one day along the road to his hotel by chance a Cretan recognized him, followed him to the hotel and immediately alerted the police who arrested him in his room.

The Cretan, according to an unconfirmed source, was called Antonios Psilakis from Rethymnon, whose father, Nikolaos, Schubert had executed as a supplier of capetan Petrakogiorgi and Antonios with two cousins he had exiled to a camp of forced labour in Germany.[843] One of the officers who was involved in the arrest of Schubert was Chaniot Kelaidis, who later recounted his experience: "Upon entering the room, I saw on the bed a leather case with his clothes and on those a pistol. I had time to grab it and put it in my pocket before the other officers saw me. I hid it and did not surrender it at the inquest which ensued". The revolver, of past technology, heavy and awkward, triggered Kelaidis' curiosity: he visited Schubert in the jails of Yenti Koule and asked him: "Why do you carry this strange thing and not a Luger or newer weapon?" Schubert, acknowledging him with an ironic smile said: "I am a 'traditional German'". The Chaniot remembered the word 'traditional' though he didn't know what it meant."[844]

During the eighties, Kostas Mamalakis was a serving soldier in the unit based in the area of Chania. A Chaniot approached him and said: "I noticed you're a good shot and familiar with handling guns. That's why I'll gift you a pistol. It has a history. Have you heard of any Schubert?"[845] Mamalakis froze upon hearing the name but pretended he knew nothing. Then the Chaniot, Kelaidis by name, told him he was a retired constable and in turn recounted how Schubert's revolver came into his hands when he was serving in the gendarmerie of Thessaloniki after the end of the Occupation. The alleged 'Schubert revolver' is a Mauser C96 type of 9mm with a long barrel and wide handle, hence the name "broomstick".[846]

It was used by the army of the Kaiser in the 1st World War and according to the German manufacturing factory at Obendorf, Kemal Ataturk ordered, in the war of 1922 against the Greeks, 350 revolvers of the Mauser C96 type specially for his officers.[847] The "Schubert revolver" bears the year of manufacture of 1920; consequently goes to support Schubert's assertions that he served in the Turkish army under Kemal and took part in the battle of Sangarios. If part of the story which Schubert narrates to the Rethymniot refugees in 1941 is true and not a fiction of the imagination, whether his or the Rethymniots, it may be there is some association between the revolver of Kemal and Schubert. Whilst the hypothesis bears plausible elements, it must be rejected by the fact that Schubert, as now evidenced, did not arrive in Thessaloniki but Eleusis and in turn was recognized and initially imprisoned at the Piraeus Aliens Centre. In any event, he would have betrayed himself if indeed he carried this outdated weapon. On the other hand, there is the possibility that Schubert's revolver ended up by a convoluted way in Kelaidis' hands as one item contained in the suitcase which Schubert, before leaving Austria, had entrusted to Katina Aggelidou. Quite simply, another element grown into the myth of Schubert's identification and arrest in Thessaloniki.

A parallel of the first version is also the following account of Meskliotis M. Batakis. According to this, in reality Schubert didn't leave with the German troops but for two years managed to remain hidden in Greece hoping the Greeks would forget him and his crimes when the moment came to flee abroad. So, early in 1947, whilst waiting at Athens (Hellenikon) airport to embark on the plane, "he is recognized by a Cretan gendarme in the guard at the airport, is arrested and driven to Chania where once tried, he is executed"[848]. At least until 2003, the date Batakis published his memoirs, Schubert's myths hold strong!

Part IV

Schubert and the Schuberites before the Courts

Chapter 1

Schuberite Trial in Athens (28 July–5 August 1947)

Witnesses and delaying tactics

On 2nd October 1946, about a year after his arrest, Sergeant Fritz Schubert was brought before the courtroom of the Special Martial Court of War Crimes of Athens under no.1 and 16 1946 orders, according to no.73/1945 Editorial act of Council to be tried for crimes he committed alone or even by others' exhortation in Crete and Macedonia from August 1941 till September 1944. In the indictment are numbered fourteen offences against him for crimes such as killings (3.000 people), systematic terror, torture, incarcerations, deportations, blackmail, rape, execution of innocent civilians, confiscation and plunder of properties, torching of villages and hamlets and lastly "the efforts to uproot the national morale of the Greeks and to taint the national synthesis of territories under occupied control".[849]

It was decided that deputy officer Fritz Schubert be tried on 31st October 1946 along with generals Bruno Brauer and Friedrich-Wilhelm Miller, his superiors in Crete and co-accused for similar crimes inevitably of a more serious nature.[850] With a memo to the respective Office of the Ministry of Foreign Affairs, the president of the Special Court Martial, lieutenant F. Papageorgiou, sought the opinion of those responsible at the Ministry whether it was "advisable that the present Schubert matter be litigated in Athens".[851] The answer of the Ministry is not known. The Court Martial decided to divide the Schubert matter from that of the generals, mainly for fear that maybe the trial would develop into an open conflict, particularly between Brauer and Schubert over the controversial questions of responsibilities. Indeed, during the course of the trial of these generals, several prosecution witnesses repeatedly referred to the relationship of Schubert with general Brauer. There was also a proposal that Schubert be called to testify. Later, at his trial, Schubert complained 'as he was not called during the trial of the German Generals Brauer and Miller to prove the lies of the former'.[852] There was also the possibility that a trial with the generals would be restricted to crimes committed more in Crete rather than Macedonia.

The court via the Royal Commissioner G. Dimakopoulos summoned an unknown number of prosecution witnesses of whom three appeared from Crete and five from Macedonia.

Additionally, the relevant local authorities submitted sworn depositions of prosecution witnesses, twenty-two from Crete – mostly from the municipality of Heraklion – and six from Macedonia, amongst which was also included the testimony of Lazaros Kommatopoulos, Schubert's most loyal and close official.[853] Dina Mantzana, Schubert's lover and one of the most important witnesses, although summoned, for unknown reasons neither appeared in court nor did she send a statement. To the testimonies of absent prosecution witnesses from Crete would be added another eight depositions from the Brauer Miller trial. Also present were five of seven summoned defence witnesses, all serving time from the municipality of Heraklion. These Schuberites turned from defence witnesses into prosecution witnesses, testifying substantial evidence against Schubert.

It is surprising to note the excessively low number of prosecution witnesses appearing from Macedonia and particularly Crete, which was basically represented by only two witnesses as the third witness, Alexandros Halkiadakis, referred to mass executions at the village of Sokaras Monofatsi, which he attributed to Schubert, though these were proved to have been committed later by others after Schubert's departure from Crete. The Cretan authorities, in order to prove Schubert's guilt, it seems relied on sworn depositions of absent witnesses and those from the trial of the generals Brauer and Miller. These statements however, which were read at the trial, had the disadvantage of depriving the court of cross examination and could harm the accused as much as the accuser. Examples of depositions where the witnesses could mix up the dates but also the identities of those committing crimes were known to the court, is shown by Schubert's acquittal from crimes for which he was accused of committing at eight villages and towns in Crete as 'not enough evidence was discovered of the guilt of the accused'.[854]

There are however sources that show that Schubert was not wholly uninvolved in some of the criminal activities where he was acquitted.

In the condemning decision of 1947, there are named for Crete twenty and for Macedonia nine, villages and hamlets where Schubert committed crimes. From this list are missing a significant number of villages which tasted the mania of Schubert and his gang, more than twenty on the Island and around ten in Macedonia (all the villages in Western Macedonia and the southern area of Lake Volvi) who were not represented at the trial.

The military and political situation then prevailing – a period of civil war – and the worsening economic climate meant travel from the provinces to Athens was difficult.

Possibly also the lack of information at the community authorities by the respective state services as regards the conduct of the trial contributed to the above villages not sending witnesses or depositions.

The Special Court Martial of War Crimes assembled in the hall of the Five-member Appeal Court of Athens (Arsakeion Building) on Monday 28th July 1947 to try the case of Sergeant "Fritz Schubert of Spyridonos born in Smyrna". The trial was conducted over five days and finished on 5th August. The panel of the court was mixed: F. Papageorgiou, lieutenant president, colonels Sp. Vyzas and S. Kotsalos and judges I. Athanasoulis and D. Economou. The duties of royal commissioner were performed by G. Dimakopouls, whilst defence counsels appointed by law were the

German educated lawyers D. Tsimpos and A. Sergopoulos. Before the proceedings started, the case of officers E. Fischer and B. Deter was separated: they were accused of oppression of economic nature against the Cretan population.

Schubert, hoping to create a good impression to the judges and the court, appeared well dressed with a dark suit, white shirt, light coloured tie, blue fabric shoes and the stance of a scapegoat: "looking like someone dragged into court for no reason".[855]

He looked indifferent, calm, cool and arrogant. He definitely had absolutely no intentions of admitting guilt and responsibilities nor of expressing regret. Strangely, for the first time after his arrest, he admitted that Smyrna was not his birthplace; rather a town of western Germany, that he had children and a wife "who were murdered during a bombardment by the enemy".[856]

This was the first time, in this court, that he had shown interest for his family, or describing them as victims of bombarding. He himself, since his arrival in Greece but particularly after settling in Macedonia, developed sexual relationships with women. In the court room the atmosphere was electric and stressed. Aside from the witnesses, relatives of the victims attended and many others anxious to hear what responses the famous Schubert would give in his description of the crimes about which they had heard so much. One of the journalists described the atmosphere during the first two days like this: "Dreadful things are being heard in the hall of the Court of Appeal where the German arch executioner Schubert is on trial. What a bloody monster he was, this pathologically disturbed criminal character? One thing I have to say: Even today his victims – those who survived and are lined up as witnesses in the courtroom – are breaking in tears as they describe what happened to their villages and the suffering of their compatriots. One or two of the victims couldn't hold back and only the composure of the guards and their quick intervention restrained them from coming to blows with him".[857]

Before the examination of the witnesses, Schubert, through his counsel, submitted an application for postponement of the trial, a tactic he repeated insistently the third and particularly the fourth day of the trial.

The first day, he complained that a German lawyer had not been appointed for him and that there hadn't been summoned as defence witnesses senior German officers under whose direct orders he had served; "a postponement of the trial is requested for a later date".[858] Indeed, he declared that he had already submitted a request to the German government that a German counsel be dispatched and he asked the court to summon his superior senior officers who were being held in allied detention camps to be examined in court, or, if their presence was not possible, to take their depositions. Schubert copied the tactics of generals Brauer and Miller who at their trial in November 1946 requested the Greek court to summon "two German lawyers who attended the Nuremberg trial".[859] In the end, at their trial two legal educated professors from the university of Munich were summoned, who, in cooperation with the Greek counsel, tried to defend the position of the generals.[860]

The voice of Crete

To begin, the commissioner Dimakopoulos read the indictment which included 23 charges of "murder, theft, plunder, destruction of communities, kidnap of civilians etc."[861]

On Monday 28th July, as the first witness approached Dim. Daskalakis, president of the community of Agios Ioannis, a small village near Kali Sykia, who gave a dark description of how Schubert and his men burned 14 women alive in flaming homes of Kali Sykia in the municipality of Rethymnon. It was an unprecedented brutality and the very peak of Schubert and his gang's criminality in Crete. The news spread like wildfire throughout the island and provoked fear and dread. "From then on Schubert became the fear and horror of women and children and the elderly"[862] concluded the witness. Schubert with this act differed from the other Germans, who generally avoided the execution and particularly the burning of women.[863] The incident at Kali Sykia returned as a title in the written deposition of the absent witness Kon. Damoulakis, who lost the mother and relative of old Damoulaki in the flames on 6th October 1943. Schubert, to the question of the court president, gave an answer which became stereotyped and repeated with every accusation against him throughout the trial: "I was not giving the orders. I was an interpreter. The Greeks gave the orders and they were the executioners".[864] The German staff sergeant adopted a line which he tried to support with three arguments:

1) That as a mere sergeant (he avoided the use of staff sergeant) in no circumstances could he breach the established hierarchy according to military regulations and give orders in the presence of his superiors,
2) That he was performing the duties of an interpreter and liaison between general Brauer and captain Kreuzer and the Greek officials of his squad[865] and
3) That those responsible for orders which led to acts of violence in Crete were the Krousonas G. Tzoulias and M. Kourakis, heads of the gang, independent of Schubert and in Macedonia Greek officers such as colonel G. Poulos, commanders of anti-communist armed teams with whom Schubert cooperated.

The second day of the trial, Tuesday 29th July, papa-Emmanouil Manousakis narrated in detail the dreadful torture to which Schubert submitted his 25 year old son Ioanni, a teacher, to reveal the hideouts of the rebels. The young Manousakis was finally transported from the village of Drapeti Monofatsi to Heraklion where he was executed along with another 49 hostages on 14th June 1943. To Schubert's reply that as an interpreter he had no right to give orders, the witness added: "Schubert had under his command a team of bloodthirsty beasts and he was unchecked acting himself at will. The residents trembled at Schubert's name".[866] During the first two days of the trial, 22 sworn testimonies were read which the Cretan authorities submitted to the court on behalf of witnesses who were not summoned or were unable to attend.

"All the witnesses refer to specific events and are categorical as regards the evil instincts of the accused sergeant. They describe with horrific details the torture to which the Cretans were submitted by Schubert when they were arrested. Under the pretence of revealing arms Schubert arrested residents, beat them and surrendered them for execution. In many cases, the witnesses testify that the executions happened by Schubert himself before the eyes of the crowd".[867]

Schubert reacted, saying that he himself hadn't been to any of the villages which the witnesses named and he added that "possibly it was some other Schubert".[868] On the second day of the trial five Cretan defence witnesses testified; "their testimonies were quite revealing so much for Schubert's activities as those of the Greek collaborators".[869] In court, attempting to alleviate their position as accomplices and cooperating in the crimes, they placed all the blame for whatever happened on the 'beast' Schubert, so becoming prosecution witnesses. The most damning of all was the 20 year old Styl. Karambatakis from Heraklion, who asserted that he was forced after his detention at Schubert's jails to enlist to the squad. Duress as the reason for enlistment to the squad had become the common ground in the defences of nearly all the Schuberites who were arrested and charged with complicity and wrongdoings. The views and information which Karambatakis and the other volunteers gave to the court were extremely valuable as they emerged from people who met Schubert close up and the terrorizing methods he used. In his testimony, Karambatakis concluded "the Germans feared him. To avoid a revolt the Cretans sent him to Macedonia".[870] The witnesses G. Maravelakis and Char. Belibasakis followed Schubert to Macedonia. The second asserted that he remained with the 'squad' from fear, as Schubert, for the smallest excuse or suspicion, "would categorize you as a communist and rifle you immediately".[871]

At the end of the defence testimonies, Schubert, showing his great disappointment remarked: "Now you've all become patriots!"[872]

The third day, Thursday 31st July, the testimonies of notable personalities of Crete who had testified at the Brauer-Miller trial were read. As they had joined in the resistance of the Island, their evidence bore great weight.[873] The testimony of Nik. Pikoulas, ex Major and director of the 2nd Office of the National Organization of Officers of Crete, was the biggest damnation against Schubert. Here Pikoulas read the decree of Brauer regarding the foundation of the hunting squad and the wide authorities granted to him. He added to his testimony the evidence that Schubert's casualties "climbed to 251 and that Schubert due to his brutalities became despised even to the Germans including military circles".[874]

The voice of Macedonia

The first day of the trial, five witnesses from Macedonia testified. The mayor Stefanos Triantafyllides, cashier of the borough of Giannitsa in 1944, gave the most crushing testimony against the accused, given he had lived through the terror Schubert had unleashed through the town; and he survived miraculously from certain death. In his deposition he described in detail the crimes of Schubert and his officials in the town and neighbouring villages.

"His men grabbed by chance anyone they felt like and he would throw the fatal blow at those who hadn't passed away. Look at the testimonies which the people drew from his sadistic ways. The beatings his men gave cannot be described, mister president. They turned those who caught into 'balloons' and they still exist, nearly three years after the period of their orgies, people still bedridden from the beating they suffered or still unable to walk".[875]

When Schubert later tried to conceal his atrocities asserting that "all this slaughter which happened at the square (of Giannitsa) was observed by the balcony by colonel Poulos and Skaperdas giving orders and supervising from there"[876], Triantafyllides gave a perfect comeback: "If there were 10 Schubert today Greeks would not exist. When he was present no one else could give orders".[877] To Kon. Bourdanis, a witness from Giannitsa, who gave a thorough description of the slaughter at Giannitsa, Schubert protested saying: "Lies, lies! I'm innocent. The security squads did everything and their capetans. Poulos and the others".[878]

The third witness, I. Galitsanos, a former butcher and present gendarme "reports with shivering details the tragedy of Hortiati".[879]

Whilst none of the few Hortiati who survived the holocaust appeared in court nor sent a witness statement, nevertheless the court judged Schubert exclusively to blame for the fire with the accusation that he "trapped most in two buildings which he torched thus murdering 145 persons".[880] Curiously it is not mentioned from the daily press then whether the judges asked Schubert why he showed such cruelty against the people of Hortiati. The president of the proceedings sufficed to ask the witness "who gave the order?" and got the reply "Schubert". Similarly, there is no mention in the daily press if Schubert tried to defend the heavy charge against him. In turn, Mih. Manos, a relative of a victim, from Asvestochori, described the terrorizing of his village on 26th July 1944 and the execution of 16 men which Schubert turned into a public spectacle, obliging many to watch. As with other cases, Schubert tried to throw the blame for mass executions on German commandants of participating divisions: "Schubert asserts that the slaughter at Asvestochori was ordered by the guard leader of the village".[881]

Athan. Stamboulides, a witness from Nea Malgara, a refugee village 27 kilometres southwest of Salonica, refers to the terror which Schubert and his men lashed out on 19th August against the residents of Nea Malgara and two other adjoining settlements. Under order of Schubert his team arrested the president of the village, Al. Katsarelia, "threw him to the ground and battered his head with their boots until he died".[882] Additionally, they executed five citizens in a ditch which they themselves had been obliged to dig.

Schubert, to the question of the president of the court, replied that "all this slaughter was done by Poulos and Skaperdas. Their gangs had entered Malgara".[883]

Finally, seven statements were read of witnesses from different villages of central Macedonia, the area of Giannitsa and western Halkidiki.

So, within three days 12 witnesses present were examined and 36 sworn statements were read of absent witnesses. The third day of the trial, Thursday 31st July, it was announced that Schubert would stand the next day. At the beginning of Thursday's session, Schubert submitted an application to postpone the trial in which he asked:

1) For a German lawyer to be dispatched from the German Government "as these appointed were unable to offer essential help"[884] and
2) Summons for examination as defence witnesses' German officers, his superiors who were held in British and American assembly camps as the Greek defence witnesses "hid the truth" and 'attributed crimes to him for which he was not responsible'.[885] Finally, Schubert referred to the court requesting justice and clemency: "Whatever I did, I did following orders. Give me the opportunity to defend myself as this was offered also to my superiors"[886] and he referred to the case of Wing Commander Alexander Andrae, the first commandant of Fortress Crete.

The court rejected his plea to postpone trial and simultaneously the satisfaction of Schubert's demands. The session was interrupted at 11:40am to continue the next day, Friday, but for unknown reasons the trial resumed on Saturday 2nd August at 11:05 in the morning.

Schubert, through his lawyers, renewed the plea to postpone the trial, asserting that the prosecution witnesses were unreliable and "prompted by patriotic hatred exaggerated real events against the accused. Their statements became cause to create unfavourable impressions against him with legal consequences".[887] He also submitted a copy application, which he relayed in German to the Minister of Justice, in which he sought postponement of the trial to enable other defence witnesses to be examined, meaning German officers. The court again rejected his plea, arguing that Schubert had the time required – two years detained – to prepare himself. Nevertheless, the accused did not give up but made also a third attempt to succeed in postponing the trial. Pretending that his Greek did not help him in liaising with his lawyers in order to defend himself more effectively, he decided to support his claim for a German lawyer reading his protest in German. In this he elaborated that his trial was of a summary nature – it lasted only five days – whereas other trials as Kalchev and Ravalli were four months.[888]

The Royal Commissioner Dimakopoulos recommended to the court to reject the plea of postponement, highlighting the fact that "after the slaughter" – he repeated that Schubert's victims climbed to 3.000 – "Schubert breathes still and polluting this hall is already his great achievement and it would be a crime to delay his punishment".[889] For the third time the court rejected Schubert's plea to summon a German lawyer and invited him to stand but he again refused. Finally, he asked that general Andrae be summoned as defence witness from Kallithea jails.

Following the rejection also of his last plea, Schubert, with all the boldness that distinguished him, addressing the judges, declared that the trial was a mockery: "I care not for my life but for justice! Both at Nuremberg and the other courts the accused were perfectly capable to defend themselves. Only my trial is processed summarily within a few days without witnesses and lawyers".[890] At the end of the session, the president of the court warned Schubert that on Tuesday 5th August the decision would be issued without his defence.

The last day of the trial, 5th August, Schubert agreed to answer questions only to clarify certain issues. He admitted that the anti-rebel force, founded in September 1943 by special written decree of Commandant of Crete Bruno Brauer, reported directly to the Military Police, acted under the lead of Krousaniotes and had two separate roles, the division of secret police and the intelligence team. He himself contributed only in recruitment and had absolutely no administrative power but merely the position of supplier, interpreter and liaison between Greeks and Germans.

In his enthusiasm to appear that he bore no responsibility for the terrorist activity of the 'Greek squad' in Crete, he referred to an incident where he tried to justify himself.

He asserted that during the last period of his stay in Crete he showed no "eagerness to follow the activities of the Greek terror squad of the people" and for this reason general Brauer 'took him by surprise and ordered to arrest him and lead him to the Secret German Police, where they gave him lobotomizing injections'.[891] So, he was transported from Crete to Athens where he was detained for several days in the sanatorium before being dispatched to Macedonia. Schubert referred to the chapter of his removal from Crete believing he would so alleviate his position, highlighting his multiple authority and psychology.

As regards the most characteristic brutalities in Kali Sykia Rethymnon and Giannitsa Pella, Schubert insisted that for the former the "Greek" of the detachments were responsible and for the second those to blame were colonels G. Poulos and S. Skaperdas, leaders of security gangs: "I was a mere sergeant. And a sergeant cannot order a Greek staff sergeant let alone a captain or a colonel Poulos. I was an interpreter. Poulos gave the orders. And now Poulos is a patriot".[892] Generally, Schubert tried to portray himself as the scapegoat of his superiors, saying with rage that "(Brauer) did everything. I saw him only three times. The third, he showed me photographs of 18 German soldiers murdered by the rebels and said that for every one murdered, 50 Greeks must be executed".[893]

Then the Royal Commissioner took the stand and referred in detail to the typical criminal activities of Schubert in Crete as well as Macedonia.

He repeated for the umpteenth time that his victims "climbed to about 3,000" and that the "natural abettor in most cases"[894] was Schubert himself. He likened Schubert to Attila as both were known as bloodthirsty terrorists and butchers who expressed their methods with the phrase "where my footsteps grass doesn't grow". After referring to the case of Smaragda Kapetanakis, the old lady from Rodakino Rethymnon whom Schubert "burned alive in an oven",[895] he concluded his address referring to the brutal dismemberment of a baby during the Hortiati holocaust. The dramatic narrative of the commissioner went as follows: "Aggeloudi led by Schubert to execution shouted to him; dog, what's going to happen to my child?' Then Schubert grabbed Aggeloudi's baby by the leg and shattered it, hitting it against a rock. Then he shouted back "That's what's going to happen".[896] Lastly, he requested of the court to proclaim Schubert guilty of all the murders attributed to him and specifically be sentenced sixteen times to death for crimes in Crete, nine times to death for crimes in Macedonia, two times to death for his general criminal activity, two times to life imprisonment, three times to temporary detainment and 20 years imprisonment for respective secondary crimes.[897]

After a short recess due to a mouth infection of the accused, the court resumed at 4.30pm when Schubert's lawyers took the stand and asked for the clemency of the court. The accused, they argued, exercised in all cases the orders of his superiors and in the circumstances the recommended death sentence "would constitute the dogma 'woe to the vanquished' and would have included a portion of national vengeance and mere traces of justice".[898] To the president's question if he had anything to add, Schubert replied "Lest God can testify that I killed with my hands"[899] and emphasised that he put his hopes in Greek justice. The five-member court, after conferring for one hour, announced its decision according to which Schubert was adjudged "guilty of all killings, brutalities, plunder and rape"[900] and they sentenced him to death 27 times. It merged all sentences into the one fatal sentence and set the place of execution as the area of Athens. Schubert heard the decision with apathy and declared he was innocent and would plea for grace. The next day, 6th August, he submitted his plea through his lawyers to the respective Commission, who issued its opinion rejecting it in early October. On 9th October, the Minister of Justice Chr. Ladas put Schubert's case before king Paul, who accepted the opinion of the Commission,[901] wiping out any hope of Schubert moderating the sentence or even his acquittal.

The issue of Schubert's blame

To the question whether Schubert committed his crimes following orders of his superiors, K. Mitsotakis, a lawyer during the Occupation at the court martial of Chania and very familiar with the workings of the administrative and legal system of the Cretan garrison headquarters, gave the following reply: "Schubert was a skiver and did what he wished. Walter, president of the German court martial of Chania replied to my arguments regarding his crimes that Schubert was fuelled by authority direct from the fortress Commandant and specifically from Brauer. The impression I have gained is that Brauer did not know exactly the nature of his activities. Brauer, in representing the Cretans, asserted that he executed communists in vengeance. For me, Schubert did what he did out of sadism and not out of military necessity".[902]

During the trial of Generals Brauer and Miller in Athens in 1946, one of the thorny issues which the Cretan witnesses repeatedly raised was who bore the blame for the dreadful crimes of Schubert and his gang. Brauer himself asserted that he found out about Schubert's crimes in the courtroom. Despite his assertions, Brauer was often notified in the form of complaints by people in high places in the Cretan community. One such person was the dean Evgenios Psalidakis, a church commissioner of the Mitropolis of Crete, who often intervened to the German authorities complaining about their criminal activities.

To his protest that Schubert executed citizens "arbitrarily with blank authority and supported by German Officers", Brauer gave him an abrupt response: "Schubert is one of the best deputies of the German army and his actions are well performed".[903] The Rethymniot Colonel Chr. Tsifakis, in December 1943, expressed the already prevailing opinion that Schubert had been authorized by Hitler himself: "Without submitting his victims to any procedures and arbitrarily he gives orders and commits with his detachment the most horrific crimes, as they say, fuelled as a deputy with power from the Fuehrer direct".[904] According to a Schuberite witness, "Schubert was uncontrollable and only after the event did the German authorities condone his activities".[905] Captain Gleblin, Schubert's superior for a while in 1943, in his statement testified that Schubert took "orders direct from commandant Bruno Brauer".[906] Last, Dina Mantzana testified: "Schubert as I discovered from him himself was active in Crete where he had committed the most terrible crimes in the world. He belonged to the German propaganda and had rights over life and death".[907]

We can conclude that Schubert in practice drew all his powers and freedoms to act as he exclusively wished from the written authority of Brauer and not from him himself to whom no term of the authority obliged him to report. As Schubert himself admitted at his trial, Brauer only saw him three times from the team's founding.

Nonetheless, Brauer and Miller were adjudged by the court to be responsible for the crimes of Schubert and his gang and condemned to death. K. Mitsotakis, in a report he submitted to the Greek national Office of War Crimes in July 1946, makes a very interesting assessment of the Brauer – Schubert relations as regards blame: "In all cases the above war crimes were executed following the orders of the same general (Brauer). The only exception perhaps was the case of Schubert who had received blank instructions to act but even his crimes are mostly attributable to the general, who condoned them albeit not ordering them directly and he repeatedly refused the distancing of Schubert notwithstanding the evident dislike of the Germans including even superior officers".[908]

Mitsotakis repeated this assessment to the author in a recent interview: "In the last analysis, the man is to blame who allowed Schubert to act as he wished Brauer bore the general responsibility even though he didn't know every detail. It's a strange case this of Schubert at least in Crete. And when Schubert left for Macedonia, nothing changed. He did what he did here in Crete".[909]

Truly Schubert's transfer to Macedonia seems to have made no significant difference to the powers he had acquired in Crete. It is unknown to which German unit he was attached after his arrival in Salonica in February 1944.

The only record in his military file appears on 29th May when he was enlisted to the machinery unit c985 of the military police which reported then to the administration Oberfeldkommandantur 395 Saloniki-Agais.[910] If Schubert is judged on the basis of Macedonian testimonies and reports which the judicial authorities of Thessaloniki assembled regarding his activities, one ascertains that generally his brutalities exceed in height and depth those of Crete. But bear in mind that the German sergeant acted in Macedonia at a more crucial period of time for the Wehrmacht and in a more sensitive region. The special commissioner of Thessaloniki, in court documents he submitted to the respective Office, makes the following comment: "During these (operations) many people were murdered or tortured in the cruellest way and many homes were robbed and burned. Generally, the presence of this mob in areas of activity likened to a wild plunder accompanying this also many tears, pain and blood".[911] The most significant change was in the area of leadership. In Macedonia, Schubert took the reins of his team more directly and took charge at every raid as he himself advised colonel Barges at their meeting in 1947: "With the passing of time, Schubert all the more directed himself the gang's operations".[912]

Thessaloniki: Schubert before the firing squad (22nd October 1947)

Thessaloniki and Crete, as previously stated, requested that Schubert be returned to the island to answer for his crimes committed there. He was moved to Crete in December 1945 but in February 1946 he was transported back to Athens to be tried as a German prisoner of war and not as a Greek collaborator. From his return to Athens until his trial, all the hopes of moving Schubert to Thessaloniki had eclipsed. And whilst Schubert, locked up in Kallithea jail, awaited to hear that he would be granted pardon, suddenly following the order of the Appeal attorney of Athens and unknown to the Minister of Justice, on 27th September he was transferred to the jail of Eptapyrgio (Yendi Koule) of Thessaloniki.[913] Once the Minister Chr. Ladas was informed of the event on 5th October he declared that "once Constitutional procedures are satisfied, I will order his immediate execution".[914] Strangely the judicial authorities of the city decided to commit Schubert to court "whilst there are reasons that the case might be postponed on technical grounds. Nevertheless it is anticipated that the beginning of the trial will attract much interest due to the appearance in court of the bloodthirsty beast".[915]

As such Schubert's move and consequent committal to court probably was of symbolic nature, in other words for the satisfaction of the assembled crowd who wished to see Schubert in chains.

On the morning of 9th October 1947, a mass of people had flooded the courtroom "to see the face of the monster which terrorized and flowed the blood of the people of Macedonia".[916] Schubert's appearance this time compared to that at the trial of July was wretched, "unshaven, dishevelled and abhorrent. He had the look of a man with his morale totally shaken. He didn't resort neither to cynicism nor shame during the process".[917]

Along with Schubert 57 Schuberites were also tried, eight imprisoned and 49 in absentia. At the start of the trial Schubert's lawyer, K. Tsitouras, submitted an objection that the Special collaborators court had no jurisdiction to try the case of Schubert who, as a foreign war criminal, had been already tried before the Special War court, the only one suitable in these circumstances. The court upheld the plea and ordered the transfer of the accused to the jails of Eptapyrgio and the continuation of the trial of the 57 volunteers of the Schubert squad.

Schubert remained imprisoned in the jails of Eptapyrgio until the morning of Wednesday 22nd October 1947, the day of his execution. In the daily press of Thessaloniki detailed articles were published regarding Schubert's last hours until his death by firing squad. Schubert, from his secluded cell waiting to die in the early morning, handed two letters to the guard to post, one to his daughter Maria who lived in Palermo with her Italian husband and the other to Colonel Johannes Barges, detained in the Kallithea jails.[918]

Also, to the guard he handed his wallet with thirty thousand drachmas and his cigarette case with the bequest 'to hand them where he knew'.[919]

Just before Schubert was transferred to the jail's offices several journalists rushed to ask him questions: "Why did you kill so many people who had done you no harm?", referring to Asvestochori, Hortiati, Giannitsa and elsewhere. The answers remained the same "These are lies! Exaggerations! I didn't kill anyone; I didn't burn any home in Crete. I was just acting under the orders of my general Muller. Each of us sustains one's fate and all of us one day will die".[920]

Until his end, Schubert appeared not only provocatively remorseless but also fanatically loyal to the idea of 'Germania' and the law of revenge: "Germany, it is said, lives and never dies. I wish it will become great again and will be able to repay its today's suffering".[921] When the guard announced to him that the priest was waiting in the office to take his confession, Schubert reacted saying: "I repeat I am not to blame for this so there is no reason for me to confess and take communion".[922] At 6:15, kneeling before the English Catholic priest[923] Schubert heard his last blessing in Latin and accepted the divine communion.

At 6:30, with fists clenched from the efforts not to faint and supported by two guards, Schubert was led to the usual place of execution. At the jail yard waited the undertaker, Emm. Malamas, whose son Schubert executed at Asvestochori on 26th July. Once he saw the perpetrator surrounded by the firing squad, in a rage he pleaded to the head guard saying: "Captain sir, I also existed as an officer and served my country loyally. I ask you one favour. This human beast who killed my only son please allow me to give the final blow to avenge the soul of my boy".[924] The officer naturally denied the favour but Malamas, a deeply wounded father, just before the order for execution, grabbing a stone shouted: "Murderer! You ate my Kostaki a 24 year old lad. The last blow I beseech you."[925] Before having time to throw the stone the guards distanced Malamas then the commissioner uninterrupted completed the reading of the judicial decision. Around 20 citizens followed the execution procedure of the squad. At the order "fire", the squad gave an end to the life of the bloodthirsty sergeant at 6:45, the moment the sun was just protruding above the heights of Hortiati.

Schubert was buried with no name, in other words without his metal identification or ΤΑΠ (Erkennungsmarke) in a mass grave at the place of execution. Later, when the German authorities arranged for the collection of remains of German soldiers who had initially been buried in different parts of Greece, (save Crete) at the central military cemetery of Dionysus- Rapentosa[926] they sought Schubert's corpse. According to the testimony of colonel Barges, Schubert's remains could not be distinguished from the other remains situated in the same mass grave of Eptapyrgio. At the Dionysus cemetery, row 1, tombstone 17, under which it is thought the remains of Fritz Schubert are entombed along with the others, there is inscribed the following epigraph: (The abbreviation OFELDW, Ober feldwebel denoting the rank of sergeant)

Chapter 2

Schuberite Trials, Ghost Trials

Thessaloniki: 'Nine present, forty-nine in absentia'

The judicial authorities of Crete and Macedonia (Thessaloniki) after the passing by the N. Plastira Government of constitutional act 6/1945 "regarding the imposition of sanctions against accomplices of the enemy"[927] and the formation of emergency Special Collaborators Courts, embarked on the difficult task of identifying and locating "traitors of the nation" who consciously became organs of the enemy as the volunteers of the Schubert gang. In Thessaloniki, the first overt interrogations of Schuberites and prosecution witnesses began immediately after the arrest and unveiling of Schubert in September 1945. First Dina Mantzana, in her testimony on 28th September 1945, named and gave evidence relating to the characteristics, status and activities of seven 'prominent' Cretans; G. Kapetanakis, G. Germanakis, G. Tzoulias, K. Economakis, N. Hanialakis, G. Maravelakis and G. Kastanakis and of the Macedons she named L. Kommatopoulos and K. Domna or Thomna.[928]

Further information relating to the Schuberites was assembled during questioning of prosecution witnesses which the police authorities carried out towards the end of September and early October 1945 for the impending trial of Schubert. To the above list the witnesses could only add a few Schuberites; the Cretans A. Mylonas and I. Gridakis and the Macedons D. Batalas, K. Kamisis and Dina Mantzana. On 17th October 1945, the special commissioner of the Collaborators Court of Thessaloniki in his report proposed, apart from sergeant "Schubert Fritz of Antoni or Konstantinides Konstantinos" they also bring to trial "all the aforementioned Greeks following the battalions Schubert, Poulos and Skaperdas".[929] Only about 15 Schuberites were known by name and until then no arrest warrants had been issued.

Of the few Schuberites added to the commissioner's list no one until then had been located or detained. The 26 year old L. Kommatopoulos was one of the first questioned in October and was soon imprisoned.[930] Immediately he used all means to get released and acquitted from the charge of collaboration. From his village Aravissos 72 villagers signed declarations in which they claimed that Kommatopoulos was forced to enlist to Schubert's gang: "he wronged no one and saved many souls from certain death as for the charge against him it is a sycophantic ploy of the communists".[931] During the process of detainment, Kommatopoulos intermittently submitted to the respective judicial committee declarations in which he argued that he served in the nationalist organization ΠΑΟ and after the attack of ΕΛΑΣ at his village early February 1944, from fear he was obliged with his wife Eudoxia to flee to Giannitsa, where he was arrested by the Germans carrying arms and was threatened with rifling. To save himself he was enlisted to Schubert's team, the purpose of which was the pursuit of communism "which today's state and nation of Greece consider a national danger and pursues anyone who pursues it".[932] Kommatopoulos justified his enlistment to Schubert's gang saying: "This action cannot be deemed a wrongdoing as it was nothing else in principle or quite simply to defend my life" and he established clearly the fact that his anti-communism was the main motive which pushed him to enlist and remain with the team till the end. He didn't fail to emphasize that 'he benefited many saving their lives and freedom'.[933] At his trial several of those he 'saved' responded to his plea and supported him. Kon. Kamisis from Asvestochori, a 54 year old rural guard, though submitted to sworn examination in December 1945, roamed Thessaloniki free until he was discovered by a Hortiati in December 1946, "I recognized him in the agency at Asvestochori, I arrested him and surrendered him to the Directorate of the Gendarmes".[934]

In his defence, Kamisis asserted that he was forced to enlist to the gang after the incident at Asvestochori on 26th July: "I followed Schubert out of fear as I didn't want to join the rebels and Schubert told us whoever wants to follow him will not be harmed".[935] He also claimed that he did not take part in the team's missions as Schubert did not consider him to be loyal to the gang. One from Asvestochori testified that Kamisis "was frivolous and got involved for booze and looting".[936] Kommatopoulos and Kamisis were sentenced to six years imprisonment.

The Schuberites in their defences generally argued that they were obliged by fear to enlist to Schubert's team. As reasons for their fear, they blamed either the ΕΛΑΣ and generally the communists or less frequently the Bulgarians who oppressed them, pursued them and threatened them with death (these cases applied only to the Macedons) or from fear of Schubert and his officials who, without reason, arrested them and threatened them with imprisonment or execution if they didn't agree to enlist. In certain cases, as with that of the youngsters I. Gridakis from Krousonas Crete and G. Xanthopoulos from Kalamaria Thessaloniki, known Schuberites deceived them with promises of money and other benefits.[937] Without exception, the detained Schuberites blamed fear and violence as the only incentives for their enlistment to the gang, evidently as a cheap excuse to alleviate their position as collaborators. Fear and violence though did not stand in the way over fifteen youngsters from three villages of western Halkidiki whom Schubert enlisted unwillingly. They managed to desert after a short stay with the gang.

The case of 26 year old from Katerini, Dionysi Batalas, can be described as exceptional. In October 1946 he ended up with Schuberites detained in the Pavlo Mela jails accused of "cooperation with the enemy done in Asvestochori and elsewhere in Macedonia".[938] More specifically Batalas was accused that at the incident of Asvestochori on 26th July he travelled to the Sanatorium and indicated to Schubert's officials which of the employees were communists, with the result that eleven of the 30 selected were executed, amongst them Panag. Tsagaris and Arist. Sakellaropoulos, both from the area of Pieria (Katerini). Batalas, as he himself mentions in his Memo before the bloody incident of 26th July, had gone to the Sanatorium with an ex captain friend, named Leviti, "to distance there some active and obtrusive communist officials, some of whom as originating from Katerini I would be able to point out to him".[939] This time Batalas intervened, so he says, so that several 'anarchical' individuals were saved. At his second visit to the Sanatorium on 26th July, the Kateriniotis offered his services and knowledge to the Schubert gang, indicating the wanted "communists". "Batalas came with others to the Sanatorium and arrested my husband", testified the widow of Tsagaris, an employee at the Sanatorium.[940]

The defence witness G. Pavlopoulos, porter at the Sanatorium, also confirmed Batalas' presence there; he claimed that Batalas intervened and saved his life and that of three other colleagues.

In the same Memo Batalas characterized the charge which the relatives of the victims brought against him "satanical fabrication against me bearing clearly the seal of communist plotting". Further, he argued that whilst the accusers Tsagaris and Sakellaropoulou "were duly poised by the communist organization", the prosecution witnesses G. Koulas and A. Fysikopoulos existed as bloodthirsty capetans of ΕΛΑΣ in the area of Katerini; they, along with two other anarchically inclined witnesses, "fabricated a classic type of slimy attack" of a nationalist. He also mentions that he pioneered the foundation of an anti-communist organization in Katerini, which over time was placed under "the divisions Kisa Batzak (Koukou). As organ of the aforementioned I received and possibly also executed German orders".[941] Batalas reinforced his Memo with a telegram plea sent to the Minister of Justice requesting "that the charge be reviewed by the Collaborators Committee of Thessaloniki" whilst as a nationalist he himself had been hunted and his 80 year old father "slaughtered by the enemy of the fatherland".[942] The court sentenced Batalas to one year in jail, the lightest sentence imposed on an accomplice of Schubert and the enemy. After a space of about a year the list of Schuberite accused nearly doubled. Three Schuberites in their depositions in 1946 gave the names of about 40 colleagues, adding evidence such as place of origin, position in the band and for some even their criminal activity.[943] In December 1946, the Special Commissioner of Thessaloniki, in the indictment he prepared for the hearing on 9th January 1947, which was finally postponed, drew up a list with 41 names of Schuberite accused of whom seven were already detained (two Cretans and five Macedons), 33 convicts (12 Cretans, 21 Macedons) and one woman not detained.

Those detained were not served with criminal charges but were generally accused that "they partook in a service by the occupying authorities and enlisted as soldiers in the Battalion of the German Schubert, by whom they were also armed and committed to the hunting and annihilation of all persons belonging to the National Resistance Organization or their colleagues, thus becoming the cause of the death of many Greeks".[944] The most famous Schuberites were convicts "prior residents of Asvestochori and already of unknown abode". The warrants for their arrest were sent to Asvestochori and later Hortiati. The scarce reports which the police divisions sent to the Special Court for the most part contained unreliable information about the wanted Schuberites. Indicatively the General Security Division of Thessaloniki in March 1948 – a month and a half after his final conviction – reports that L. Kommatopoulos "followed the German armies and is already situate in Germany!"[945]

Even worse, the gendarme's Administration of Drama in April 1951 certified that N. Mantzana, who in the meantime had married a policeman and resided in the village Konopina of Aitolokarnania, remained with Kapetanakis in Germany and that G. Tzoulias had escaped to America.[946] These constitute just a few of the many inaccuracies which the document contained about other Schuberites.

For the first time, after a written recommendation by the Special Commissioner, the three-member Special Appeal Assembly decided on 26th April 1947 to commit "before the courtroom of the Special Court as per article 9 A.N.533/45 the … ".[947] There follows a list of the names of 58 men and women of whom nine were detained and 49 were convicts (30 Macedons and 19 Cretans). The case file was based on questioning and particularly depositions of witnesses examined from Asvestochori (16 of total 32) Giannitsa, Hortiati, Karpi and Stathi – the last two villages lie on the eastern slopes of mount Paiko – and from villages of western Halkidiki. The villages lying on the southern side of lake Volvi were not represented. The Special Assembly ordered the continuation of the detention of accused and the arrest of the remaining "residents of Hortiati and already of unknown abode". It is not known whether the police authorities of Hortiati or Asvestochori, who took receipt of the arrest warrants, proceeded to take steps to locate and arrest the convicts.

During questioning in early 1946 the Schuberites St. Diktapanides and G. Xanthopoulos gave evidence, mostly inaccurate, about the places of origin of many of the Macedonian convicts as Koxenoglou, Tatoglou or Katoglou from Aravissos, D. Kosmides, N. Papadopoulos and Korkanidi from the area of Kilkis. Another Schuberite, St. Giannoglou from Nea Gonia, despite being questioned by the police division of Nea Kallikrateia in August 1946, remained free till his death in March 1952.[948]

The Schuberites convicted in absentia K. Domna from Komotini, G. Politis from Dravisko Serres, Chr. Tsakirides from Koudounies Drama, Pan. Kantartzides (correct Katirtzides) from Petralona Chalkidiki, G. Papoutsis and Vas. Papamanolis from the area of Drama and Dina Mantzana from Agrinio Aitolokarnanias, were arrested and detained during the period 1951–1952 but law 2058/1952 're pacification measures, allowed retroactive release and acquittal of those convicted of collaboration. It was then the "genuine nationalists" were released, as were the last accomplices of the enemy.[949] Indicatively, Mantzana was arrested in Agrinio and detained in the jails of Eptapyrgio on 9th September 1951 to be released after twenty days.[950]

When Chr. Tsakirides was finally arrested in 1969, the court barred his life term "because the decision was rendered unfulfilled and was barred completing twenty years".[951] Ant. Triantafyllides from Kavala, 18 years old, was arrested in Thessaloniki by EAM and imprisoned in a hostage camp of ΕΛΑΣ in Ardea (Aridaia) where, most likely early in 1945, he was executed along with other collaborators.[952]

Chr. Kyzirides and his colleague Andr. Xanthopoulos encountered the people's nemesis. They were arrested in Kalamaria and transported to Hortiati, where the enraged crowd observed their lynching in the central square of the village.[953] Finally, the process of Schubert's trial was set for 9th October 1947, a few days after his transfer to Thessaloniki.

As mentioned above, the attempt to try Schubert along with 58 men of his team did not succeed due to the court not having jurisdiction to adjudge his case. After his departure from the hall, it was discovered that a large number of prosecution witnesses were missing. Of the 42 summoned, only 16 appeared, most from Asvestochori. The notable absentee from the trial was Giannitsa. The climate of civil war created serious problems for those summoned to testify against collaborators and accomplices of the enemy. Aside from the fear that they could be characterized left wing or communists, the fact that many collaborators were either acquitted or released without serving their imposed sentence so as to become enlisted in various state services, particularly the army and security gangs, had a negative effect, with many not appearing at trials once summoned.[954]

The judges heard from 13 from Asvestochori a rehash of the same incidents and names; Schubert, Germanakis and Kapetanakis and more rarely Batalas. The 49 year old Nik. Boubousis appeared particularly frank in his testimony, saying that "of these present I remember no one save Kapetanakis and Germanakis. Germanakis did the killings".[955] Finally, Pan. Tzavaras, captain of the Aliens Division of Thessaloniki, gave the answer to the dilemma of the court, testifying that he had managed an inquiry into the case and recognized witnesses who could assist.

Then the president of the court interrupted the trial and postponed judgment "of the respective cases indefinitely until the summons and appearance of all witnesses mentioned in the indictment" and particularly those summoned from Giannitsa.

At the final trial, on 13th January 1948, the number of accused remained the same as in October 1947, that is 48 convicts and 10 detained as follows:

1) Lazaros Kommatopoulos of Savva, 29 years old, farmer, resident of Aravissos, Pella,
2) Eudoxia, wife of L. Kommatopoulos, 24 years old, housewife, resident of Aravissos,
3) Dionysios Batalas of Vasileios, 29 years old, farmer, resident of Katerini,
4) Georgios Xanthopoulos of Konstantinos, 23 years old, labourer, resident of Kalamaria Thessaloniki,
5) Konstantinos Kamisis of Evangelos, 57 years old, labourer, resident of Aravissos,
6) Ioannis Gridakis of Philip, 20 years old, tailor, resident of Krousonas Heraklion,

7) Dimitrios Alatzas of Ioannis, 25 years old, farmer, resident of Kyrianna Rethymnon,
8) Stylianos Diktapanides of Dimitrios, 45 years old, tobacco producer, resident of Kallifyto Drama,
9) Georgios Koutoudis, rural police, resident of Giannitsa,
10) Anastasia, wife of G. Koutoudis, housewife, resident of Giannitsa.

For the defence of the present accused six lawyers were appointed and 17 defence witnesses who, for the most part, testified in favour of D. Batalas and L. Kommatopoulos. Of the 23 prosecution witnesses half represented Asvestochori, a village which due to its proximity to Thessaloniki was always a supplier of a large number of witnesses whilst the remainder testified for Hortiati, Giannitsa and the villages Stathis and Karpi in the area of Goumenissa. At this trial, no witnesses came forth from the villages of west and north Halkidiki.[957]

As at the trial of October 1947, characteristic of the testimonies was the vagueness the lack of relevance and a tendency to standardize information. From the start it was clear that on this day Schubert and his close officials were being retried in absentia. Kommatopoulos was the contentious character. The witness Nik. Tomaras, a lawyer, was informed that "of the accused Kommatopoulos and Kapetanakis were the leaders of events at Hortiati"[958], contrarily the defence witness Pan. Varvarides from Nea Apollonia gave false evidence that L. Kommatopoulos at the incidents of Asvestochori and Hortiati "was to be found in N. Apollonia".[959] Of interest is the remark of St. Triantafyllides from Giannitsa about Kommatopoulos that, whilst present at the slaughter of Giannitsa, "he did not take part in the executions", also about Koutoudis that "from fear he enlisted to Schubert's battalion as he was threatened with execution by the Germans".[960] Particularly noticeable is the tendency of the prosecution witnesses to provide favourable evidence to Schuberites known to them or compatriots who didn't belong to Schubert's immediate circle. Again, other witnesses felt the need to make a comment about one of the accused present, albeit the remark was a generalization or was vague. One from Asvestochori added that G. Xanthopoulos "wore a uniform and weapon" and guarded the prisoners whilst another tried to blame everyone saying: "the accused, present or not, were all there at the place of execution".[961]

As the witnesses were not clear, specific and decisive they created an uneasiness within the court and the agitation of the president of the Special Court Manesi who, in disappointment, announced: "we want evidence to accuse someone".[962] It was a 'ghost trial', as described by a journalist as it developed into a parade of names of absent accused. In the end, the accused denied the charges on must points and counsel requested the acquittal of their clients. The court issued its number 2 decision according to which the following Schuberites present were deemed punishable: L. Kommatopoulos, K. Kamisis and D. Alatzas to six years imprisonment, I. Gridakis to three years imprisonment, St. Diktapanides to two and a half years imprisonment, G. Xanthopoulos to two years imprisonment, and last D. Batalas to one year imprisonment. (As he had been detained for over a year, he was free immediately) All accused were deprived of their civil rights for life. G. Koutoudis, his wife Anastasia and Eudoxia Kommatopoulos were deemed innocent due to doubtful evidence.

Convicted in absentia to death were G. Germanakis, G. Kapetanakis, Kon. Economakis and G. Tzoulias from Crete, to life imprisonment the Cretans Ant. Mylonas, Nik. Halianakis (correct Hanialakis), Dim. Kouluris, and the Macedonian St. Giannoglou. The rest, about 70% of the accused, were sentenced to six years imprisonment and deprivation of their civil rights for life.

These were the Cretans G. Karellis, Dim. Koinakis, G. Belivasakis (correct Belibasakis) G. Maravelakis, Math. Mouskouras, G. Kastanakis, Nik. Kantzalakis (correct Katsalakis), Dim. Christodoulakis, Nik. Manousakis, Drakos Pirounakis, Emm. Avgoustakis, and Eleft. Petromanolakis and the Macedons Konstantina (Dina) Mantzana, Ioan. Lazaris or Lazarides, Ioan. Korchanides, Dim. Kosmides, Chr. Kyzirides, Chr. Tsakirides, Pan. Kantartzides (correct Katirtzides), Ioan. Salpasides (probably Salpatsides or Salpahtsides) with his sons Christos and Vasileios, Chr. Tatoglou or Katoglou, Prodr. Koxenoglou, Stavros Giannoglou, Kon. Konstantinou with his wife and brothers Nik. Konstantinou and Geor. Konstantinou, Nik. Papanikolaou, Kon. Domna (Thomnas) or Donos, Vas. Papamanolis, G. Varveris, G. Politis, G. Papoutsis, Kyros Grammatikopoulos, Nik. Papadopoulos, Andr. Xanthoulis or Xanthopoulos, Dion. Haralambous and Dim. Papastoios.[963]

It is worth noting that the court placed 38 of the aforementioned Schuberites under one umbrella and convicted them with the same sentence on the basis that they all had similar criminal history. Whilst the present sources don't assist in determining the extent of each one's guilt, they do define the distinction of one small group with criminal activities in their records. To this group belonged the Cretans D. Christodoulakis, Nik. Manousakis, G. Belibasakis, E. Petromanolakis, D. Avgoustakis, D. Pirounakis, N. Hanialakis and G. Maravelakis and of the Macedons K. Grammatikopoulos, N. Papadopoulos, and P. Koxenoglou. Undoubtedly their punishment according to their activities should have been much more severe. In fact, the sentence imposed by the Special Court of Heraklion for their activities in Crete was death for the first seven of the group and 20 years imprisonment for Maravelakis.[964]

Crete: Justice and Punishment

The information that the collaborators' court documents in the municipality of Heraklion had been destroyed[965] by order of the magistrate Avgoulea made the search at Heraklion futile. For this reason, it was difficult to determine the process of locating, arresting and trying the men who served in the Schubert gang. On the issue of pursuing and punishing the Schuberites, Crete differed greatly from Macedonia.

Firstly, the Schuberites in Crete, after the departure of the German forces from the island, could not argue, as the Macedons, that they were working with the enemy to fight communism. So, unlike what happened in Macedonia and other parts of mainland Greece, the collaborators did not enjoy the same protection by state bodies and their compatriots. The Cretans nurtured untamed hatred against the "Gestapo", as they usually named the Schuberites, and generally the collaborators. The mania of the clan leaders against the accomplices is explained in part by their attempt to reinstate their patriotism which the premature founding of Schubert's gang with Greeks had seriously hindered. Secondly after the liberation in many villages of Crete the resistors bypassed the judicial process and adopted the traditional law of vendetta to punish many of the Schuberites. Third, the Cretans, particularly in the villages around Heraklion, were able with more certainty to identify, name and relate to the criminal activities of far more Schuberites than the Macedons. The explanation lies mainly in the fact that about 70% of the Schuberites were enlisted from Krousonas (45%), from the city of Heraklion and from few villages of the provinces of Malevizi and Monofatsi. It would be very difficult for a Schuberite to hide on Cretan soil.

The case of the young I. Gridakis is interesting, as he himself gave detailed information to the Special Commissioner of Thessaloniki in his deposition in May 1946. His comments describe an individual who, to avoid punishment, resorted to irrational behaviour. It is worth noting that his fanatically Germanophile father, Philip, had dressed him early on in Hitler's uniform as he was destining him to join the German army.[966] According to his testimony, his compatriot G. Tzoulias influenced him at the age of 16 to enlist to the Schubert gang to "earn an adequate income" as a tailor.[967] Truly throughout his term Gridakis was used as a tailor but for a long period he performed the duties of footman to Schubert. He followed Schubert as far as Yugoslavia where, along with other Schuberites, he enlisted to the gang of the nationalist leader Draza Mihajlovic and in 1945 returned to Greece via the International Red Cross. Finally returning to Crete after the departure of the German forces, Gridakis was arrested and in February 1946 brought to trial. One of the defence witnesses was Aristodimos Mihelidakis from Krousonas, a rebel of ΕΛΑΣ who testified that Gridakis has been imprisoned by ΕΛΑΣ along with other Schuberites in the hotel "Berlin" awaiting trial as a Gestapo.[968]

Fortunately, Mihelidakis intervened and reassured the officials of ΕΛΑΣ saying that he did not think that (Gridakis) had "done anything in Crete"[969] and so saved him from likely execution. After his conviction in Heraklion, he was transferred to Thessaloniki where he was confronted with the possibility of a second trial without the support of the witnesses he had in Crete and to prove his innocence he thought up the following story: he argued that he deserted in the summer of 1944 from Schubert's gang and went to Thessaloniki where he found work in the tailor's of his" compatriot Emmanouil Mantidakis, Ermou 4". Again, according to him, during the EAM reign he was discovered by EAM in Thessaloniki and threatened with trial as a rebel. As he insisted that he had harmed no one "ΕΛΑΣ roamed him round different villages where Poulos (Schubert) division was active to recognize him". Upon ascertaining that no villager recognized him to incriminate him, he was set free.[970] The story of Gridakis' roaming, apart from sounding unlikely, has common elements with the story of his arrest by ΕΛΑΣ in Crete.[971] As previously mentioned, Gridakis was sentenced to three years imprisonment by the Special Collaborators Court of Thessaloniki.

The 20 year old Dim. Alatzas from Kyrianna Rethymnon, in his attempt to justify his enlistment to the Schubert gang, related two versions as regards the motives which pushed him to dress as a Schuberite. When in July 1946 he first appeared before the Special Court, he narrated the issue of his enlistment in general terms as it happened: in the autumn of 1943 after a row with his father, he moved to Heraklion to find work.

At the cafe where unemployed people often assembled, a man from Heraklion approached him; Antonis Mylonas, a Schuberite, as he later discovered, and he suggested he follow him if he wanted to serve in the Gendarmes to crack down on black market trade. He led him to the offices of the German police where he introduced him to Schubert and his officials as a newly selected member of the gang. After being detained a few days, Alatzas dressed in German uniform and later followed Schubert to Macedonia.[972]

In May 1947 with the flames of civil war blazing, Alatzas, locked up in the Pavlo Melas jail, did what many other Macedonian Schuberite colleagues did; that is, he used communism as an excuse to justify his enlistment to Schubert's gang and so withdrew his previous statement to better his treatment in the pending trial. In his memo to the Special Assembly, he fabricated the following incident: from his village he went to Heraklion to find work. On the way someone asked to see his identification: "he reckoned I was a suspicious active communist or anarchist and ordered me to follow him to his office. There I was placed before Schubert. After questioning me as a suspicious foreigner in those parts he threatened he would lock me in his jailhouse unless I accepted to enlist to his gang in the pursuit of the black-market trade."[973]

He then dressed in German uniform and was armed. Note that the checks of identification of travellers, wayward peddlers and others suspected of being communists or liaisons of the rebels was a trusted method used by the battalion in Macedonia. Alatzas adapted this tactic to himself, alleging duress as the reason for his enlistment.

It is not clear whether Alatzas was convicted by the Special Court of Rethymnon, but in a court document of 1945 he is named as 'a collaborator'. Following decree, he was moved to Thessaloniki and after questioning in December 1946 committed to trial. However, a few days before the trial on 13th January 1948, the Rethymnon court, by its decision of 9th January, acquitted Alatzas of all charges.[974] The respective court in Thessaloniki after receiving the decision for unknown reason lifted the charge and conviction of Alatzas and ordered his release. On 2nd March 1948, Alatzas was set free after serving only a small part of his six-year imprisonment.[975]

Almost all the Schuberites arrested and detained were tried before the Special Collaborators Court of Heraklion. From recorded testimonies, Eleftherios Kallergis or Skolindakis, a 33 year old priest from Keramoutsi Malevizi, was one of the first to be detained in November 1944.[976]

In the summer of 1945, Haralambos Steiakakis was detained, a resident of Avgeniki who was charged that "dressed with German army uniform he transported men of Schubert's hunting gang to respective arrests and executions of Greeks patriots".[977] All witnesses agree that Steiakakis was enlisted as a driver of a requisitioned vehicle to enable him to maintain his family and that the rebels did not execute him as he was of limited intellectual capacity. He was convicted to imprisonment 12-year time. At around the same time, the cases of five Heraklian Schuberites were tried in absentia: Nik. Moukouna (also Mouskouras) from Chryssavgi, suburb of Heraklion, Ioan. Markopoulos, Geor. Papadakis, Ioan. Manousakis also from Chryssavgi and Dim. Antonakakis. Of the four prosecution witnesses one was a Schuberite, G. Karellis, and another, Miltiades Drosos, a collaborator from Heraklion. All witnesses restricted themselves to generalizations and standardized phrases that the accused were dressed in German uniform and took part in executions, looting and raids on different villages of Crete. On 24th November 1945, they were sentenced to death.[978]

The 20 year old Ioan. Fil. Ieronymides from Krousonas was detained in October 1945. For unknown reasons, Ieronymides, along with Kallergis, was detained until March 1948 when they were tried with other Schuberites. The 23 year old Georgios Karellis from Heraklion was the first known Schuberite to be convicted in 1945 to life imprisonment, with the charge that he effected "arrests, abuse and executions" of citizens.[979]

As aforementioned, the 18 year old Ioan. Gridakis in February 1946 was convicted by the Special Court of Heraklion to three years imprisonment. Immediately after his conviction, the court ordered the transfer of Gridakis and Karellis to Thessaloniki to be tried for crimes committed in Macedonia.[980] As Karellis had been chosen as a defence witness in Schubert's trial, he was held in the Chania jail without finally being transferred to Thessaloniki. Finally, Nikolaos Manousakis had become "an organ of the Germans at Larani Monofatsi" prior to his enlistment to the Schubert gang, which he later followed to Macedonia. Manousakis belonged to the close circle of Schubert, performed the duties of a medic and committed numerous crimes. In March 1946, for his activities in Crete he was sentenced to death by the Special Court of Heraklion and in absentia to six years imprisonment in January 1948 by the respective court of Thessaloniki.[981] It is unknown why Manousakis was not transferred to Thessaloniki though his name appears early on in the lists of the Thessaloniki Court. He is the only one who appears to have been executed by the Greek state.[982]

The judicial authorities of Heraklion drew up a list of 22 Schuberites from the municipality of Heraklion whom they committed to trial on 23rd November 1946. Eleven of these were sentenced in absentia to death: Georgios Tzoulias, Dimitrios Tzoulias (probably Stylianos Tzoulias as Dimitrios does not exist) Konst. Axotakis, Georgios Frangiadakis, Ioannis Papamanousakis (the same person with Ioanni Evag. Manousakis executed in Macedonia), Dimitrios Belibasakis (possibly the same with

Georgios Belibasakis also active in Macedonia), Emmanouil Aplatanakis, Demetrios Kontaxakis, Stylianos Axantonakis, Matthaios Xystrakis and Iraklis Protogerakis.

Of the Schuberites present they convicted Ioannis Katriadakis to death, Christos Andrigiannakis, Evangelos Nikolaidis, Stavros Syntihakis to life imprisonment, Georgios Maravelakis to 20 years limited imprisonment, Konstantinos Papamathiadakis to 15 years limited imprisonment and Stavros Bairactaris to five years imprisonment "for national unworthiness". Ioannis Aplanatakis, Ioanni Pangalos Menelaos Saridakis and Niki Voulgaris were acquitted. A journalist noted that for some accused the "decision seemed exceptionally lenient by the general opinion"[983] and that H. Andrigiannakis and K. Papamathaiakis were roaming free in their village (probably Tympaki Mesara) until the day of the trial. At least 50% of the named 'Schuberites' in a relative press article are totally unknown to other sources and this raises suspicion that some of these don't satisfy the criteria to be described as Schuberites. They may simply have been acting as accomplices or organs of Schubert and the Germans.

The largest and last trial of Schuberites was conducted on 30th March 1948 before the Special Collaborators Court of Chania. The Court decision named 14 detained and 21 Cretan convicts who served Schubert either armed or informers.

The indictment which does not differ from that of the Special Court of Thessaloniki is as follows: "spurred by common gain they have confessed to each other their mutual involvement during the period of the enemy occupation, undertaking service to the occupying authorities and acting in an oppressive way for the people, these who enlisted in the division of the German Officer Schubert, armed by him they took part in endless executions of Greek patriots and facilitated the cause of the occupation".[984]

The Special Court of Chania tried the case of the 35 Schuberites based on the committal Decree 239 of 1947 of the Special Court of Heraklion. It is not known for what reasons the Heraklion Assembly transferred jurisdiction to the respective court of Chania though all the accused were residents of Heraklion. In all probability the transfer of the trial to Chania was decided for security reasons to avoid the slaughter of the accused by relatives of victims and fanatic activists, as occurred at the trial of the Somaraki collaborators from the village of Sarhos Heraklion.[985]

For the division of liability and respective sentences of the accused, the court categorized the crimes into two main groups: 1) undertaking service for account of the enemy and 2) executing violent acts against the Greek people punishable according to law 533/1945 and amendments of 1946. Seven of the detainees were deemed innocent due to doubts: Dimitrios Vas. Kapsalis, 32 years old from Anogeia Alexandros Emm. Amargianatakis, 28 years old, former policeman from Heraklion and the Krousaniotes Stavros Geor. Tzoulias, 34 years old, Ioannis Nik. Makatounis or Tzoutzouroukos, 70 years old, Evangelos Ioan. Makatounis or Tzoutzouroukos, 20 years old, Antonios Emm. Kokolakis, 27 years old and Ioannis Fil. Gridakis 20 years old.

The last had been convicted earlier at Heraklion and Thessaloniki, but submitted a plea to be released before serving the remaining time of his sentence. The court acquitted Ioan. and Evag. Makatounis, father and son, Stavros Tzoulias and surprisingly I. Gridakis from the charge that they served in the Schubert gang in uniform and took part in executions of citizens.[986] Gridakis' acquittal was possibly due to his declarations that he was intending to enlist to the Greek campaign assembling at that time to be dispatched to Korea. He was killed in Korea.

The crimes which appear to have been committed by D. Kapsalis, Ant. Kokolakis and Alex. Amargianitakis were generally denouncing patriots. Save for Gridakis the other six were not uniformed Schuberites but collaborator accomplices.

On the remaining seven detainees the court imposed heavy fines. The priest Eleftherios Kallergis was sentenced to death for acts of violence against the Greek people and 20 years limited imprisonment for undertaking duties "by the enemy". First and foremost, Kallergis became one of the close associates of the despised Hartmann, "he was registered to Hartmann's intelligence and espionage services and equipped with identification signed by Hartmann".[987] Then papa-Lefteris armed and German clad followed Schubert in raids against civilians and took part in executions even of women as at Kali Sykia and Kallikratis. Further, he was deemed guilty of the charges that in cooperation with other Schuberites in 1943 he brought on the death of 11 Krousonas patriots.[988]

The same sentence was imposed also on Georgios Mic. Anastasakis, 27 years old, from Stavrakia Malevizi and Pavlo Nik. Syngelaki, 29 years old, from Kato Viannos. Emmanouil Ioan. Spanakakis, 24 years old, from Gagales Monofatsi and the Krousonas Ioannis Fil. Ieronymides were sentenced to life imprisonment for violent acts and 20 limited years for undertaking service for the enemy. The charge against Ieronymides that along with other Schuberites in August 1944 he took part in the execution of 15 men from the village of Sarchos Malevizi has particular interest as regards its reliability. The judicial decision names 19 companions of Ieronymides who allegedly took part in the execution squad on the 22nd August 1944.[989] Of these, 13 co-accused had absolutely nothing to do with these executions as from early 1944 they were absent from Crete in Macedonia, whilst the other six were convicts. The young Ieronymides was the only one present at the trial. There is however the detailed testimony of the captain of the Military Police of Heraklion, Richard Haar, relating to the execution of the 15 Sarhos, who stated that the executions were decided and conducted at Sisarcha by a German squad under the orders of captain Ipten who took part during this period in the destruction of Anogeia.[990]

Last of all, Savvas Evag. Koutantos, 40 years old, president during the occupation of the village of Kamari Malevizi doesn't appear to have been a uniformed Schuberite, rather a trusted accomplice of "the Tzoulias, of Schubert and the organs of the Gestapo". He was arrested and detained in Heraklion in December 1944 and committed to trial with the charges that "he became a conscious organ of the enemy to promote his propaganda highlighting the cause of the occupier; he also conducted a memorial for the German fallen at Stalingrad and provided the enemy systematically information about individuals and organizations".[991] He was punished with 20 years' imprisonment as a denouncer and propagandist. The last convicted to temporary sentence of 27 years was named Nikolaos Mic. Haralambakis, 30 years old, from Komes Pediados, whose relationship with the Schubert gang is not clarified in the court documents. Haralambakis was deemed responsible for the imprisonment and abuse of a resistor's family from Kato Symi Viannos and for the brutal looting of his property.[992]

The most notorious Schuberites, all uniformed and armed, and accused of heinous crimes were convicted to death in absentia. The prizes go to seven from Krousonas, the hard nucleus of the gang serving Schubert from the beginning of his professional career in Crete in June 1942: Georgios Mic. Tzoulias, Stylianos Mic. Tzoulias, Dimitrios Mic. Christodoulakis or Stivaktakis, Ioannis Kon. Epanomeritakis or Koutoutos, Haralambos Dr. Agiomyrgianakis, Stergios Nik. Agiomyrgianakis and Emm. Makatounis or Tzoutzouroukos. The remaining 14 absent accused originated either from Heraklion: Georgios Kokkinis or Athinaios, Ioannis Kambas or "Turk" Ioannis Mouskouras, Ioannis Evag. Manousakis (Chrysopygi) or other villages of the municipality of Heraklion: Georgios Ioan. Ambadianakis and Emmanouil Avgoustakis from Stavrakia Malevizi, Georgios Ioan. Savoidakis from Megali Vrysi Malevizi, Drakos Pyrounakis from Gagales Monofatsi, Emmanouil Mic. Aplanatakis, Eleftherios Petromanolakis and Nikolaos Hanialakis from Garipa Monofatsi, Georgios Romanos and Grigoris Ant. Goumenakis from Agious Deka Kainourio and Georgios Ioan. Germanakis from Miamou Kainourio.

All the accused were sentenced twice to death for cooperation with the enemy and acts of violence against citizens. The court separated G. Tzoulias, I. Epanomeritakis and G. Savoidakis upon whom they imposed triple death sentences "for acts of denouncing Greek citizens to the enemy".[993] All three, but mainly G. Tzoulias with Savoidakis, through different periods of the Occupation denounced to Schubert and the Germans about 230 persons, many of whom were abused, imprisoned, banished or even executed, "and their villages wholly or partially torched and demolished by the Germans".

The denouncing of 117 persons only from Anogeia Mylopotamos are mentioned who played a part in the horrific destruction of the village on August 13th 1944.[994]

The decision of the Special Court of Chania leaves no area of doubt that the most crimes were committed by the trio from Krousonas: G. Tzoulias, D. Christodoulakis and I. Epanomeritakis.

They were convicted that along with other Schuberites they had a role in the execution of about 100 citizens, men and women, in different villages of Heraklion and Rethymnon during the most bloodstained period of activity of the squad during the last four months of 1943.

In their history, aside from executions, are listed terrorizing of villages, threats, torture, snitching, imprisonment and blackmail of citizens, looting properties and torching of homes.[995] It is worth noting that none of the above convicted served the sentenced time. After the Civil War, those still imprisoned were released and many were rewarded by the state in civil or military positions.

The end of the blood circle at Krousonas

Haralambos Giannadakis, one of the clan leaders of the team "Satana" in his memoirs, which he wrote non sine ira et odio (not without anger and hatred) against his Schuberite and Gestapo compatriots, admits that "from the many crimes of the enemy all us rebels of Crete hardened to adopt similar reprisals".[996] The decisions on collaborators' executions were taken quickly, "then we had given orders to the rebel courts and they shot without too many procedures. So, we raised the courage and morale of the people of Crete. At the various executions of traitors we gave them favours, as we say 'option', in other words to choose themselves in what way they wanted their death sentence".[997] Indeed the 'capetan' himself revealed that the rebel teams of Heraklion, after the departure of the Germans from the city on 12th October 1944, had decided to enter the prisons where around 400 collaborators were held to execute them on the spot.

The secret was exposed and the Military Command of the island obstructed their plan.[998]

Of the 46 from Krousonas who were associated in any way with Schubert and the Germans, only six were tried by an official court whilst the rest who were arrested became victims of the rage and vengeance of their compatriots. (v. Appendix II, Table A) When some rebels from Anogeia up in the hills wished to tease their Cretan colleagues saying: "you still have a lot of work to do yet down in Krousonas" they received the reply: "We've killed ours and killed them over again but yours you haven't been able to kill them the first time or the second",[999] meaning the collaborators of Anogeia in comparison to the Krousonas were few.

The vengeance turned particularly against the Tzoulias, resulting in their family being wiped out in entirety. Today the name Tzoulias has almost disappeared from Crete. The decimation began with the innocent and infirm. At Giofirakia the rebels slaughtered the elderly Sofia, wife of the already murdered president Michael Tzoulias and mother of the Tzoulias, together with their 16 year old son Ioanni and her grandchildren "in their grandma's apron". Of her daughters, Styliani, the fiancé of Kon. Makatounis the Krousonas rebels first raped her, they transported her to the village cemetery, where they ripped her stomach "and threw her still alive onto the melting pot of the cemetery".[1000] Another sister they executed after first abusing her. Nikolaos, the eldest of the five sons of Michail Tzoulias, was the recognized head of the family and of the Germanophiles of Krousonas.

Whilst counted amongst the Schuberites, he never wore German uniform nor took part in raids and as per common admission never took out a gun to kill someone but "functioned in the Schubert gang from above, as a coordinator, adviser and snitch".[1001] Nonetheless he was considered the most dangerous collaborator of all the Schuberites and Gestapo due to his close cooperation with persons in high places in the German service of espionage – counterintelligence of Heraklion and particularly the notorious commandant of the 3rd Office major Hartmann. He was also known amongst the high echelons of Cretan administration and society in Heraklion. About him Schubert himself testified in 1945 that "the general informer of the Germans and cooperating with Hartmann was Nikos Tzoulias, resident of Hrysonos".[1002]

Nikolaos Tzoulias, after the departure of the German armies from Heraklion in mid October 1944, for his own safety, settled in Athens hosted by his compatriot Troulinos from Heraklion. After the liberation of Crete in May 1945, Tzoulias was arrest after being denounced by his own landlord. Whilst being transported in handcuffs to Heraklion for questioning and trial, two Cretans boarded the ship "and fired two bullets, one in the chest and one in the temple".[1003]. He was murdered – they say by one Krousonas St. Fountoulakis, nephew of general G. Fountoulakis, the Military Administrator of Crete in 1945 – to stop him revealing known names who played the activists and highly placed individuals who communicated with the German Hartmann.[1004]

Capetan Giannadakis pursued his enemies with fanaticism and pride and when he surprised them, apart from his revolver he used his knife with which he beheaded his victims to show vengeance and brutality. The capetan gives a detailed description of how, on 15th September 1944 he managed, defying the danger of the German guards, to enter a tavern at "Tambakaria-Stomio" west of Heraklion. There the hefty Schuberite Manolis Makatounis or Tzoutzouroukos, known also as "Bagolas" was drinking: "So carrying my revolver in my pocket I entered and with a leap I'm standing on the table opposite the traitor. He pulls his revolver but doesn't have the time to use it as he was first hit by me with a bullet in his head. We struggled, he was wounded and I grabbed my knife and slaughtered him. The traitor gurgled with his head cut off".[1005] Then he carried Makatounis' head and hung it at Metohi of Georgios Grigorakis at the place where they say Makatounis had executed him on 10th September 1943.[1006] Later his head was placed at the church of Agios Haralambos at Krousonas 'so the souls (of the victims) could see it and rest in peace'.[1007]

Giannadakis' act inspired one rebel to write a song which the rebels of the Satana team sang: "Giannadakis we want the Reaper (of Death) with a cleaver to cut the heads of Gestapo night and day".[1008]

From the family of Emm. Makatounis or Tzoutzouroukos the rebels of Krousonas spared the life of his wife; not however his sons, the seven-year-old Philip and the fifteen-year-old Ioanni, at whose execution their mother was present at the Bodosaki school of Heraklion, which was at that time used as a collaborators' jailhouse. Of the younger brothers of Emm. Makatounis, the Krousonas executed in cold blood Stylianos, 22 years old, Konstantinos, 30 years old, Nikolaos, 32 years old and Haralambos, 34 years old.[1009] The only ones who managed to escape from the Krousonas' gun or knife were the relatives of Makatounis Ioanni, 67 years old and Evangelos, 25 years old, father and son who were discovered in their hideout and were surrendered to the judicial authorities. In November 1945, they were committed to trial with the charges that they undertook services under Major Hartmann and committed endless crimes, such as denouncing seven residents of the village Kalesa, blackmail and endless looting of villagers, abuse and executions of patriots. Specifically, the monk Agathaggelos Stratakis testified that the accused, as Schuberites, forced him to surrender his weapon and in turn transported him to Heraklion before Schubert who pitied him and set him free.

Another witness reported the blackmail of villagers of Kalesa by Evangelos Makatounis to enlist to Schubert's gang.[1010] Whilst both (Makatounis) were sentenced to death, they remained in jail until July 1947 when they were committed again to trial by the decision of the Special Court of Heraklion. At the final trial in March 1948 the Special Court of Chania totally unexpectedly relieved them of all charges and acquitted them.[1011] During the period of eight months which passed from the issue of the decision in July 1947 until the execution of the final trial, the civil war – possibly other factors – was a historical coincidence which contributed to the acquittal of the two Krousonas and also the release later of all the accused Schuberites and their accomplices.

The third Krousonas family which supported Schubert with four members was that of Ioanni Makridakis. His children, Emmanouil, 25 years old, Georgios or 'Manaras' and Nikolaos or 'Italos', 29 years old, served under Schubert in Crete. Emmanouil and Georgios were arrested in December 1943 by rebels of the Bantouvas clan, were beaten up badly and, bloodied from knife wounds, were transported to the area of Larani, southeast of Heraklion, and thrown into a ditch, in fact a 'bottomless hole' to lose all trace. Emmanouil died on the spot but Georgios managed, notwithstanding the knife wounds and injuries from the sides of the ditch, to climb out and was taken to the nearest German hospital of Ambelouzo, where he was treated and lived to an old age "with the marks of the knives around his abdomen".[1012]

The third brother, Nikolaos, though in German uniform, was arrested by the Germans for some serious wrongdoing (probably theft of skins or meat) and dispatched in 1944 to Mauthausen where he became "smoke and ashes".[1013]

Another two Krousonas were executed violently by men of the Allied division of intelligence at their hideout on Psiloritis. Nik. Baltzakis had been sent to the Middle East where he was trained by the English as a saboteur. Upon returning in late autumn 1943, his relatives persuaded him to jump camp and dress as a Schuberite.[1014] Agents of the Allied division managed in June 1943 to trick Baltzakis and his companion Milt. Katsalakis and led them in uniform and armed into the lion's den, the hideout of the rebels of Psiloritis. Whilst Baltzakis was looking up high for the British aircraft to appear with supplies, unsuspecting, he was shot in the back of his head by three Cretans. The Briton John Lewis surreptitiously killed Katsalakis with a quick head lock, breaking his neck and causing an instantaneous death.[1015]

Schuberite fugitives overseas

Most Schuberites who fled outside Greece, whether following Schubert or the German armies during their departure from Greece, for the most part returned to

Greece during different periods of time. Indicatively, around 30 Schuberites who escaped from Schubert to Croatia, nine months later crossed the Greek border pretending to be unemployed workers from Germany, without being submitted to even basic controls. It is not known what happened to the remaining, approximately 30, Schuberites, whom Schubert placed in a German work camp when in February 1945 he arrived in Vienna. It is substantiated however that four "prominent" Krousonas Schuberites: Stylianos Tzoulias, Ioannis Epanomeritakis or Koutoutos, Stergios and Haralambos Agiomyrgianakis, at least till 1948 resided in the city of Dortmund, Schubert's birthplace, at the address to which Tzoulias in his letter asked that they write to him.[1016] For their arrest and extradition, the Ministry of Justice sent, in March 1948, a respective document to the Ministry of Foreign Affairs. A year later no evidence that any action had been taken by the Ministry was given to the British authorities under whose control the area of Westfalen was administratively run. I. Epanomeritakis was the only one of the team who returned later to Greece, was arrested in Athens and in turn convicted in Chania to 16 years imprisonment.

From the jails of Corfu, after the threat against his life by one Ant. Xylouris, he was moved to Patras jail where this time the communists tried to kill him, but Chronis Kalyvianakis from Livadia Mylopotamos intervened and saved him.[1017] Possibly to purge himself of his criminal acts, after his release he denied worldly affairs and became a monk at the monastery of Agios Panteleimon on Agio Oros where he passed away in 2009.

Of the other fugitives, Styl. Tzoulias lived the rest of his life in Germany whilst his brother Georgios Tzoulias seems to have settled in Belgium where he also died.[1018] The brothers Nikolaos and Dimitrios Mathaiakis from Elia Pediados, Heraklion, fled to the eastern tip of Africa to the hamlet Muhoroni in Kenya.[1019]

Georgios Kapetanakis was one of the select members in the close circle of Schubert in Macedonia. According to the testimony of Mantzana, Kapetanakis carried "the rank of sergeant and was deputy to Schubert".[1020] He and G. Germanakis were the most bloodthirsty perpetrators of Schubert's orders and during the absence of their chief they had the right of life and death over their victims. In Macedonia, Kapetanakis became well known, particularly for the torture to which he submitted persons he deemed suspect. For his crimes he was sentenced to death in absentia by the Special Courts of Chania[1021] and Thessaloniki[1022].

Just before his extradition by the Greek authorities from Italy where he had fled in 1945, suffering from depression, he committed suicide on 4th May 1949, falling from a window of the clinic where he was being treated at the Lipari islands (Aeolian) north of Sicily.

Kapetanakis, the son of Panayiotis and Maria, was born in 1907 in the village Moulete (today's Chryssavgi) Kissamo around 60 kilometres west of Chania. At this village in May 1941, the villagers killed German parachutists and secretly buried them outside their village. In November of 1943, G. Kapetanakis, 36 years old, "was a loser, clever but a traitor. He always got involved in quarrels and caused problems with the locals. Unmarried, he lived with his parents and worked on the family fields. His brother Yiannis, a resistor, nearly killed him to save the village".[1023] His cantankerous ways were, it seems, the main reason to provoke his distancing and the aversion of his compatriots whom to avenge he denounced to the German service of espionage-counter espionage of Chania that they killed the parachutists during the Battle of Crete. On 19th November a German force surrounded the village, assembled the residents and asked them to reveal the spot of the mass grave and those responsible for the murder of the parachutists. As everyone remained silent, the Germans selected 25 men and four women, whom they transported to the Agia jails where during questioning they submitted them to harsh torture to confess. The women yielded and admitted that the 'patriots' and not the residents killed the parachutists. Finally, on 14th December, from the selected men the German Court Martial sentenced three to death: Nikolaos K. Kouridakis, president of the community Vardi G. Kouridakis, rural police and Dimitrios Andr. Kouridakis, secretary. Two men and one woman were sent to the concentration camp of Mauthausen from where only the woman later returned. The Kouridakis were executed above the graves of the parachutists.[1024]

During the events at Moulete it is reported that Kapetanakis, "during the process of questioning by the Germans himself badly tortured Greek prisoners"[1025] To save himself from the rage of his compatriots he enlisted to Schubert's gang and "left early for Heraklion, otherwise we'd have killed him".[1026]

After Schubert's departure from Crete early in January 1944, Kapetanakis is not mentioned as having taken part in the gang's raids on villages of Heraklion or elsewhere in Crete. Note he was the only notorious Schuberite from the municipality of Chania. In Macedonia, during the reorganization of the team, Schubert promoted Kapetanakis to the position of deputy and 30 year old G. Germanakis, also newly selected, to the position of the most loyal execution staff, whilst the veterans Krousonas G. Tzoulias and D. Christodoulakis remained in lower ranks. After his criminal doings in Northern Greece, Kapetanakis "moved to Italy from where he sent a letter to his compatriot and successor Antoni Botonaki. The letter was submitted to the Appeal Magistrate to request respectively his extradition".[1027] Following measures by the diplomatic representatives of the Ministry of Foreign Affairs, the Italian police, in September 1947, arrested Kapetanakis in the city of Bari where he had married an Italian from a Cretan mother with whom he had one daughter. In turn, he was locked up in the "concentration camp of foreign refugees"[1028] at the Lipari islands until his case for extradition was tried by the Rome Appeals court. Whilst still detained in the camp he attempted to try his hand again as an informant, denouncing this time Greek 'communists' he met at the camp.

So, in April 1948 he sent to the Greek Government Commission in Bari a terribly incoherent letter in which he named detainees as 'red snitches' and advised them to request more details about their past from the Piraeus Police Directorate.[1029] Evidently with this letter Kapetanakis tried to win favours from the Greek authorities, hoping that his anti-communist inclination would help his case in a very critical period of the civil war. As the time for his extradition approached and his anti-communism did not meet the anticipated reaction, his depression deteriorated to such an extent as to lead him to suicide.

So closes a page from the dramatic period of the German occupation of Greece, at the centre of which was the brutal and criminal character of Fritz Schubert and the activities of his underground gang which assembled from Greek accomplices of the Germans.

Acknowlegements

With many many thanks to Niki Karapiperi from our hometown Andros Island in Greece, who put me in touch with the Fotiou family. Alexandra Fotiou, the original Greek author's daughter and her family for encouraging and supporting me throughout my translation project. Eleftheria Velioti and Anna Pavlova whose patience and goodwill in formatting and the like was indispensable. Lastly, my wife, Rika and three children, Angelika, Alex and Nino for their youthful input on numerous occasions.

Most grateful to you all.

Notes

1. At football matches, the people of Chania often insult those from Heraklion calling them "Schuberite Kastrinians" (www.artablogs.gr). According to Panagiotis Mantakas from Chania (recorded telephone interview, Chania, 3.5.2008) "we call the Heraklians Schuberites". Interesting that in Cretan dialect 'schubero' means an 'animal, beast'. In villages in the region of Paggaio of Eastern Macedonia, the term, 'you act like Schuber' denotes a 'hard, revengeful, unrepentant person' v. Stratos Theocharis, recorded telephone interview, Vrasna, 9.3.2007.
2. Anonymous, "The bastards of Hitler who slaughtered with music", The Pontiki, 19.10.2006.
3. Mark Mazower, email to the author, 18th July 2001.
4. Nea newspaper, 23.9.1998.
5. Constantine Mamalakis, recorded telephone interview, Heraklion, 26.3.2005.
6. Panagiotis Lambrou. Email to the author, Heraklion, 10.6.2010.
7. Tasos Kostopoulos. https://www.goodreads.com/el/book/show/22845577.
8. Nicholas Fotiou. recorded interview, Marathousa, 14.8.1979.
9. John Tsolakis. recorded interview, Nea Apollonia, 14.8.1979.
10. Vaggelis Karamanolakis "Private and Public: the experience of Civil War Avgi, 20.9.2009.
11. Theofilos Tsolakis, recorded interview, Nea Apollonia, 16.6.1999.
12. Manolis Frangiadakis, private letter to the author, Heraklion, 18.12.2001.
13. Stratos N. Dordanas. The innocent blood. Retaliation of German Occupation authorities in Macedonia, 1941–1944, Athens, 2007.
14. Ibid. pages 24–25.
15. Thessalonikeon Polis. "Crime & Punishment: the 'Macedonian' Frits Schubert (1941–1947)" issue 20, 2006, p.66–103.
16. Constantine Mamalakis, recorded phone interview, Heraklion, 26.3.2005.
17. Versions of Schubert's Greek origins exist in the article of Anglocretan Stevens Smith "Frits Schubert" Haniotika Nea 2.8.1998 and journalist I. G. Manolikakis, Golgotha of Crete, Athens 1951 p.111–121.
18. Hagen Fleischer, recorded telephone interview, Athens 28.10.2006.
19. Historical Archive of Foreign Ministry (IAYE) 1949.
20. ASKI. 1947.
21. DIS. Report on Rethymnon, 1943.
22. IAMM. 1944.
23. Michael Matsamas, recorded telephone interview, Chania, 29.1.2006.
24. John P. Papadakis, recorded phone interview, Rethymnon 13.12.2007.
25. Asonitis, "Like Schubert?" Eleftherotypia 28.10.2001.
26. Manolikakis.
27. George Kavvos, German-Italian occupation and resistance of Crete 1941–1945 Heraklion 1991.
28. Har. Giannadakis, Memoirs, Heraklion 1987 and Memories of the past, Heraklion 1995.

29. J.A. Diskant "Scarcity, Survival and Local Activism: Miners and Steelworkers, Dortmund 1945-8", Journal of Contemporary History, 24 (4) (1989), 549.
30. Ibid., p.553.
31. Stadtarchiv Dortmund ... 2006. The information relating to the Schubert family his profession, his presence in the Middle East and return to the homeland, the moves of the family, the relevance and his enlistment in the army, was sent, after correspondence to the author in the form of search reports (Recherchenberichten) by D. Knippschild, head archivist at the community archives of Dortmund. A quick search of the telephone directory revealed 124 residents with the surname Schubert.
32. Ulrich Trumpener, Germany and the Ottoman Empire, 1914–1918, Princeton 1968, p. 68. Of same "German military aid to Turkey in 1914: An historical reevaluation ", Journal of Modern History, 32 (1960) 145–149.
33. Wiki / Gallipoli_star.
34. Efi Allamani and Christa Panayiotopoulou, "The armistice of Mudros and its consequences', History of the Hellenic Nation, vol.7, Ekdotiki Athinon, Athens 1978.
35. levantine.plus.com ... In the commercial guide of Smyrna of 1926 there is advertised the German Company Max Unz, import-export representatives as also reference to Deutsche Orient Bank.
36. Hagen Fleischer, recorded telephone interview, Athens 28.10.2006. Also, Stadtarchiv Dortmund, 2006.
37. Manolikakis p.111. The author describes his 'work' as service to the Turkish army most probably of Kemal.
38. Information about Schubert's presence in Smyrna also exist in the archives of the Italian Consulate of Smyrna. The Mirone family reference bears the no. N.134/I/M with the note about Giovanna 'marriage to a German' (Letter to the author, no.815 from Consul M. Tommasi, Smyrna, May 17th 2006).
39. Alexander Kitroeff, The Greeks in Egypt.
40. Stadtarchiv Dortmund ... letter to the author, Dortmund, March 15th, 2006.
41. Bundesarchiv, Berlin, October 13th 2005. A photo copy of Schubert's party id was sent to the author, following correspondence, by Heinz Fehlauer, researcher of the federal Archive of Berlin. When Schubert was detained in Kallithea jails, he declared that in Alexandria he resided at 57 Aboukir Street. v. Archives of K. E. Mamalaki, "Sworn testimony of Fritz Spyridon Schubert "Kallithea Jails, 18.10.1945. Abou Quer avenue as Federigo street today exist in the luxury precinct of Smouha near the center.
42. Stadtarchiv Dortmund, April 13th, 2006.
43. Deutsche, (WASt): Berlin, June 16th, 2005. The information relating to Schubert's military records emanate from the 'metal id tags' or ΤΑΠ (corpse recognition tags) which, after liaising with the author, were collected by Stephan Kuchmayer, researcher of the Archives of Berlin.
44. Hagen Fleischer, "the geopolitical plans of nazi Germany in postwar Crete".
45. Το Βήμα, 29th July 1947. Also, Μακεδονία & Ο Ελληνικός Βορράς 29th July 1947. The information regarding his position is probably inaccurate as Schubert then was only a corporal.
46. Andrae served as Commandant of Crete from July 1941 to the end of September 1942.
47. Archives of K. E. Mamalaki "The Special Court Martial of War Criminals, Decision no. 1, Athens, 5th August 1947".
48. Manolikakis, p. 112. The report bears the date 28th June 1945.
49. Recorded interview, Ottawa (Canada), 1st March 2005. Schubert's girlfriend Chrysoula K, orphaned by her mother, was a 22years old girl living in a house next to Economakis

with her Greek-American father and three siblings. Due to the bankruptcy of her father, the family we're struggling in times of strife. It seems Schubert took advantage of her economic situation and with food as an allurement – possibly also using force – he seduced the young Chrysoula, who in 1944, paid for her short affair with shaving, shamed naked through the streets of the city, she was abused by the liberating factions.

50. Konstantinos E. Mamalakis, recorded telephone interview, Heraklion, 17.2.2005.
51. Konstantinos Mamalakis, recorded telephone interview, Heraklion, 26.3.2005. Mamalakis account is based on the information relayed by Captain R. Stockbridge.
52. I. G. Manolikakis, p. 111.
53. On July 28th 1947, the first day of Schubert's trial in Athens, the issue of his Greek origin was raised. According to the daily press only Το Βήμα of 29th July 1947 mentions that he was born 'of a Greek mother'. In the other papers he is merely characterized as a 'Frankolevantine'.
54. There exists also the version that the Turkish girl was an employee of P. Konstantinides: v.rwf.gr.
55. Stevens Smith, "Fritz Schubert", Χανιώτικα Νέα, 2nd August 1998. Also, The History of my Captivity, 20th July – 28th April 1945, Montreal 1997 p. 47–48. In an interview Smith assured the writer that 'the information I have emanates from Rethymniot informers whose source was Schuber first hand. If they added their own additions, we do not know'. Stevens Smith, recorded telephone interview, Montreal 7.6.2007.
56. Behind the myth of Greek origin which Schubert moulded may also lie feelings of inferiority created within him whilst associating with Greeks of Turkey. Indeed, many testify that Schubert expressed his anti-Greek feelings showing particular animosity against the refugees of Asia Minor who were for the most part venizelikoi and cooperated or supported the Resistance. v. Georgios Xylouris, recorded interview Krousonas, 28.6.2006 and Anna Devreli, recorded interview, Salonica, 20.8.2007.
57. Socrates A. Prokopiou, Stroll through Old Smyrna, 2nd edition, updated and illustrated p. 53–58.
58. Georgios Karras, recorded telephone interview, Heraklion, 7.11.2006.
59. Georgia K., recorded interview, Avgeniki, 29.6.2006. This lady who asked to remain anonymous, whilst still a child in Heraklion knew the Konstantinides family and remembers her mother's explanations. A few years ago, she became the owner of the house in Avgeniki where Schubert resided.
60. Ioannis P. Papadakis, recorded telephone interview, Oros, 13.12.2007. The source is one of the eight children of a victim Pantelis Papadakis.
61. Dim. Gousides, "From the Nazi were saved those who fled to the mountains" To Βήμα, 2.9.1970.
62. There are many and varying views and remarks about Schubert's Greek, being broken and slang to fluent with a heavy Smyrnan or Turkish accent. Schubert does not appear to have learnt Greek in any school rather with Greeks with whom he associated for about twenty years in Smyrna and Alexandria.
63. Georgios Karras, recorded telephone interview, Heraklion 7.11.2006.
64. Antony Beevor, Crete. Also, Martin van Creveld, Hitler's Strategy, where the author cites exact numbers of casualties: 2,071 dead, 2,594 wounded and 1,888 missing so "operation MERKUR" cost more casualties than the whole campaign against the Balkans.
65. Ibid.
66. Mark Mazower.
67. Ibid., p. 236. Also, Manolikakis p. 94.
68. Beevor, p. 237.
69. Ibid., p. 238. The total number of dead rose to 3,500 and over 30 villages totally routed.

70. Kavvos, p. 35.
71. Ibid., p. 33–34.
72. Ibid., p. 31–32. Also, Beevor p. 237–238 and Report of the central committee of the ascertainment of brutalities in Crete, Municipality of Heraklion (or Kazantzaki Report).
73. Stratos N. Dordanas, The blood, p. 200.
74. Kavvos, p. 105.
75. Hagen Fleischer, The geostrategic plans, p. 135.
76. Charles P., King, p. 120.
77. Beevor, p. 271 The base of the Siena division was at Neapolis Lasithi.
78. Kavvos p. 341.
79. Ibid., p. 103–104.
80. Hagen Fleischer, "Occupation and Resistance, 1941–1944", History of the Greek Nation, vol. 8, Εκδοτική Αθηνών, Athens 2000, p. 14.
81. Ibid., p. 30. Also, Kavvos p. 65.
82. Kavvos, p. 65, 69, 75–76. The remaining projects were the construction of an airport at Kastelli Pediados and underground fuel bunkers at Peza Pediados Heraklion and Vamvakopoulo Kydonia Chania.
83. Haralambos Giannadakis, Memoirs, p. 76–77.
84. , p. 101. Beevor, p. 289.
85. Ριζοσπάστης, 20.11.1946.
86. Haralambos Giannadakis, Memoirs, p.75. Fermor's letter was published in Καθημερινή, 27th May 1981.
87. Hagen Fleischer, "Occupation and", p. 31.
88. Manolikakis p. 148–160 where details are listed relating to the resistance movement and the different armed gangs through Crete.
89. Kazantzakis Report p. 105. Also, Kavvos p. 77 who calculates the remaining allies up to 10,000 whilst A. Beevor p. 218 mentions 5,000.
90. Kazantzakis Report p. 103–106.
91. Ioannis Papadakis, recorded telephone interview, Oros, 13.12.2017.
92. Ελεύθερη Γνώμη, 19.12.1945. It is testified that Cretans interested in asking Schubert about his collaborators, assembled a number from the Remedial Jails of Chania.
93. Georgios Papadakis, recorded interview, Oros, 7.11.2007. At the interview were present also other members of the Papadakis family who offered their testimony regarding their father's murder.
94. At the Oros incident the German clothed accomplice was a Cretan from Rethymnon. The witness refused to disclose the name of the Rethymniot to the writer.
95. Vasileios Haronitis, recorded interview, Heraklion 29.6.2006.
96. Haralambos Giannadakis, Memoirs p. 63.
97. Kazantzakis Report, p. 98.
98. Manolikakis, p. 118.
99. Beevor, p. 281. Also, U.S. War Department, Handbook on German Military Forces.
100. Beevor, p. 263–264. Also, Kavvos p. 230,786. Hartmann's first name is not reported.
101. Kavvos, p. 796,802. It appears Hartmann had been adopted by a German family in Thessaloniki, spoke faultless Greek, served as deputy consul in Salonica, became a representative of German engines in the city and a fanatic supporter of nazism. In his statement Schubert names him German Major "with the pseudonym Hartmann and real name Ruggiero". Walter Leuchs, the General Consul of Germany in Salonica disagrees with the above, emphasizing that 'someone not a seasoned diplomat but a trader with an

Italian name would not be able to assume a role in the German consulate at that particular time'. Email to the writer, Thessaloniki, 18th February 2009.
102. Deutsche Dienstselle Berlin (WASt), Berlin, 16th June 2005. Schubert's military records only refer to his departure from the 433rd Regiment on 18th July 1942. His enlistment most probably happened in December 1941 or latest January 1942 immediately after the Division settled in Crete. Schubert claimed in 1946 that he served from 1942 to 1943 in the 162 'infantry division' whose existence is not recorded in Crete. Possibly he confused it with the 164th infantry Division. v. K. E. Mamalakis archive, "Sworn testimony of the accused Fritz Schubert", Kallithea Jails, 18th October 1946. Also www.lexicon-der-wehrmacht.de.
103. Pier Paolo Battistelli, Rommel's Afrika Korps. Tobruk to El Alamein, Oxford 2006, p. 36.
104. Kavvos, p. 65.
105. Fleischer, "Occupation", p. 30.
106. Manolikakis, p. 112. Also, Beevor p. 263–264. Also, Manolis G. Polioudakis, The National Resistance against the German-Italian Occupation in Crete, 1st June 1941 to 30th June 1945, Rethymnon 2002 p. 83–84.
107. Stergios G. Spanakis, Cities and villages of Crete, vol. B, Heraklion 1991, p. 444.
108. Beevor, p. 96–97. Also, Konstantinos Giannadakis, recorded telephone interview Heraklion, 2.6.2008. According to Giannadakis, the German intelligence had in its possession many documents of Pendlebury containing his plans as regards Krousonas.
109. K. E. Mamalakis archive: "Report of the examination of witness Richard Haar", Heraklion, 16th June 1945. Also, Kavvos p. 788–794.
110. Georgios M. Xylouris, recorded interview, Krousonas, 28.6.2006. Also, Konstantinos Mamalakis, recorded telephone interview, Heraklion, 1.3.2008. Soultatos, a candidate in the elections of 1933 of the Peoples Party often used the prewar paper, 'Εθνικό Κήρυκα', in Heraklion for the dissemination of his Germanophile ideology emphasizing that the Germans would return one day as conquerors for the good of mankind.
111. Konstantinos Fanourakis, National Resistance of Krousonas. Memoirs, Heraklion 1999 p. 70 forming part of the preface (p. 69–79) of Georgios Xylouris.
112. Konstantinos Giannadakis, recorded telephone interview, Heraklion, 2.6.2008. It is strange why Tzoulias and a few other Krousaniotes of the Peoples' Party armed with English weapons from Grigorakis-Satana in the resistance against the Germans during the Battle of Crete in May 1941.
113. K. E. Mamalakis Archive: "Report of ex Commander of Gendarmes of Heraklion Captain Polioudakis Ioannis" The Report bears no date and was probably drafted while Polioudakis was imprisoned at the Jails of Heraklion in November 1944.
114. Michail Nik. Tzoulias had five sons, Nikolao, Georgio, Kaniori, Konstantinos Stylianos and Ioannis and two daughters. Their ancestors derived from Epirus and settled in Krousonas during the Revolution of 1821. v. Georgios Xylouris, "The upbringing of the Tzoulia family" Αλλαγή, Heraklion 25.9.1992. Note that the Tzoulia and Tzouliadakis families not only were not related but were ideologically of opposite factions.
115. Georgios Xylouris, recorded telephone conversation, Krousonas 24.6.2008.
116. Fanourakis, p. 22.
117. Ibid., p. 74–75.
118. Georgios Xylouris, recorded interview, Krousonas, 28.6.2006.
119. Giannadakis, Memoirs p.105. Also, Kavvos p. 198.
120. Fanourakis, p. 78.
121. Kavvos, p. 202.
122. Giannadakis, Memories, p. 110–111.

123. Konstantinos Giannadakis, recorded telephone interview, Heraklion, 2.6.2008. It is noteworthy that of the 62 hostages executed on 3rd and 14th June outside Heraklion as retaliation for the murder of accomplices and allied sabotaging, the 13 were from Agia Varvara, the largest number of casualties from any other village or town in Crete. Also, Kavvos, p. 202–220.
124. Markos G. Polioudakis, p. 83.
125. Grigoris M. Sifakis, email to the writer, Salonica 13.4.2010. It is not known for exactly what reason M. Sifakis was arrested possibly along with others from Agia Varvara about a month and a half before the execution of Germanophile accomplices by rebel clans. It is likely that Sifakis' name was included in a list of patriots composed by a resistor of Bantouva, Kon. Katsifaris, which list ended up in the hands of the German gendarmerie early spring 1942.
126. Manolikakis, p. 114.
127. Georgios Xylouris, recorded telephone interview, Krousonas 24.6.2008.
128. Kyriakos Kritovoulides, Memoirs. Cretans, Athens 1859 (?), p. 146.
129. Giannadakis, Memories, p. 21.
130. Antonis K. Sanoudakis, Church and Resistance, Knossos, 1993 p. 204.
131. Georgios Xylouris, recorded interview, Krousonas, 28.6.2006 v. addendum of same in the essay of Konstantinos Fanourakis p. 74–79.
132. Beevor p. 208. Also, Giannadakis, Memoirs.
133. Panagiotis Kanavakis, recorded interview, Heraklion 28.6.2006.
134. K. E. Mamalakis, archive.
135. Kavvos, p. 799–809 where there appears a detailed list with the names of German and Italian war criminals referred to trial. Note the name Jagdkommando was given with the league's founding in August 1943. Manolikakis, p. 114 who counts the crimes of Schubert till August 1943 'exceeding 1,000'. Kavvos, p. 230 refers to 'squads of Schubert's league'.
136. Giannadakis, Memoirs, p. 21.
137. Ibid., p. 11–13.
138. K. E. Mamalakis, archive, "Testimony of Michail Filippou Kourakis" 20th April 1944 M. Kourakis who was imprisoned by ΕΛΑΣ, testified that Germanophile covillagers encouraged him to enlist to Schubert's gang.
139. Konstantinos Giannadakis, recorded telephone interview, Heraklion, 2.6.2008. The view that Schubert's victims were few is corroborated by a comment of General Alexander Andrae made to the historian Hagen Fleischer, 'If I remember well, he told me he met him (Schubert) in jail. If Schubert had caused havoc in Crete, he would know as Andrae served as Commander in Chief of Crete till September 1942' v. Hagen Fleischer, recorded telephone interview, Athens, 28.10.2006.
140. Manolis Batakis, Memories, Chania 2003, p. 163. The writer was present at Schubert's speech, but managed to escape and be saved. According to Batakis the team was mixed consisting of Germans and 'Krousonas traitors. Also, Ioannis Batakis then 15, had hidden in a large 'trunk' in the next-door room of the school from where he could hear Schubert questioning and ordering his men to form a phalanx and pour salt on the wounds of the victims' feet. v. recorded telephone interview, Meskla 11.8.2008.
141. Ο Ελληνικός Βορράς, 30.7.1947. Other members of the gang most likely were the Krousaniotes: Sterg. K. Agiomyrgianakis, Haralambos Dr. Agiomyrgianakis, Kon. E. Axotakis, Kon. G. Axotakis, Sterg. Vergetakis, and Kon. I. Makatounis or Tsoutzouroukos. v. Giannadakis, Memoirs p. 107. Schubert in his testimony at the Chania jails refers to an attack from his base at Avgeniki on the villages of Mesara accompanied by 15 "special agents" v. Kavvos, p. 229.

142. K. E. Mamalakis archive, 'Report of ... Polioudakis Ioannis', Heraklion, no date.
143. Haralambos Giannadakis, Memoirs p. 63. Also, Kavvos p. 792–793. In his statement, the sergeant of the Military Police R. Haar deals thoroughly with the wide network of Greek agents within Hartmann's espionage nexus.
144. Army General Staff – Directorate of Military History (or ΔΙΣ). "Report of activities EAO 'Petraka', Chania 18.1.1950, p. 252. Kavvos, p. 174.
145. ΔΙΣ, vol. 6. "Saboteurs of rebel clans in Crete", Crete 27.7.1944, p. 61.
146. Kavvos, p. 231–232.
147. George Psychoundakis, The Cretan Runner, London 1955, p. 156–157. Apart from this version, there is maintained another version transmitted traditionally through the Gyparis family. Here Thymakis visits the farm of Gyparis along with an accomplice of Schubert, named Komna, who pretended he was a wanted fugitive by the Germans and sought asylum at the farm. They convinced Gyparis that 'they wanted to join the resistance and visit an English hideout'. Gyparis, knowing Thymakis as an Anglophile, believed them, offered them a meal and in turn revealed the weapon armory and the English hideout. Then the double-crossers gave the signal to those standing by, Schubert and his gang, who surrounded the spot, arrested Gyparis, found the weapons and executed him on the spot. Giannis Psychountakis, a partner at the farm, managed to escape. v. Kon. Gyparis, interview with Epim. Platsidakis, Chania, 23.5.2008.
148. Kavvos, p. 198.
149. Battistelli p. 10. By the end of August, the military material was transported by ship to Tobruk and by mid-August was supplemented with air transfer of detachments from the Cretan Guard Division the former 164th Infantry Division. v. Kavvos, p. 251.
150. Manolikakis, p. 112.
151. Kavvos, p. 198.
152. Marlen Von Xylander, Die Deutsche. Freiburg 1989, p. 36. Also, Kavvos, p. 199.
153. Kavvos, p. 204.
154. Beevor, p. 286.
155. Kavvos, p. 208. Polioudakis ordered all divisions of the gendarmerie to post his order of 14th June 1942 'at all central spots in villages and to the furthest huts' Lieutenant (Wili) Wilhelm Krohn, directing the Secret Police of Heraklion testified at the trials of Generals Broier and Miller that apart from Polioudakis, he who contributed to drafting the list of 50 Heraklian victims on 14th June was the lawyer Nik. Meimarakis, an important agent of the Germans. v. Ριζοσπάστης 15.11.1946 and Nikos K. Karkanis, The traitors of the Occupation, Athens, 1981, p. 364.
156. Georgios Frangoulitakis (Skoutelogiorgis), The cross eagles of Psiloritis. Heraklion 1991, p. 83.
157. Giannadakis, Memories, p. 11. Also, Fanourakis, p. 25–26. The executions are dated between 5th and 16th June 1942. Aside from Spyridakis detained at Agia, the remaining five were the first victims of Krousonas.
158. Beevor, p. 261. Also, Kavvos, p. 213.
159. Ibid., p. 263.
160. Kavvos, p. 219.
161. Το Βήμα, 30.7.1947, unnamed, "The trial of the German executioner of Crete Schubert."
162. K. E. Mamalakis, Special Martial Court of War Crimes, decision no. 1, Athens 5th August 1947.
163. Το Βήμα, 30.7.1947.
164. Μακεδονία, 29.7.1947. Also, Manolis Karellis, Historical notes. Heraklion, p. 212.
165. Frangoulitakis (Skoutelogiorgis), p. 62.

166. Ibid.
167. Kavvos, p. 124.
168. Ibid., p. 168 wherein the Order of Commander Broier of 20.2.1942. From the beginning of the Occupation, those wanted by the German authorities used forged documents, issued by local gendarmerie and local authorities. The forgers whether individuals or civil servants were threatened with referral to martial courts and the worst of punishment.
169. Ibid., p. 133.
170. Antonis Sanoudakis, Zaharia Bantouvas. The Civil War, Knossos, 1995, p. 63.
171. Ibid., p. 64.
172. Ibid., p. 65. Examples of persons who used German but also Turkish to win Schubert's forbearance are scarce. Professor K. Gardikas with his German saved a few Petralonites, P. Paschalides, a Turkish speaker helped many covillagers in Nea Apollonia as also Turkish speaking G. Theodoridis, a Heraklian chemist whom Schubert spared from the blackmailing threats of a Schuberite.
173. Ibid., p. 67. Also, K. Giannadakis, "The imprisoned patriots in the light", Μεσόγειος, 15.12.2008.
174. Evangelia M., interview with K. E. Mamalakis, Avgeniki 15.6.2008. Evangelia or Valio M., then around 17, met Schubert under unusual circumstances. Schubert often flirted with her watching her sweeping her yard at Venerato. A bold move though revealed his true intentions. Without her knowing he took her sandals from the cobbler, where she had left it for repair, and so obliged her to go to his office and ask it back. Then he 'pounced in her'. Fortunately, though at that moment, three army clad tall Schuberites suddenly entered the office and upset his plans. Schubert irate jumped to whack them round the face. In the comic scene created, Evangelia grabbed the opportunity to disappear taking back her sandal.
175. Frangoulitakis (Skoutelogiorgis), p. 86.
176. Kavvos, p. 235. The author who often makes mistakes as regards the date of events, puts the incident at Grigoria at June 9th 1942.
177. Ibid., p. 234. Magiasis was stabbed during his trial in Heraklion in 1946 by the Anogeian Geor. Vrentzos avenging his brother Michail whom Magiasis executed at Psiloritis in August 1943, v. Kavvos, p. 365.
178. Ibid.
179. Ibid., p.178. M. Porphyrogenis was active in Crete from spring 1942 till the end of 1943. He made great efforts to organize and unify the various resistance gangs, armed or otherwise, in Crete, under the umbrella of EAM. His attempts weren't rewarded with complete success as some parties, in the towns and villages, objected to the communist ideal which EAM progressively adopted.
180. K. E. Mamalakis archive, Special Court Martial of War Criminals, Decree No.1, Athens 5.8.1947. It is not known if the Italian soldiers belonged to Schubert's team or more likely they took part in the attack as members of the German unit.
181. Konstantinos Mitsotakis, recorded interview, Athens 2.6.2006.
182. Kavvos, p. 251.
183. Beevor, p. 290.
184. Fleischer, "Occupation … ", p. 30. Beevor, p. 271 estimates the German-Italian forces more than 75.000 men.
185. Kavvos, p. 268.
186. Ibid., p. 343.
187. Ibid., p. 312.

188. WASt: Personal veranderung. The transfer was effected on 3rd April v. letter to the writer, Berlin 16.6.2005.
189. www.lexiconwehrmacht. Also, Kavvos, p. 783. Conclusive evidence confirms the fact that Schubert served in the Military Police (Feldgendarmerie) and not the Secret Field Police, the GFP or SS, as mentioned in newer sources. Schubert himself declared at his trial that he belonged to the Military Police (Ελευθερία, 6.8.1947). Also. von Xylander, p. 117 Last in Macedonia Schubert served in the motor division c 985 of the military Police.
190. His increased powers within the Gendarmerie immediately after his joining in April 1943 made such an impression that some British agents, as Captain Ralph Stockbridge date him founding the "Hunting Commandos" back to this period v. Kavvos, p. 801.
191. http ... redcap.... "German Military Police".
192. Nikos A. Kokonas, Crete, 1941–1945. Rethymnon, 1989, p. 102.
193. K. E. Mamalakis archive, "Report of German war criminals active in Crete and particularly in the Municipality of Heraklion", Heraklion 28th June 1945. Also, Kavvos, p. 794 and Manolikakis, p. 113.
194. K. E. Mamalakis archive, "Report of Polioudakis Ioannis, Heraklion undated.
195. Manolikakis, p. 114.
196. K. E. Mamalakis archive, Special Court Martial. Athens 5th August 1947. Also, IAYE, 1949, Special Court of Collaborators of Chania. 30th March 1948.
197. Giannadakis, Memories, p. 46. Note the writer blames the executions of the five Krousoniotes exclusively on covillager Schuberites/Gestapo.
198. ΓΑΚ Heraklion: Special Court, 24.11.1945.
199. Kavvos, p. 783. At his interrogation on 8th June 1945, Gleblin asserts, as does Polioudakis that he himself ordered the imprisonment of Schubert, though in reality they both probably testified to Hartmann who also had personal reasons to imprison him.
200. Manolikakis, p.114. The writer refers that Schubert remained in the jails of Agia for one month.
201. K. E. Mamalakis archive, "Testimony of Markos I. Fantakis". Also, Kavvos, p. 802.
202. Spanakis, p. 532.
203. Batakis, p. 153. The Mesklian writer describes the incident in detail.
204. Artemios Stamatakis, recorded telephone interview, Meskla 19.5.2008.
205. Batakis, p. 162. Also, Ioannis Batakis, recorded telephone interview, Meskla 11.8.2008. The German spy Tzimis lived at the home of Tsamadakis.
206. Ibid., p. 163.
207. Karellis, p. 188.
208. Kavvos, p. 356.
209. Ibid., p. 320.
210. Kostopoulos, p. 16.
211. Ibid., p. 21.
212. , p. 357.
213. Karkanis, p. 351.
214. Manolikakis, p. 114. Also, Kavvos, p,229.
215. Hagen Fleischer, recorded telephone interview, Athens, 28.10.2006.
216. Konstantinos Mitsotakis, recorded interview, Athens, 2.6.2006.
217. Stratos N. Dordanas, "German authorities of the Occupation and Greek administration ", Vassilis K. Gounaris-Petros Papapolyviou, The price of blood. Thessaloniki 2001, p. 97.
218. Kavvos, p. 329.
219. Stratos N. Dordanas. Greeks against Greeks. Thessaloniki 2006, p. 37.

220. Archive of Hagen Fleischer, the Letter of Johannes Barge "In relation to the death of Friedrich Schubert former sergeant of the Military Police". Lage, 31.8.1951.
221. Kokonas, Crete, p. 96. Also, von Xylander, p. 117.
222. K. E. Mamalakis archive. Special Court Martial of War Criminals, Decision no. 1 Athens, 5th August 1947.
223. K. E. Mamalakis archive, National Organization of Cretan Officers, 1945. Also, Kavvos, p. 794. The "Report" belonging till 2008 in the Kavvos archive, consists of 12 large typed pages with a prologue about the composition and operation of various departments of the German army, also detailed lists of German and Italian prisoners of war who are categorized according to position and service. Last is added a list of the officers of EOK executed by the Germans.
224. Ριζοσπάστης, 19.11.1946.
225. Fanourakis, p. 30.
226. Πατρις, Heraklion, 9.11.2004: Anonymous, 'The memories of bestialities rekindled Nazi'.
227. Ibid.
228. Michail Matsamas, recorded telephone interview, Chania 29.1.2006. Also, Penelope I. Doudoulaki, Memories, Chania, 2008, p. 73.
229. Giannadakis, Memoirs, p. 101. Also, Frangoulitakis (Skoutelogiorgis), p. 81. Kokonas, Crete, p. 96. The number of volunteers differs according to sources and grows up to 200 men.
230. Manolikakis, p. 115. Also, Kavvos, p. 229. The sources exaggerate the numbers of recruits from prisons which in reality must have been small. Of the 112 names in Tables A and B (v. Appendix II) none seem to have been recruited from criminals released.
231. Το Βήμα, 30.7.1947. The testimony of K. Karabatakis, though unconfirmed may to an extent be true.
232. Batakis, p. 152. Also, Kavvos, p. 229 and Beevor, p. 295.
234. Kavvos, p. 793.
235. Giannadakis, Memories, p. 12. The writer uses the terms "Schuberite" and "Gestapitis" alternately without giving any explanation. Note neither the Gestapo nor the SS came to Crete.
236. Ibid., p. 51. The Schuberite I. Epanomeritakis solved the property differences he had with N. Sfakianakis from Keramoutsi by executing him outside his house.
237. Ibid., The Schuberites dug the floor of his pharmacy and stole the money.
238. Georgios Xylouris, recorded interview, Krousonas 28.6.2006.
239. Fanourakis, p. 30.
240. Collaborators Documents: "Sworn examination of witness Nikolaos Fanariotis", Nea Kallikrateia, 3rd August 1946.
241. Sanoudakis, Zaharias, p. 64. Reference to the terrorizing of the village Metohi Vorou, July 1942.
242. IAYE, folder 135. Chania 30th March 1948. Refers to the Schuberite attack on the village of Petrokefali Heraklion in July 1942. Also, Batakis, p. 152, attack on the village of Meskla Chania in July 1943. On both occasions the Schuberites were German clad.
243. As regards the dress of the Schuberites confusion prevails. For the most part sources talk of German and Italian uniform. The court references in Thessaloniki note the Schuberites 'wore uniform resembling the German to distinguish them' v. Collaborators' Documents. Thessaloniki, 26th April 1947. The disagreement seems has arisen from the fact that the lower ranking Schuberites wore Italian uniform whereas the higher ranks and generally the team's older volunteers wore German uniform.
244. Μακεδονία, 30.5.1947. The volunteers of Colonel G. Poulos wore German uniform with Greek markings.

245. Beevor, p. 281.
246. Το Βήμα, 30.7.1947. The testimony of the Heraklian convict K. Karambataki.
247. Ibid., p. 264. Also, Kon. Gyparis, interview, Chania, 7.1.2009.
248. K. E. Mamalakis archive. "Sworn testimony of Fritz Schubert", Kallithea Jails, 18th October 1945.
249. Kavvos, p. 792.
250. Ibid., p. 794. The Cretans believed that in his prerogatives Schubert exceeded the German hierarchy of Crete and reached the rank of H. Himmler, head of the SS even Hitler himself: 'drawing apparently the powers directly from the Fuhrer v. Chr. Tzifakis "Report N. Rethymnon", Rethymnon, December ,1943.
251. Ibid., Note the episode between Schubert and Haar must be dated between May and June 1943 as Schubert was still a lieutenant and Haar a sergeant heading the Krousonas jail.
252. Giannadakis, Memories, p. 22. Also, IAYE, Chania, 30th March 1948. In the documents are noted the various acts of violence which the Schuberites committed in small or larger groups under the leadership of the deputies.
253. Konstantinos Mitsotakis, recorded interview, Athens, 2.6.2006.
254. Collaborators Documents: Special Court of Collaborators of Thessaloniki, Decision no. 519, Salonica, 26th April 1947.
255. Ελευθερία, 6.8.1947. Also, Ο Ελληνικός Βορράς, 6.8.1947.
256. Dordanas "German authorities", p. 95.
257. Kostopoulos, p. 21.
258. K. E. Mamalakis archive, "Statement of Marco I. Fantaki", Chania. Kavvos, p. 802 where the witness is named Fiotakis. Both names are known in the area.
259. K. E. Mamalakis archive: Special Collaborators Court of Thessaloniki, Decision no. 1, Thessaloniki, 5th August 1947.
260. Manolis Pantinakis, The province of Agios Vasileios, Rethymnon, 2006, p. 383.
261. Ριζοσπάστης, 29.7.1947. Reference to the statement of Dim. Daskalakis, community official of Agios Ioannis Rethymnon. In his testimony the Rodakiniotis priest Geor. Sfakianakis (Sifakakis is wrong) exaggerates the strength of the gang to 200 plus men. See also Kavvos,p. 413 who corroborates the testimony of Sfakianakis.
262. Pantinakis, p. 385, includes the statement of G. Sfakianakis.
263. Ibid., p .387. Also, Kavvos, p. 413. Some sources dramatize the events highlighting that Kapetanaki was thrown alive onto a lit stove where she was incinerated.
264. Ibid., p. 389. Brauer's order provides proof that Schubert's operations at Rodakino met his approval.
265. In the decision of the Special Martial Court it is a mistake that the executions took place in October 1943.
266. Municipality of Chania, registry death certificate of Emmanouil Mantakas, vol. B (1943). Also, Ioannis Mantakas, recorded telephone interview, Chania 2.5.2008.
267. Municipality of Chania, Registry Office, death certificate of Georgios Manousakis. Also, death certificate of Emmanouil Manousakis vol. A.
268. Manolikakis, p. 115.
269. Emmanouil Nikoloudis, recorded telephone interview, Chania, 2.5.2008.
270. The General Commander of Crete, I. Passadakis in his defense mentions that he intervened to save Skoulas when he was arrested for anti-Nazi activities v. Passadakis, Athens, 1948, p. 8.
271. Manolikakis, p. 115. Also, ΔΙΣ, Chania, p. 369.
272. Ριζοσπάστης, 26.11.1946. Also, Karkanis, p.,373 wherein the statements of the lawyers St. Kelaidis and P. Nikolikakis, both from Chania, at the trials of generals Brauer and Miller.

Most conclusive of all was colonel Chr. Tzifakis who in his Report highlights '.. in the city of Chania in the middle of the market and without any justification were murdered by a German deputy the butcher brothers Manousakis and the teacher Mantakas' v. ΔΙΣ, Rethymnon, December, 1943, p. 37.

273. ΔΙΣ, 'Report of the intelligence team of Chania', Chania, p. 368. Schubert avoided moving around Chania as he had been informed of the threats against his life.
274. Ριζοσπάστης 22.11.1946. Also, Karkanis, p. 371. Testimony of K. Mitsotakis at the trials of the Generals.
275. Manolikakis, p. 115.
276. Kavvos, p. 298.
277. Ioannis Mantakas, recorded telephone interview, Chania, 2.5.2008.
278. Kavvos, p. 150. Exceptions are Lieutenant Colonel Ant. Beteinakis from Archanes and I. Kazantzakis from Pyrgos who led secret resistance organizations in their environs without however any particular activity.
279. ΔΙΣ, vol.6. 'Report of the actions against the Bantouvas organization', Heraklion, 20.8.1945, p. 174.
280. Hagen Fleischer, 'Occupation', p. 31.
281. ΔΙΣ, "Reports of the activities of the armed teams of Eastern Crete", Heraklion, 9.5.1950. Report of Colonel Nik. Plevris. The other organizations of EOK in Rethymnon and Chania were created in the summer of 1943 along the lines of that of the municipality of Heraklion.
282. Kavvos, p. 271, Letter of 20th March 1943 of Patrick Leigh Fermor, head of the English Mission to the appointed members.
283. Ibid., p. 268.
284. K.E. Mamalakis archive, "Report, Heraklion". The report dated 28th June 1945 was sent to the Military Command of Crete and signed by eight members of the National Organization of Cretan Officers in the prefecture of Heraklion. Also, Kavvos, p. 794.
285. Ριζοσπάστης, 9.11.1946.
286. Kavvos, p. 395.
287. ΔΙΣ, vol.6. "Reports", Heraklion, 9.5.1950, p. 280. The report was prepared by Colonel Nik. Plevris and sent to ΓΕΣ (or ΔΙΣ, N. Plevris).
288. Beevor, p. 291.
289. ΔΙΣ, N. Plevris, p. 277.
290. Ibid., p. 277. Also, Beevor, p. 289.
291. ΔΙΣ, N. Plevris, p. 280.
292. Beevor, p. 291. Also, Karellis, p. 191. General Wilhelm Miller at his trial mentions 11 dead, 30 wounded and 12 prisoners of the total force of two units in conflict with the rebels v. Ελευθερία, 3.12.1946.
293. Kavvos, p. 392. Capetan Bantouvas in his Report does not mention the killings of the Germans at the guard post of Kato Symi and deludes himself about an all-day battle on 11th September against 4.000 Germans leaving 222 dead! He also asserts that the 15 German prisoners after questioning by the English, were executed 'for military reasons' Finally he adds that he departed for Egypt assisted by the English for health reasons. The Report contains many inaccuracies and exaggerations v. ΔΙΣ, "Reports of the national liberation party of Crete" Heraklion 20.8.1945.
294. Beevor, p. 290. Also, Kavvos, p. 393.
295. Kavvos, p. 404.

296. Ibid., p. 395. Archimandrite E. Psalidakis in his letter to M. Bantouvas on 16th September mentions 350 casualties. General Miller was found responsible by the court for the murder of 471 persons at Viannos, v. Ριζοσπάστης, 10.12.1946.
297. Ibid., p. 394.
298. Ibid., p. 405.
299. ΔΙΣ, N. Plevris, p. 283.
300. Ibid., p. 278.
301. Kavvos, p. 417.
302. Ibid., p. 417.
303. Ibid.
304. ΔΙΣ, N. Plevris, p. 284.
305. Kavvos, p. 419. The remainder were A. Beteinakis and reserves Emm. Paterianakis and Pan. Berkis against whom existed valid evidence that they cooperated in the operations of Bantouvas at Viannos.
306. ΔΙΣ, N. Plevris, p. 285.
307. Kavvos, p. 420.
308. Ibid.
309. Ibid.
310. Ibid., p. 437.
311. Giannadakis, Memories, p. 89.
312. Alekos Mathioudakis, On the road to freedom, Rethymnon, 1997, p. 99.
313. N. A. Kokonas, The Cretan Resistance, Rethymnon, 1994 p. 73.
314. Ελευθερία, 6.8.1947.
315. Kokonas, The Cretan Resistance, p. 102.
316. Kavvos, p. 413.
317. Pantinakis, p. 179.
318. ΔΙΣ, "Reports of the activities of EAO Petraka", Chania 18.1.1950, p. 252. Some sources refer to two conflicts, the first on 4th October with the patrol of the Sellia jails and the second the next day with a German detachment from Rethymnon.
319. IAYE 1949. Special Court of Collaborators of Chania. Chania 30th March 1948, p. 15.
320. Kazantzakis Report, Heraklion 1983, p. 56. Another version that Schubert accompanied the Germans and upon his return from Tsilivdika in the afternoon he stopped at the village, p. 181.
321. Pantinakis, p. 191.
322. Andreas S. Stavroulakis, Heartaches and agony of the Occupation, Chania, p. 194. According to the testimony of the community president, Manolis Gryntakis, the choice of women was not by chance but based on a list of names which a snitch in the village gave to the German guard of Sellia and indirectly to Schubert himself.
323. Pantinakis, p. 181.
324. Ibid.
325. Ibid., p. 197.
326. Karkanis, p. 385.
327. Kavvos, p. 410.
328. Kokonas, Crete, p. 96. The Allied Military fearing reprisals from the Germans upon Bantouvas arrival on the island, did not allow him to return to Crete, notwithstanding his attempts, till September 1944.
329. Kazantzakis Report, p. 58.
330. K. E. Mamalakis archive, Special Court Martial of War Crimes. Regarding the supplies to Bantouvas v. Kavvos, p. 411.

331. Ibid. Reference to the raid of Schubert with 40 men and a force of around 500 Germans.
332. Spyros Manouselis, recorded interview, Kallikratis, 19.5.2008. The witness 14 years old then, remembers that the Schuberites differed from the Germans because they have 'Italian weapons and clothing. Dirty little men from Mesara'.
333. Stelios Giannakakis, recorded interview, Kallikratis, 11.5.2008.
334. Stavros Manouselis, recorded interview, Kallikratis, 19.5.2008.
335. Stelios Giannakakis, recorded interview, Kallikratis, 11.5.2008.
336. Kazantzakis Report p.58. Also, Kavvos, p. 414.
337. Bundesarciv-Militararchiv, 8.10.1943.
338. K. E. Mamalakis archive. Also, Kavvos, p. 414.
339. Kavvos, p. 414. This testimony is not corroborated by another source.
340. K. E. Mamalakis archive. According to other testimonies, G. Grigorakis was executed by a Krousonas or a group of them in September 1943 v. Giannadakis. Chania 30th March 1948.
341. Kavvos, p. 415.
342. Ibid., p. 373. Also, Beevor, p. 295.
343. Georgios M. Milakis, recorded interview, Heraklion, 19.5.2009.
344. Emm. Symianakis, "The execution of Lasithians by the Germans" Λινιές, monthly journal of the Association of Lasithians of Heraklion, Heraklion, October 2003.
345. Ibid.
346. Kavvos, p. 415. Also, K. E. Mamalakis archive. The victims at the villages of Kritsa, Tzermiado and Miamou numbered 16 persons and not 30 as assessed in the British "Report" v. Kokonas, Crete, p. 184.
347. Spanakis, p. 537.
348. Giannadakis, Memories, p. 22.
349. Emmanouil G. Manidakis, recorded interview, Miamou, 10.4.2007.
350. Ibid.
351. Ibid. Germanakis didn't follow Schubert and his gang through Yugoslavia to Austria but with 10–15 Cretans escaped in October 1944 from Axiochori Kilkis and appears to have enlisted to one of the security battalions, possibly that of Michail Papadopoulos or Michalaga which was active then in Western Macedonia. After the Occupation, he possibly hid in Athens where his family had moved. Today in the areas of Athens, three Germanakis are listed with the father's name G(eorgios) (v. OTE entry Germanakis).
352. K. E. Mamalakis archive, "Testimony of Georgia widow of Iosif Kasapakis" (no place and date). Also, Kavvos, p. 802. Witness statements, as Kasapakis' and Grylaki's constituted part of G. Kavvos Archive which the various authorities of Crete submitted to the Office of the Military Command of Crete who in turn relayed them to the probe Office of Kavvos at Chania. Kavvos copied these statements missing out details such as time and place to use them in the narration of his book.
353. Ibid., "Testimony of Vasiliki widow of Markos Grylakis' (without place and time). There remains an unconfirmed report that around the villages Maza and Fones, Schubert for a while used the village Tzitzifes in Apokorona as a temporary base. English agents checked correspondence destined for Schubert at Dim. Stylianakis' home, who acted as postman between Chania (Agia Jails) and Tzitzife. The incidents at Maza and Fones probably relate to Schubert's stay at Tzitzife, v. Doudoulakis, p. 90, report of Emm. D. Stylianakis.
354. K. E. Mamalakis archive, 5th August 1947. Also, Konstantinos Mamalakis, recorded telephone interview, Heraklion, 20.2.2008.
355. Κρητικός Κήρυξ, Heraklion, 1st January 1944. v. App. I, First Announcement.
356. See above, p. 103.

357. Ibid. E.K.A.K. is the mistaken abbreviation for the correct E.A.K.K. or 'Greek Detachment Hunting Criminals' which later when Schubert brought the detachment to Macedonia was adapted to 'National Detachment of Pursuit of Communists' v. Ριζοσπάστης, 30.7.1947.
358. Kavvos, p. 415. According to Kavvos, the Chief of Staff of Fortress Crete sent Schubert in person with all his squad to destroy the newly formed armed team of ΕΛΑΣ under Captain Kritona Kyanidi who surprised Schubert by ambush resulting in the capture of two Schuberites which obliged Schubert to return immediately to Chania.
359. Batakis, p. 168.
360. Ibid., p. 169.
361. Kokonas, Crete, id, p. 102.
362. Batakis, p. 170.
363. Artemios Stamatakis, recorded telephone interview, Meskla, 11.8.2008.
364. Known are the names of three captured: Kon. Axiotakis from Krousonas, Geor. K. Triantafyllakis from Asites and Geor. D. Saloustrou or Hatzigiorgi from Anogeia.
365. Batakis, p. 171.
366. Karkanis, p. 158.
367. Ριζοσπάστης, 6.11.1946.
368. Το Βήμα, 6.8.1947. Ελευθερία, 6.8.1946.
369. Von Xylander id, p. 117, footnote 72. A few days before his departure, Schubert released from the Jails of Heraklion two prostitutes Katy Aidonopoulou, 33 years old from Teta Artas and from Drama Nitsa Georgantopoulou 35 years old who it appears were preferred whores. v. Μεσόγειος, 26.6.2008, p. 17.
370. Kokonas, Crete, id., p.101 Also, von Xylander id., p. 117, footnote 71.
371. Κρητικός Κήρυξ, Heraklion, 7.1.1944. Passadakis, a fanatic executor of the Germans, with no patriotic inclination even at the worst reprisals as those at the provinces of Viannos in September 1943, always took the side of the perpetrators and criticized the Cretans with the warning, 'if you don't denounce the criminal individuals, the community is an accomplice and responsible for mass reprisals' v. 'Proclamation to the Cretan people', Κρητικός Κήρυξ, Heraklion, 20.9.1943.
372. Kavvos, p. 412. Brauer's plea was published in the press on 17th November 1943.
373. Ibid.
374. Κρητικός Κήρυξ, Heraklion, October / November. The church bells were deemed an anti-German weapon of the villagers who used them to warn the men to flee to the hills before the German detachments had time to blockade their village.
375. Kavvos, p. 461. In his announcement in April 1944 on the occasion of the abduction of General Karl Kreipe, Commandant Brauer reminded the Cretans of the 'promulgated policy of pacification, peace and security for the population' which he had pursued since October 1943.
376. Κρητικός Κήρυξ, Heraklion, November 8th 1943.
377. v. Appendix I. First Schubert Announcement.
378. Schubert at this point is consistent with the tactics which the General Administrator I. Passadakis threatened the Cretans immediately after the horrendous events at Viannos and before the German authorities decided to promote the plan of placating and reconciliation in October 1943. v. Κρητικός Κήρυξ, Heraklion, 20.9.1943.
379. v. Appendix I. Second Schubert announcement.
380. Ibid., January 1st 1944.
381. Kavvos, id., p. 412. The plea was announced on 17th November 1943.
382. Kokonas, Crete, p. 102.
383. Κρητικός Κήρυξ, Heraklion, 18th January 1944.

384. Passadakis, id., p. 12. The 'political apology' was composed in 1947 by friends of Passadakis when he was imprisoned.
385. K. E. Mamalakis archive, "Letter of Tom Dunbabin or Ioanni" 17.12.1943. In the end, papa-Kallergis' contacts with resistance organizations in the hope he would jump to the opposite camp did not bear fruit. v. G. Kalogerakis, Anogi, February-April 2005, p. 4.
386. Kokonas, Crete, id., p. 101.
387. Ibid., p. 102. Kokonas in the Greek version of the British Report evidently is mistaken when he refers to Schubert departing 'a few days later, on 2nd January 44'. (cf. Crete, id., p. 102) Note that G. Tzoulias on 10th January was still in Crete as on this day he released eight Krousaniotes from the Heraklion Jails v. Μεσόγειος, Heraklion, 26.6.2008, p. 17.
388. ΔΙΣ, "Reports of the activities of the team of espionage and intelligence of the municipality of Chania" (no place and time), p. 369. The Report was submitted to ΓΕΣ by Captain Marko Spanoudaki, member of EOK, responsible for the Office of intelligence of the municipality of Chania.
389. Καννος, p. 429.
390. Ibid.
391. Kostopoulos, id., p. 19. The 'Gendarmes Squad of Chania' was assembled on 17th February 1944 and dissolved the end of September 1944. In German documents of the time the squad is mentioned as 'the Greek battalion in pursuit of Papagiannakis rebels.
392. Collaborators Documents: "Defense of the accused Dimitrios Alatza" Thessaloniki, 25th July 1946.
393. Deutsche Dienststelle Berlin, 29.05.1944, letter of archive keeper Stephan Kuehmayer to the author, June 16th 2005.
394. Collaborators Documents: "Defense of the accused Ioannou Gridakis", Thessaloniki, 25th May 1946.
395. IAYE 1949, Special Martial Court of war Criminals: 'Indictment against Fritz Schubert', Athens, 2nd October 1946.
396. Karkanis, p. 384. Schubert's victims in Macedonia number between 300 and 320.
397. Καννος, p. 794.
398. The report is signed by Colonel N. Dimotakis, Director of Intelligence of Υ.Π.Σ.
399. K. E. Mamalakis archive, Athens, 5.8.1947.
400. IAYE, 1949. Chania, 30th March 1948.
401. Giannadakis, Memories, p. 44.
402. Ριζοσπάστης, 10.12.1946. Also, Karkanis, p. 377.
403. Μακεδονία, 30.7.1947.
404. Μακεδονία, 29.7.1947.
405. Μακεδονία, 28 and 29.7.1947.
406. Το Βήμα 29.7.1947.
407. Ο Ελληνικός Βορράς, 29.7.1947.
408. Konstantinos Mitsotakis (IKM), 'Minutes of Meeting, Athens 1946.
409. Panayiotis Kanavakis, recorded interview, Heraklion, 28.6.2006.
410. Konstantinos Mitsotakis, recorded interview, Athens, 2.6.2006.
411. Emmanouil Portalakis, recorded interview, Heraklion, 28.6.2006.
412. Konstantinos Mitsotakis, recorded interview, Athens, 2.6.2006.
413. K. E. Mamalakis archive, "Report of the examination of witness Richard Haar" Heraklion, 16th June 1946. Also, Καννος, p. 797.
414. See above p. 97.
415. Stavros Manouselis, interview, Kallikratis, 19.5.2008.
416. Ioannis Papadakis, recorded telephone interview, Oros, 13.12.2007.

417. Ibid.
418. ΓΑΚ. Documents of the Special Court of Collaborators: Minutes and decisions Heraklion 1945–1946.
419. Dordanas, Greeks, p. 330–336.
420. Nikos Marantzides. 'The armed nationalist leaders of the Occupation in Northern Greece' The other Captains. Armed anti-communism during the Occupation and Civil War. Athens, 2006, p. 45–47. To the area of Giannitsa after 1922 moved 783 Pontian families from a total 6,854 refugee families.
421. Ibid., p. 66.
422. Dordanas, Greeks, p.170–190. Also, Jacob Hondromatides 'Traitors of the Occupation' Historical Issues volume 17(2008) p. 62–71 and 'The black shadow in Greece. Nationalist and fascist organizations in Greece interwar years and the German Occupation 1941–1944' Martial History (Athens, 2001) p. 75–80. Hondromatides points to Schubert's group joining that of Poulos with Veroia as their base (p. 77). Schubert remained independent merely cooperating on occasions with Poulos.
423. Stratos N. Dardanos, 'Greeks against Greeks: George Poulos and his volunteers', 1st Assembly of Tsotyli, the civil wars: local aspects of the Greek Civil War, Tsotyli 16th June 2001, p. 11.
424. Ibid., p. 15.
425. Dordanas, Greeks, p. 191–206.
426. Stratos N. Dordanas 'The opponents of ΕΛΑΣ in the Giannitsa area'. Memoirs of the Occupation and Resistance: A Contribution to the history of Giannitsa during the German Occupation (1941–1944), Seminar, Giannitsa 17th October 2004.
427. Ibid. Anticommunist leaders in German occupied Central Macedonia.
428. Ibid.
429. Ibid., The innocent blood, p. 336.
430. Dordanas, 'Anticommunist leaders in German occupied Central Macedonia.
431. Thanasis Mitsopoulos, In the Macedonian hills, The 30th division of ΕΛΑΣ, 5th edition, Athens, p. 297. Also, Tasos Hadzianastasiou, 'The nationalist lords in Bulgarian occupied Macedonia and Thrace' in Marantzides, p. 303.
432. Thanasis Kallianiotis 'The anticommunist captains in West Macedonia (1942–1949)' in Marantzides, p. 242.
433. Ibid., p. 244–245.
434. Mitsopoulos, p. 312.
435. Kallianiotis, 'The anticommunist captains in West Macedonia (1942–1949)' in Marantzides p. 245. Also, Mitsopoulos, p. 304–305.
436. Mitsopoulos, p. 293. Mitsopoulos dates the establishment of the leaders Haseri, Tsarouchidi and Skaperdas at Giannitsa to early July 1944.
437. Marantzides, 'The armed nationalist guards of the Occupation in northern Greece', ditto, p. 33.
438. Ibid., p. 42.
439. Dordanas, The blood, p. 364.
440. , as above, p. 55.
441. Dordanas, The blood, p. 381. Koukos was the primary example of an organized Turkish speaking village which from spring 1943 was established as one of the most powerful anticommunist bastions of Macedonia.
442. Eleftherotypia, 26.10.2003.
443. Dordanas, The blood, p. 366, 487, 503.
444. Ibid., p. 516.

445. Dordanas, 'The enemies of ΕΛΑΣ in the area of Giannitsa'. Memoirs of Occupation and Resistance: Contribution to the history of Giannitsa during the German Occupation (1941- 1944), Giannitsa 17th October 2004, p. 3. Also, Dionysios Kasapis, recorded telephone interview, Giannitsa 23.1.2007. Also, Dimitris Hatzivrettas, 'Giannitsa: 14th September 1944', Memoirs of 1944, Seminar, Giannitsa 17th October 2004.
446. Mitsopoulos, p. 657.
447. Ibid., p. 492, 514.
448. George Boskos, recorded interview, Giannitsa, 2.10.2008.
449. Marantzides, 'The armed nationalist', p. 42.
450. Mitsopoulos, p. 185. The resistance executed some Bafrans and burnt several homes.
451. The recruits of Schubert at Giannitsa were Lazaros Kommatopoulos with his wife Eudoxia, Chr. Tatoglou, P. Koxenoglou, N. Papadopoulos, all from Aravissos, I. Salpasides with his two sons, St. Diktapanides, Chr. Tsakirides, G. Korkanides, D. Kosmides, G. Koutsoudis, G. Varveris, G. Politis and B. Papamanolis from provinces of Kilkis, Drama and Serres.
452. Savvas Michaelides, interview, Petralona, 26.6.2007. Lazaros Kommatopoulos appears to owe his close tie to Schubert to the fact he knew the teacher and recent lover of Schubert, Katina Aggelidou from Sandali, Pella.
453. George Boskos, recorded interview, Giannitsa, 2.10.2008. Also, Mitsopoulos, p. 186.
454. Dordanas, The blood, p. 302.
455. Dionysios Kasapis, recorded telephone interview, Giannitsa 23.1.2007.
456. Salonica Appeal court Traitors' Documents: 'Report of sworn witness examination of Stefanos Triantafyllides, Giannitsa, 1st October 1945. (Henceforth the source of information will be stated only as 'traitors documents' and it will be implied that they originate from the Salonica Appeal Court).
457. Hatzivrettas, p. 3.
458. Traitors Documents: 'Report of the examination of witness Stavros Katsoulea' Giannitsa, 29th June 1946.
459. Ibid.
460. Traitors Documents: 'Report of sworn examination of witness St. Triantafyllides' Giannitsa, 2nd July 1946.
461. Traitors Documents: 'Report of the examination of Stavros Katsouleas, Giannitsa 29th June 1946.
462. The 28year old Aggelidou remained 'engaged' to Schubert until end September when replaced by 24year old Dina Mantzana, the daughter of a doctor in S. Skaperdas guard.
463. Traitors Documents: Administration of municipal Police of Giannitsa no. 26/1/2g 'Regarding activities of war criminal, German Schubert', Giannitsa, 25.6.1946.
464. Ibid., 'Report of sworn examination of witness St. Triantafyllides', Giannitsa, 2nd July 1946.
465. Ibid., 'Report of examination of witness Stavros Katsouleas', Giannitsa, 29th June 1946
466. Ibid., 'Report of sworn examination of witness Stefanos Triantafyllides', Giannitsa, 1st October 1945.
467. Ibid.
468. Traitors Documents. Division of National Security of Salonica no.8/22/104, 'About the criminal Schubert' to the Martial Command of Salonica, Legal Department, Salonica, 4th August 1945.
469. Traitors Documents. Police Dept. of Halkidiki, no. 26/I/3, 'Concerning the activity of war criminal Schubert Fritz' Polygyros 8th January 1946. The exact relationship is uncertain of Schubert with the unit known as 'Topographic Service'. After his move from Giannitsa to Halkidiki, Schubert allegedly was 'placed' under the control of the German unit to which a small team of cartographers belonged. Most likely, these were no more than 10–15 in

number. Similarly, unit 511 of the Cretan Guard Administration amounted to 14 persons. v. ΔΙΣ, vol. 5, file 911/Δ/2, doc. no. 5. 'Daily force and war force of all positioned troops on the island Chania 1.7.1944, p. 49.
470. Ibid.
471. Traitors Documents. 'Sworn examination of witness Athanasios Kazakis', N. Kallikrateia, 9th August 1946.
472. Georgios I. Zografakis. Information-witnesses-evidence regarding the National Resistance in Halkidiki, Polygyros, 2006, p. 235.
473. Ibid., p. 234–236.
474. Athanasios Tzirinis, recorded interview, Nea Gonia, 1.10.2008.
475. Traitors Documents: 'Sworn examination of witness Ath. Kazaki', N. Kallikrateia, 9th August 1946.
476. Athanasios Tzirinis, recorded interview, Nea Gonia, 1.10.2008.
477. Traitors Documents: 'Sworn examination of witness Stavros Giannoglou', N. Kallikrateia, 4th August 1946. Apart from Giannoglou, the other recruits were Kaldis, Mandinos and Parashos.
478. Traitors Documents: Administration of Halkidiki police, national security division Polygyros, no. 26/I/3, 'To the higher directorate of central Macedonia police, security division', Polygyros, 8.1.1946.
479. Sources often confuse this 'battle' of Nea Gonia with that of Krini between a German force and the 2nd division under capt. Kitso on 12th September 1944.
480. Traitors Documents. Police station N. Kallikrateia no. 21/1/4, 'regards the activity of war criminal German Schubert Fritz' to the subdivision of police N. Moudania, N. Kallikrateia, 17th December 1946. The incident is also mentioned by the president Ath. Kazaki. G. Papadopoulos only describes Kitsos as head, v. recorded telephone interview, Nea Triglia 19.7.2007.
481. Traitors Documents: 'Sworn examination of witness Ath. Kazakis', N. Kallikrateia, 9th August 1946.
482. Zografakis, p. 76. Deposition of Kassandran Riga Stambouli, prominent member of ΕΛΑΣ.
483. Parmenion I. Papathanasiou, For the Greek North. Macedonia 1941–1944. Resistance and tragedy, vol. 1, 2nd edition, Athens, 1997 p. 441.
484. B.A. Vasilikos, Halkidiki, Salonica 1938, p. 76.
485. Papathanasiou, vol. 1, p. 461.
486. Ath. Frontistis ΠΑΟ., Panhellenic Liberation Organization. History and contribution to the National Resistance 1941–1945, Salonica, 1977, p. 275. Also, Papathanasiou, vol. 1, p. 453.
487. Papathanasiou, vol. 1, p. 447.
488. Zografakis, p. 249.
489. Ibid., p. 462–463. On September 30th 1943, Skordas retaliated against the Marathiotes, who had previously arrested and kidnapped a Rizioti resistor during his stay at relatives. The incident at Marathousa caused such turmoil at the headquarters of ΠΑΟ and ΕΑΜ of Macedonia beckoning the imminent competition of the opponents in battle.
490. K. Konstantaras, Struggles and pursuits, Athens, 1964, p. 77.
491. E. Polemistis, Under the light of truth. The resistance organizations of Northern Greece, Salonica 1948, p. 44. Also, Frontistis, p. 274–275 and Konstantaras, p. 83.
492. Pericles Selidis, 'The unknown diaries of a resistor', Eleftherotypia, 14.4.2007. Selides, who served in the 2nd division of the 16th Regiment of Vermio, under capt. Kolokotroni notes 'the battle was at mount Hortiati with the men of ΠΑΟ but it didn't last long and

they scattered' Regiment 13 and 27 under K. Mitsos and A. Tsamalouka respectively had camped during this period at the heights of Hortiati, v. Papathanasiou, vol. 2, p. 588–591.
493. Vaios Kalogrias, 'Armed teams of autonomous leaders and nationalist officers in the area between Strymon and Axios (1941–1944)', Nikos Marantzides, The other Captains. Armed anticommunists in the years of Occupation and Civil War, Athens, 2006, 168–170.
494. Zografakis, p. 76.
495. Ibid., p. 75, 261.
496. Papathanasiou, vol. 1, p. 226.
497. Ibid., vol. 2, p. 875. 'The Summarized Order of active forces in the Peninsula of Halkidiki' bears no date, but no doubt was published just before or immediately after the Allied invasion at Normandy in June 1944.
498. X. Kotzageorgi – G. A. Kazamias, 'The ramifications of the Bulgarian Occupation to the economy of Eastern Macedonia and Thrace' in Xanthippi Kotzageorgi-Zymari. The Bulgarian Occupation in Eastern Macedonia and Thrace 1941–1944. Establishment-configuration-ramifications, Salonica, p. 112. Ibid., p. 308–310, v. army maps showing the allocation of Bulgarian forces in Halkidiki.
499. Papathanasiou, vol. 1, p. 450–451. Listed are detailed diagrams by Athan. Skorda of the German-Bulgarian fortifications at the straits of Rentina/Stavros.
500. Athan. I. Hrysohoou, The Occupation in Macedonia. The effects of Bulgarian propaganda, vol. B, 1943 & 1944, Salonica, 1950, p. 395.
501. Pericles Selidis, p. 9, writes 'we passed (the men of the Kolokotroni division) through Nyfopetres, the Lake of Langada and Volvi' to camp at Riza, at the northern heights of Holomonda towards the end of November 1943. Kolokotronis remained in Halkidiki for about two months.
502. Hrysohoou, p. 137.
503. Nicholas Yiouldasis, recorded interview, Ottawa 22.3.2007. Near Vavdos were stationed a unit of about 30 Germans around the magnesite mines, which was transported to Germany by ship.
504. Kotzageorgi-Zymari, p. 308–309. The maps show that the 3/4th divisions of the 41st Regiment had control of the coastal belt of the whole gulf of Kassandra, but do not determine whether these divisions bases were at Gerakini and Nikiti.
505. Hrysohoou, p. 145, 401, 402.
506. Zografakis, p. 166.
507. X. Kotzageorgi, 'Bulgarian integration policy regarding education, language and culture in Eastern Macedonia and Thrace' in Kotzageorgi- Zymari, p. 83–106.
508. Dordanas, The blood, p. 303.
509. Zografakis, p. 183.
510. Chrysohoou, p. 401. The author refers to Bulgarian divisions on missions from Nea Apollonia (more accurately from lake Volvi Nea Apollonia) Stavro and Stratoni. Passing Marathousa they asked for the surrender of three EAM officials, who had escaped to the mountains. At Arnaia, as ten incriminated had hidden, they held their relatives whom they released the next day.
511. Eudokia Galanou-Tsekoura, recorded telephone interview, Salonica, 12.5.2007. The Bulgarian expeditionary division made a stop the same day, June 2nd at Marathousa where the commander warned the local committee that 'their village would soon need to cater for Greek battalions', a sure indication of the cooperation between Germans/Schubert and Bulgarians, v. Dimitris Tsolakis, recorded interview. Marathousa, 13.6.1999.
512. Traitors Documents: 'Sworn examination of witness Stavros Giannoglou', Nea Kallikrateia, 4th August 1946.

513. Traitors Documents: 'Sworn examination of witness Athanasios Kazakis', Nea Kallikrateia, 9th August 1946.
514. Christos Poiratzides, recorded interview, Petralona 9.3.2007. Most information about the events at Petralona come from Poiratzides, a Schuberite deserter. Also, John Papadopoulos, recorded interview, Petralona, 1.10.2008.
515. Ibid.
516. Traitors Documents: 'Sworn examination of witness Panagiotis Katirtzides', Nea Kallikrateia, 9th August 1946. For recruits v. Section II, Diagram G. All deserted at Nea Apollonia. To Nea Kallikrateia, Schubert brought as a hostage Theodoros Efthimiou who they say he planned to execute. His wife, who was pregnant then, pleaded to Lazaros Kommatopoulos, who intervened to Schubert managing to secure his release. v. Savvas Michaelides, recorded interview, Petralona, 1.10.2008.
517. Zografakis, p. 235.
518. Traitors Documents: National Security Division of Salonica, 'Regarding the war criminal Fritz Schubert' Salonica, 4th August 1946. According to another account reverend Grigoris was arrested on the road between Nea Silata and Krini with a chance trader G. Minoglou. During the period of EAM, reverend Grigoris was jailed at Polygyros, then later found hanged, apparently suicide.
519. Heracles Kazakis, recorded interview, Krini 1.10.2008.
520. Ibid.
521. Athanasios Tzirinis, recorded interview, Nea Gonia 1.10.2008.
522. John Kehagias, recorded interview, Krini 1.10.2008. Apart from M. Moustaka and G. Soubasis, the other recruits were Antonios Tzirinis, Miltiadis Gavanas, George Koutsoudis and a Tsakalos. They all deserted from Nea Apollonia and took refuge at ΕΛΑΣ Halkidiki.
523. Traitors Documents: National Security Division of Salonica, 'Regards the war criminal Fritz Schubert' Salonica 4th August 1945.
524. Traitors Documents. 'Sworn examination of witness Nik. Fanariotis' Nea Kallikrateia, 3rd August 1946.
525. Filippos Kotsantas, recorded interview, Peristera 4.10.2008.
526. Ibid. According to another source, Peristera had one victim. v. Nikolaos Fanariotis, note 53.
527. Traitors Documents: 'Sworn examination of witness Nik. Fanariotis', Nea Kallikrateia, 3rd August 1946.
528. From Galatista were recruited two youngsters, Argyrios Sakelaris and a Stergios who both escaped from Nea Apollonia with others from Halkidiki.
529. Panagiotis Varis, interview, Livadi 18.10.2008.
530. Kleanthis Venetopoulos, Place of origin: Livadi Halkidiki, Salonica 1998 p. 259. From the summer of 1944, a division of ΕΛΑΣ Halkidiki kept their hideout in the woods of 'Kerasies' between Petrokerasa and Livadi. Venetopoulos' home was used as the headquarters during the last three months before the liberation.
531. Panagiotis Varis, recorded interview, Livadi, 18.10.2008.
532. Traitors Documents: Administration of Giannitsa Police no. 26/I/2g, 'regarding the actions of war criminal German Schubert Fritz' Giannitsa, 25th June 1946.
533. Traitors Documents: 'Sworn examination of witness Nik. Fanariotis', Nea Kallikrateia, 3rd August 1946.
534. Ibid.
535. Christos Poiratzides, recorded interview, Petralona, 9.3.2007.
536. Theofilos Tsolakis, recorded interview, Nea Apollonia, 18.6.1999. Also, Theofilos Kokkotas, recorded interview, Nea Apollonia, 24.6.2006.
537. Papathanasiou, vol. 2, p. 460, refers to the assembly of the core of the organization.

538. Zografakis.
539. Maria Grammatikou-Halkia, recorded interview, Giannitsa, 31.7.2007.
540. Eudokia Galanou-Tsekoura, recorded interview, Thessaloniki, 1.4.2004.
541. Theofilos Kokkotas, recorded interview, Nea Apollonia, 24.6.2006.
542. Ibid. On 8th June, following a tip-off, eight young girls from the ΕΠΟΝ were arrested to whom Schubert, once brought to his office, gave the following warning 'Listen here. If I get to hear of anything, you won't get off, I'll wipe you out' v. Anna Devreli, recorded interview, Salonica, 27.6.2006.
543. John Tsolakis recorded interview, Nea Apollonia, 14.8.1979.
544. Leontis Paschalides, recorded telephone interview, Nea Apollonia, 21.10.2005.
545. Ibid.
546. Anna Devreli, recorded interview, Thessaloniki, 20.8.2007.
547. Theofilos Tsolakis, recorded interview, Nea Apollonia, 16.6.1999.
548. John Tsolakis, recorded interview, Nea Apollonia, 14.8.1979.
549. Marathousa forms part of the nucleus of Zervochoria. Today Zervochoria, Palaiochora, Geroplatanos, Krimni, Marathousa and Riza form a unified municipality.
550. Museum of the Macedonian Struggle: Research Centre of Macedonian history and evidence (KEMIT). Census tables 1913–1940.
551. Grigoris Varveris, recorded interview, Marathousa, 16.10.2004.
552. Konstantaras, p. 71.
553. Mitsopoulos, p. 575, 753. 30year old capetan Stratos with enlistments augmented the division to 120 armed men whom he added to the team of capetan Zaharia Zagoritis from Arnaia thus assembling an important force 'exceeding 200 men approximately' at the battle of Vrasta in November 1943. Haritides abandoned with his division Halkidiki for Krousia beginning February 1944 v.Konstantaras, p. 83.
554. Zografakis, p. 69. Hence the spot 'Kakavos' is also named as a lair of ΕΛΑΣ at Holomonda.
555. Ibid., p. 369.
556. Grigoris Varveris, recorded interview, Marathousa, 16.10.2004.
557. Niki Routsi, recorded telephone interview, Polygyros, 14.3.2004.
558. Dimitris Tsolakis, recorded interview, Marathousa, 13.6.1999. Also, Nikolaos Fotiou, recorded interview, Marathousa, 14.8.1979.
559. Grigoris Varveris, recorded interview, Marathousa, 16.10.2004. There is also an untested source that the horsemen had no relation to the Schuberites v. Nikolaos Samaras, recorded interview, Marathousa, 8.10.2004.
560. Ibid.
561. Dimitris Giataganas, recorded interview, Melissourgos, 16.10.2008.
562. Ibid.
563. Dimitris Tsolakis, recorded interview, Marathousa, 13.6.1999. V. Tsoukalas, for professional reasons, had moved with his family to Marathousa some years before.
564. Spyros Fotiou, recorded interview, Thessaloniki, 15.8.1979.
565. Dimitris Tsolakis, recorded interview, Marathousa, 13.6.1999.
566. Traitors Documents: 'Sworn examination of witness Stavros Giannoglou', N. Kallikrateia, 4th August 1946. In his narrative he refers no doubt to the raids of 18 and 19th June.
567. Nikolaos Fotiou, recorded interview, Marathousa, 14.8.1979.
568. Theofilos Tsolakis, recorded interview, Nea Apollonia, 16.6.1999. Boris Tsolantzevits, resident of Profiti and his sons Socrates and Christos in 1947 were committed to trial with the accusation that they had become 'willful organs of the enemy (Bulgarians) to disseminate their propaganda'. The court acquitted them. V. Thessaloniki Appeal, Special

Collaborators Court: Collaborators Decisions 1–500, Decision no. 424, Thessaloniki, 15th April 1947.
569. Athanasios Chrisohoou, p. 397.
570. Dimitris Tsolakis, recorded interview, Marathousa, 13.6.1999.
571. Spiros Fotiou, recorded interview, Thessaloniki, 15.8.1979.
572. Ibid.
573. Zografakis, p. 221–223, 317.
574. Olga Haideftou, recorded interview, Marathousa, 8.10.2004. Those arrested were Kitsos (Christos) Haideftos with his wife Sofia and his 15year old daughter and the 25year old Olga Haideftou with her baby. Some Marathiotes believe that Haideftos, during the burning of the village, showed Schubert the homes of the resistors. The accusation based on suspicions rather than facts.
575. Ibid. The phrasing of Haideftou 'the boys snatched, the pillows in blood' refers to the injured Schuberite the Sunday at Marathousa who was lain in the Community office on pillows and sheets brought by the then president Anagnostis Kaisis.
576. Ibid.
577. Dimitris Tsolakis, recorded interview, Marathousa ,13.6.1999.
578. At the plundering operation of Marathousa, it seems, partook the Metaxan Theodoros Katsikas, former president of Nea Apollonia and a dubious character. Fearing ΕΛΑΣ in 1944 he abandoned the village with his family and settled in Thessaloniki. It is unknown what ties he had with the occupying authorities of the city. Active between Thessaloniki and Langada, he worked in the livestock trade 'making many gold sovereigns', exploiting the plunder of animals from armed collaborators and the overriding conditions of black money (A. Hatzigeorgiou, recorded interview, Thessaloniki, 16.10.2004). There are indications that Katsikas played a negative role in representing the injured villages during the trials of the Schuberites and their leader. v. Nikolaos Samaras, recorded interview, Marathousa , 8.10.2004.
579. Nikolaos Samaras, recorded interview, Marathousa, 8.10.2004.
580. Olga Haideftou, recorded interview, Marathousa, 8.10.2004.
581.. Andreas G. Devrelis, recorded telephone interview, Nea Apollonia, 15.10.2005.
582. Dimitris Tsolakis, recorded interview, Marathousa, 13.6.1999.
583. Olga Haideftou, recorded interview, Marathousa, 8.10.2004. At the memorial of 'Platana' erected in 1989 there are named 26 fatalities with the inscription' and other unknown warriors'. Engraved are five (of the six) resistors, all non Marathiotes, who were murdered by the Bulgarian cavalry on 19th June, eight EAMite officials, all non Marathiotes, seven of whom were executed on 20th June at the spot 'Platana'. Cornelios Eliades, an EAMite from Melissourgos, was arrested at the block of Melissourgos on 18th June and later executed at Nea Apollonia. Of the 13 Marathiotes named on the marble, 11 were victims of 19th June, V. Tsoukalas victim of 18th June and Sp. Haideftos of Mavrogiorgos, a shepherd, killed some other day by a German car at the spot 'Yankov' of Holomonda. Amongst the executed were two traveling traders arrested on 19th June near Marathousa and executed at 'Platana' without being named on the memorial. In all, the number of victims amounts to 29 persons. So, from the memorial are missing the names of the salesmen and one murdered rebel.
584. Niki Routsi, recorded interview, Polygyros, 14.3.2004.
585. IAMM, Archive of Nikolaos Dea: Directorate of Food of the Provinces, Control and Inspection Service, 'Report on our trips to the provinces from 15–21 September 1944 'Thessaloniki, 23.9.1944, p. 5.
586. Vasileios Voyiatzis, recorded telephone interview, Marathousa, 3.10.2006.

587. Georgios Voyiatzis, recorded telephone interview, Nea Raidestos, 8.12.2006.
588. Voyiatzis, recorded interview, Marathousa 17.10.2006. S. Baharides who is considered to have played a dubious role during Schubert's stay in Nea Apollonia, became it seems the scapegoat for the holocaust of Marathousa. He was tried as a resistor at Holomonda and executed after the destruction of the village.
589. Niki Routsi, recorded telephone interview, Polygyros, 14.3.2004.
590. Dordanas, The blood, p. 201.
591. Traitors Documents: 'Sworn examination of witness Stavros Giannoglou, Nea Kallikrateia, 4th August 1946.
592. Georgios Voyiatzis, recorded telephone interview, Nea Raidestos, 14.9.2005.
593. Traitors Documents: 'Sworn examination of witness Panagiotis Katirtzides', N. Kallikrateia, 9th August 1946.
594. Savvas Liapis, recorded interview, Nea Madytos, 18.6.2006.
595. Konstantinos Sofis, recorded interview, Nea Madytos, 18.6.2006.
596. Ibid.
597. Traitors Documents: Stavros Giannoglou, Nea Kallikrateia, 4th August 1946. Giannoglou states that at an assembly of his men at Nea Apollonia, Schubert asked 'Whoever wishes to be released and go back home, should leave the line' Four men pulled aside amongst whom the two Cretans and two Halkidikiotes. The latter, tipped off, deserted immediately so got off but the Cretans delayed and were executed. The episode has no date attributed but probably happened early July and refers to the fate of the Cretan peddlers from Nea Madytos, as they also became victims of Schubert's trap.
598. Archive of Modern Social History (AΣKI), Archive EΔA, file 219, 'Report of the District Committee of Halkidiki at the Macedonian Office', 30.7.1944. In the report is stated 'At N. Madytos the Collab. killed 8 (of which) 3 local officials'. Apart from the three aforementioned, the remaining victims of the village were Har. Adaloglou, Stratos Ladopoulos, I. Tsiftis, Mic. Tintonis and Nik. Kalbenis.
599. Traitors Documents: 'Law suit of Stavros Ant. Arnaoutelis against Asterios Sar. Koumboyiannis', Salonica, 19th July 1945.
600. Traitors Documents: 'Sworn examination of witness Anastasia Valavani, Langada, 4th August 1947.
601. Theofilos Kokkotas, recorded interview, Nea Apollonia, 24.6.2006.
602. Ibid. The communal secretary I. Matselas (known as Matsalas) was an ex-policeman and brother-in-law through sister to metaxan Th. Katsikas. During EAM days Matselas was executed with other collaborators at Holomonda.
603. Theofilos Kokkotas, recorded interview, Nea Apollonia, 11.12.2006. Apart from Zahos those executed were Dim. Karakasis and Kon. Karadimitriades.
604. Dordanas, The blood, p. 531.
605. Theofilos Kokkotas, recorded interview, Nea Apollonia, 24.6.2006. The whole narrative regarding the ambush of Kitsos relies on the contribution and experience of Th. Kokkotas.
606. Traitors Documents: 'Examination of witness Eleni Akassi' Thessaloniki 13th November 1945. The suspicions around the betrayal of the ambush turned against Mic. Akassis, a moderate member of the local EAM, whose wife and daughter, imprisoned in Schubert's jails, had been allowed free immediately after the ambush. His wife Eleni later testified as defense witness at the trial of Schuberite Lazaros Kommatopoulos. After the occupation Akassis became an active member of the Maides organization. v. Theofilos Kokkotas, recorded telephone interview, Nea Apollonia, 28.9.2006.
607. Maria Grammatikou-Halkia, recorded telephone interview, Giannitsa, 31.7.2007.

608. Theodore Valahas – Daphne Theochari, Hortiati, 2nd September 1944. Whatever remains of that day, it is a memory, Hortiati 570, 2008 p. 46, witness A. Ioannidi or Platona.
609. Dordanas, The blood, p. 529–530.
610. Traitors Documents, Minutes and Decisions, vol. 2, (201–450), Meeting of 9th October 1947, No. 430–433, 'Sworn deposition of Vassili Papasteriou'.
611. Stavros Tsiotsis, recorded interview, Asvestochori, 22.6.2006.
612. Rodolfos Sahinis, recorded interview, Thessaloniki, 29.5.2005. The 14year old Sahinis happened to be on holiday with his family when he chanced upon the group of children to the right of the park. At some stage, the fake shots became so dense and frequent to panic many there. A German guard saw Sahinis terrified hiding behind a tree and, waved him to follow leaving him behind the tyre of an abandoned truck before allowing him to later return to the crowd.
613. Ibid.
614. Spyros Tsiotsis, recorded telephone interview, Asvestochori, 21.8.2007. The daily press states that he who intervened to the German captain was called Eugenikos, an attorney from Thessaloniki v. Φως, 10.10.1947.
615. IAYE 1945, file 5, 1: Office of Nat. Security No. 8006/79/495, 'Report of crimes and events of 1st August 1944', Thessaloniki, 2.8.1944.
616. Φως, 10.10.1947.
617. Dordanas, The blood, p. 531. There is concern in the sources whether the 30 selected men for punishment came from the Sanatorium (Μακεδονία και ο Ελληνικός Βορράς 14.1.1948) or from the crowd in the park (Το Βήμα, 29.7.1947) The latter seems more probable.
618. Το Βήμα, 30.7.1947. Statement of Schuberite G. Delibasakis (read Belibasakis).
619. Traitors Documents: 'Report of sworn deposition of witness Konstantinos Kamisis' Thessaloniki, 18th December 1945.
620. Anna Devreli, recorded interview, Thessaloniki, 27.6.2006.
621. Ibid. It is the first report of a Cretan Schuberite leading the way in a team who wished to desert. Apart from Manousakis, no other Cretan is mentioned. The origins of another, one Dardanos, is unknown.
622. Christos Poiratzides, recorded interview, Petralona, 9.3.2007. The ΕΠΟΝitissa Amalia Flamourtzoglou 'was beyond suspicion, as she aided everyone. She was like a mother and sister. She even boiled water for us to wash our hair' testifies C. Poiratzides. To the good times she created with the Schuberites apparently contributed her friendship to Prodromos Koxenoglou from Aravissos. Apart from snitching on the Schubert league to EAM, she helped many Halkidikiotes Schuberites who used the well near her home pretending they were washing or drinking cold water. Poiratzides deserted with the help of Amalia on 30th July and surrendered to the 31st Regiment of ΕΛΑΣ from where he later left.
623. Ibid. Mavrides, the most anxious of the Petralonites often asked of his villagers to help him desert but to no avail. Most likely, Mavrides heard either from Flamourtzoglou or Katina Aggelidou herself that the deserters would have to leave that evening as the next day Schubert was preparing arrests. There are accounts that after the Germans left, Mavrides managed to find Aggelidou in Thessaloniki to thank her for her help as, according to his own testimony 'it is she who fed us. She sheltered us and other youngsters from Schubert'. He was saddened that the EAMites later executed her, v. Savvas Michaelides, recorded interview, Petralona, 1.10.2008.
624. Traitors Documents: 'Sworn examination of witness Panayiotis Katirtzides', N. Kallikrateia, 9th August 1946. There is reference that with the desertion of Schuberites from Petralona and Krini helped the 'wife' of Schubert Katina Aggelidou. Various reports circulated about her detection, arrest and death. The most plausible version is the testimony of St.

Triantafyllides, who states that 'the Elasites arrested her and executed her in the old market of Giannitsa'. The truth is that she was lynched by the crowd. v. Traitors Documents: 'Report of sworn examination of witness Stephanos Triantafyllides, Giannitsa, 1st October 1945.
625. Christos Poiratzides, recorded interview, Petralona, 2.3.2007.
626. Ibid.
627. Anna Devreli, recorded interview, Thessaloniki, 27.6.2006.
628. Anna Devreli, recorded interview, Thessaloniki, 27.6.2006.
629. Ibid.
630. Ibid.
631. Ibid.
632. Theodoros Glavas, recorded interview, Nea Apollonia, 8.10.2004.
633. Ibid.
634. Anna Devreli, recorded interview, Thessaloniki, 27.6.2006.
635. Ibid.
636. Ibid.
637. MA, RH19. 'Unternehmen sudwestlich Saloniki', 22nd August 1944.
638. Karkanis, p. 382–383.
639. MA, RH 19. 'Unternehmen, 22nd August 1944.
640. Traitors Documents: Centre of foreign Aliens of Thessaloniki, 'Report of examination of witness Dina or Konstantina Madzana' Thessaloniki 28th September 1945 (from now on 'Traitors Documents, Dina Madzana'). The deposition of Madzana contains valuable and detailed information about her role in Schubert's league until his departure through Yugoslavia to Austria, her adventure with Schubert as her return to Greece in September 1945.
641. Dordanas, The blood, p. 544.
642. Thanasis Mitsopoulos, p. 349.
643. Ibid., p. 353. Throughout the time Schubert was determining in Axioupolis the positions of the anticommunist battalions, a force of about 800 infantries in the area of Giannitsa, the leaders of ΕΕΣ were summoned to a meeting for the reorganization of its command in light of the German departure.
644. Traitors Documents, Directorate of Police of Kilkis, National Security, no. 26/2/2E, Kilkis, 6th February 1946.
645. Ioannis Kromlides, recorded telephone interview, Gorgopi, 17.7.2011, Kromlides, 17year old then, was an eyewitness to the described events from start to finish and his memory remains active and strong. Most of the narrative of events is based on his statement.
646. Ibid.
647. Evangelos Papanastasiou, recorded telephone interview, Nea Moudania, 16.6.2011. Papakonstantinou, 14 years old then, was eyewitness to the events until the selection of the 12 to be executed.
648. Traitors Documents: Dina Madzana.
649. Ioannis Kromlides, recorded telephone interview, Gorgopi, 17.7.2011.
650. Ibid. According to I. Kromlides, the father was recruited to the league after Schubert agreeing to his suggestion that he wear Schuberite uniform instead of his son.
651. Traitors Documents: Dina Madzana.
652. Ibid.
653. Valahas-Theochari p.87. The fact that the village had 2,265 residents comes from the 'Report' of Hortiati of Emil Wenger, the Swiss representative of the International Red Cross in Greece. See also Michail Stamatelatos and Foteini Vamva Stamatelatou, Geographic

dictionary of Greece, Ερμής ΕΠΕ, Athens, 2001 where the number of residents in the census of 1940 mentions about 1,800.
654. Νέα Ευρώπη, 3 and 8th June 1941. To the uprising contributed also political unrest of the residents with authorities.
655. Anastasios Trondzios, recorded telephone interview, Hortiati, 12.1.2009. Also, Valahas-Theochari, p. 30–31.
656. Ibid., p. 162. The photo was taken on 30th August 1943.
657. What happened (32 years ago) at Hortiati', Τα Νέα, 25th September 1976. Testimony of Georgios Mittas, liaison then of EAM who refers to 15 Hortiati being enlisted then in ΠΑΟ.
658.. Kalogrias, 'Armed teams of independent warlords and nationalist officers in the area between Strymon and Axion' in Nikos Marantzides. The other captains. Anticommunist armed forces during the years of Occupation and Civil War, Athens, 2006, p. 139.
659. Selidis, p. 9. In their report, Mitsou and Tzamaloukas do not refer to an attack of ΕΛΑΣ. v. Papathanasiou, p. 596.
660. Valahas-Theochari, p. 31.
661. Τα Νέα, 25th September 1976. According to G. Mitta, the first ΕΛΑΣ division at Hortiati was established by a student from Veroia.
662. , p. 532.
663. Mitsopoulos, p. 516.
664. Ibid., p. 342, 514–515.
665. Dordanas, The blood, p. 525–526.
666. Mitsopoulos, p. 342–345.
667. Dordanas, The blood, p. 529.
668. Zografakis, p. 77. The deposition of Rigas Stambouli, a resistor from Kassandra who held an important position in the ranks of ΕΛΑΣ Halkidiki.
669. Konstantinos Paschaloudis, recorded telephone interview, Thessaloniki, 11.8.2010.
670. Georgios H.Gouramanis, The historical Hortiati, Hortiati, 1988, p. 45. The writer states that the unit was camped 'ten days before' from 2nd September i.e. from 23rd August.
671. Valahas-Theocharis, p. 59.
672. Konstantinos Paschaloudis, recorded telephone interview, Thessaloniki, 7.8.2010.
673. Ibid. Paschaloudis enlisted to ΕΛΑΣ in spring 1944 and for a while served as a political member at the Exemplary Unit of Youth of Hortiati G. Valahas (capetan Foteinos) until the latter's transfer in August to the 13th Regiment of Kilkis when he took over the command of the Youth Unit.
674. The source of the narrative consists of a series of recorded telephone interviews given by Konstantinos Paschaloudis in Thessaloniki on August 7, 11, 27th 2010 and October 22nd 2010.
675. Valahas-Theocharis, p. 59. Capetan Hortiati in his Report speaks of their installation towards the end of August in the area of Hortiati, 'our divisions have begun leaving the mountains and are being advanced to the outskirts of Thessaloniki.
676. Georgios Gouramanis, p. 45–47.
677. Elli Almetidou-Koutsiali, The holocaust of Hortiati, Thessaloniki, p. 48.
678. Valahas-Theocharis, p. 119, where is listed the order no. 1329/25.9.1945 of the Misdemeanor Council of Thessaloniki.
679. The Greek North, September 19th, 1976, Statements of M.H. and Anast. Zeka.
680. Konstantinos Paschaloudis, recorded telephone interview, Thessaloniki, 7.8.2010. Theodore Valahas (v. recorded telephone interview, Thessaloniki, 3.11.2008) asserts that Floria,

Hortiati and Tromaras, the last in absentia, were convicted to many years in jail but were pardoned by the Government of Th. Sofouli early 1946. The assertion is unconfirmed.
681. The archive of capetan Hortiati (G. Kirkimtzis) published in 2008 by Theodore G. Valahas (p. 129-160) consists of original documents written by third parties and personal narratives.
682. Ibid., p. 131-32, 134, 137. Protests to capetan Hortiati from bordering villages like Lakkia, Agios Vasileios, Langadikia Kavalari and Filyro.
683. Ibid., p. 134. The report probably dates to the last days of August.
684. Athanasios Kyroudis, recorded telephone interview, Thessaloniki, 16.1.2009. The EAM A. Kyroudis, 26 years old in 1944 was one of the suppliers of the unit of capetan Floria at 'Kastanies'.
685. Valahas-Theocharis, p. 34. The official responsible was called Giannis Loutzioudis In the account of lieutenant St. Draga it becomes very clear how sensitive capetan Kitsos was towards the requests of farmers and breeders to protect them from animal thieving. A unit of capetan Kitsos relieved the breeders of Agios Prodromos from a looting band of Bulgarians.
686. Ibid., p. 138.
687. Anastasios Trontsios, recorded telephone interview, Thessaloniki, 12.1.2009.
688. The Greek North, 19.9.1976. Also, Anastasios Trontsios, recorded telephone interview, Thessaloniki, 12.1.2009.
689. The Greek North, 19.9.1976.
690. Tamiolakis, employed by the Ο.Υ.Θ. in 1969 researched the archives of the Organization and in 1985 published the results in a paper, History of Water Supply in Thessaloniki, University Studio Press, 1985 In the book he dedicates (p.28) a paragraph to the Hortiati incident of 2nd September. In 1987 in an EPT broadcast about the Thessaloniki supply, I. Staninos briefly recounts the incident of 2nd September from the spot at the aqueduct 'Kamara' (v. DVD of I. Tamiolakis made available to the writer).
691. Ioannis Tamiolakis, recorded telephone interview, Thessaloniki, 19.8.2010.
692. Every Friday: An. Trontsios, recorded telephone interview, Thessaloniki, 12.1.2009. Every Saturday, G. Trontsios, The Greek North, 19.9.1976 and G. Gouramanis, p. 32. Twice a week: S. Panilas, IAYE, file 4 (1945) 'sinistre du village Hortiati' (paper E. Venger). Every fortnight: G. Mitas, Τα Νέα, 15.9.1976 and K. Paschaloudis, recorded telephone interview, Thessaloniki, 7.8.2010.
693. The Greek North, 19.9.1976, testimony of G. Trontsios and Valahas-Theocharis, p. 95, report of capetan Hortiati. The description of the Greek car is the similar with the one of K. Paschaloudis.
694. IAYE, 'sinistre, Hortiati', S. Panilas mentions three employees whilst Giannis Tamiolakis names five amongst whom Al. Sotirchopoulos who is verified to have traveled with the German car. Possibly Tamiolakis names all the employees scheduled to travel but some in the end were absent for any reason.
695. The Greek North, 19.9.1976, testimony of G. Trontsios. Also, Valahas-Theocharis, p. 95, evidence of capetan Hortiati. The 18year old G. Farsakides (Valahas-Theocharis, p. 101) involved in the ambush refers to 'the German open vehicle'. His information not always reliable.
696. The sources generally agree with that of G. Trontsios. If no driver is mentioned then either the chemist or one of the military police did the job of driving. I. Tamiolakis is the only one who raises the figure of Germans involved to five, three military police the driver and the Austrian chemist. Of these the chemist was killed, three imprisoned and one wounded German escaped to Asvestochori.
697. Dordanas, The blood, p. 532. The ruling bears the date, 12.7.1944.

698. An. Trontsios, recorded telephone interview, Thessaloniki, 12.1.2009.
699. The first who specified the time of arrival, 9.00 for the Greek and 9.30 for the German car, was S. Panilas in his statement to the representative of the international Red Cross on 7th September 1944 v. IAYE, 'sinistre, Hortiati'. Since the above times became accepted by many. On the other hand, V. Rikoudi (Valahas-Theocharis, p. 72) and G. Gouramanis (Gouramanis, p. 32) use the phrase 'a little later' to declare the time space between the Greek and German car. K. Paschaloudis states that the fire shots against the German vehicle were heard at 'Kastanies' about five minutes after the shots at the first car (recorded telephone interview, Thessaloniki 7.8.2010). Capetan Hortiati in his first note writes that 'the two cars 'arrived simultaneously v. Valahas-Theocharis, p. 94.
700. The Greek North, 19.9.1976. Trontsios during his interview, possibly due to a memory loss, lapsed into inaccuracies, one relating to the existence of resistors in the village. Further neither he nor any other from Hortiati knew of the ambush at 'Kamara' on that day.
701. Valahas-Theocharis, p. 131. A community official at Hortiati in a letter to the command of the 1st unit states that the German lead ordered the authorities of the village 'by 4pm to assemble all the animals. The event dates to 20 or 27th August.
702. Athanasios Kyroudis, recorded telephone interview, Hortiati, 16.1.2009.
703. Almetidou-Koutsiali, p. 26. Also, Valahas-Theocharis, p. 72.
704. Valahas-Theocharis, p. 100. According to the resistor Farsakidi, Rikoudi upon discovering the car 'probably had to do with Greeks' (note the wording) took a shot in the air to call it down, a detail Rikoudi hushes up, though capetan Hortiati corroborates this, v. ditto, p. 95.
705. Konstantinos Paschaloudis, recorded telephone interview, Thessaloniki, 27.8.2010.
706. Ibid., p. 84. Tamiolakis names him Rizopoulos. He also mentions two technicians Nestora and Molyvopoulo as passengers of the truck. The testimony is not verified.
707. Gouramanis, p. 32. The existing sources differ as regards the number of passengers, wounded, detained and the Germans who escaped.
708. Konstantinos Paschaloudis, recorded telephone interview, Thessaloniki, 27.8.2010.
709. Valahas-Theocharis, p. 78, statement of EAMite Athan. Kyroudis.
710. Ibid., p. 77.
711. Ibid., p. 74. Capetan Hortiati, mostly for his personal convenience, staged amongst others the presence of capetan Floria at the village v. ditto, p. 93.
712. The Greek North, 19.9.1976. There is the testimony that whilst 45year old Areti Zekka advised an activist neighbor to abandon the village, she herself remained and became a victim v. Valahas-Theocharis, p. 78.
713. IAYE, 1945, 'Report of crimes and events of 12.9.1944', Thessaloniki, 13.9.1944. They testify to 14 and 32 military vehicles. If indeed 14, then the German force neared 200 soldiers including 80 Schuberites.
714. Almetidou-Koutsiali, p. 24, statement of Maria Aggelinoudi. Also, statements of Vasiliki Gouramanis, p. 27, Eleni-Gouramanis-Nanakoudi, p. 29 and George Logaritis, p. 30. In their statements the word 'noon' has wider meaning. In slang dialect it describes the early afternoon.
715. Ibid., p. 26. These were the first trucks which arrived at Hortiati from their base, Asvestochori. A little later, arrived a few more from Thessaloniki. So, the vehicular unit of Asvestochori and Schubert's gang had up to two hours to prepare and travel the eight kilometres to Hortiati. One version, that the German authorities had already scheduled the destruction of Hortiati for 2nd September and 20 (others say 32!) vehicles waited ready for the order to advance on Hortiati immediately, is based on doubtful and hypothetical

evidence. v. interesting and pioneering research by Theodoros Valahas, 'The crime was foregone', Hortiatis 570, September-October 2009.
716. Ibid., p. 29.
717. Το Φως, 10.10.1947.
718. Gouramanis, p. 34.
719. Ibid., p. 33. Badatsios in spring 1944 with 16 Hortiati took part in a meeting of the local EAM to elect the military and political lead. v. Valahas-Theocharis, p. 41.
720. Almetidou-Koutsiali, p. 36.
721. The Greek North, 14.1.1948.
722. Almetidou- Koutsiali, p.31.
723. IAYE 1945. 'Sinistre du village Hortiati', statement of Maria Aggelinoudi. Also, Valahas-Theocharis, p. 90.
724. Almetidou-Koutsiali, p. 32, statement of Maria Aggelinoudi.
725. Ibid., p. 39.
726. Theodore Valahas, recorded telephone interview, Thessaloniki, 2.7.2009.
727. Το Βήμα, 29.7.1947, testimony of I. Galitsanou. Ibid., 2.9.1970, of Vaiou Daoudi.
728. Νέα Αλήθεια, 3.9.1945.
729. ΕΘ, Minutes and Decisions. 'Sworn testimony of Panayiotis Sarvanis.
730. Dordanas, The blood, p. 536.
731. Vaggeli Plakas, The holocaust at Hortiati of 2nd September 1944. 60 years later: memory and duty, Thessaloniki, 2004, p. 45.
732. Theodoros S. Zervas, Lawsuit for damages as a result of emotional distress before the Court of Thessaloniki, 29th August 2001.
733. IAYE. 'Sinistre. Hortiati', testimony of Eleni Koukaroudi.
734. Ριζοσπάστης, 6.8.1947.
735. Archive of K .E. Mamalakis: Special Court Martial of War Criminals, Decision No. 1, Thessaloniki, 5th August 1947. It was not proven that he raped Georgia Koukaroudi 19 years old, Anastasia Ritsioudi, 29 years old, Anastasia Simoni, 16 years old, and Areti Sotiriou, 18 years old. All these women were either burned or murdered.
736. Traitors Documents: 'Sworn examination of witness Stavros Giannoglou, N. Kallikrateia, 4th August 1946. According however to the testimony of L. Kommatopoulos, I. Kambas was executed by order of Schubert 'because he deceived a girl at Asvestochori. v. Traitors Documents: No. 1756, Secretariat of Special Court of Thessaloniki, Archive Division, Thessaloniki, 6th June 1961. The testimony of Kommatopoulos seems most reliable.
737. IAYE. 'Sinistre. Hortiati', testimony of Ioannis Karatzis (read Kirkimtzis).
738. IAMM, 'Report regarding our trips to the Provinces'.
739. Dordanas , The blood , p. 539.
740. Collaborators' documents: Report of the examination of witness Anastasios Zeka, Thessaloniki, 1st October 1945.
741. Collaborators documents: Sworn testimony of witness Odysseus Dyseakis, Heraklion, 31.1.1945.
742. Neue. Zeitung, Nordheim, Westfalen, 26.9.2006.
743. Int. Comm. of Historians (1993), The Waldheim Report.
744. Ute von Livonius, electronic mail to the author, Freiburg, 27.5.2006.
745. http://www.wissen.spiegel.de.
746. Waldheim Report, p. 185.
747. Dordanas, The blood, p. 541.
748. Waldheim Report p. 185–186.
749. IAYE. 'Sinistre. Hortiati '.

750. Willi Pohlmann was the last command of the Gendarmerie 501 division (Feldgendarmerie 501) of the Military Administration of Thessaloniki-Aegean, v. Dordanas, 'The German', p. 120.
751. The official title was 'the National Detachment of the pursuit of Communists' (E.A.K.K.).
752. The Greek North 1.8.1947. Note a few days later, on 14th September, at Giannitsa with Garrison command captain Pesko, colonel Poulos and other gang leaders Schubert had the general command to commit the murders described below.
753. Neue Rheinische Zeitung, Nordheim, Westfalen 26.9.2006. Evidently Rondholz ignores the written authorization which Garrison command Bruno Broyer gave Schubert in August 1943.
754. Dordanas, The blood, p. 523. The Fuehrer's telegram to the Military Command of the Southeast Forces is dated 24.8.1944. Interesting as regards the issue of the management of 'surprise attacks by the resistance are the directives of General Wilhelm Miler, Command of the Garrison of Crete and former supervisor of Schubert who on 14th August 1944 emphasizes that 'to show we are capable of imposing our strength over the whole Island we cannot anymore maintain any qualms against innocent men, women and children. Speedy action is the primary rule for the successful and effective imposition (of retaliatory measures) v. ΔΙΣ 'Guidance for the management of surprise attacks of the resistance', Crete 14.8.1944, p. 97.
755. Ibid., p. 470–471.
756. Dimitris Hatzivrettas, p. 470–471.
757. With reference the anticommunist commands and their activities in central Macedonia, v. Marantzides, p. 72.
758. Anna Konstantinidou, 'Day of the holy Cross 1944 at Giannitsa', Φίλιππος, vo. 33.
759. Georgios Boskos, recorded interview, Giannitsa, 2.10.2008.
760. Traitors Documents: Dina Madzana.
761. Dordanas, The blood, p. 544.
762. Ibid.
763. Georgios Boskos, recorded interview, Giannitsa, 2.10.2008.
764. Traitors Documents: 'Report of examination of witness Stavros Katsouleas ', Giannitsa 29th June 1946. Katsouleas then served as justice of the peace at Giannitsa.
765. IAMM, Archive of Nikolaos Dea. 'To the International Red Cross, Personnel Division – Thessaloniki', Asvestario, 17.9.1944. Testimony of Georgiadis, president of Food Supply of Giannitsa.
766. Traitors Documents: Dina Madzana.
767. Traitors Documents: 'Report of examination of witness Stavros Katsouleas', Giannitsa, 29th June 1946.
768. Traitors Documents: Dina Madzana.
769. Το Βήμα, 27.7.1947. Statement of Giannitsiotis Kon.Bourdanis, owner of liquor store.
770. Traitors Documents: Dina Madzana. Skaperdas saved Thomas Giannos and Fotios Tsilis, who had survived the beating. v. testimony of Stavros Katsouleas. Giannitsa 29th June 1946.
771. Konstantinidou, p. 11.
772. Dionysios Kasapis, recorded telephone interview, Giannitsa, 15.9.2006.
773. IAMM, Archive of Nikolaos Dea, v. 765.
774. Το Βήμα, 29.7.1947.
775. Traitors Documents: 'Report of examination of witness Stavros Katsouleas, Giannitsa 29th June 1946. The victims were wealthy landowners and businessmen of the city: Th. Maggriotis, Th. Athanasopoulos, G. Kiourtsoglou, I. Papachristoudis, Emm. Kaimakis, P. Petrides, H. Dioudis, M. Milios and D. Dimoulas.

776. Konstantinidou, p. 11–12.
777. Traitors Documents 'Report of examination of witness Stavros Katsouleas, Giannitsa, 29th June 1946.
778. Konstantinidou, p. 12.
779. Ibid.
780. Ibid. Commandant Max Peschko satisfied his passion for alcohol, visiting almost daily the liquor store of Maximos Papadopoulos and the home of mayor Maggriotis who kept his own vines. Some Giannitsiotes justify the disregard or weakness of Peschko to save Maggriotis and Papadopoulos 'that captain Schubert was a confidant of Hitler and had the power to arrest even higher-ranking officers of the Wehrmacht, if they didn't help along his criminal path' v. Dionysios Kasapis, recorded telephone interview, Giannitsa, 15.9.2006.
781. Traitors Documents: 'Report of sworn examination of witness Stephanos Triantafyllides, Giannitsa, 1st October 1945. The hatred of Schubert towards the local authorities dates from his first stay at Giannitsa in the spring of 1944. According to testimonies, the reason behind his hatred was his distancing from Giannitsa and the fact that the authorities issued ID cards to the resistors with fake names.
782. K. Papakonstantinou, 'The chronicle of 14th September 1944', Kambos Echo, 5.10.2005.
783. Το Βήμα, 6.8.1947.
784. Traitors Documents: 'Report of sworn examination of witness Stephanos Triantafyllides, Giannitsa, 1st October 1945.
785. Ibid.
786. IAMM Archive of Nikolaos Dea. 'Report of our trips to the Provinces from 15–21st September 1944' Thessaloniki, 23.9.1944 These details were given by the Giannitsiotes to Emil Wenger, representative of the International Red Cross.
787. Ibid. It seems that after the execution of their brother Dim. Papaioannou, one Giannitsiotis was taken by some Schuberites to the women to identify the Papaioannou sisters, whose father had already been executed as a communist. There is not a shred of truth in what Th. Mitsopoulos writes (v. Mitsopoulos, p. 368) about rapes and barbarities of Poulikoi and Germans (Schuberites) acting on 'young and beautiful girls' of Giannitsa.
788. Ibid. On the victim's monument is written a total number of those executed to be 110, but many of these are not named.
789. Traitors Documents: 'Report of sworn examination of witness Stephanos Triantafyllides ', Giannitsa, 1st October 1945.
790. Traitors Documents: 'Report of sworn examination of witness Panayiotis Haritides', Giannitsa, 1st October 1945.
791. Traitors Documents: 'Report of sworn examination of witness Stephanos Triantafyllides' Giannitsa, 1st October 1945. Even before the massacre Schubert demanded of the bakery owners that they make 500 loaves for the men of the Battalions.
792. Traitors Documents: 'Report of sworn examination of witness Stephanos Triantafyllides, Giannitsa, 1st October 1945.
793. Traitors Documents: Dina Madzana.
794. Traitors Documents: 'Report of Events' No. 26/I/2c, Directorate of Police of Giannitsa, Giannitsa, 25th June 1946.
795. IAMM, Archive of Nikolaos Dea, No. Intro.262, file 5: 'Report of our travels to the provinces from 15–21 September 1944, Thessaloniki, 23.9.1944.
796. Mitsopoulos, p. 370.
797. Traitors Documents: Dina Madzana.
798. Ibid.
799. Ibid.

800. Stratos N. Dordanas, The blood, p. 552.
801. Το Φως, 23.10.1947.
802. Traitors Documents: Dina Mantzana.
803. Stratos Dordanas, "Anticommunist warlords in German occupied Central Macedonia" in Nikos Marantzides, The other capetans. Anticommunist warriors during the Occupation and Civil War, Athens, 2006, p. 76–77.
804. Ibid.
805. Ibid. Not the actual takeover which took place on 11th October, rather an attack by ΕΛΑΣ against Krya Vrysi just before 28th September when there were skirmishes in and out of Chalkidona between divisions of ΕΛΑΣ and volunteers of Poulos with casualties on both sides. v. Mitsopoulos, p. 390–395.
806. Traitors Documents: "Report of sworn testimony of witness Ioannis Germanopoulos", Salonica, 29th September 1945.
807. Ibid.
808. Traitors Documents: Dina Madzana.
809. Ibid. According to the Schuberites Giannoglou and Kamisis, Germanakis with his men were enlisted in Papadopoulos' gang, without it being clear which of the three Papadopoulos. Most likely that of Mihalagas in Western Macedonia. v. Stratos Dordanas, Greeks, p. 474.
810. Traitors Documents: "Sworn examination of the witness Stavros Giannoglou", N. Kallikrateia, 4th August 1946.
811. Traitors Documents: Dina Mantzana.
812. Ibid.
813. Ibid.
814. Dordanas, The blood, p. 572.
815. Traitors Documents: Dina Mantzan.a
816. Mazower, p. 357.
817. Traitors Documents: Dina Mantzana. Henceforth there follows a strict series of events as recounted by Mantzana in her defense.
818. Ibid.
819. Ibid. Evidence is lacking to support the view that Schubert showed forged 'papers' as passport or travel documentation to the police authorities at Eleusis airport.
820. Ibid.
821. Ibid. Note Mantzana during her stay in Athens remained at the 8th High School until 20th September.
822. Ibid.
823. Ibid., p. 94.
824. Traitors Documents: 'Report of the examination of witness Christos Betsis', Goumenitssa, 1st June 1946.
825. The inquiry undertaken at the Austrian archives, division of the state Opera (Oesterreichisches, Wien) showed that a ballerina with the name Anna Pinter or Pinther does not exist. V. letter no. 1034212/0002 to the author, 2009.
826. Traitors Documents: Court Decisions, 1947.
827. Traitors Documents: Remedial Jails of Eptapyrgos, "Release Order", Thessaloniki, 9th November 1951. Mantzana was arrested in Agrinio on 31st October 1951, but the Special Court of Patras on 2nd November issued 'a release order' allowing Mantzana free in a week.
828. Sarantos P. Antonakos, "An executioner of the SS in the hands of the Greek police", Illustrated History, 96 Athens (June 1976), p. 94–97. Of the same The Calvary of a nation, Sparta 2001, p. 501–502. Antonakos' exact sources cannot be checked and verified.
829. Ibid., p. 96.
830. Ibid., p. 97.

831. Ibid. A colonel G. Economou is mentioned as collaborating in the assembly of the Security Battalions in the Peloponnesus, around Corinth but it is not known how he knew Schubert.
832. Ibid.
833. Nikos A. Kokonas, British spies in Crete 1941–1945. The policy and strategy of the Allied Secret Forces and their agents, Athens 1991, p. 92.
834. Ελεύθερη Γνώμη, 21.9.1945.
835. Ibid., 22.9.1945.
836. Kokonas, British, p. 92.
837. Ελεύθερη Γνώμη, 19.12.1945.
838. Giannadakis, Memoirs, p. 106–107.
839. Ελεύθερη Γνώμη, 5.1.1946. Also, Eleni Haidia, "The punishment of collaborators, 1945–1946" in Mark Mazower, After the War, p. 58.
840. George C. Kiriakopoulos, The Nazi, p. 217.
841. Ibid., p. 222. Many Cretans still believe Schubert was arrested and condemned in Thessaloniki, v. Πατρίς, 29.10.2005 and M. Matsamas, recorded interview, Chania, 29.1.2006.
842. Konstantinos Giannadakis, recorded telephone interview, Heraklion, 2.6.2008.
843. Kiriakopoulos, p. 222.
844. Konstantinos Mamalakis, recorded telephone interview, Heraklion, 17.2.2005.
845. Ibid.
846. Archive of K. E. Mamalakis, no. 0549.
847. Ibid.
848. Batakis, p. 172.
849. Historical Archive of the Ministry of Foreign Affairs (IAYE) 1949. Special Court Martial of War Criminals, 'Indictment against Fritz Schubert, born in Smyrna and residing in Vienna', Athens, 2nd October 1946.
850. IAYE 1947, file 117, Athens, 3rd October 1946.
851. Ibid.
852. Ο Ελληνικός Βορράς, 8.6.1947.
853. K. E. Mamalakis archive. Athens 5th August 1947.
854. Ibid.
855. Το Βήμα, 29.7.1947.
856. Ibid. Schubert's family from 1941 had settled permanently in Palermo of Sicily which underwent heavy bombarding prior to surrendering to the allies in August 1943. By September 1947 Schubert was informed by his wife that she was residing with their younger son in a refugee camp near Rimini. v. Hagen Fleischer archive. Letter of Colonel Johannes Barge, 31.8.1951. In 1951 Johanna Schubert lived in Genoa Italy at Via Rodi 6B. Also, Deutsche (WASt), email to the author, Berlin, 4.7.2005.
857. Ελεύθερη Γνώμη, Heraklion, 29.7.1947.
858. K. E. Mamalakis archive. Athens, 5th September 1947.
859. Ριζοσπάστης, 2.11.1946.
860. Stratos N. Dordanas, 'Crimes of war. Historical Conference, Chania, May 26th 2006, p. 4.
861. Hagen Fleischer archive: letter of Johannes Barge: 'Regarding the death of Friedrich Schubert' Lage, 31st August 1951.
862. Το Βήμα, 29.7.1947.
863. Karkanis id., p. 363.
864. Ibid.
865. Kreuzer was in charge of the operations of the Military Police of Crete v. Πατρίς, Heraklion, 9.11.2004. Also, Kavvos, id., p. 797 refers to a colonel Kruzer (sic) commandant of the 47th Regiment of 22nd Division based at Ambelouzo Mesara Heraklion.
866. Μακεδονία, 30.7.1947.

867. Ibid. The majority of the absent witnesses came from the municipality of Heraklion (40%) whilst the remainder were divided nearly equally between the municipalities of Rethymnon and Chania.
868. Contemporary Social History archive (ΑΣΚΙ). The testimony that some Schubert also in the police served then in Crete is untrue.
869. Ριζοσπάστης, 30.7.1947.
870. Ελευθερία, 30.7.1947.
871. Το Βήμα, 30.7.1947.
872. Ibid.
873. Ριζοσπάστης 1.8.1947. The statements originated from members of the National Organization of Crete Sp. Tamiolakis, lawyer of Chania, N. Plevris, colonel from Heraklion, P. Nikolakakis, doctor of Chania, K. Mitsotakis, lawyer at the German court martial of Chania, N. Pikoulas, major from Heraklion, Evag. Drymis, mayor of Heraklion, K. Polychronakis member of EOK and Bruno Brauer, Commandant of Crete.
874. Ελευθερία, 1.8.1947. Also, Ριζοσπάστης, 19.11.1946.
875. Το Βήμα, 29.7.1947. Also, Ελεύθερη Γνώμη, 29.7.1947.
876. Ριζοσπάστης, 6.8.1947.
877. Ibid. There is presented a second version according to which two instead of ten Schubert are mentioned.
878. Το Βήμα, 29.7.47. Ελευθερία, 29.7.1947.
879. Το Βήμα, 29.7.1947. Naturally Galitsanos was not a live witness of the events but extracted the information from his surviving compatriots.
880. K. E. Mamalakis archive. Athens, 5th August 1947.
881. Ελευθερία, 6.8.1947.
882. Collaborators documents. 'Regarding the arrested German Fritz Anton Schubert' Thessaloniki, 3rd November 1945. Also, Ριζοσπάστης, 1.8.1947.
883. Ibid. In reality in the mission the aforementioned leaders did not take part rather the volunteer divisions under the nationalist Aristeidis Papadopoulos.
884. Ελευθερία, 1.8.1947.
885. Ibid.
886. Ibid. Alexander Andrae had been jailed from January 1947 in Kallithea jails where he met Schubert with whom most likely he discussed the issues relating to their impending trials. Andrae's trial was held in December 1947 and during the last stage a German lawyer was involved. He was convicted to life imprisonment and following the granting of grace was left free early 1952.
887. Ελευθερία, 3.8.1947.
888. The Bulgarian officer Andon Kalchev, founder of the paramilitary organization Ohrana and leader of the Komiti with Italian and German support armed Slav speaking militia in villages of Kastoria-Florina and cooperated with the Italian captain Giovanni Ravalli who served at the Guard Headquarters of Kastoria. In 1946 both were convicted in Athens to life imprisonment for crimes against the Greek population. v. Dordanas, The blood, id., p. 388.
889. Ριζοσπάστης, 3.8.1947.
890. Ελευθερία, 3.6.1947.
891. Ibid.
892. Ριζοσπάστης, 6.8.1947. v. Karkanis, id. p. 386.
893. Ο Ελληνικός Βορράς, 6.8.1947.
894. Μακεδονία, 6.8.1947.
895. There are two versions as regards S. Kapetanakis' death. According to a Rodakino priest G. Sfakianakis 'they threw (Kapetanakis) into the fire' (burning house) along with Despoina

Vardaki. According to another testimony these women were thrown into an oven from where they escaped with severe burns v. Pantinakis id., p. 387, Kavvos, Karkanis.
896. Ριζοσπάστης, 6.8.1947. According to available sources, the two-year-old Athanasios Aggeloudis (correct is Aggelinoudis) and his mother Evangelia, 22 years old were led to the oven of Gouramanis where they were cindered along with other women and children. The incident, as narrated by the commissioner is unknown.
897. Ελευθερία, 6.8.1947.
898. Εμπρός, 6.8.1947.
899. Το Βήμα, 6.8.1947.
900. K. E. Mamalakis archive. Athens, 5th August 1947.
901. Ελευθερία, 10.10.1947 and 16.10.1947.
902. Konstantinos Mitsotakis, recorded interview, Athens, 7.6.2006.
903. Kavvos, id., p. 784. The report of the examination of dean Psalidakis is shown unchanged.
904. General Military Staff Office – Military History Directorate (ΔΙΣ).
905. Ελευθερία, 30.7.1947: testimony of St. Karambatakis.
906. Kavvos, p. 784.
907. Collaborators documents, Thessaloniki, 28th September 1945.
908. Dimitrios P. Dimitrakos, Kostas Mitsotakis, Political Biography: 1918–1961.
909. Konstantinos Mitsotakis, recorded interview, Athens 7.6.2006.
910. Deutsche Dienststelle (WASt): Veranderung Meldungen, letter to the author Berlin, May 24th 2005.
911. Collaborators documents: judicial committee. Decision no. 519, Thessaloniki, 26th April 1947.
912. Hagen Fleischer archive, "Regarding the death of Friedrich Schubert", Johanes Barges, Lage, 31.8.1951.
913. Ο Ελληνικός Βορράς, 2.10.1947. Also, Μακεδονία, 5.10.1947.
914. Μακεδονία, 5.10.1947.
915. Ibid., 9.10.1947.
916. Ο Ελληνικός Βορράς, 10.10.1947.
917. Ibid.
918. Johannes Barge from June 1943 to May 1945 served as commandant of various infantry regiments of Fortress Crete and chief of staff to general Georg Benthack the last garrison command. In February 1946 the British surrendered Barges to the Greek authorities to stand trial. At Kallithea jails he met Schubert with whom he empathized so in 1951 he notified Schubert's daughter Maria and the German authorities regarding the trial and execution of Schubert. Note Barges was set free in October 1950 and returned to Germany. (v. Hagen Fleischer archive, Lage, 31.8.1951).
919. Μακεδονία, 23.10.1947.
920. Ibid.
921. Ibid.
922. Ο Ελληνικός Βορράς, 23.10.1947.
923. According to another version, the priest was named Jenner and was probably an American of Anglican doctrine. v. Hagen Fleischer, recorded interview, Athens 28.10.2006.
924. Ο Ελληνικός Βορράς, 23.10.1947.
925. Ibid.
926. This cemetery, situated 30 kilometres north of Athens was founded in September 1975 and contains 9.905 graves of German soldiers murdered in mainland Greece during the Occupation.
927. Greek Government Gazette, no.12, Athens, 20th January 1945.
928. Collaborators documents: Dina Mantzana.

929. Collaborators documents. Thessaloniki, 17th October 1945.
930. Ibid., Thessaloniki, 23rd October 1945.
931. Ibid., Aravissos, 15th October 1945.
932. Collaborators documents. Thessaloniki, 3rd February 1947.
933. Ibid., Thessaloniki, 3rd February 1947.
934. Ibid., Thessaloniki, 14th January 1947.
935. Collaborators documents. Thessaloniki, 18th December 1945.
936. Μακεδονία, 13.1.1948.
937. Collaborators documents. Thessaloniki, 28th May 1947.
938. Collaborators documents, Thessaloniki, 21st October 1946.
939. Ibid., Thessaloniki, 15th October 1946. A considerable number of employees of the Sanatorium originated from Katerini and the area who as former employees of the Sanatorium of Agia Petra Monastery of Olympus had been transferred to the Sanatorium of Asvestochori before the Occupation.
940. Ibid., Thessaloniki, 13th January 1948.
941. Collaborators documents. Thessaloniki, 15th October 1946.
942. Ibid., Thessaloniki, 25th September 1947.
943. Collaborators documents: "Testimony of accused Stylianos Diktabanides" Thessaloniki, 12th January 1946. Diktambanides names 29 Schuberites. Also, Xanthopoulos names 30 men of Schubert's gang. Also, Gridakis names 32 Schuberites.
944. Collaborators documents. Thessaloniki, 12th December 1946.
945. Ibid., Thessaloniki, 4th March 1948.
946. Collaborators documents. Drama, 17th April 1951. According to oral reports Tzoulias settled in Belgium and Kapetanakis had already committed suicide in Italy.
947. Collaborators documents. Thessaloniki, 26th April 1947.
948. Collaborators documents. N. Kallikrateia, 4th August 1946. Also, death certificate. Nea Gonia, 10th March 1952.
949. Eleni Haidia, "The Punishment of Collaborators. "and Mark Mazower, After the War. Princeton and Oxford 2000, p. 55. Also, Stratos N. Dordanas, "Pool of Siloam", Καθημερινή, 9.3.2009.
950. Collaborators documents. Thessaloniki, 9th November 1951.
951. Collaborators documents. Thessaloniki, 1st April 1969.
952. Ibid. Ardea, 31st January 1945.
953. Theodoros Valahas, recorded telephone interview, Thessaloniki, 2.7.2009.
954. Kostopoulos, id., p. 102.
955. Collaborators documents. Thessaloniki, 9th October 1947.
956. Ibid.
957. Collaborators documents. Thessaloniki, 13th January 1948.
958. Ibid.
959. Ibid.
960. Ibid.
961. Ibid.
962. Ο Ελληνικός Βορράς, 14.11.1948.
963. Collaborators documents, Thessaloniki 13th January 1948.
964. Ελεύθερη Γνώμη, 8.3.1946 and 24.11.1946.
965. Konstantinos Mamalakis, recorded telephone interview, Heraklion 14.5.2005. The collaborators' archive, which was recently discovered at the First Instance Court of Heraklion is today housed at ΓΑΚ of Heraklion.
966. Georgios M. Xylouris, recorded interview, Krousonas, 28.6.2006.
967. Collaborators documents. Thessaloniki, 25th May 1946.

968. A hotel "Berlin" is not mentioned in the sources. Possibly meant is the "Brittania' of Chania.
969. Collaborators documents. Heraklion, 15th February 1946.
970. Ibid., Thessaloniki, 25th May 1946.
971. Ibid., Heraklion, 15.1.1946.
972. Collaborators documents, Thessaloniki, 25th July 1946.
973. Ibid., Thessaloniki, 18th May 1947. A witness from Kyrianna testified that Alatzas argued with his father and left for Heraklion to enlist in the German police v. collaborators documents. Rethymnon, 13th October 1947.
974. Collaborators documents. Rethymnon, 9th January 1948.
975. Ibid. Thessaloniki, 2nd March 1948.
976. Historical archive of the Ministry of Foreign Affairs (IAYE). Chania, 30th March 1948.
977. ΓΑΚ Heraklion. Heraklion, 30.9.1945 and 1.10.1945. Steiakakis must have served in the Schubert gang till at least 10th October 1943, the date on which he was accused of acting with other Schuberites in violent acts.
978. Ibid.
979. Collaborators documents. Heraklion, 24th October 1945.
980. Collaborators documents. Heraklion 9th March 1946.
981. Ibid. Manousakis listed in his diary 'the crimes which the Schuberites committed in Macedonia and their cooperation with Bulgarian and German detachments' v. Ελεύθερη Γνώμη, Heraklion, 8.3.1946.
982. Antonis Sanoudakis, Zaharia Bantouvas id., p. 55. Manousakis was already Germanophile from the First World War. His execution had been scheduled by the Bantouvas clan early June 1942 but because of German reprisals during the harvest had been postponed.
983. Ελεύθερη Γνώμη, 24.11.1946.
984. IAYE. Chania, 30th March 1948.
985. Five members of the Somarakis family were chopped to pieces by relatives of the victims in the courtroom as they weren't satisfied with the decision of the court.
986. IAYE. Chania, 30th March 1948.
987. Ibid.
988. Kavvos id., p. 793. Heraklion, 16th June 1945.
989. Ibid., p. 556.
990. Ibid.p. 556 and 794. According to unconfirmed oral testimony, Ieronymides took part in the execution at Sarchos along with Epanomeritakis and Stergios and Haralambos Agiomyrgianakis. (v. also Konstantinos Mamalakis, recorded telephone interview, Heraklion 25.6.2009).
991. IAYE, 1949. Chania, 30th March 1948, p. 14.
992. Ibid., p. 30.
993. Ibid., p. 27.
994. Ibid., p. 12. Also, Kavvos id., p. 793, testimony of Richard Haar in which the Tzoulias are characterized as 'above any description traitors' Haar, sergeant of the Military Police, deserted and surrendered to the Greek authorities of Heraklion and in June 1945 gave a detailed report. From 1942 he served at different posts in Crete, one of which the guard of Krousonas where he remained as commandant from March to November 1943. In his testimony he names and characterizes several Cretan close accomplices of Schubert and the Germans.
995. Ibid.
996. Giannadakis, Memoirs, p. 101.
997. Ibid., p. 34,36.
998. Ibid., p. 80.
999. Georgios Xylouris, recorded interview, Krousonas, 28.6.2006.

1000. Αλλαγή, Heraklion, 15.9.1992, p. 5. Also, Konstantinos Mamalakis, recorded telephone interview, Heraklion, 26.5.2009.
1001. Georgios Xylouris, recorded interview, Krousonas 28.6.2006.
1002. K. E. Mamalakis archive. Testimony of Fritz Schubert, Kallithea jails, 18.10.1945.
1003. Georgios Xylouris, recorded interview, Krousonas, 28.6.2006. v. Kavvos id., p. 791, where lieutenant R. Haar testified that Nik. Tzoulias gave information to Alex Bauer, the director of the Office of espionage in Heraklion in 1944 about Fountoulakis.
1004. Giannadakis, Memoirs, p. 53.
1005. Giannadakis, Memoirs, p. 61.
1006. Konstantinos Mamalakis, email to author, Heraklion, 26.6.2009. Also, Giannadakis, Memoirs, id., p. 13 who considers Emm. Makatounis responsible for the murder of Georgios Grigorakis.
1007. Konstantinos Mamalakis, recorded telephone interview, Heraklion, 25.6.2009.
1008. Giannadakis, Memoirs, p.,62. It appears that Giannadakis slaughtered 'symbolically' Filippos Gridakis, the Germanophile community president at the Police Station of Krousonas where he had filed for protection. v. Giannadakis, Memoirs id., p.34.
1009. Konstantinos Mamalakis, recorded telephone interview, Heraklion, 25.6.2009. Also, Kostas Epanomeritakis, Αλλαγή, Heraklion, 15.9.1992.
1010. ΓΑΚ Heraklion, Heraklion, 25.7.1947.
1011. IAYE. Chania, 30th March 1948.
1012. Mamalakis, recorded telephone interview, Heraklion, 9.5.2008.
1013. Μεσόγειος, 27.6.2008, p. 17 v. K. Mamalakis, recorded telephone interview, Heraklion, 2.3.2008.
1014. Kokonas, Crete, p. 96. According to the official British Report, Baltzakis was arrested by Schubert and obliged to enlist to his gang.
1015. K. E. Mamalakis archive: testimony of rebel Eleft. Kalitsouna to K. Mamalakis. According to another version, Baltzakis and Katsalakis who served in the mixed Garrison of Krousonas were persuaded by three Krousonas resistor secret agents to plot with the Italian soldiers and kill their German colleagues. The plan failed and the Italians now vulnerable escaped taking the two Schuberites with them who were led by a rebel liaison to Psiloritis. v. Konstantinos Giannadakis, Μεσόγειος, 27.6.2008, p. 16.
1016. IAYE. Heraklion, 22nd March 1949. Later during the sixties, the son of Epanomeritakis, Konstantinos from Heraklion visited his father in Geseke of Westfalen, a city northwest of Dortmund, where he met also the other three from Krousonas.
1017. Konstantinos Mamalakis, email to author, Heraklion, 23.9.2010.
1018. Georgios Xylouris, recorded telephone interview, Krousonas, 24.6.2008.
1019. IAYE. Chania, 30th March 1948.
1020. Collaborators documents: Dina Mantzana.
1021. IAYE. Chania, 11th October 1945.
1022. Collaborators documents. Thessaloniki, 13th January 1948.
1023. Ioannis Kouridakis, recorded telephone interview, Chryssavgi, 8.5.2008.
1024. Kavvos id., p. 389.
1025. IAYE. Voukolies, 3rd December 1947. It is reported that Kapetanakis sent a letter to the bishopric of Kissamo for a certificate that he was single.
1026. Ioannis Kouridakis, recorded telephone conversation, Chryssavgi, 8.5.2008.
1027. IAYE. Voukolies, 3rd December 1947.
1028. IAYE. Centro Lipari, May 4th 1949. It refers to Kapetanakis' suicide.
1029. IAYE. Rome, 8th May 1948. Kapetanakis' letter is attached to this document.